£9·50 H3

720·11

D1477145

University of Strathclyde
SCHOOL OF ARCHITECTURE
INFORMATION ROOM

Models and Systems
in Architecture
and Building

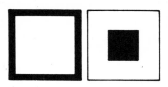 **Land Use and Built Form Studies**

University of Cambridge Department of Architecture

LUBFS Conference Proceedings Number 2

Models and Systems in Architecture and Building

Edited by Dean Hawkes

University of Strathclyde
SCHOOL OF ARCHITECTURE
INFORMATION ROOM

The Construction Press Ltd

Acknowledgement

The Martin Centre is grateful to Applied Research of Cambridge Limited
for supplying the administrative support which made this conference possible.

© 1975 The Martin Centre for Architectural and Urban Studies

ISBN 0 904406 09 1

No part of this book may be reproduced in any form
without permission (except for short extracts for
review purposes).

Published in 1975 by
The Construction Press Ltd
Lunesdale House,
Hornby, Lancaster LA2 8NB,
England.

Contents

Editorial

University of Strathclyde
SCHOOL OF ARCHITECTURE
INFORMATION ROOM

This conference, held in Cambridge in September 1973 was the second annual conference to be held by the centre for Land Use and Built Form Studies in the Department of Architecture at the University of Cambridge, England.* The centre was established in 1967 and was initially under the Directorship of the then Professor of Architecture, Sir Leslie Martin. In a paper presented at the Royal Institute of British Architects in January of that year Sir Leslie powerfully argued the case for the development of a strong, theory-based approach to architectural research and practice.

"... the architect has a special task; in my view it is to study the potentialities of the built form in an increasingly rational manner and to extend this everywhere by speculative thought. The ultimate problem for the profession is that of setting out the possibilities and choices in building an environment. And in that field the crisis will not be solved by technical advance alone, or by picturesque images. At bottom it is a crisis of lack of understanding. Our task is to try to make that understanding more complete."

In essence this statement represents the guiding principle of the work of the six years which elapsed between the foundation of Land Use and Built Form Studies and the date of this conference. Inevitably over such a period individual pieces of work will follow paths which were not envisaged at the outset, new themes will emerge and, in some instances, initial aims will not be realised. All of this has occurred, but underlying the work has been the unifying goal of studying "the potentialities of the built form."

The idea behind this conference was, in the first place, to register the main concerns and emphases in the centre's work at the building scale. This was, however, only a part of the intention because two other important themes were identified. On the one hand the work of the centre has been seen to relate, through both its aims and its methods, to work which has grown-up independently in other places both in this country and abroad. On the other hand we have begun to see work which started out as research within the framework of an academic institution move on through phases of further development in the outside world and so into application in practice. It was with these three considerations in mind that the conference was planned.

In addition to stating the aims of the conference it is equally important to stress what it was *not* about. Many of the papers discuss or describe the use of the computer as an aid or tool in architectural research or practice, or in the building process. In spite of the frequency with which these references occur the conference was not about computer aided design. Both the subject matter and the discussion extend well beyond the limits of that term or of any of its synonyms. The title *Models and systems in architecture and building* potentially embraces a wide range of subject material. For this reason it is worthwhile attempting in this Introduction to define the particular meanings which are attached to the key words *model* and *system* in this context.

Models and mathematics are often seen to be inseparably linked, and the connection between mathematics and the digital computer is now too familiar to be remarkable. There are, however, valuable uses of the concept of a model in both architectural theory and practice beyond the highly specific notion of mathematically expressed relationships programmed for manipulation on a computer. These other uses are an important part of the material of this conference. There is also a tendency to imagine that models and their use in architecture and building are the invention of the last decade or so, in some way dependent for their existence upon the development of appropriate and often complex mathematical formalisms. Such models do, of course, exist and serve valuable functions in many areas of research and practice, but a number of papers, for example those by Steadman, Hawkes and Mitchell, offer evidence of both a broader definition and a much longer history of the underlying notion encompassed by the term "model". This is done by pointing to other forms of representation which may be used, even invoking the name of Vitruvius, and by offering reminders of the now lengthy history of the use of mathematically expressed relationships in certain areas of building design.

The second key word is *system* and it is particularly important to establish the meaning which is attached to this since the introductory paper by William Hillier is, in effect, a challenge at the philosophical level of the validity of the "systems" approach to architectural design, through an argument presenting the virtues of the alternative "structural" point-of-view. Later on in these proceedings the word *system* is found used in conjunction with the word *building* in the titles of three papers, by Richens, Ehrenkrantz and Goodman, in which context its meaning is transformed from a generalised philosophical concept to a more specific and, in the general sense, well understood approach to the design, planning and construction of buildings. We are dealing therefore with two meanings of this word. The first is conceptual in which case, most simply stated, a system is "a set of elements standing in inter-relations." (cf. Bertalanffy, L. von (1968)

---

*In 1974 the research activities of the Department of Architecture were re-organised under the title of the Martin Centre for Architectural and Urban Studies.

General System Theory, chapter 3). The second is the specific use of the term to define an approach to *building* which, in one way or another, makes use of a finite and precisely defined set of standard elements.

With these definitions in mind there now follows a brief commentary on the proceedings themselves. The aim of the papers given on the opening day was to establish the broad framework within which the contributions of the following sessions would find their place. The challenge represented by William Hillier's paper to one of the fundamental assumptions implicit in both the title of the conference, and in much of the Cambridge work, has already been referred to. Philip Steadman also deals with important philosophical ideas in his consideration of the value, in the development of architectural theory, of Karl Popper's definition of three "worlds",

"World" one, the objective world of material things, "world" two, the subjective world of minds and "world" three, distinct from but entirely dependent upon the first two, a world of "objective knowledge".

Dean Hawkes' paper relates directly to the group of four later contributions on *Environment* and sets out to present the long history of development and use of models in this area of building design as the basis for the development of a prescription for the preferred form of such models. Ed Hoskins' contribution relates the process of design to the process of building production by viewing a model of a building as a central component in an information processing system to serve both the analysis of performance, which is an essential part of design, and the accumulation and processing of data which is necessary in the effective control of the production process.

The material of the four working sessions of the conference is organised under four headings. The first is *Description* and opens with William Mitchell's paper *'Vitruvius Computatas'* in which the influence of the computer upon architectural form is viewed

"as a direct continuation of the classical academic tradition of elementary composition which embodied an Aristotelian conception of form."

This is no narrow academic point, but one of general and fundamental importance since it represents a warning against the easy assumption that computer systems in architecture can be regarded as being formally neutral and may therefore be left to satisfy their own internal, technical criteria. Their foundations must be firmly based upon a profound understanding of the nature of architectural form. The other papers in this group are concerned with the technical problems of constructing effective computer representations of buildings. Janet Tomlinson presents a particularly clear "basic primer" on the relationship between the nature of the problem and the means by which it may be solved. The papers by Jennifer Jacobsberg and Peter Hayward are both based upon "real world" experience in the design and development of computer systems for immediate application in "live" building programmes. The major point which emerges from these and which serves to illustrate both Mitchell's theoretical argument and Tomlinson's discussion of general principles, is the closeness of the relationship which exists between problem and solution in this area. Both papers show how, even within the context of highly formalised and rationalised approaches to building, the associated computer systems are extremely complex.

"Such a system is only possible where the building geometry is well-defined and co-ordinated."(Jacobsberg)

"A very large part of the cost of using computers to assist in the design process is the cost of data preparation. This militates against one-off application programs." (Hayward)

The second group of papers come together under the heading of *Environment.* The common link between them lies in the fact that each illustrates, in its individual way, an important new direction in the general consideration of environmental problems in architectural design and research. This might be described as the shift from the traditional empirical basis of design techniques towards the acceptance of a more theoretical viewpoint. Neil Milbank's paper on predicting the thermal environment is founded upon the statement that,

"Recent developments in the theory of thermal response and a greater understanding of comfort requirements lead to better predictions of the way users will react to the thermal environment in buildings."

Michael Delany's paper on road traffic noise takes the form of a comparative discussion of the merits of alternative techniques of analysis and prediction, of empirically-based models, small-scale physical representations and the potential of computer techniques based on fundamental theory. Richard Stibbs describes his work on the prediction of illumination in buildings by the development of a computer model based upon the integral equation theory first proposed by Spencer and Stakutis in the United States in 1951. This work is an example of the way in which the potential of the computer allows important, but mathematically complex, theoretical contributions to be brought closer to the point of practical application. The final paper in this group, Julian Hunt on aspects of wind flow near buildings, also discusses both experimental and theoretical approaches.

Each of these papers helps to make an important point in the way in which it relates advanced theoretical work in its field to the pressing problems of everyday design. In this they illustrate a balanced view which acknowledges the inescapable relationships which exist between problems, solutions and tools in design.

Space and *activities* together form the subject of the third group of papers. Under this heading the four papers adopt widely differing points of view. Keith Ray describes an approach to modelling the "classical" problem in this field, the relationship between spatial organisation and functional performance. The basis of the work is the evaluation of input physical plans and operational policies for large and complex hospital organisations, with output in the form of traffic matrices showing journeys classified by origin, destination and type. Charles Eastman in his paper adopts a more "architectural" approach and discusses the nature of a computer system which *infers* specified relationships and constraints from input spatial arrangements, indicating automatically to the designer those situations which fail to satisfy either his own expressed design objectives or the requirements of fire and building codes and so forth. The third of these papers, by Tom Willoughby, examines the notion, once seen to be potentially the most obvious and exciting outcome of the marriage of architecture and computers, of the automatic generation of building forms. The proposition made by the paper is that it is both more cost effective and logical to use the computer to generate numerous plans within the limits of loosely defined constraints, and then subject them to further evaluation, rather than to try and search for the "best possible" solution by progressively tightening the constraints. There is a close link between these arguments and the work described in the final paper in this group from Crispin Gray and Ed Hoskins. This describes the generation of alternative forms of hospital building within a set of predetermined geometrical and functional constraints, concentrating on one particular aspect of hospital layout; the economic and efficient disposition of departments in a way which minimises inter-departmental circulation. No attempt is made to find the "best" hospital, but rather to make economical use of the computer to generate a number of sensible alternatives. On the basis of further evaluation one of these may then be selected for development into the final complete design.

The common thread running through these papers is their emphasis on the significance and value of evaluation in the process of architectural design. By accepting this it can be shown that a practical and economic compromise may be achieved between certain concerns and aspirations in building design and the use of computer aids.

The four papers which make up the final group are concerned in various ways with aspects of *building systems.* Geoffrey Hutton argues that building systems may, by analogy with natural organisms, be seen with advantage as evolving species which have their nature determined by the degree to which they satisfy user requirements, in the widest sense of the term. This proposition is used to support a case for an approach to building based upon

"... closed technical, material and economic
solutions .. "

The second paper, from Paul Richens, is very different in presenting a technical description of the development of a working computer system for an existing building system. This is in essence a *detailing machine* which allows the architect to describe a sketch design for a building to the computer and to receive back a fully detailed set of working drawings. This in itself is an impressive technical achievement and the techniques used deserve close study, but there are important aspects in the interaction between the worlds of hardware and software, related to the discussion of *Description* in the first group of papers, which should not be overlooked. Drawing upon a wealth of experience in the development and applications of systems, both hardware and software, in building in the United States, Ezra Ehrenkrantz explores in his paper the relationship between these two uses of the term within the framework of rigorous

cost and performance constraints. His account of his work with the Veterans' Administration hospitals programme makes a fascinating comparison with Howard Goodman's description of the British work on the development of the Systems Health Building Programme. Each piece of work is clearly the product of its particular cultural, economic and technological environment, but there is a remarkable similarity in the nature of the fundamental problem as it is seen on both sides of the Atlantic.

"We are faced with problems which are widespread —rising costs, the time that it takes to get the building up and finding that the building is obsolete by the time it is occupied." (Ehrenkrantz)

"We are concerned with not only the reduction in the time that it takes to design a hospital, but also in a reduction in the time that it takes to prepare the brief and the production material. The best average which was generally being achieved within the Service was four and a half to five years between thinking about having a hospital and cutting the first sod on site. We wanted to offer a system which would reduce this time . . . We are now in a position where, assuming maximum use was made of our systems, a building could be conceived and built within five years." (Goodman)

This is a problem which experience suggests defies satisfactory solution by conventional design and contractual procedures. Neither paper confronts the fundamental question of the desirability of institutions and buildings of this scale, that is not their job although it is not an issue which should be ignored, but because these workers have accepted the challenge of this scale of operation as it was laid before them they have been inspired to make stimulating contributions to the development of serious thought about the nature of architectural design which may well prove to benefit work at other scales.

The general objectives behind the conference were outlined earlier. Insofar as certain aspects of the work at Land Use and Built Form Studies during its first six years have been presented alongside other academic work with which it shares certain common factors and work from practice to which it has either directly or indirectly contributed, these objectives have been fulfilled.

A concern which is expressed by a number of contributors shows a desire to relate the new techniques and approaches to the continuing process of development of a rational basis for architectural design. In his paper referred to at the outset, Sir Leslie Martin showed how in some of the works of the pioneers of modern architecture,

"the developing theory became dogma . . . The speculative thought that could have extended the range of built forms into totally new environments dried up . . . It is speculation that makes rational thought live; and it is rational thought that gives speculative invention its basis and its roots."

There are encouraging signs in the underlying atti-tudes which inform the work presented here that this lesson has been heeded. It is not superfluous however to remind ourselves, in conclusion, of the danger which may lie in wait if models and systems come to acquire the status of a new dogma. □

Part 1

Overview

Introductory remarks

William Howell

It is an old campaigner's dictum that time spent on reconnaissance is seldom wasted. Anyone involved in the design process could extend that, and say that time spent in simulation is seldom wasted. A designer, like a campaigner, starts with the reconnoitring operation — the gathering of data and the definition of all the parameters within which his future actions must take place. Then, again like the campaigner, he has to formulate courses of action, or more precisely sets of actions, which react on the data and upon each other. The more that blind guesswork can be eliminated, the greater the likelihood of success in either type of enterprise. This can only be done by displaying, in the form of some kind of analogy, the results of various sets of choices.

Perhaps before leaving my campaigning simile, we might pay a passing tribute to Nelson, who, as well as being a master of reconnaissance (despite pitiful resources—"Send me more frigates" was his perennial cry to the Admiralty), ensured success by endless 'design' sessions in his cabin with all his captains, in which every possibility was, literally, modelled, and everyone knew not only what options to go for initially, but which further options to adopt in the light of the developing situation. As you no doubt know from your history books, after one celebrated, and more or less redundant message (except, perhaps, from a purely theatrical point of view), the entire battle of Trafalgar was fought without the necessity for any further discussion or instruction. All the options had been examined in advance and every possible response evaluated.

I would like to give a brief backward glance (and perhaps the odd sideways glance) at the situation in the general run of practice.

Perhaps I should say, in parenthesis, that some of the papers which follow are by practitioners who have already been involved in sophisticated design methods, as well as by those active in devising emergent techniques of an even more sophisticated kind.

Faced with this futuristic display, the general run of practice amongst whom I, perhaps in company with one or two others, class myself, feels a bit like Australian aborigines, chipping away at their flint arrowheads, and gazing through the barbed wire at the Woomera range. What they see may open up fascinating speculations for the future, but probably seems a bit remote from the problem of getting a kangaroo for supper.

We are all, of course, brought up to model, mainly in 2-dimensions in the form of drawings. (Actual 3-dimensional models seem very seldom to be used as design tools, are usually made after all the decisions are taken (i.e. too late) and are more to do with public relations than with design method).

I have always been a passionate drawer, because it is such a remarkably effective (though at present somewhat unfashionable) medium for exploring three-dimensional spaces and structures, and the inter-relationship (and conflicts) between elements—not only effective but cheap, easily reproduceable, conveniently postable and, above all, malleable. It is in this connection that I recently remarked to someone that I thought the computer would prove the biggest design breakthrough since tracing paper—a remarkable medium, which not only facilitates modification, but preserves layer upon layer of record of earlier conformations. Curious that it has only been in wide use for about a hundred years, when it came on the scene as the biggest design breakthrough since the eraser. How anyone retracted from drawing board error prior to that I've never been able to envisage.

It is through this non-capital-intensive, unsophisticated medium that much effective work is done daily on the classic design cycle of hypothesis, appraisal, modification and re-appraisal.

We have a dictum in my office, 'When in doubt, draw it out', and we draw maniacally, gratifyingly and extremely unprofitably; everything is explored, this way, that way, sideways, upwards. And there are still bits we don't draw, and they are the bits that usually go wrong.

The actual process of drawing has a kind of therapeutic, perhaps one might say catalytic, effect on the designer which, if drawing becomes superseded, may have to be replaced by something else. Like knitting between print-outs. I suspect that there is a kind of gestative lapse of time which is not susceptible to being 'saved'.

Many of us use, in addition to drawings, various do-it-yourself kindergarten kits as design aids during the exploratory stage—little bits of cut-out coloured cardboard, blocks or whatever. One significant factor in such an operation is the extent to which the medium moulds the message. For instance, if you cut out bits of cardboard to represent all your room shapes, what shape do you make them? If rectangular, do you adopt a common depth, so that they will fit when arranged contiguously? If you do so, you are exploring ways of arranging accommodation in a flat-fronted building. You may miss whole sets of arrangements based on an indented facade and a stepped section—an elementary example, but illustrative of the way design tools pre-empt certain solutions. I'm sure that later on, when we hear about computer-aided systems, we shall find the same thing happening.

There is, of course, a solid Luddite stratum in every design profession, which will cling panic-stricken to time-honoured routines. But even the most hardened feet-dragger will surely give up his handicraft drawing-board activity when he is offered, connected to this malleable, recordable, transmittable, visual simulation, instantaneous facts on floor area, total enclosed volume, area of total external envelope, daylighting standards, cost. At present we have got near this situation in some instances in which the range of elements, choices and geometrical systems are pretty simple; it is attractive to speculate on the elaboration of these, at present, relatively primitive systems.

I have mentioned cost, and you will see that economic modelling is less well covered in our programme than other aspects. So far as I am aware the vast amount of effort that has been put into the computerisation of bills of quantities has not greatly improved the quality of information from quantity surveyors, nor the accuracy of their forecasts nor the responsiveness of their in-contract cost monitoring. All that seems to have happened is that some quantity surveyors seem to go around in bigger cars.

I recently took to task the sales manager of some new solve-all-your-problems building product, who appeared in my office with a repulsive brochure filled with examples of his product used on one absolutely awful building after another. I tried to persuade him that the only effective way of selling anything to architects (and I am saying this here because I believe it to be as true of ideas as of plastic rain-water goods) is to launch it through good architecture. An ill-designed building that proclaims that it was evolved by some pretentious design method would have done well to keep quiet about it—a thoroughly counter-productive exercise. It doesn't make people feel any better about the building, and discredits whatever thinking went into the design system.

It is interesting to think of the various recent projects incorporating radical environmental systems—all alas unmemorable, because with depressing regularity they seem to have become embedded in dreary, undistinguished architecture. It is hardly surprising that their message falls on stony ground.

So let me end with this parting thought,—that we dedicate ourselves to propagating more sophisticated design methods through the medium of more environmentally sophisticated, more humane and more delightful buildings. That is, in the end, the only way to give credibility to our propositions. □

The architecture of architecture

Foundations of a mathematical theory of artificial space

Bill Hillier and Adrian Leaman

'The essential unit entity in biology is not the isolated individual, but the continuous configuration in space-time which connects a parent individual to its descendants, or more generally the union of such configurations relative to species which have among themselves functional interactions.'—Rene Thom[1]

'One must force the frozen circumstances to dance by singing to them their own melody,'—Karl Marx[2]

Where do intentions come from?

Intentions are a favourite theme in architectural discourse. Not only are they said to be the starting points for design, but also that which distinguishes architecture as an art from architecture as a science. Since science deals with how things are, not how they should be, architectural 'intentions' are said to be the responsibility of the individual designer, or the bodies who instruct him, and architectural science is asked to concern itself with the perfectibility of a process, a methodology for the realisation of pure intentions.

But where do intentions come from? At the very least, intentions must exist by virtue of the prior existence of mental representations of a morphology—that is, some set of related forms—linked to search procedures for the production of design conjectures. These are the structures the designer thinks with rather than things he thinks about, as unconscious as the syntactic and semantic structures of language. The designer's dependence on them is easily forgotten. Too often the concept of 'intention' serves as a means of preserving this amnesia at the level of theory. It locates the designer in a void, rather than in a universe of discourse already highly structured through the history of the morphology on which he acts. It desocialises the theory of design, and renders central questions—such as how the individual acts of the designer transmit essentially social experiences—inaccessible to systematic enquiry.

As soon as the relation between the manifest morphology of architectural forms and the designer's imaginative activity is recognised in theory, the conceptual system of 'intentionality-cum-methodology', with its separation of ends and means, breaks down. It is the essence of any design activity that ends and means are linked into a single conceptual system. Any reference to ends is already resonant with means, and vice versa. It is this unity that makes design possible.[3] The existence of a morphology is the precondition for an imaginative and creative activity. The study of that morphology is therefore the study of the conditions within which design is possible. This is the theme of the paper.

But if architecture-as-activity is only possible because architecture-as-things exists, then there is more than a little inconsistency in arguing first that architecture is unlike science because it is concerned both with ends and means, and second that 'intention' can be separated out as the special preserve of non-science. But this conceals a more important oversight. Science has been concerned with systems which incorporate 'intentional' or 'purposeful' behaviour for nearly two hundred years, more or less since the notion of function became a main theme in the scientific investigation of natural forms. The notion of function as a creator of form, in a suitable environment, led to a new understanding of the importance of time, resulting eventually in the vast new perspective of evolution theory. Architecture, in spite of its predilection for organic analogies, has not yet passed through a parallel emancipation. It continues to operate in three-dimensional space, rather than in four dimensional space-time. The belief in the autonomy of intention in architecture is by and large an illusion resulting from the removal of time from the morphological field on which architecture acts, and with which it thinks. The re-introduction of time has the effect of making architectural science, potentially, and if we wish it, co-extensive with architecture, and makes it possible to study how the initiatives of the individual designer are linked to the higher-order systems by which each society constructs an artificial environment in its own image.

Physical time and biological time

Two distinct conceptualisations of time, one rooted in physics, the other in biology, have co-existed in science since the last century. The physical view of time developed through the notion of irreversibility. Any reversible process was shown to be accompanied by an irreversible sub-process, which continues in the same direction regardless of the direction of the main process. The irreversible sub-process is the progressive loss of energy available for work. At a general level, this is identified as the tendency to increased disorder, or entropy, in any system. The formulation of the concept of entropy thus led to a physicalist interpretation of time with an arrow pointing in one direction only. This concept might be conveniently referred to as *entropic time*.

Biological time was quite different, and in important ways opposite to the entropy interpretation. Darwinian evolution demonstrated that the variety of observable species was not to be accounted for in terms of the variable effects of the environments, but through the successive transformation of species into new species. Prior to Darwin 'environmental' determination was the scientific orthodoxy (formerly held by Darwin himself) with transformationism an improbable metaphysics. The transformational time defined by an evolutionary process was not marked by any kind of regular clock, not even the cosmos itself. It required no exogenous frame. It was defined by the successive appearance of new forms, in which the next was possible only because the last had occurred. This can be referred to as *morphogenetic time.*

Both concepts use nature to record time with unique directionality. But there is a difference. Entropic time is a time of observers located outside a system, able to observe changes in relations within the system and call them entropy. Morphogenetic time is time internal to the system, of the nature of its being a system and its form of organisation. It yields a space-time unfolding into greater rather than less organisation, eventually giving, as is the case with biological evolution, systems which are so logically complex that they see themselves, and begin to construct their own evolution.

Through the agency of physical analogue and statistical mechanical models, the physical view has dominated environmental studies. At a theoretical level this dominance had been reinforced by the adoption of 'general system theory', which attempts to reduce biological (or morphogenetic) time to physical (or entropic) time, in order to gain the advantages of the more easily available calculus associated with the latter. This has led to a generation of non-morphogenetic models which are in effect highly conservative, even leading to the covert introduction of 'social darwinism' which reduces evolution theory itself to physical time by emphasising the mechanics of natural selection at the expense of morphogenesis.

The loss of the morphogenetic theme is a high scientific (perhaps also social) price to pay for the instrumental advantages of a calculus. But there is another less obvious loss, and that is the possibility of bringing 'intentions' and 'purposes' within the domain of scientific enquiry. The notion of a system which projects a future state of itself by means of some set of 'symbols' (that is, entities that represent other entities, in an informational sense), which do not resemble the projected state as much as act as instructions for building it, is as old as Leibniz, and today offers the general explanatory framework for the study of living organisms at most levels of resolution. It provides a general theory of the means by which nature realises both the continuous production of structurally stable forms, and, in the longer view, morphogenetic transformation. To think of symbolic projections of future states in any system as being solely to do with extra-scientific 'intentional' behaviour (and in architecture to reduce this to the individual imagination) is clearly the result of taking too limited a view of the system, in effect taking it out of its temporal context. What appears at any moment in time as 'intentionality' is itself a possibility, created by the unfolding of that morphogenetic system up to that point in time. To say, for example, that a clock fulfils the purpose or intention 'to tell the time' may be adequate in everyday language, but from a scientific point of view it is misleading. To 'tell the time' is not a construct which exists independently of the artificial morphology defined by 'clocks'. It is a conceptual 'intention' existing only by virtue of the prior existence of that morphology of clocks unfolding in space-time.

The morphogenetic analysis does not of course solve the problem of 'is' and 'should' although it constrains it within a more limited field. But it does introduce a useful new category: the category of the 'might'. Any morphology must be defined as a set of possibilities, not all of which necessarily exist. The actual is not uniquely possible, but an instance of the possible. A morphological set may be thought of as existing either as a distribution of variety regardless of time, or as an ordered, evolutionary series with a unique time direction. It is noteworthy that, at a sufficient distance from our own society, this framework of analysis is normally adopted. An archaeologist or an anthropologist will not see 'intentions' or autonomous 'purposes', but an evolving morphology which links social action and thought to artificial things. The scientific study of contemporary artificial systems—it might be called the archaeology of the present—requires a parallel distancing.

Morphologies and codes

Any science, natural or artificial, has for its object a morphology that exhibits similarites and differences in space-time. The invariances, local and evolutionary, of the set is the object of theory. A theory takes the form of a model, made of symbols, which attempt to represent the space-time morphology as a set, or series of transformations. Operations on the symbols should reproduce, or be mappable into, the observed transformations in the morphology. If this is successful, then the invariances of the morphology might be held to be recaptured in the symbols, and a theory to exist. But to evaluate success, it is necessary to converse with the morphology without the intermediary of symbols, that is, we must displace it physically in some way (experiment), or simply observe it. The theoretical-practical duality of any scientific endeavour follows naturally from these considerations, as does the logical similarity of superficially different types of theoretical activity. For example, in one case the symbolic model may be an equation, the space-time morphology certain series of states of falling bodies, and the mode of direct conversation experimentation; and in another the symbolic model may be a series of sentences in natural language, the morphology human societies, and the mode of direct conversation systematic observation. In all cases however the results of science are structures of symbols which represent morphologies.

If natural morphologies are already internally structured (that is generated) through the mediation of symbol-like entities, then it follows that a scientific theory may actually take the form of simulation, in artificial symbols, of some structure of 'symbols' that already appears to exist within nature itself. The 'genetic code' is an example.

If the morphology in question is artificial rather than natural—say, language—then the situation is still more convoluted. First, any invariance in the morphology, which a theory of that artificial system will attempt to recapture, must be assumed to have already arisen through the agency of active and cognitive behaviour on the part of human beings, or their collectivities. Secondly, it must be assumed that some, or even all, of these invariances are already 'understood' in the same sense that the syntactic and semantic structures of language are understood, and in everyday use, without this 'understanding' being externalisable. Indeed it is largely through such autonomically 'understood' structures that language permits—to use Chomsky's memorable phrase—a 'rule-governed creativity'.

Many artificial morphologies exhibit these paradoxical properties of being autonomically 'meaningful' and usable while resisting scientific explanation as to how this is possible. Systems which are entirely non-mysterious in everyday life remain more inaccessible to scientific understanding than much of nature. Languages, cities, societies, cultural systems, architecture, even knowledge itself all illustrate this paradox. As a consequence special sciences have come into existence to study these systems, namely the sciences of the artificial. The branch known as structuralism explicitly studies what is already 'known' in the autonomic sense, that is it tries to reconstruct the conditions in which such 'knowing' is possible.

The morphologies that exhibit these paradoxical properties have one attribute in common: each either is, or contains, a system of social signification. It is this, rather than the physical nature and form of the morphology that renders it opaque to present scientific understanding. In the case of architecture, the problem resides in how architecture 'works' in relation to society. How and why do different societies at different times construct and transform artifical space, and what is the effect of these transformations. How can the *intelligibility* of artificial space be accounted for and reconstructed?

The concept of 'code' is useful in analysing such morphologies. The word 'code' has two slightly different meanings. It can be a structure of rules governing a particular morphology, say, a set of permissible behaviours. Or it can be a structure of rules for making translations, either between differently structured domains of the same morphology (as in the case of a code for transmitting secret information) or between two dissimilar morphologies (as in the case of a morphology in space-time related to an abstract or semantic morphology—language for example). The latter is the important one from the point of view of artificial morphologies which serve as signifying systems, since the formal requirement for intersubjective intelligibility to be available through such a system is that transformation within the space-time morphology should be systematically related to transformations in the semantic morphology. This would be the minimum structure necessary for such a system to transmit meaning.

If, in addition to the intelligibility requirement, the further stipulation is added that the morphology should work as a 'rule-governed creativity'—that is algorithmically, rather than on a basis of one-to-one mapping—then it implies that each of the dissimilar morphologies related in the code must possess its own internal structure, and that the translatability between the two must be at a level of parallel structural transformations, and not at the level of looking up forms in a dictionary which assigns a unique 'meaning' to each. Language exhibits this property in

both its domains. Words tend to be organised into syntagms and syntaxes. The 'semantics' embody, at the least, a bundle of interpretive schemes for dealing with reality and capable of 'solving problems' introduced by unfamilar experiences. Structures of this type are the subject matter of categorical algebra, and the best way of representing them formally is by treating the morphologies as the domains of an algebraic structure. A simple, yet mathematical, interpretation of the concept of 'meaning' is yielded through such formal structures of relationships.

Levi-Strauss has written extensively on the algebraic bases of cultural signifying systems, and has ascribed their existence to inherent properties of the human mind. The foregoing considerations suggest that his analysis is unnecessarily extreme. If account is taken of the 'dissimilar domains' structure of such codes, and the 'internal structure' requirement, then it is clear that during the evolution of the system there would be a need at each stage to maintain translatability between domains, and this could only be based on a formal translatability between the—possibly different—structures within either domain. In other words, a need for an algebraic mappability would ensure that at each stage of evolution, the whole system, and each domain separately, would retain an algebraic form by being related to the other. The space-time morphology would be internally ordered through the evolution of structurally stable states as it moved from simpler to more complex forms. The internal code of this morphology would be an abstract deposit of these structurally stable states. The concepts of structural stability and morphogenesis are keys to the nature of artificial codes, and translatability between dissimilar domains can be suggested as an alternative general theory for the algebraic nature of codes.

The concept of code thus offers a framework for the scientific analysis of artificial morophologies that is both rich and rigorous. It links together, in a natural way, aspects of the subject matter that are normally well separated and even thought incompatible. For example, it links the social and historical aspects to the mathematical. It links the study of modes of creating artificial space to the study of its intelligibility. It links the notion of underlying formal structure to that of a rich variety at the observable level. It links existent and past states to possible and non-existent states. The code is the means by which the unfolding of a morphology in space-time 'passes through the head'. By studying the history of that unfolding, and in particular its structurally stable states, in relation to the societies that produced them, we are in all likelihood studying the means of our own awareness of space, that is the cultural intelligibility of the morphology of artificial space.

The analysis of an artificial system on the basis of the concept of code requires three related studies. First, the study of a morphology and its internal rules of evolution, giving what might be termed an absolute or 'mindless' unfolding of that morphology. This, for convenience, may be called the syntactic domain. Second, the study of a semantic field to which the morphology refers, in a signifier-signified relation. This may be called the semantic domain. And third, the study of the translatability relations. The concept of code might be held to refer simply to the last, the translatability relations, but since these are meaningless without the two domains, then it is better to refer to the whole structure only as the code.

Statistical stability and structural stability

Science, being concerned with the introduction of novel artificial structures and relationships, namely those between symbolic systems and morphological domains, takes the form of a dialogue between the formal capabilities of symbolic systems and the morphological domains they aim to encapsulate. This requires the scientist to be aware of the *constructive* effect of symbolic systems on the world they describe. The universe seen through symbolic systems is likely to reflect the internal properties of that symbolic system. This can happen in mathematics as well as natural languages. Social scientists, for example, have mistaken the forms of the calculus, with its central notion of continuous concomitant variation, for mathematics itself, and even for science itself. Only relations, however few, reflecting this structuring effect of the dominant symbolic system were permitted to be 'scientific'. The use of structural mathematics in related fields like anthropology, and the growing knowlege of catastrophe theory,[4] are only slowly leading to an awakening from this 'dogmatic slumber' of the social sciences.

Awareness of this danger suggests that it is useful to establish a metacritique of the types of formal language available, and the properties of morphologies to which they might refer. In general, three types of property that morphologies present can be distinguished and referred to the properties of symbolic systems. First there are *logical* properties (for example: 'existing', or 'not being something else') which are, quite simply, the minimum properties of all objects. To this domain there corresponds the symbolic system of logic, which deals with those properties of objects which they share with all other objects. Second, there are *measurable* properties, the separating out of which was Galileo's great contribution to theoretical physics i.e. his 'primary' properties, as opposed to the 'secondary' properties which we imposed upon the object through our mode of perception. To these correspond the mathematics of quantity. Third, *semantic* properties, namely those which result from significant connectedness within and among morphologies, a subset of which map into human cognition, and are called 'meaningful'. To these there correspond the mathematical structures we normally think of as algebraic. The relations among, and mutual reducibility of, these different types of mathematical structure are of course of great importance in the history of epistemology, but they are not our theme here. Here this distinction is introduced in order to clarify the role of statistics in modelling artificial systems.

Statistics is essentially the logic of aggregates. Like logic, it requires only that a set of objects has a property, say, of corresponding to a point on a continuous scale, or of adopting, at any point in time, one of two fixed states. Then, given that the process is random, meaning that there is no connection between objects or events (no significant connectedness, or semantics), statistics can make good predictions about the behaviour of such aggregates, since in large enough samples these will approach statistical stability as expressed, for example, in a normal distribution curve. Where the process is non-random, for example when the events in a sequence are such that an event is influenced by previous events in the sequence (as in a sentence for example), then we introduce more algebra into the equations.

The importance of this randomness requirement is not always realised. It implies that when a set has a strong internal structure or is observed only in small numbers, then its properties or behaviour will less easily conform to the basic pattern of statistical stability. Structure is the enemy of statistical stability. To use a simple example, if we regularly patronise a coffee house, and the strength of the coffee varies from being very strong to very weak and back again, rather than oscillating around a mean strength, and this holds even for a large number of visits, then we know that the process is non-random, and that some stable structure has interfered in the system to produce statistical disorder—that is, a stable deviation from the normal distribution curve that a random process of coffee-making would produce. For example, there exists a rota for coffee-making on alternate days and the different coffee-makers make it wrongly in a different way. This relation between structure and statistical disorder at the level of resolution at which we first seek it is of the utmost importance. Moreover, for large numbers, it is essential that the interference structure should be structurally stable, or it would not produce interference in the statistical stability of the sample.

This quickly leads to qualitative break-off points in the type of order we can hope to find in a system. Consider a simple spatial example of swimmers depositing towels on an undifferentiated beach. The order in such a system could be described, for large numbers, in terms of some probable spatial distribution of clustering taking into account such factors as point of entry to the beach and so on. But take those swimmers away from the beach and put them in a more complex environment, say, wooded dunes, and give them a packet of sandwiches and a qualitatively different situation appears. In this case the distribution will be largely determined by a new stable structure, namely that the swimmers will locate themselves by finding realisations in the rich environment for a model 'in the head' which tells them what a picnic place is like. Although we have only increased the degree of differentiation in the system, it is clear that our concept of order must be of a different kind from the statistical one that worked in the less differentiated case. The situation is still highly ordered, but not in terms of a statistically stable distribution on a surface.

In social science it is these structurally stable deviations from statistical stability that should be studied. Statistical disorder is interesting because it requires us to look for such a structure. In this case the possibility of a purely statistical order acquire a very useful role as a starting place, since it tells us what the system would be like if it were random, that is if it lacked semantic properties, that acted as structurally stable interference effects in the statistical stability. The task of any science is to arrive at a random process in respect of its morphology, that is, to name and relate all structure that produces non-randomness, such that what remains in the space-time manifestation of the morphology is random and therefore epiphenomenal. Codes are structurally stable producers of non-randomness.

Function and form in architecture

That buildings are 'functional' and 'meaningful' is self-evident, but it is equally self-evident through the morphogenetic analysis, that 'function' and 'meaning' exist and are intelligible by virtue of the evolution of a morphology of built forms. This requires us to make a further fundamental distinction in the study of artificial systems, one which is familiar in linguistics but not in sociology or architecture. This is the distinction between the morphology itself, as it exists at any point in time, and the individual or corporate appropriation and use of that morphology. The first corresponds to what the linguists call the level of language, which is a structure of social conventions independent of the individual; the second corresponds to speech, or the individual appropriation of the existing morphology. The natural linkage of the higher order, supra-individual morphological domain with the individualised, but still structured appropriation of it that linguistics proposes, works well for architecture, and leads away from the mystique of 'intentions' without sacrificing creativity.

A conceptual difficulty arises with architecture because the morphology of forms exhibits what we might call 'negative redundancy' in relation to function: that is, nearly everything functions in more than one sense. This can be understood by looking at the evolution of built form in terms of a fundamental duality: that buildings at once function as modifiers of the relation between man and nature and as modifiers of the relation between man and other men. But this duality is not strange. In fact it is normal. All systems by which mankind changes its relation to nature are also elaborated into systems of social signification. We might consider eating as an example. Eating fulfils an energy transfer need, but at the same time it is embedded into complex and pleasurable cultural forms. In social terms, the functional nature of all such artificial systems is to exhibit this duality. To restrict its function to the physiological aspects desocialises the morphology and renders it unintelligible.

The matrix of these dualities, man-nature and man-man, and 'language' and 'speech', constructs the four function model of architecture.[5] At the level of 'speech' or 'design', the man-nature relation is the climate modification function of the building; at the level of 'language' or 'morphology' it becomes the resource modification function. The man-man relation at the lower level is the level of interaction between activity and space; at the higher level it is space as a social language constructed through the properties of the morphology. This paper is concerned with the last named, the man-man relation at the level of the 'language as a whole'.

In all such artificial systems the existence of the language-like morphological level is the precondition for the speech-like 'design' level. To try to consider design independently of its morphological domain which makes it possible is like trying to explain speech without understanding the structure and properties of language. The important question is: *how* is it that higher order morphologies are constructive of speech or design acts? Is it simply by providing a set of morphological images which can be transmitted? Or is it important that, in architecture as in language, this relation should work algorithmically, and not on a one-to-one basis, in which case we must assume it has a more abstract nature? Again the concept of code comes to our assistance. One aim of the second part of this paper is to show how and why the transmission is algorithmic and abstract, rather than imagistic and one-to-one. In explaining this we shall use the notion of code to link sociological and logico-mathematical properties, and in effect to give a sociological and historical interpretation to the formal properties of built form which are embedded not so much in the morphologies as in the relations defined by morphologies. It is the abstract nature of this transmission structure—the code—that links the generation of built form to our understanding of it. It passes through the mind both ways.

The hypothesis is that the relation of human behaviour and cognition to artificial space is governed by an evolutionary code, which explains both our modes of constructing space and the way it is intelligible to us. The morphology therefore exhibits the properties of social language. The abstract code will account for the similarities and differences in the morphology, and show how our understanding of them depends on a matrix of socio-spatial abstractions. From an empirical point of view, the code can be seen as a structurally stable interference in an otherwise random statistical order, existing at the level of interaction between activity and space. In terms of architecture as a whole, the analysis is incomplete, since it does not deal with the man-nature side of building. Nevertheless, it offers a framework for integrative analysis of both aspects.

The logic of space

The research programme implied by this theoretical perspective is therefore concerned with the reconstruction of a code which produces structurally stable differentiations in the forms of artificial space, and can be thought of as equivalent to a theory of that morphology. The test of such a theory is its ability to map observable transformations into transformations within the symbolism in which the theory is embedded.

This is an orthodox, hypothetico-deductive scientific strategy, but its epistemological stance is quite different from that of system theorists. The meta-theoretical statements of system approaches normally argue that all models are relative to the observer's intentions and purposes.[6] This is not self-evidently true. A covert anthropomorphism underlies the relativistic modesty of system modellers. Surely nature itself has its own models? The genetic code is not relative to observers, since epistemologically speaking we cannot doubt the existence of some such structure. The genetic code may be thought of by us as relative to our sign systems, and the conceptual schemes they imply. But from a scientific point of view such structures exist in nature as 'internal' models, and much of modern biological research is concerned to reconstruct them.

In the domain of the artificial, these concerns are reinforced. Language may be considered as an example of a structure which undoubtedly has a formal structure independent of observers (indeed it is that which gives it its creative usability by individuals). A model for a grammar may be wrong, but this does not imply an epistemological relativity. The difference between 'structuralist' and 'system theoretic' approaches in the sciences of the artificial is given by this distinction between what might be called 'internal' (structuralist) models and 'external' (system theoretic) models; this in turn links into the distinction between morphogenetic time (internal models) and entropic time (external models).[7] The research strategy implied by the internalist programme could be characterised approximately as treating reality as the print-out from a computer, and trying to deduce or reconstruct the program.

Another way of looking at it is to suggest that the Galilean hypothesis (that physical reality *is* mathematical, and that equations are more than useful instruments) is being transferred from the natural to the artificial world. If artificial reality is indeed logic-mathematical in some sense, then it should not be thought surprising. Mathematics and logic are themselves artificial, and since they attempt to deal with the formal and abstract properties that are not written on the surface of things, at the same time as representing our cognitive operations on things, then it would be no surprise if foundational ideas in mathematics were also pervasive structuring forms in artificial domains. Both in biology and artificial sciences, structuralism is founded on this anticipated isomorphism.

In the case of artificial space, the point acquires force through a simple analogy between spatial and logical forms. The simplest gesture of artificial space is that of defining a barrier. A barrier distinguishes two types of space from each other. If no distinction were required, then no barrier would be required. This corresponds exactly to the basic gesture in the logic of classes, that is drawing a distinction by putting a barrier between concepts. Moreover, in space as in logic, this gesture can be made either in terms of distinguishing two types of space both with positively different properties, or in distinguishing one positive type and its complement or negation, that is lacking the property. Again by making a barrier permeable, we define a relation between types of space. The clarity introduced into formal logic by Venn diagrams might be thought of as illustrating this close analogy between space and logic. Finally it could be argued that, like logic, architecture begins with simple spatio-logical gestures in three-space, then elaborates them into many-dimensional structures in logical space. It is through this that in building walls and holes we build intelligibility and complexity.

Spatial surfaces and aggregation modes

In all artificial systems which construct inter-subjective 'meaning', the question arises as to the level of resolution at which this meaning is principally decipherable. In language, for example, it is *not* the level of the word. Any word is prolific with possible meanings, as any check with a dictionary will show. Language nevertheless manages to achieve unambiguous definition of the meaning of a particular word by extensive use of the context of the word, including the other words around it, the epistemological context of the speech act, and such extra-verbal cues as style and gesture. These are not gratuitous and decorative aspects of language, but technical devices for fixing meaning across a semantic field that is vastly larger than it would be if word and meaning were in one-to-one correspondence.

From the point of view of words, the sentence is the minimum viable meaning form although even this still requires all the context variables. This appears to have an interesting correspondence with the way in which people and architects experience artificial space. Architects both design buildings and tend to see buildings as the basic unit of environmental experience. The architectural culture can be virtually defined in terms of the tendency to select a particular building from an aggregate and give it unique attention. For the layman, unless he shares the architectural culture, the situation is usually different. His experience is usually at the level of 'place', that is the general properties of the location and situation in which he finds himself.

Given that buildings, like words, may be rich with possible meaning in themselves, another promising analogy with language suggests itself. Everyday experience of space appears to be much more at a level comparable with the sentence, that is the aggregate of buildings in a particular location. This is confirmed by the way in which spatial terms and their associated social semantics are embedded in the unconscious semantic structures of language, in which words like 'village', 'suburban', 'urban' and so on are spatial descriptions which carry with them a mode of social existence. They appear to constitute, as it were, islands of structural stability in the socio-spatial code.

No term exists in architectural discourse for this level of experience, and certainly no technical term. Since it appears that the elementary level of environmental experience may be that of the 'sentence', or characteristic aggregate, a new term is needed. The term *'spatial surface'* is suggested. The primary level at which the socio-spatial code expresses itself through the language of the morphology of artificial space is this 'spatial surface'.

It might appear that in moving up the scale of complexity, an insuperable problem of formal description is likely to arise. Are spatial surfaces not infinitely variable? In certain ways they are, of course, but in terms of certain structural properties they are much simpler to describe than buildings. As is normally the case with hierarchically organised systems, micro-state complexity yields a macro-state simplicity. In some fields it is very difficult to say how this happens (picking up a cup of coffee for example, is a simple macro-state gesture involving phenomenal micro-state complexity), but in the case of artificial spatial surfaces it is relatively simple. Their general structural properties are given by the way in which the spatial surface is generated. These processes of generation can be termed: *aggregation modes*. That aggregation modes take relatively few basic forms can be seen by considering a little more closely the logic of spatial elaboration.

Buildings are normally thought of as enclosing space. But they also define external space. They do so individually, but more importantly as aggregates they define higher-order spaces. An aggregation mode is a rule structure concerned with what can and cannot be done after space has been enclosed, both in the substantive proximate space, and in the marginal spaces

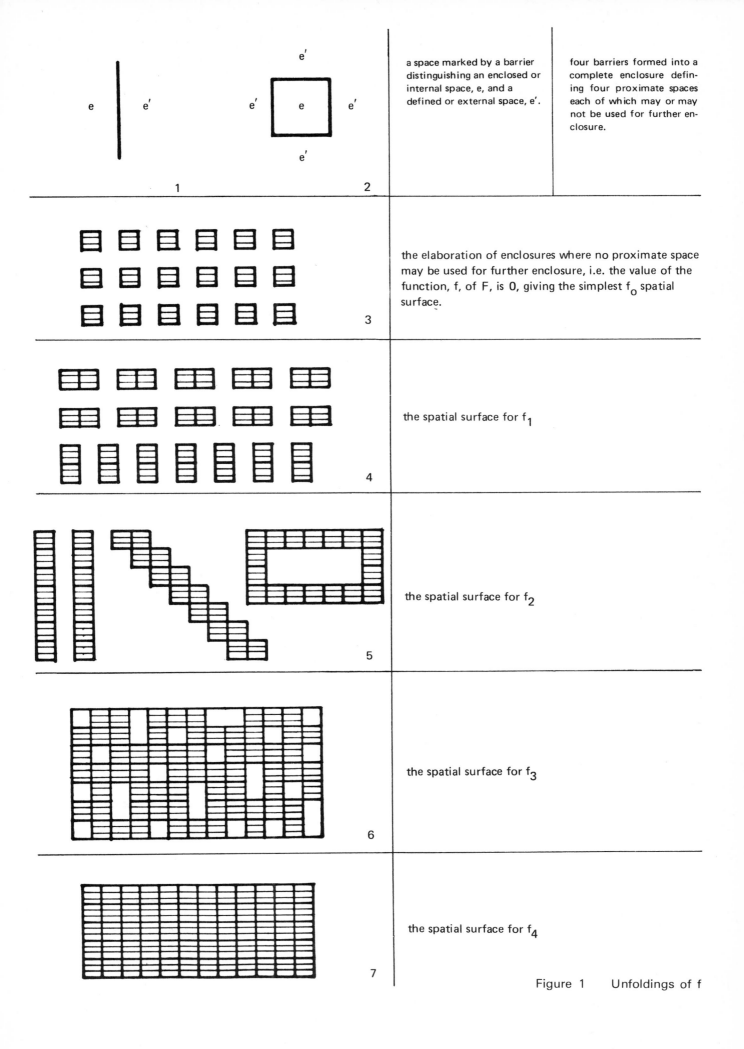

a space marked by a barrier distinguishing an enclosed or internal space, e, and a defined or external space, e'.

1

four barriers formed into a complete enclosure defining four proximate spaces each of which may or may not be used for further enclosure.

2

the elaboration of enclosures where no proximate space may be used for further enclosure, i.e. the value of the function, f, of F, is 0, giving the simplest f_0 spatial surface.

3

the spatial surface for f_1

4

the spatial surface for f_2

5

the spatial surface for f_3

6

the spatial surface for f_4

7

Figure 1   Unfoldings of f

defined by the shape of the building. It is these socially defined rule structures which give rise to the characteristic structural differences in spatial surface, and it is at this level that the morphology of artificial space acts as a social language. Aggregation modes, it will be seen, are invariant under changes of style, technology and decoration. They provide the rudimentary schemes on which decoration may elaborate. It is aggregation modes which account for the manifest homology of socio-spatial forms distributed through different cultures in time and space. Also the major transformations in the morphology of space that are occurring today are through the dramatic effects of changes in the aggregation modes, and their social semantics.

It will be noted that a radical change in the mathematical strategy is implied by these concepts. A generative approach is to be substituted for a descriptive one. This is a major simplification, since it is argued that *the structural properties of spatial surfaces on which 'meaning' (and therefore the usage code) hangs are given by the generative rules for that spatial surface.* This generative approach applies both to the local (in space and time) generation of a spatial surface, and to the evolution of the code itself on an evolutionary scale.

The concept of system also changes with this approach. The task is not to describe a system as it is presented to an observer, in order to introduce better external controls on its further development, but to understand *how the system generates itself, and produces its own internal order,* that is its structurally stable states and processes within an evolution of a socio-spatial morphology. In such a system there are no simple elements, only relations between morphological and semantic domains. Moreover it has already been shown how complex a barrier is, seen from a logical point of view. The secret of the evolution of such systems, and that which solves the problem of relations between micro-states and macro-states, is that the 'simplest structures' (rather than 'elements') of such a system contain within themselves structural variables which lead, when simplest structures are combined together, to variable unfoldings into higher order systems. It is the object of the next stages of the paper to argue that these unfoldings possess stages of structural stability in both morphological and semantic domains of the code, and in the translatability relations.

The 'system' described is, of course, a large, incomplete and evolving abstraction, which is not directly observable (any more than the equation for a falling body is observable); moreover it is probable that no complete embodiment of the 'system' exists on the ground, but that nevertheless it is the means by which what does exist on the ground, with all its local and historical contingency, is intelligible. At this stage it is clear that a virtual reversal of the concept of 'model' is involved, since it is argued that this abstraction is the most 'real' thing, and that the realisation in space-time—the artificial spaces we see—are 'models' for this abstract structure of relations. But such a reversal is familiar. This is the concept of model used in mathematical logic, where a 'model' for a structure of logical symbols is a realisation in some mathematical domain.

This might be thought an intellectual extravagance, were it not that this coincides precisely with our present understanding of how language works, and how it relates to acts of speech and understanding. It appears that we need a paradigm in which the whole of language and its semantic field is in action with every linguistic act. It has, for example, been demonstrated that in order to decode certain sentences exactly—which in practice are not difficult but which a computer cannot manage—it is necessary for the decoder to have access to virtually the entire field of knowledge of the speaker[8] If artificial space is intelligible, there is no reason why it should not be because a knowledge of the whole code is embedded in our representation of the morphological field, such that as with language, the whole structure can be action in interpreting environmental experience. How this relation of the whole code structure to the particular situation and experience is constructed will also be part of the subject matter of the ensuing section.

Elementary syntax of spatial surfaces

The general form of a code is that two dissimilar, internally structured domains are linked by translation rules, such that transformations within one domain can be mapped systematically into transformations in the other. Where one domain is morphological and the other abstract, a syntax-semantics distinction can conventionally be used. This duality of a morphological reality and a domain of abstract 'meaning' characterises artificial space, but it is also necessary to make a further sub-division within each domain into two further sub-domains, giving four domains in all.

It has already been observed that the simplest architectural gesture, the indication of a barrier, yields an already complex structure, namely a relation between an enclosed and non-enclosed space formed by a barrier, both being mapped into a semantic domain. The four domains of the code are all present in this structure:

(1) logical differentiation of types of space, that is the reasons for enclosure or non-enclosure
(2) the barrier arising from (1), the act of differentiation, forming enclosures and defining non-enclosures
(3) the permeability of enclosures in relation to non-enclosures and other enclosures
(4) rules governing what may happen next in the proximate spaces defined by the enclosure

The hypothesis is that each domain has an internal structure, such that its transformations can be mapped into transformations in all other domains.

Call logical differentiation A, barriers forming enclosures E, permeability P and rules for further elaboration F. For purposes of initial exposition, let each of A, E, and P and F adopt one of two states: the positive state, A, E, P and F and the negative state A', E', P' and F'. Thus A or A' distinguishes a reason for being E or E', enclosed or non-enclosed, implying P or P', the form of permeability between enclosed and non-enclosed (or enclosed and other enclosed) and a rule F or F', which says whether or not a further enclosure can be constructed in the proximate space to the enclosure. This gives an overall structure:

$$[[A \lor A'] \rightarrow [E \lor E']] \rightarrow [[P \lor P'] \rightarrow [F \lor F']]$$

This represents the logical form of the simplest arch-

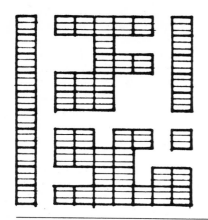

a randomly produced spatial surface for f_3 (P), that is f_3 subject to the constraint of accessibility for all second-order interior spaces showing typical second-order forms produced.

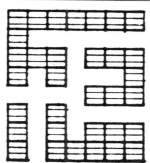

a further example of a randomised process subject to f_3 (P).

ground plan of section of a squatter settlement in Old Delhi showing schematic conformity to f_3 (P) in terms of general types of second-order spaces.

source: Payne G: Functions of Informality: a case study of squatters settlements in India, *Architectural Design,* Aug. 1973.

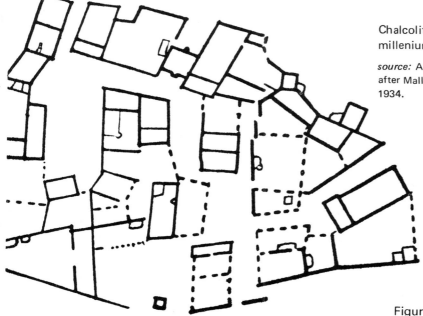

Chalcolithic village at Tell 1 Tuleilat Ghassul, 4th millenium BC, showing schematic conformity to f_3 (P).

source: Anati E: *Palestine before the Hebrews,* Cape, 1963, p 308, after Mallan A. & Koppel R: *Tuleilat Ghassul, Vols. I & II,* Rome, 1934.

Figure 2   Unfoldings of f_3 (P): formal and real

itectural gesture. Conventionally, E and P may be thought of as syntactic, since they refer to the ordering of physical entities, A and F as semantic since they refer to ordering of abstractions.

For the sake of simplicity assume that a complete enclosure is made of four barriers in the form of a square. This is the basic unit of operation, and carries with it all the structure in the above expression. Let A be such that for *each* barrier a rule F or F$'$ governs what may happen in the external space beyond the barrier, namely F, 'free to enclose again', or F$'$ 'not free to enclose again'. Thus for each *completed* enclosure, A determines a function f, which may have a value from 0-4 according to how many of its barriers may be built against. Thus for an enclosure with f_0 none of its four barriers may be built against; an f enclosure may have one of its four barriers built against, and so on up to f_4 which may have all its barriers built against. A space, defined by an enclosure, is assigned, through the act of enclosure, a rule which says whether or not the proximate space is free to be built upon or conserved. A randomised process is then assumed to operate, using these rules and structures, in a finite, isotropic space until the space is as densely filled as possible subject to the rules and structure.

Examples of the outcomes of such operations are given in *figure 1*. Obviously for f_0 the result is a series of free-standing pavilions because each time an enclosure is completed no wall may be built against any other. The surface is full when no more enclosures can be fitted in without touching each other. For f_1 the results are rather similar, but the units are semi-detached; f_2 is more interesting—the more familiar constructions of streets and squares as well as a variety of zig-zag shapes are derived; f_3 is more maze-like, constructing a series of courtyards usually some of unit size, and some of twice unit size; f_4 eventually fills the whole spatial surface. Each of these is topologically distinct, f_0 is a ball; f_1 two joined balls, f_2 is a line including a line joined to itself i.e. a circle; f_3 is a kind of net; and f_4 is a dense block. It is interesting to compare these results with those of March on the floor-space index of different configurations.

All this is straightforward but illustrates a point that may not be so obvious. A relatively random process of aggregation, given that there is a simple rule, can produce complex, recognisably different and structurally stable higher-order aggregations.

Matters may be complicated by introducing a further factor, namely a permeability constraint P, which says that all defined spaces shall be accessible to each other and from the outside. This has the effect of making the spatial surface appear more lifelike. When P is applied to f_3, for example, the spatial surface generated is very similar to such structures as the squatter settlements of Delhi and the Chalcolithic village at Tuleilat Ghassul *(figure 2)*. The typical sub-surfaces (e.g. two short parallel lines, a U-shape, an isolated block) of these real forms are generated by the formulas f_3 (P) operating in an otherwise random process. These simple examples illustrate the idea of *a model in which the mode of generation is said to be the model's structure.*

Such structures can be termed the first order unfolding of the syntax. They offer an initial simplified ap-proximation of some of the properties that we might wish to characterise as those of spatial surfaces, and show these differences to be, from a simple-minded and purely mathematical point of view, a set of transformations. This may be more theoretically interesting than it is lifelike, because only part of the total code has been utilised, and also because it has only been applied at one level. The spatial surfaces generated would go on endlessly unless stopped by an arbitrary barrier, or some rule for making finite, structurally stable higher order structures out of the unfolding of the syntax. The next stage of the argument therefore concerns the production of structurally stable higher order unfoldings, which we will call the 'elementary forms' of artificial space, since this is what we believe them to be.

The rule for the generation of elementary forms out of the syntactic process for the production of spatial surface is close to the heart of the argument: it is that once a rule has produced a structure, the rule can then be applied to the structure itself. In other words, the rule operates continuously, and it can make itself more complex objects to work on. This is the key to the syntactic evolution of spatial form. In fact this rule has already been covertly used in moving from barriers to enclosure i.e. use barrier to make the simplest closed form. When four barriers make an enclosure, rules can then be applied to the enclosure as a whole. This operation of 'same rule, more structure' will also be useful in the discussion of the semantic evolution of artificial space. It is the key to the generation of extremely complex, but structurally stable, forms out of simple operations, and shows in principle how the code both produces and renders intelligible the highly complex forms of space that we experience in every-day life.

The next problem is therefore to define what new structure has been created, and what is the effect of continuing to apply the rules in a process which includes the new structure as well as the old. Most of the new structures are self-evident, the set comprises variously connected aggregations of enclosures, some discontinuous, some continuous in varying degrees. These are shown in *figures 1 and 2*. One more new structure is less obvious. Whenever there is a defined space which is non-free, that is, one that is conserved empty, there exists what could be termed an 'open space barrier', which is of indeterminate depth. A secondary, or notional barrier has been created at some distance from the barrier which defined the space, which exists whether or not it is fixed or marked on the map. In the case of an f_0 structure, this open space barrier extends all the way round the enclosure, and by implication, a more complex structure has already been created than appeared to be the case.

If this notional barrier around the f_0 is completed by being fixed, or even built as a physical barrier, then one of the two major elementary forms had been created, namely the pavilion surrounded at a distance by a secondary barrier *(figure 3_1)*. This is termed the 'inout' elementary form, since the enclosure governs a set of open spaces in a relation that is both in-to-out, and one-to-many. That this form has an inverse is well known to all who have seen the motif of Land Use and Built Form Studies. The set of continuous enclosures around a perimeter, enclosing an open space in an out-

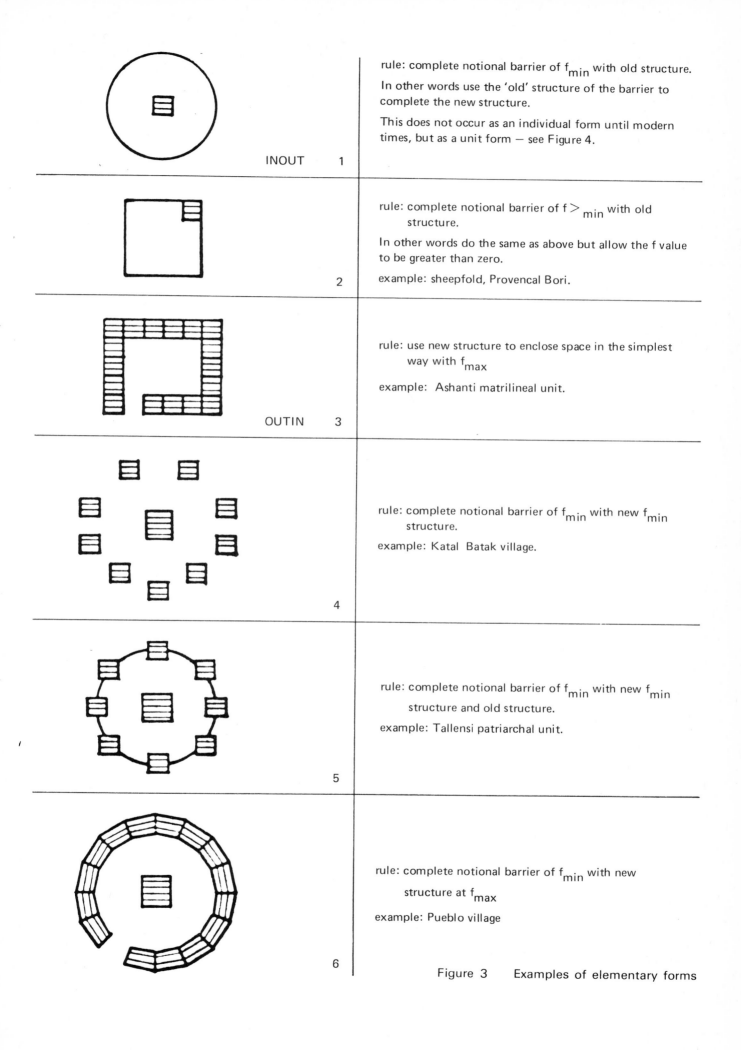

INOUT   1

rule: complete notional barrier of f_{min} with old structure.

In other words use the 'old' structure of the barrier to complete the new structure.

This does not occur as an individual form until modern times, but as a unit form — see Figure 4.

2

rule: complete notional barrier of $f >_{min}$ with old structure.

In other words do the same as above but allow the f value to be greater than zero.

example: sheepfold, Provencal Bori.

OUTIN   3

rule: use new structure to enclose space in the simplest way with f_{max}

example: Ashanti matrilineal unit.

4

rule: complete notional barrier of f_{min} with new f_{min} structure.

example: Katal Batak village.

5

rule: complete notional barrier of f_{min} with new f_{min} structure and old structure.

example: Tallensi patriarchal unit.

6

rule: complete notional barrier of f_{min} with new structure at f_{max}

example: Pueblo village

Figure 3   Examples of elementary forms

to-in, many-to-one relation can be termed the 'outin' elementary form. Its generation in the syntax is equally simple. It is the unique product of the rule: maximising the value of f at the first order level, use whatever structure exists to make a second order enclosure *(figure 3$_3$).*By contrast, the rule for the inout form is: minimising the value of f at the first order level, use whatever structure exists to make a second order enclosure. Thus the syntax produces these two primary elementary forms literally as inverses of each other. It is noteworthy that both forms have a 'double boundary structure', that is one in which two boundaries must be crossed to move from 'outside' to 'inside'. The generation of double boundary structures is of pervasive importance in the evolution of the urban spatial surface.

They are however only the two simplest outcomes of the second order generative process. *Figure 3* illustrates a further selection of elementary forms that may be generated at the second order level, together with their generative rules. So far as can be seen at this stage—that is prior to any exhaustive programme of generation and testing against real world data—these unfoldings offer a syntactic taxonomy for a large proportion of village and semi-settled forms that have become familiar in recent years through the ethnographic and photographic works of Rudovsky, Fraser and others.[9] A full interpretation of these villages as socio-spatial systems however requires also the semantic component of the argument (discussed later) as well as a study of local and historical contingenices of the normal technological and environmental kind.

A further distinction is critical to the further evolution of complex spatial systems. This is the distinction between what can be termed multiple and unit forms. A multiple form is one that is generated as an aggregate following a rule. Once it exists however it is clear that it can itself be a template for further similar forms, without the process of generation needing to be repeated every time. Again this idea has been implicitly used between the level of the barrier and that of the enclosure. The unit form is therefore a multiple form used as a template. An example would be the in-out elementary form used as a template for a large institutional building. A section of more complex unit forms is given in *figure 4.* All these forms exist in Banister Fletcher,[10] except one which exists only in multiple form, and which is crucial to the evolution of urban form.

The distinction between unit and multiple forms is of fundamental importance in the evolution of higher order structures, since it permits a design-like activity to be an intrinsic part of the evolutionary process. In fact it is tempting to view design—when seen within the scope of an evolutionary morphology—to be precisely to do with the use of templates, as opposed to the auto-generation of form following rules. A designed form is of its nature defined as finite, as opposed to self-ending as is an auto-generative, rule governed form. The consequences of this for the design of a town are interesting, since it appears to suggest a third category between designed order and contingent chaos: namely that of an auto-generative order of a process subject to generative rules. The form of towns as we know them is certainly of this kind. A paper is in preparation demonstrating the syntactic evolution of urban form, showing that it appears, in its familiar forms, as a fourth order unfolding, a conclusion which is paralleled in the semantic unfolding. This offers a natural and internal theory of the equifinal production of urban form by societies relatively independent of each other, and also for its structural stability until modern times. It also offers a formal set of reasons for the rapid transition from early settled life in villages to the first elaboration of proto-urban forms. Much work however remains to be done, and initial hypotheses are all that can be offered within this paper.

Semantics of spatial surfaces

The work of Piaget has revitalised the question of the relation between mathematics and life. By showing that structures of algebra and logic can serve as models of explanation for cognitive behaviour—he offers them literally as 'internal' models of intelligence—and that these may originate in the concrete operations of the infant (more precisely, in their co-ordination), Piaget has linked the foundations of mathematics to the foundations of behaviour and thought. Structuralist linguistics and anthropology suggest that this approach can also be applied nearer to the surface of perceived reality, and that mathematical structuralism may provide as fertile a form of explanation in the non-natural sciences as it does in the natural sciences. An underlying theme of this paper is that the many domain structures of categorical algebra may provide models for 'meaning' and intelligibility in artificial systems.

The discovery that mathematical apparatus used in advanced areas of natural science can also serve as internal models for the cognitive behaviour of children and the social arrangements of 'primitive' people (group theory for example is used both in theoretical physics and in the study of kinship systems) is not a surprising convergence if proper account is taken of the duality of any cognitive process, between the figurative properties of the universe as it presents itself to our perceptions, and the ordering operations which the perceiving subjects applies to that universe to give it intelligibility. Classification, for example, one of the simpler cognitive processes, exhibits this duality by requiring two mental gestures to complete an act of classification: first, an intensional act by which the defining property, or intension, of a class is named; then an act of enumeration in terms of that property by which the extension of the class is established. The intensional act refers to the operational ordering of phenomena in terms of some structured view of reality in the subject, the extensional act to the figurative properties of entities enumerated in terms of that ordering.

This duality shows that any cognitive process must be seen as a dialogue between the ordering operation of an active subject, and the morphological properties of the universe. 'Primitive' people, in bringing order and intelligibility into their universes, naturally make use of the logico-algebraic ordering apparatus of 'intelligence'. That they do so, and do so at the level of observables, and also that they construct their artificial signifying systems using the same apparatus, has been the theme of Levi-Strauss. The discovery of logico-algebraic structures as ordering principles in primitive cultural systems is not surprising. They arise

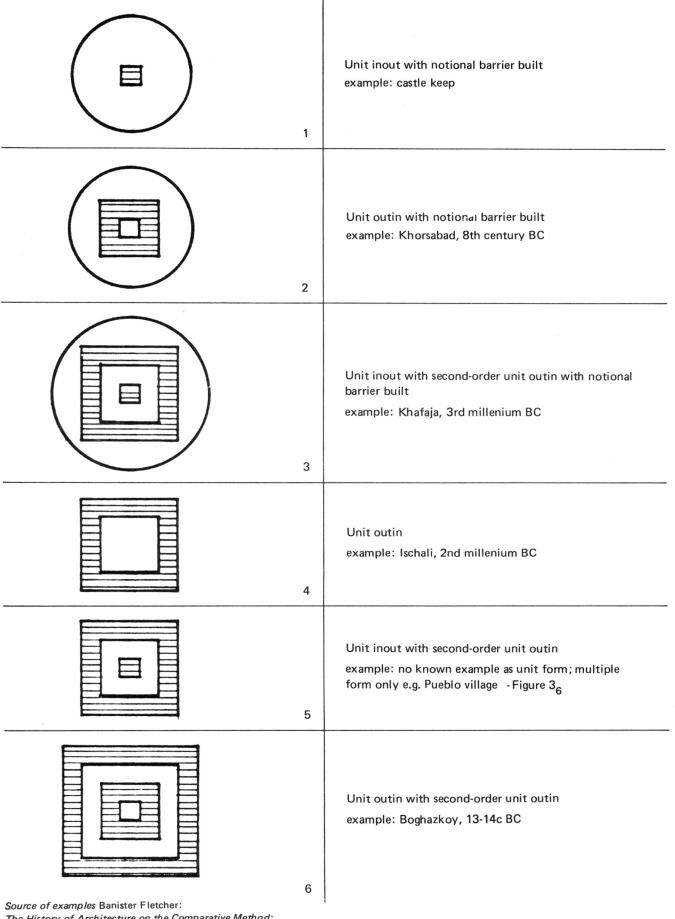

1   Unit inout with notional barrier built
example: castle keep

2   Unit outin with notional barrier built
example: Khorsabad, 8th century BC

3   Unit inout with second-order unit outin with notional barrier built
example: Khafaja, 3rd millenium BC

4   Unit outin
example: Ischali, 2nd millenium BC

5   Unit inout with second-order unit outin
example: no known example as unit form; multiple form only e.g. Pueblo village - Figure 3_6

6   Unit outin with second-order unit outin
example: Boghazkoy, 13-14c BC

Source of examples Banister Fletcher:
The History of Architecture on the Comparative Method:
London, Athlone 1961. First published 1896

Figure 4   Examples of unit forms

from the operational side of cognitive activity. However, such a simple ordering process, limited to observables, inevitably generates anomalies, which the elaborate strategies of myth attempt to explain away.

By contrast, science is intolerant of anomaly and looks beyond the inconsistent surface of things for internal ordering processes. But science also adopts a dual strategy, reflecting the dual nature of the cognitive act. It makes explicit its idea that there is 'significant connectedness' in the morphologies that are its object. In other words science lays bare its theories in order to test and, if necessary, change them. Secondly, science makes explicit its own operations by constructing formal symbolic systems which embody the operational aspects of cognition. These are laid out besides the exposed theory so that tests of the mapping between the two can be made and may be explored in an externalistic way. In doing so science progressively discovers and elaborates the internal transformability of mathematical structures, and increasingly these provide models for the transformability of natural morphologies (and, like language, provide in themselves objects of interest for scientists to study).

This leads to the identification of two levels for the application of logico-mathematical structures. First, the *everyday level* of their *unconscious* and unreflective application in order to produce, out of the observable universe, intelligibility and significance. This results in the continuous construction of artificial systems of significance which we call 'cultures' which embody the transformability of logico-algebraic structures, discovered through cognitive action. Secondly, the *scientific level* of the *conscious* exploration of the transformability of logico-algebraic structures in relation to hypothesised internal ordering properties of morphologies. When we apply the second to an understanding of the first, as when anthropologists study primitive peoples, or psychologists experiment with children, we discover an unexpected isomorphism between mathematics, including its transformability, and real life. It is clear on closer inspection that this should not suprise us.

These considerations may help to understand what often appears as a basic paradox in the relation of logic and life: logico-algebraic structures appear to be of the nature of all artificial systems, yet to explain none fully. Logic, it appears, is too pure to represent the internal ordering of artificial systems like cultures. The requirement appears to be that imperfection should be taken account of in an ordered way.

But this apparent paradox only results from the covert assumption that the logico-algebraic structures of cognitive operations are actual properties of the universe to which the operations are applied. For example, to say with respect to any binary distinction that an object either has or has not the property, Y, is a statement about cognitive operations upon the world, not about the world itself. With respect to logical 'truth' the misunderstanding is more far-reaching. Logical truth is a production of the symbolic system of logic, and says nothing about the world to which it refers. To produce 'scientific truth' from 'logical truth' requires a perfect mapping between the domain of logical symbols and the real world, but this mapping would itself have to be represented in a perfectly map-pable set of symbols, and this leads to an infinite regress.

With regard to the man-made semantic universes we call cultures, a parallel point can be made. Just as the logical operation of the constructive subject does not imply a parallel ordering of the real universe, so the logical method of constructing systems of signification does not mean that the resultant semantic field will itself exhibit such a simple ordering. It is much more likely to exhibit the result of a logico-algebraic procedure operating in a universe which consistently fails to respond to the simplicity of its operations. The initial question should be: how can logico-algebraic operational structures cope with the continual discovery of the imperfect results of its own perfect operations, and a universe that continually poses problems for our logical activity?

The history of 'thought about thought' is full of the awareness of such imperfection. The Chinese Yin-Yang symbol—a disc divided in an S-shape, but with each half of the division carrying a remnant of the other—expressed its dominanace in Chinese thought. Leach has commented on the importance of anomalies in classificatory schemes in, for example, providing animal categories for swearing and other purposes.[11] In physics itself, the imperfection of a process came to be seen as its most important physical property. There are many other examples.

Boolean algebra (taken here as the simplest paradigm for logical operations) however is founded on the exclusion of imperfection. This exclusion is expressed through the Boolean concept of 'negation', and the related concept of 'universe'. In any universe, U, with objects, x, then the property p or not-p accounts for all objects in the universe:

$$[x : p(x)] \cup [x : \neg p(x)] = U$$

and this is true for an extension of the universe. The structure of assumptions says that a universe exists (not necessarily a 'universal' universe, but perhaps a defined universe of discourse) and that the operation of negation in terms of any property divides that universe into two parts with no remainder.

In terms of the cognitive duality, it is clear what is happening. Boolean algebra provides a procedure for handling the extensional side of cognitive activity, taking for granted both the universe and the intensional structures representing this universe in the subject. If anything, it is a process for re-ordering the relationship between the two according to a simplified but more rigorous rule system. It provides a model for the establishment of pure and logical relationships, but says nothing about either the universe to which it refers and takes for granted, or about the intensional structure of the subject which it also takes for granted as a source of defining properties for the extensional activity that it orders. The Boolean is an external model builder unlikely to recognise that his simplified, but purified, operations say nothing about the universe itself, nor about the intensional structure through which we order it.

However, in approaching the semantic fields of artificial systems, it is exactly the intensional aspects that are the object of interest. It is not clear what contribution the Boolean model could make to such a study; first because it is extensional and reformist rather than intensional and analytic; and secondly because it assumes the existence of a universe, when the semantic analysts must seek to understand how such a universe can come to be *constructed* through the logico-algebraic activities of individuals and societies. If he assumes the universe and models it, a Boolean externalist implicitly assumes that the logico-algebraic ordering structures which generate the universe are as simply represented in the universe itself. Such an approach invariably breaks down under an apparently unmanageable complexity.

It appears then that logic, as we have it, does not present useful models for the recapture of the internal logical order of the semantic fields through which the artificial universe is experienced. What appears to be required is a procedure which does not assume, but investigates, the relationship between a logico-algebraic ordering procedure, and a universe which resists its simplicity. The scientific model of the *dialogue* between the formal symbolic and morphological domains appears to be exactly what is required. The semantic fields resulting from such an enquiry would not simply be ordered in logico-algebraic terms, but would be the resultant of a dialogue between logico-algebraic structure and a universe with infinite morphological variety. Since modern science characteristically represents a shift from an interest in extensional structure to an interest in intensional structure, such a procedure would be in keeping with the spirit of science.

The question may therefore be put directly: what would be the effect of running a logico-algebraic structure, as similar to a Boolean algebra as possible, in a universe which resisted its simple discriminations at every turn? The answer is, so far as can be seen, that a paradigm for the evolution of semantic universes and their structurally stable states is discovered. The following paragraphs attempt briefly to characterise such a structure, which appears to yield an account of the semantic evolution of spatial forms. Within the scope of this paper, formal considerations are dealt with briefly, since the mathematical and axiomatic aspects of the approach are dealt with in another paper in preparation, concerned solely with this subject.

The formal system proposed is called 'semantic algebra'. It has many of the structural properties of a Boolean algebra, although its outcomes are quite different and adjustments are made all the way through, following the requirements of changes in the axioms. For the purposes of the following explanation, the general structure of Boolean algebra is assumed as a starting point, although this assumption is not made in the axiomatic version of the system.

The perfection of Boolean algebra is embodied in the Boolean concept of negation and its linked concept of universe, which are expressed in the fundamental equations: $A \cap A' = \emptyset$ from which it follows that $A \cup A' = U$. Semantic algebra introduces a new *axiom of imperfection* $A \cap A' \neq \emptyset$ from which it follows that $A \cup A' \neq U$. In a semantic algebra no construction of A, A', $\cap$ and $\cup$ can constitute a finite universe, from which it might be suggested that the 'universal universe', U_u, cannot exist: $U_u = \emptyset$. This gives the *axiom of non-existence,* which states no universe exists, nor anything in it exists, until it is made.

The axioms of imperfection and non-existence mean that any dichotomy implies that an object can be made which embodies *both* the positive and negative properties (the axiom of imperfection); and that a semantic universe is one that is constructed, *not* one that is found and subsequently ordered. In other words nothing in a semantic universe exists until it is made, *not even the universe itself* (the axiom of non-existence).

More precisely, the concept of negation and universe have both been 'localised', to conform to the requirements of constructive and unfolding systems, as opposed to systems that already exist. In semantic algebra the term 'universe' is used to mean the set of objects constructed by the operations of semantic algebra, which means that a series of universes is created as the algebra 'unfolds'.

The localisation of the concept of negation is the foundation stone of semantic algebra. As Wittgenstein notes, in real life negation appears to *imply* what is negated, but 'not the *assertion* of it'[12] (our emphasis). In fact three types of binary dichotomies recur throughout language. The first is what can be termed the 'positive inverse'. The 'positive inverse' of the verb 'give', for example, will be an equally definitive gesture in the 'opposite' direction, as realised in the verb 'take'. Secondly, there is a 'universal' or 'logical' negation of the verb 'give' which is simply expressed as 'not give', or in other words everything in the universe which is not 'give'. Boolean algebra depends on 'universal negation'. The third possibility is that the verb 'give' also has a negation which is inextricably linked with the term negated, but says nothing at all about the remainder of the universe. For the verb 'give' this 'local negation' is the verb 'keep'. 'Keep' *implies* the notion of 'give' but does not assert it. 'Keep' raises the possibility of 'give' only to deny it. The relation of 'keep' to 'give' is an example of the paradigm of *local negation* which is the basic concept of negation used in semantic algebra. In the same way, the concept 'zero' is the local negation of 'number'.

The concept of 'local negation' raises a further possibility which the other forms of negation do not appear to possess. A concept may be combined with its local negation to construct a more complex concept. In relation to 'give' and 'keep', for example, the construction 'give keep' has one of its realisations in the verb 'lend'. This operation of construction resembles the Boolean operation of intersection, although with quite a different result. This homology can be clarified by means of a Venn diagram, as in *figure 5*, which illustrates both the operations, 'local negation' and 'intersection', and the concept of a local universe. The construct 'givekeep' is said to be the universe of its members, 'give' and 'keep' and itself.

A semantic algebra is a procedure for unfolding a simple concept like 'give' into a complex semantic field. It consists of one object, namely a concept of logos, two operations, namely local negation and intersection (the combining of an object with a local negation), and a rule that states that all operations that are possible must be carried out. The result of this structure is an unfolding series of universes of more and more complex objects and structures, which are offered as an internal model for the evolution of complex social concepts out of simple individualised

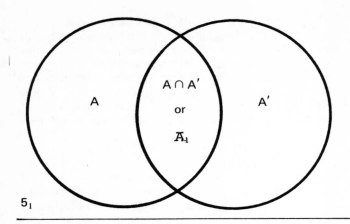

$\mathbb{A}_1$ = first universe of A

5_1

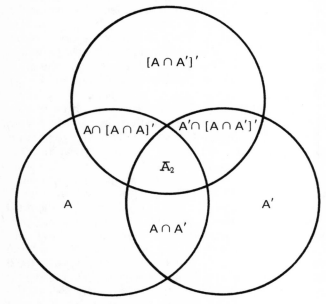

$\mathbb{A}_2$ = second universe of A

5_2

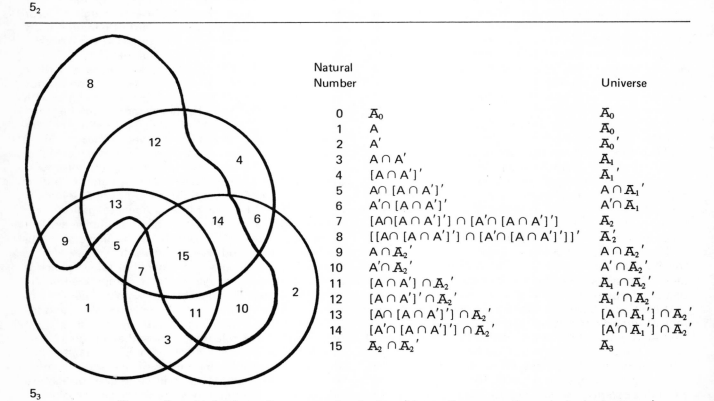

Natural Number		Universe
0	$\mathbb{A}_0$	$\mathbb{A}_0$
1	A	$\mathbb{A}_0$
2	A'	$\mathbb{A}_0'$
3	$A \cap A'$	$\mathbb{A}_1$
4	$[A \cap A']'$	$\mathbb{A}_1'$
5	$A \cap [A \cap A']'$	$A \cap \mathbb{A}_1'$
6	$A' \cap [A \cap A']'$	$A' \cap \mathbb{A}_1$
7	$[A \cap [A \cap A']'] \cap [A' \cap [A \cap A']']$	$\mathbb{A}_2$
8	$[[A \cap [A \cap A']'] \cap [A' \cap [A \cap A']']]'$	$\mathbb{A}_2'$
9	$A \cap \mathbb{A}_2'$	$A \cap \mathbb{A}_2'$
10	$A' \cap \mathbb{A}_2'$	$A' \cap \mathbb{A}_2'$
11	$[A \cap A'] \cap \mathbb{A}_2'$	$\mathbb{A}_1 \cap \mathbb{A}_2'$
12	$[A \cap A']' \cap \mathbb{A}_2'$	$\mathbb{A}_1' \cap \mathbb{A}_2'$
13	$[A \cap [A \cap A']'] \cap \mathbb{A}_2'$	$[A \cap \mathbb{A}_1'] \cap \mathbb{A}_2'$
14	$[A' \cap [A \cap A']'] \cap \mathbb{A}_2'$	$[A' \cap \mathbb{A}_1'] \cap \mathbb{A}_2'$
15	$\mathbb{A}_2 \cap \mathbb{A}_2'$	$\mathbb{A}_3$

5_3

Figure 5   Unfolding of a semantic algebra (Venn diagrammatic and algebraic forms)

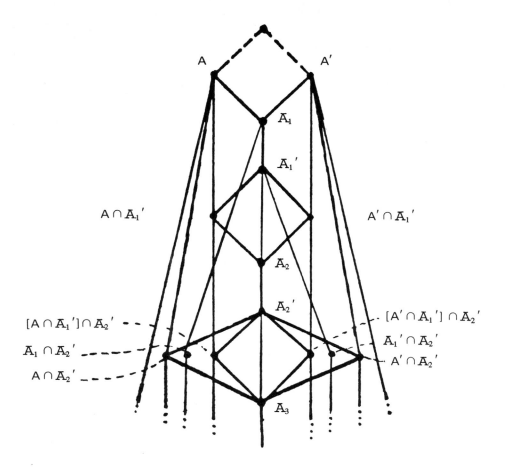

Figure 6   Unfolding of a semantic algebra to third universe (graph theoretic representation)

gestures and states.

Given the construction of the first universe shown in *figure 5₁*, the operations are then applied again. Since it can be shown that double negation is not equal to affirmation in a semantic algebra, and that neither the initial object nor its local negation are part of the local negation of the first universe, the unfolding proceeds by creating a new object outside the existing structure (the local negation of the first universe), followed by the intersection of this structure with all previous structure with which it can intersect without tautology, that is without being reduced to an earlier structure by resorption (for example the intersection of A with A∩A' is A∩A', but the intersection of A with [A ∩A'] is the structure A ∩ [A∩A']. *Figure 5₂* shows the construction of the second universe, and *figure 5₃* a third universe though here numbering is used to show that the unfolding can be mapped one-to-one into the natural numbers, and is therefore denumerable.

This unfolding structure possesses many properties that may not be obvious at first sight. First, any universal structure (identified by the heavy capitals e.g. $Ā_1$, $Ā_2$, $Ā_κ$, contains as part of itself all previous structures in the unfolding. This corresponds to semantic reality, in that terms ('village' 'town' etc.) represent exactly such complex, many-faceted concepts, hence the difficulties encountered in defining them indicatively.Also, through this property a link may be forged between semantic algebra and information theory. Second notions like 'forgetting' and 'remembering' are representable, in that a local negation of a universe 'forgets' the internal structure of that universe, by treating it as a 'gestalt', but then 'remembers' previous structure by intersecting with it to make new structures. In the same sense, the act of 'design' forgets the internal structure of a multiple form, by treating it as a unit form, this internal structure then being remembered by active elaboration and usage. Third, the unfolding is modelled on the same principle as the spatial syntax outlined in the previous section: namely that the same operation may be applied to structures generated by operating on simple objects. to produce more complex structures. This provides a possible key to the retention of isomorphism between dissimilar domains as artificial universes evolve. Fourth, it allows the logico-algebraic construction of semantic fields which to the experiencer exhibit rich properties of ambiguity and denseness. Fifth, the graph representation *(figure 6)* shows that a semantic algebra resembles the 'inverted pyramid hanging by its vertex' suggested by Piaget as the proper intuitive model for human knowledge. Sixth, a semantic algebra provides a paradigm for context sensitivity in a meaning system in that any structure is intelligible as itself, and as a member of its local universe, paralleling the intuitive understanding of, say, being in a village and being in a particular space in a village.

The seventh property is more remarkable. The sequence of operations on the non-universal structures has the effect of reproducing exactly the same unfolding in the higher order universes. In other words a simple, algebraic relation between hierarchic levels appears to be generated. This is an interesting result, because understanding relations between levels in hierarchies is a leading problem in many scientific

Universe

Universe		
G_0		logos 'give'
	G	to give
	G'	to keep
G_1	G ∩ G'	to keep by giving i.e. to keep the symbolic value of giving (lend is a modern version) to the generalised other.
	[G ∩ G']'	the generalised other's keeping of the symbolic value of giving i.e. effectively, to be required to give to the higher order subject's keeping (taxation is a modern version); obligation
	G∩ [G ∩ G']'	the act of giving to the higher order subject; ceremonial giving, as it were, to the set of social reciprocities (de-based modern version: the charity dinner) (old version: ceremonial gift exchange)
	G'∩ [G ∩ G']'	to give to the dead, who embody the generalised other, the higher order social subject, but who keep without reciprocation; sacrifice (modern version: flowers on graves)
G_2	[G∩ [G ∩ G']'] ∩ [G'∩ [G ∩ G']']	generalised ritualistic exchange as a means of regulating social relations (modern version: buying drinks, sending cards etc.)

Figure 7   Unfolding of the verb 'give' to second universe

areas.[13]

Finally, semantic algebra shows how the concepts of structural stability and morphogenesis may exist and be ordered in a semantic field. This suggests a possible relationship to the work of Rene Thom on morphological archetypes in language[14], since semantic algebra suggests a logico-algebraic regularity in the production of complex social concepts out of individualised primitives, and offers a paradigm for relating Thom's exploration of the semantic basis of language to the complex semantic system in daily use. Of course, language itself remains largely at the level of the first, or at most the second, universe. More complex unfoldings are not those represented in words but in cultural systems. As far as architecture is concerned, the thesis is that artificial space represents one of the systems within which these more complex socialised concepts are represented, in particular the unfolding of the verb 'to be'. This gives it a certain primacy as a social language, and suggests that architecture may be much more important to society than the social scientists, with their mechanistic metaphors, have allowed it to be. Artificial space is, literally, a language in which society says things which are too complex to be said in words.

A worked example of the unfolding of a complex social semantic field from a simple individual gesture is given in *figure 7*. This example is used because the second universe of 'give' is 'general ritualised exchange' which appears as a structurally stable regulator in most pre-trade societies. The reader's attention is drawn to Marcel Mauss's book 'The Gift' where such systems are examined in detail, in which the exchange of objects and services is used as a primary set of social signifiers, to regulate relations within and between societies. A theory of the ubiquity as well as the structural stability of such forms is offered by the semantic algebraic interpretation.

One further point of some importance is illustrated by this unfolding. In its simple forms the verb 'give' requires a simple, probably individual subject, the 'giver'. But as the concept unfolds into its higher-order structures, a higher-order subject is required, an 'inter-subjective subject'. This suggests that the tendency to personalise society, and to ascribe to it thought processes, while being undesirable and naive, may not be entirely devoid of structural reference. In the language of artificial space such 'intersubjective subjects' are identifiable, as the unfolding of the verb 'to be', in relation to its various syntaxes, creates structurally stable states at its universal stages of unfolding. Such stable states are recorded in language in 'gestalt' terms like 'dwelling', 'village', 'town', 'city' and so on.

The general form of a semantic algebra is best illustrated by considering the unfolding of the verb 'to be', given in *figure 8,* in relation to the different meanings assigned to the word, or phrases incorporating it, in everyday language. The initial meaning is to be physically present in a place, to 'be here', to be present in real space. The local negation uses the idea of physical presence in real space, but negates it. Both initial terms therefore relate to those aspects of our existence by which we are *connected to an immediate environment.*

The next term and its local negation refers to those aspects of our existence by which we are *independent*

Universe

Universe		logos 'be'	spatial interpretation
A_0			
	A	be present	places for people to be
	A'	be absent	places for things to be
A_1	$A \cap A'$	be in domain of representations, symbols etc. to be 'in your head'	places where people can be in their heads e.g. asleep, a garden etc.
	$[A \cap A']'$	for there to be a space of representations in which you are not i.e. in 'society's domain of representations	a sacred space where you are not in normal time, but where sacred things are
	$A \cap [A \cap A']'$	to be physically in a space of society's representations and symbols	a ceremonial and profane activity space in which you both are physically and in society's domain of symbols
	$A' \cap [A \cap A']'$	not to be physically, but to be in society's domain of representations only i.e. to be a name only, to be dead	a burial ground in which you are not, in which you become a thing with a name
A_2		a simple society	a village

Figure 8   Unfolding of the verb 'be' to second universe; logical interpretation and spatial interpretation : 'A'

of immediate environment, that is the world of internal representations and symbols. This might be thought of as the world of 'logical space' as opposed to real space. Everyday language uses the verb 'to be' in relation to logical space through such sentences as 'I am in the Communist Party', by which we say we are 'present' in an abstraction.

The following term and its local negation are constructed from the intersection of the two foregoing, in that *the world of representations and symbols is also constructed into real space.* It is possible to enter physically certain spaces which constitute real space realisations of logical space. Architecture participates in the realisation of such spaces. Its central theme is the mapping from logical into real space. The universe, A_2, is the structure comprising all three terms and their local negations.

Semantic algebra provides a model for the unfolding of all four domains of the code, namely logical differentiation, rules for elaboration, enclosure, and permeability. All four are given up to the second universe in *figures 8, 9, 10 and 11.* Socio-spatial theory, it could be conjectured, arises from the dialectical relationship of the unfoldings of A and E.

Elementary relations in the AFPE code

The code properties of a spatial surface—differentiation, barriers, permeability and rules for elaboration—can be called 'logical properties', intelligible through understanding rather than through simple perception. The properties of any particular spatial surface result from an unfolding of E and P, through F which is given by A. F 'carries' the structure of A from the level of the simplest structure to the level of the spatial surface. Alternatively, it can be said that A is logical space, E is real space, and A is mapped into E through F and P. This may be represented by $A \xrightarrow{F \ P} E$ (hence the acronym AFPE code). Either way F, and its function, f, are basic to the decoding of a spatial surface, that is finding its generative formula. At a schematic level, the variability of spatial surfaces is given by relatively few relationships among the four domains, in interaction with certain social variables.

Call a random process a 'mindless' syntactic generation of a spatial surface out of E, unconstrained by any F, and by implication ignoring A (P being unimportant at this stage of the argument). If such a random process is allowed to generate an artificial spatial surface on a previously undifferentiated surface, the value of the function f of F will be seen to be maximal as the space approaches maximal denseness. In other words, a random process without a value ascribed to f is seen in time to be equivalent to f_4, or f_{max} *It follows that insofar as the value of f remains less than maximal for a dense and stable spatial surface, then some structurally stable mechanism has intervened.* The maintenance of a structure of non-built or open space is therfore an indicator of exogenous ordering of some kind.

This leads to a distinction between two forms of density: semantic density, and syntactic density. Semantic density exists when a spatial surface has been fully elaborated according to its generative formula. This will imply a greater or lesser degree of syntactic density, that is the degree to which the space is physically dense in that no further structure may be physically placed on the surface. By definition, an f-minimal surface will approach semantic density long before syntactic density, whereas an f-maximal surface will arrive at semantic density at a point much closer to syntactic density. An important result of this is that an f-maximal surface can therefore embody much more semantic content than an f-mimimal surface, which arrives at density at a much earlier stage of elaboration. This is subject to the real life constraint that if f is f_4, and the surface is dense, then no spatial surface exists in an experiential sense, only a series of discrete interiors. Thus there is always some exogenous ordering of spatial surfaces.

Two fundamentally dissimilar lines of development for spatial surfaces arise from this distinction: those in which the value of f is minimal, in which case there is relatively strong exogenous ordering; and those in which the value of f is maximal, in which case the exogenous ordering is relatively weak, and the ordering of the spatial surface is more internal and syntactic. A natural relation with social variables follows. Insofar as a society uses space as a set of signifiers of social order, it will do so in terms of some exogenous ordering of the spatial surface in which values of f will be lowered or minimised; insofar as space is freed from the constraint of acting as a signifier for social order, its aggregates will tend to be syntactic and f-maximal. Thus the use of space for representing social order tends to minimise f, whereas a more instrumental or free elaboration of space tends to maximise f. The invariance of this relation in the code is shown by the tendency, even in the densest urban spatial surfaces, for the main buildings embodying the social order to be surrounded by an open space barrier. The general differences in the spatial surfaces between the City of London, where only two buildings have open space barriers, and the City of Westminister where many buildings have open space barriers is given by this simple formula. The City of London reaches semantic density at a point much closer to syntactic density than the City of Westminster.

The difference between f-minimal and f-maximal spatial surfaces is the simplest and most general example of differential aggregation modes. It is best illustrated, as are the relations to underlying social variables, by the contrast between the spatial surfaces of pre-settled and settled societies, extensive documentation for which now exists in the archaeological and anthropological record.

Pre-settled societies, as studied by anthropologists, normally utilise space as one of the signifying systems for that form of social solidarity characterised as 'mechanical' by Durkheim, that is a social solidarity dependent on symbol and ritual rather than on functional interdependence through extensive division of labour[15]. In general such societies impose a strong exogenous and symbolic order on space, leading to f-minimal spatial surfaces at first and second order levels.

This ordering begins to change with the advent of settlement. Settlement (as is too rarely observed by those who discuss the relation of social and spatial process) is a spatial act, meaning the fixing of work to place and the transition from a discoverable and untransformed local environment to one artificial and transformed. Settlement means that social space ceases to be primarily symbolic and becomes increasingly instrumental. The formative influences on settled space derive not from the symbolic systems of social order but from instrumental systems of survival and work. Lacking strong exogenous ordering of space, the spatial forms and the aggregate surfaces of the maximal values of f are progressively discovered and elaborated.

Since settled societies bring with them an inheritance of social complexity, the semantic content of the spatial surface does not change, but finds an alternative syntactic expression. At Catal Huyuk, the earliest known urban spatial surface, which is syntactically f-maximal, A is unfolded entirely in interiors and no use is made of the higher order spaces generated by f-maximal unfoldings. The whole of the second universe of A, including its A_2' form, the shrine, is unfolded at Catal Huyuk through differentiation of interior spaces, Urban form proper develops from the discovery and elaboration of the higher-order spaces of f-maximal syntaxes, which then become the bases for higher-order developments. The building block of the urban spatial surface is the f-maximal elementary form (the multiple outin form), which is also the basic form of an agricultural settlement, and the normal form for farms throughout the world. This however gives only one side of the formula for the urban spatial surface. Following Weber's definition of the city as a 'fortress/market'[16] , a parallel duality exists in the spatial form. Insofar as the city is a fortress, concerned with external and internal social order, then the spatial outcomes are f-minimal at all levels. Insofar as the city is a market, concerned with productive work and exchange, then the spatial surface is f-maximal. This socio-spatial duality is a universal in classical urban forms, invariant under technology, style and decoration.

Various other simple relations of this kind appear to hold. For example, matrilineal societies tend to the f-maximal first and second order (multiple outin) forms, wheras patrilineal societies use f-minimal first and second order (multiple inout) forms. Why this should be so may be clarified by consideration of the duality in the simplest spatial gesture of making a barrier, that is the duality of E and E'. An enclosure can either be a gesture of inclusion, E, or a gesture of exclusion, E'. The inclusive gesture faces 'inward' and does not preserve an open space beyond the barrier. The exclusive gesture, on the other hand, faces 'outwards' and defines an open space barrier beyond the indicated barrier. In a primitive military encampment, for example, this gesture is made twice: a gesture of exclusion, preserving an open space barrier, is made around the central building where spoil is kept; and then the exclusion gesture is repeated at the second order level of encampment boundary, where an open space barrier is again preserved. It is noteworthy that the exclusion gestures refers initially to things, and the inclusive gesture to people, and this relation holds throughout the unfolding. A monument, for example, is not a simple spatial object but a highly complex one, defining only an open space barrier, and having no interior. The association of the exclusion gesture with the male role in society and the inclusion gesture with the female, provides a rich field of study both from the point of view of the battle of the sexes seen as the earliest form of struggle between classes[17] . Town

form is in effect a highly evolved synthesis of these contradictory lines of social and spatial development.

Urban form proper can virtually be defined in terms of an absence of open space barriers which have been, as it were, removed and placed on the outside of the town. It arises only after the exclusion gesture A_4' the building of a town wall, creates the conditions in which previous internal exclusion structure can be forgotten. At this point, the central citadel turns into a set of free-standing public buildings in a continuous landscape, and the internal court spaces of multiple outin aggregates open outwards and become side streets. The coming alive of the streets and the continuity of the elaboration of space through universes up to the fifth, are the distinguishing marks of the urban spatial surface proper, as contrasted to the spatial surfaces of proto-urban forms, as occurred for example in pre-Colombian American and in early Egypt[18].

The difference between an exogenously ordered f-minimal spatial surface and one internally ordered and f-maximal, leads to another major dimension of the social meaning of artificial space, again so far as can be seen, an invariant in all cultures: namely the difference between sacred and profane space. A sacred space is highly structured in an intensional sense; it is fixed and finite, its 'meaning' is in its structure and it is exogenously defined. A profane space on the other hand has extensional variety rather than intensional structure; it is non-fixed, and proliferates new aspects and forms of itself; its 'meaning' is in its variety rather than its structure and its structure is richly syntactic, rather than exogenously ordered. It uses syntactic possibilities to proliferate semantic content rather than using semantics to order syntax. Structure and variety are of course indissolubly connected in any meaning system, but one may be maximised at the expense of the other. Both are sought after for example by tourists; in fact the two poles perfectly characterise the type of spatial structures frequented by tourists: the places of maximal intensional structure, and the places of maximal extensional variety.

It is not possible within the scope of this paper to offer a complete account for the evolution and code form of the urban spatial surface, but a few notes on some of its more interesting logical properties are pertinent. First it is a *combined* unfolding maximising f for the most part, minimising it for certain areas. The f-maximal areas are subject to: (a) a high degree of permeability; linked to (b) the maximal elaboration of marginal space (that is space left over by enclosures at first and second order level; and (c) subject to the structure given in *figure 12* which represents a simple linking of two semantic algebras, producing both 'normal' forms (verticals and horizontals) and 'special' forms (crossovers), the 'crossovers' being the forms of space that most characterise 'urbanness' in the sense that the tourist will seek them out.

Of particular interest in this model are the 'marginal' spaces, that is, the 'by-product' external spaces resulting from building specific space for relatively tied uses. Marginal space is generated continuously by f-maximal aggregation modes, and if no inhibiting rule exists, such space 'tends to use', and secondary elaborations of the space appear. The elaboration of marginal space is one of the keys to the

Universe

E_0		logos 'E'
	E	an enclosed space
	E'	a non-enclosed or defined space; an external space defined by the act of enclosure
E_1	$E \cap E'$	a transition space, both enclosed and defined (e.g. a garden or yard)
	$[E \cap E']'$	a social space set apart, and symbolically closed in normal time (e.g. a sacred space)
	$E \cap [E \cap E']'$	a space set apart yet accessible and symbolically open in normal time (e.g. a public open space)
	$E' \cap [E \cap E']'$	a non-space set apart as a marker of defined space only (e.g. a monument)

Figure 9   Unfolding of 'enclose' 'E'

Universe

P_0		logos 'P' — 'permeable'
	P	permeable, having a hole to pass through, (e.g. an ordinary door)
	P'	not permeable (e.g. a continuous wall)
P_1	$P \cap P'$	permeable, but not to go through (e.g. a window)
	$[P \cap P']'$	a symbolic barrier (e.g. a church door)
	$P \cap [P \cap P']'$	an open gate, symbolic entrance permeable in normal time, (e.g. entrance to public open spaces)
	$P' \cap [P \cap P']'$	the sealed entrance (e.g. entrance to a tomb)

Figure 10   Unfolding of 'permeable' 'P'

Universe

F_0		logos 'F'
	F	free to enclose again
	F'	not free to enclose again
F_1	$F \cap F'$	free to elaborate symbolically (grow flowers, place gnomes etc.)
	$[F \cap F']'$	not free to elaborate symbolically (since society's symbols are already present e.g. statues)
	$F \cap [F \cap F']'$	free to enclose again, but only with transient structure for profane public purposes which must be dismantled after use (e.g. a place to put up stalls, fairgrounds etc. (a village green))
	$F' \cap [F \cap F']'$	totally preserve as it is (e.g. the space around central public buildings, monuments etc.)

Figure 11   Unfolding of rules for enclosure 'F'

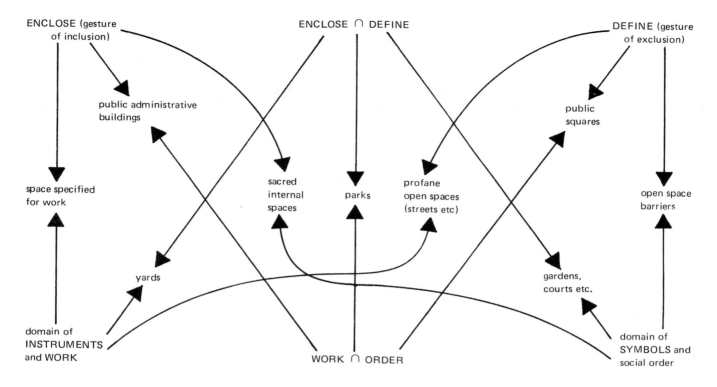

ENCLOSE (gesture of inclusion)

ENCLOSE ∩ DEFINE

DEFINE (gesture of exclusion)

public administrative buildings

public squares

space specified for work

sacred internal spaces

parks

profane open spaces (streets etc)

open space barriers

yards

gardens, courts etc.

domain of INSTRUMENTS and WORK

WORK ∩ ORDER

domain of SYMBOLS and social order

Figure 12   A semantic field, giving simple linking of two semantic algebras

richness of the urban spatial surface in the profane areas of the town, and reconciles multiple use patterns with the natural predominance of space that is specified for a particular use. Also interesting are the 'ambiguous' spaces, since their nature is to be subject to the rule 'both build and not build'—that is build, but only non-permanent structures, e.g. mobile markets and fairs. This ambiguous rule is a good demonstration of the importance of ambiguity in the elaboration of spatial surfaces, and how ambiguity can nevertheless be generated—and recaptured—in a structured way.

The logical nature of the modern transformation of urban space can also be clarified a little. The shift in general is from (a) the outin aggregation forms to the inout forms; leading to (b) the proliferation of pavilion forms in an open landscape surrounded by open space barriers (c) the consequent freezing of most marginal space and secondary elaboration (d) the establishment of clear, unambiguous demarcations and boundaries, where previously a structured ambiguity prevailed and (e) loss of continuity in the surface. In general these changes could theoretically result from the simple instruction in the code: prime all terms, that is make all gestures gestures of exclusion. The new open spaces of the city are not made free by this transformation, but on the contrary subject to a strong exogenous order.

Such an explanation of the changing logic of the urban spatial surface would appear to be explicable through the given relations to social variables. It could be argued that the urban spatial surface was the spatial equivalent of 'organic solidarity', that is a society dependent for its internal structure not so much on symbols as on functional interdependence induced by the extensive division of labour. Organic solidarity requires the functional integration of space, and therefore all f values are maximal wherever possible in the

urban spatial surface, subject to the existence of a ruling authority whose structures are f-minimal. It appears that in the current transformation space tends to be f-minimal rather than f-maximal, and it can therefore be hypothesised that a structurally stable exogenous order is being imposed, which represents a concern for social order rather than for work. A general impoverishment and fixity would result from this, and a greater emphasis on aesthetics combined with a dislike of non-formal elaboration of space. All these properties appear to be present in current spatial orthodoxies, especially those whose prime concern is with aesthetics.

An explanation for this could be that the type of division of labour that exists today is dissimilar in type to that of the urban organic solidarity. In the phase of industrialism, people do not create patterns of functional interdependence by making relations with each other, but instead each individual makes an arrangement with a focal point. A series of pyramids rather than a network is the result. The emphasis is on the individual, with a unique relation to his focal point, but lacking lateral relations with his fellow men of a direct and functional kind. In such a situation, a society might be expected to return more and more to conditions of mechanical solidarity, and use symbolic means more and more to stabilise the social order and yet confirm the separation of members from each other. This would link the primary role of media in our type of society with the transformation of space into what it was prior to large scale settlement, namely a signifying system presenting the social order in a society dependent on such mechanical solidarity devices for its cohesion. In such a situation it is difficult to see how architecture could function other than as a device for covert social control. Indeed this has been the primary theme in the social discussion of spatial form for the past one hundred or more years.

The theme of the double boundary is also important to the modern transformation. The f-maximal outin aggregation mode generates double boundary structures from the inclusion gesture, giving buildings surrounding a space in a many-to-one relation, whereas the f-minimal pavilion forms currently in use, with their open space barriers, generate double boundary structures from the exclusion gesture. In the latter case open space becomes a no-man's-land between the inhabitants and the outside world, rather than a communal interior space, permeable to the outside yet unique to the inhabitants. In semantic algebraic terms, the open areas surrounding a block of flats are $[E \cap E']'$ (exclusion), whereas the street was $E \cap E'$ (inclusion form).

These changes in terms of open space barriers, double boundary structures (and multiple boundary structures of the urban spatial surface), marginal space and its elaboration, permeability, strength of boundaries and classifications, show how profound the change is in the logic of space in our time, and how fundamental its discontinuity from spatial history since the beginning of human settlement. These changes are related to social changes, and the sources must be sought in the debate on the relation of space forms and the maintenance of order. In this situation, the synthesis of space as a means of achieving social order with the architectural imagination, as manifested in the work of Le Corbusier and others, might be thought inimical to the evolution of spatial surfaces that reproduce the richness and social viability of earlier structurally stable forms.

However it is possible that this present situation, in which the new logic of space arises from the generalisation of the exclusion gesture, and the negative aspects of spatial evolution, will be superseded by changes which are now beginning. Most probable is that the urban spatial surface, which was abandoned with the town itself, will return (or will be 'remembered'), but without finite urban forms which led us to think that building outside their limits had to follow extra-urban aggregation modes. The result will be not the universal garden city, but the discovery of new and richer forms of the urban spatial surface. The evolution of such forms of artificial space will depend on understanding the internal generative structures of a non-imposed spatial order, in which the complex of rules for its manufacture will be distributed in the society rather than located in a single focus, and in which the role of designer will be the generation of structurally stable unfoldings rather than the imposition of exogenous order. ☐

References

1. Thom, R: *Comments* by Rene Thom on C. H. Waddington: Basic Ideas in Biology: in Waddington (ed.): *Towards a Theoretical Biology 1*, Edinburgh, 1968
2. Marx, K: given in Fromm, E: The Theory of Mother Right for Today in *The Crisis of Psychoanalysis*, Cape, 1971
3. Hillier, B. & Leaman, A. J. : How is Design Possible?: *Architectural Research and Teaching*, Vol. 3 No. 1, Jan. 1974
4. Thom, R : Topological Models in Biology: in Waddington, C. H. (ed) *Towards a Theoretical Biology 3*, Edinburgh 1970
5. Hillier & Leaman : How is Design Possible?: op. cit.
6. see, for example, Echenique, M : *Models: a discussion : Architectural Research and Teaching*, Vol. 1 No. 1, May 1970 pps 25-30
7. Hillier, B & Leaman, A. J. : *Structure, System, Transformation: Transactions of the Bartlett Society*, Vol. 9 1972-1973, pps 36-77
8. Winograd, T: *Understanding Natural Language*, Edinburgh, 1972
9. Rudovsky, B : *Architecture without Architects:* Academy Editions, 1964
   Fraser, D : *Village Planning in the Primitive World*, Studio Vista, undated.
10. Fletcher, B : *The History of Architecture on the Comparative Method*, London, 1961, 1st edition 1896
11. Leach, E : *Anthropological Aspects of Language: Animal Categories and Verbal Abuse:* in Maranda P (ed): Mythologies, Penguin, 1972
12. Wittgenstein, L : *Tractatus logico-philosophicus*, Routledge, 1922, para. 4.0641 and *Philosophical Investigations*, Blackwell, 1953, para. 447
13. Pattee, H. H. : *The Problem of Biological Hierarchy:* in Waddington, C. H. (ed): *Towards a Theoretical Biology 3*, Edinburgh, 1970
14. Thom, R : *Topologie et Linguistique:* mimeo
15. Durkheim, E : *The Division of Labour in Society*, Macmillan, 1933, Free Press, 1964
16. Weber, M : *The City*, Free Press, 1968
17. e.g. Mellaart : *Catal Huyuk*, Thames & Hudson, 1968
18. Fromm, E : op. cit.

Acknowledgement

The authors wish to acknowledge the help of the following: Professor Pat O'Sullivan of UWIST for making key suggestions that led to the development of semantic algebra; Professor John Musgrove of UCL School of Environmental Studies for providing an academic milieu in which this work could advance; the MSc students of 1972/3 of the School of Environmental Studies at UCL to whom we owe too many debts for individual acknowledgement, and in particular to Mick Bedford, who drew the diagrams and criticised the text. ☐

Models in our heads, models in the material world, and models in the world of objective knowledge

Philip Steadman

The title of my paper is a long one, and I shall spend some part of my time in explaining what I intend to convey by it. The last two words give the clue to the paper's intention. *Objective Knowledge* is the title of Sir Karl Popper's latest collection of essays [1]. My purpose is to try to set some ideas about the process of design and the study of designed objects into the framework of a view of the development and accumulation of human knowledge which might be described as broadly 'Popperian'.

The word 'model' is used here in the broadest sense, to mean any kind of representation, image or simulacrum of some object or phenomenon. In the present context the reference is of course specifically to models or representations of buildings and other artefacts, and to models of the functional environments for which these buildings or designed objects are intended. 'Models in the material world' would thus be representations of buildings or artefacts in drawings, diagrams, photographs, in written or otherwise encoded marks on pieces of paper, or as solid material models made out of cardboard or wood; and 'models in our heads' would of course be mental images or pictures of these same buildings and objects. These types of model are situated respectively in what Popper refers to as 'World 1', the objective world of material things, and 'World 2', the subjective world of minds. Popper's theory of knowledge involves the concept of a third world, however, distinct from these first two but entirely dependent on them, a 'World 3' of 'objective knowledge'.

World 3 is a world of 'objective structures which are the products, not necessarily intentional, of minds . . . but which, once produced, exist independently of them.' [2] It is, in Popper's own words, 'the world of intelligibles, or of *ideas in the objective sense;* it is the world of possible objects of thought: the world of theories in themselves, and their logical relations; of arguments in themselves; and of problem situations in themselves.' [3] This world is embodied, physically, in books, documents, pictures, records, social structures, in physical artefacts of many kinds; it embraces language, art, science and indeed the whole of inherited culture. It has an autonomous existence which is relatively independent of the thoughts and opinions of individual men. It is knowledge that is in many cases not even *known* by individuals.

One of the examples which Popper gives to illustrate the point is a book of logarithm tables, which no one man, it is safe to say, carries in his head, or ever has done —not even Napier. It is possible, indeed, for modern tables of logarithms to be prepared by computer. And yet the knowledge comprised in such tables is of enormous practical importance and in daily use by engineers for all kinds of real world projects. Even with less mechanical and repetitive subjects than logarithms, it is still quite possible for authors not to know in detail the contents of their own work, let alone for their readers. And when these authors die, their works may sit on library shelves for years, centuries even, before they are re-read and their significance appreciated.

A good example from the history of science is Gregor Mendel and the papers he wrote in the 1850s on his studies of plant breeding: to which Darwin was ironically enough given references at the time of their publication in a bibliography sent to him from Germany, references which he included in an article for the *Encyclopaedia Britannica,* without having seen the papers themselves. Had he done so they would have provided him with one missing and vital component of his theory of evolution, an understanding of the mechanism of genetic inheritance. It was only around 1900 that Mendel's work was rediscovered and the modern science of genetics set under way.

It should be emphasised that Popper's use of the word 'objective' to describe this knowledge is intended to convey this relative autonomy from the subjective knowledge of individuals; but not, and here the term is possibly misleading, that 'objective knowledge' is necessarily always any truer or that it is completely free from bias, distortion or inconsistency. There is nevertheless a sense in which the knowledge comprised in libraries, in books, in scientific papers—objective knowledge (perhaps 'collective knowledge' would be an alternative term)—is more important than the knowledge in men's heads; because it is more permanent, more complete, it is directly available to criticism and study, it is accreted cumulatively as the result of the efforts and experiences of many generations, and it is relatively more secure and less subject to accidental disturbance and degeneration.

It follows that the 'world of objective knowledge' in the design context would comprise, in general, scientific or other knowledge not only about actual existing or historical buildings and artefacts, but about hypothetical, future or possible designs. And models in this world, World 3, would be *theoretical* models, whether mathematical in structure or else formulated in language or in some other symbolic representational form; in any case parasitic upon the material world, World 1, and upon the world of minds, World 2.

Now that I have explained the title of my paper I would like to go off on an apparently different tack, and talk about the subject of evolution: and I hope to converge back on Popper and objective knowledge in due course. It is possible roughly speaking, and rather artificially, to distinguish four stages in the evolution of life on earth, these stages characterised by the different ways in which useful information or knowledge is obtained by organisms about their environment—or one should say environments—and this information passed on to their descendants. The first stage, and lasting for the greatest amount of time, is that represented by the evolution of plant life and of a great number of the lower animal species.

In this case information is passed on from one generation to the next through genetic heredity in the manner demonstrated by Darwin and by the mechanisms first elucidated in the experiments of Mendel. If we consider the question of adaptation of form and behaviour in organisms, adaptations which confer fitness' on the individual—that is to say appropriateness to circumstances and way of life—we can say that in a certain, rather metaphorical sense, embodied in these adaptations is 'knowledge' which the organism possesses about its environment. This is not conscious knowledge, of course, but nevertheless these adaptations arise, are selected as a result of there being certain regularities, certain constant features in the environment over long periods of time—the continuing presence of various chemical materials, the regular cycles of the days and the seasons, stable levels of temperature, the continued existence of other species, themselves only slowly changing, constituting either potential food, potential competitors or potential predators, and so on. And thus each adaptation, each aspect of fitness for unchanging or repeated circumstances, can be seen to represent a kind of inductive generalisation, and so a prediction on the part of the organism, that 'as things have been on many occasions in the past, so they will be again in the future'. That these predictions may naturally be upset by rapid, large scale and, it goes without saying, unforeseen changes in the environment, is illustrated by the failure of species to adapt to such catastrophes and by their resulting extinction. It was Samuel Butler's notion that heredity in all species, and not just those with brains, was a kind of 'unconscious memory' of the ancestral past; he wrote a book with that title in which he developed his theory. In a strictly metaphorical sense this expressed an important truth about adaptation.

This is the first stage in our four stages of evolution then. The second stage is marked by the evolution of a new and very special type of adaptive organ, the brain. Previous to this the animal, in the early stages of the evolution of the nervous system, is capable of responding instinctively to a fixed range of environmental situations, each of which provokes automatically a fixed response through a mechanism which is innate, inherited, and involves an action which does not have to be learned. This remains true of many of the functions controlled by the 'lower' parts of the brain in evolutionarily more advanced species, including ourselves. But at a higher level, the possession of a brain allows the animal to learn from its experience over the course of a lifetime. It learns through trial and error, that is to say through conditioned response. By repeated and in principle quite possibly random

behaviours, the animal learns that some of these behaviours result in failure, others in success or in some advantage, and the successful behaviours are 'reinforced', they are retained, they are learned. Adaptations of behaviour which were previously instinctive and acquired through natural selection over many thousands of generations are now produced in one generation only. J. W. S. Pringle and W. Ross Ashby among others have pointed out this important formal parallel between the mechanisms of adaptation in learning and in evolution. The brain is essentially an organ which is 'adapted to being adapted'; it is a means of accumulating adaptations.

Now the simple 'trial and error' process of learning characteristic of lower animals, in which essentially random behaviours are tested for their efficacy in the given environment, is clearly a very inefficient not to say dangerous method of acquiring knowledge about that environment—although initially and in the simplest case this is the only possibility available. As the memory of various ploys and strategies is accumulated, however, it seems that the brain has ways—not yet very well understood—of coordinating all this remembered information into a more or less coherent representation of the external world; into an internal, mental *model* of the world, in which various behaviours may be tried out in theory, as it were, without the risks which would attend the testing of these behaviours in actual practice.

This conception of the brain as containing a representation or model of the external world seems to be due largely to the philosopher Kenneth Craik. In his book *The Nature of Explanation* [4], Craik states that 'One of the most fundamental properties of thought is its power of predicting events'. He shows in several illustrations how the possession of an internal, mental model of the world would appear to explain the way such predictions can be made, in the whole range of applications of human thought but particularly in scientific predictions, and in design.

Amongst biologists and experimental psychologists a view of the brain as constituting a model of the surrounding environment of the creature is associated particularly, perhaps, with the names of C.F.A. Pantin and J. Z. Young as well as with many others. The complex behaviour of insects such as ants, wasps and bees appears to indicate that even with their very small brains these animals possess maps or models of the regions around their nests or hives. As J. Z. Young has written, the characteristics of the neural network which constitute memory 'must in some way be made to correspond to features of the environment, the function of the memory being to recognize certain events when they recur in the world around.' [5] Representations of the world of the detail and subtlety which must be available to higher animals, Young argues, must depend on the existence of some code whereby the memories afforded by the sense impressions can be organised into coherent patterns. 'It would be entirely reasonable', he suggests, 'that such a code be determined by heredity.' 'The requirement is that the memory shall contain an alphabet suitable to set up representations of those situations that the animal is likely to meet in its lifetime . . . Experiments have shown that the frog's retina reports to the frog's brain only certain features of the visual world, features that are likely to be of 'interest' to a frog. Presumably a frog's brain contains a simple alphabet that will allow storage of information about a few such simple changes. Heredity may well be able to provide the necessary simple set.'[6]

Whatever the structure of a model in the brain of the external world might be, and however it is built up through heredity and through learning, there can be no doubt that its adaptive and selective significance is enormous. Such a model is not static, but is used to predict the future. As Pantin says, the implication is that the animal can 'try out' consequences which have not yet occurred. 'In operation the model in fact allows some degree of extension into the future. In the past it utilizes memory, but memory which is not purely static records of particular past configurations, simple sequences in time, but the sequences of many dimensions in time, from whence rules governing the probable future can be inferred.' Here is the beginning of inductive reasoning proper. The animal is in effect enabled to draw the conclusion *mentally* that 'as things have been on many occasions in the past, so they will be again in the future'. The process of learning from its beginnings in trial and error becomes now a much less haphazard business, since the internal representation of the external environment allows the formation of plausible behavioural 'hypotheses' in relation to this model which have a greater probability of being correct, clearly, than when they were formed at random.

To recapitulate, we have now considered two of the four stages in evolution which I have referred to earlier; organic evolution before the emergence of the brain, and the evolution of the brain itself. The third stage is the beginning of the evolution of culture in man. Here the process of learning takes on a quite new dimension, because of the development in man of symbolic language for conveying information. With language it becomes possible for parents to teach their children by 'telling' as well as 'showing'; so that the accumulated experience of each generation in coping with the problems of life can be passed on to the next, and so be carried down in ways other than via genetic heredity. For many animal species, each generation meets the world no better prepared than its predecessor (or only marginally so, through genetic evolution). But human beings can, through language, develop a collective historical sense and memory, build up a body of oral tradition, and pass on their hard-won skills and knowledge through the instruction and education of their children, through religious customs and taboos, through art and artefacts, through social organisation, in short through culture.

It seems reasonable to extend the idea of a mental 'model' of the environment held by the individual brain, and to say that different human cultures embody in their tradition, their beliefs, their religion and their art, a kind of shared image or representation of the world as it appears collectively to each particular society. In some degree the model or models are externalised then, are given physical form outside the individual brain. And just as tools and useful artefacts may be viewed as adaptive extensions of man's physical body—Samuel Butler, who was fascinated by this idea, referred to tools as 'extra-corporeal limbs'—so works of art or of literature can be seen as extensions of man's conceptual apparatus, and in

some degree externalisations of the mental pictures he has of his environment—'environment',that is to say, in the broadest sense, and not simply naturalistic or representational pictures of surface appearances of things, but aids to understandings of the world's internal structure and workings.

The fourth phase of evolution, the one which we humans are now involved in, is not entirely distinguishable from the earlier stages of cultural evolution; but is characterised particularly by the use of written language for the recording and transmission of 'hereditary' cultural information. Previously, experience could be passed on from generation to generation in some degree in the form of physical artefacts and works of art, but otherwise largely by teaching and through oral tradition, the limits of which process were imposed by the capacity of one memory to store information and of the next to learn. But with the introduction of written records, and subsequently their copying in large numbers through printing, these limits could be transcended, and the possibility arose of a cumulative growth and storage of knowledge and experience in books and libraries—indeed, to come back to Popper, of the growth of 'objective knowledge'. The most outstanding and characteristic feature of this last phase of cultural evolution is, of course, the rise of organised science.

At this stage you might well be asking, 'What has all this to do with design and architecture?' I shall try to answer that question by reference to a diagram with which you may be familiar from Christopher Alexander's *Notes on the Synthesis of Form*.[7] I will argue that the underlying metaphor of that book is evolutionary, that its epistemological basis is biological. Alexander's argument, you will I am sure remember, started from the premise that traditional methods of design have become inadequate to cope with the great complication of modern design problems, where the systematic interaction and interrelatedness of a great range of factors render unworkable a simplistic division of the problem into manageable parts according to preconceived categories. Alexander contrasted the essentially successful designs of artefacts and buildings, as he saw them, in primitive or what he called 'unselfconscious' cultures, and in traditional craft production, with this apparent failure on the part of present-day or 'selfconscious' designers to arrive at equivalently well-adapted solutions.

This thesis of Alexander's is indicated diagrammatically in the figure, where in 'unselfconscious' design processes the form of the designed object interacts directly, according to Alexander, with the functional context for which it is designed. To take an example, in the design of a simple primitive house; the house is erected, and found, when it is occupied, to have certain defects. When a new house is built, the previous design is copied exactly, but with the exception that small changes are made to remedy the observed defects. The process goes on with repeated copying and variation through many cycles. It is not important to the process that the changes made are necessarily the right ones immediately to correct the design's failures. In fact it is even possible for variations which are introduced accidentally into the design through slight inaccuracies of copying, to turn out to be im-

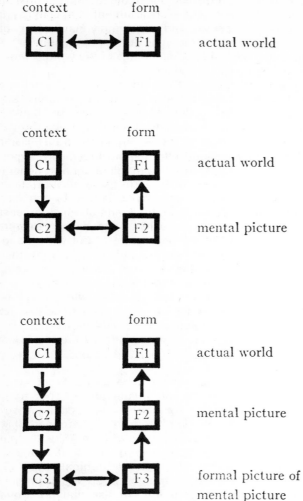

context   form

C1 ⟷ F1   actual world

context   form

C1   F1   actual world

C2 ⟷ F2   mental picture

context   form

C1   F1   actual world

C2   F2   mental picture

C3 ⟷ F3   formal picture of mental picture

Figure 1

provements. What *is* important to the success of the process is that there be repeated copying together with only slight variations; that successful variations be selected for; and that the 'context' of the design, as Alexander calls it, the functional programme, or the environment, remain substantially unchanged over long periods of time. This is the case in primitive and stable societies, and there is ample archaeological and historical evidence to show that the gradual development and improvement of tools and other artefacts has taken place in exactly this manner—though less evidence admittedly for buildings, which have not survived in historical series in such great numbers.

It is clear that what Alexander is talking about, and it is not his idea but goes back to the mid-nineteenth century, is the *evolution* of tools or designed objects by a process very analogous to organic evolution. Alexander uses the term 'good fit' to describe the work of W. Ross Ashby on homeostasis and Ashby's experiments with an 'adaptive machine' of his own equivalent of biological fitness in the relation of organism to environment. What is more, the whole question of the mechanism by which 'good fit' is produced, is discussed by Alexander in relation to the work of W. Ross Ashby on homeostasis and Ashby's experiments with an 'adaptive machine' of his own invention, the Homeostat, whose purpose was precisely to illustrate by means of an electrical/mechanical model the processes of adaption of behaviour produced through variation with sel-

ection in organic evolution; or by random trial and error in learning.[8]

Of course tools do not evolve in their own right, as do organisms, but *are evolved* through the agency of man. Much confusion has resulted over the failure to make this obvious distinction between the two processes. I would suggest that what Alexander has shown in the top part of his diagram would strictly speaking apply only to organic evolution, whereas technological evolution or the evolution of artefacts should more properly be represented as in the second level, where the agency of man in the process is quite clearly shown.

It is important to note nevertheless that the 'hereditary information', as it were, which is passed from one 'generation' of artefacts to the next, is not exclusively transferred through the medium of men's minds and memories. This information, the accumulation of experience which, say, the design of a good knife blade embodies, is comprised within the physical form of the object itself, which acts as a model from which the design of a new blade is copied. There is some fascinating internal evidence in support of this observation provided by George Sturt's account of the craft production of farm wagons, in his book of reminiscences, *The Wheelwright's Shop.*[9]

Sturt describes how many features of the 19th century wagon—which seemed to be very specially adapted to their function in ways which he could not immediately appreciate—could not be explained to him by the men who made the wagons. They *did not know* the rationale for the details of the designs, but simply used templates and copied old wagons. And yet, as Sturt discovered through persistent analysis, there turned out always to be very sound structural or functional reasons for the very complex features of the construction, despite the fact that the wheelwrights were not consciously aware of these reasons.

The second part of Alexander's diagram indicates the 'selfconscious' process of design, in his phrase, where the designer carries in his head a 'mental picture of the form—that is of the designed object—and a 'mental picture' of its context, and tests the one against the other in his imagination. It is clear that what Alexander is talking about here are mental models of designs and their functional environments—models in designers' heads, that is. His argument about the failure of current 'unselfconscious' design methods is based on the proposition that these mental models are inadequate; they fail to correspond to the real features of the situation, and they fail to predict with sufficient accuracy the anticipated performance of the form under the conditions of its anticipated context.

In the third level of the figure, Alexander introduces what he calls 'formal pictures of mental pictures'. We might take some slight license here and use this level of his diagram to signify externalised models of buildings or artefacts and their contexts or environments: that is to say, material, 'World 1' models such as drawings or three-dimensional solid representations, as well as the theoretical 'World 3' models which would be embodied in these or other, say written or mathematical, forms. This is not quite what Alexander meant by 'formal pictures of mental pictures' but is I think arguably what he should have meant.

Instead of this though, what Alexander actually describes in *Notes on the Synthesis of Form* as his proposed remedy for the purported failures of current design procedures, and what he is in fact referring to in this diagram as a 'formal picture of a mental picture', is something very peculiar. Instead of making a plea for the construction of more reliable or more precise explanatory and predictive models of architectural situations—of building designs and their environments—which is what the logic of his argument seems to be leading to, instead of this, the formal picture or model he proposes constructing is not of form and context at all, but only of the imagined interrelationships between those points or aspects where the one fails to fit the other (what he calls 'misfit variables').

From a logical point of view that is surely very paradoxical. In order to imagine these 'misfits', so-called, it must be that the designer has at least some image or mental picture, both of form and of context, in order that he can envisage such a 'misfit' at all. He can only be in any degree precise about the nature of this misfit, and in what ways it might be causally inter-related with other misfits — other points at which form and context are not well adapted or adjusted — insofar as he is prepared to be precise about exactly what form, what detailed design, he is proposing to fit to the given functional context.

Other authors have pointed to this curious feature of Alexander's work, and have suggested that a psychological understanding of this fact of Alexander's 'telling the right story but pointing the wrong moral', as one might say, is to be found in his anxiousness to devise a method where the criteria by which a design and its 'fitness' were judged would be, as he hoped, objective and absolute; and also where the supposedly erroneous preconceptions and fixed ideas of the designer would not be allowed to interfere in the creation of new solutions. Both these aims of Alexander's are misguided, and are based on underlying misconceptions.

It is worth observing two points from a biological perspective here. First that in the biological sense, as well as in an analogous technological sense, 'fitness' is a relative attribute. There is no sense in which any organic species is absolutely 'fitter' than any other. An overall measure of fitness is given in effect by reproductive success and survival, but this is a resultant rather than a definition of fitness, and within this the fitness conferred by any particular adaptation is entirely a matter of the particular ecological niche which the species occupies at some point in time—the availability of foods, the locality, the climate, the presence of other species in competition, and so on—and so what confers fitness at one time or place may not do so at another. Equally with artefacts or buildings, there can be no absolute measures of performance or of the appropriateness of a design for its function; but only measurements against some stated aims or criteria, that is in terms of some subjective scales of value.

The second biological observation is that, taking an evolutionary view of the progress of architectural design, the notion that there is virtue in a designer trying to rid himself wholly of preconceptions, even if this were in any sense possible, becomes patently absurd. Preconceptions, that is to say accumulated knowledge about existing or past types of solution, are all the designer has got to work from; and his business must be to apply this knowledge to changed conditions, to identify the failures or problems of past designs, and adapt old solutions to answer new problems.

The basic difficulty facing the present-day designer, which Alexander pointed to in his contrast of 'unselfconscious' with 'selfconscious' processes of design, nevertheless still stands. The success of the 'unselfconscious' process depends crucially on the great stability of primitive cultures, and the fact that the functional context or set of conditions which any given artefact was intended to answer to, did not substantially change over long periods of time. It was thus possible for the method of trial and error in actual practice, that is to say prolonged experiment with the actual buildings or tools themselves, to yield good results. This is not practical when the functional programmes for buildings or artefacts change at a greater rate, because the experience gained about one building or tool through its being tried in use cannot be applied directly in the next, where the requirements are very different. Instead, some more generalised *theoretical* and ultimately scientific understanding is required of the factors which determine performance, and their interrelationship.

Here then is the function of models. Whether these be mental or physical models, whether they be loose and informal, hazy mental pictures, or formalised, externalised representations in material or mathematical shape; their function is in increasing our understanding of the way in which buildings or tools perform, and so as a consequence providing a basis for predictions about the performance of buildings as yet unbuilt, or tools as yet unmade. These predictions are made by 'running the model faster than the world' so to speak. Of course this does not imply any absolute prohibition on testing designs in actual practice and learning from these tests; and this can be a useful exercise, and with many smaller products and even, say, with the design of cars is exactly what is done, very successfully. But the difficulty in experimenting with buildings in general is that they are too big, too expensive, and it takes too long.

In conclusion then, and to come back to Popper and 'objective knowledge'; I hope I have made a convincing case that the logical direction of Alexander's argument should have led towards work on the continuing development of more accurate, probably mathematical models of designed objects and their contexts, offering deeper understanding and a more trustworthy means of prediction, than those models which have served designers previously. Some progress in this direction is to be reported in the various papers given later in this conference. While in some ways the philosophical substructure of *Notes on the Synthesis of Form* reflects the influence of Popper, the conclusion which Alexander by contrast actually comes to in the book is certainly far from Popperian. The progressive accumulation and evolution of collective knowledge in art as well as science, including the creative production of works and insights of great originality and novelty, as Popper sees it, does not demand a complete break with the preconceptions or mental categories of the past, nor an ignoring of the solutions already known to past problems. Quite the opposite. It is not without significance that the subtitle to Popper's book is 'An evolutionary approach'; and Popper presents in the book the picture of a continuity in the growth of knowledge, and of the fundamental analogy between adaptations of the organic body with the adaptations represented by mental pictures of the world and by scientific theories, of the kind which I have tried to suggest briefly here.

The special virtue of 'objective knowledge', as Popper argues, is the fact that it is collective, made public, its assumptions are made clear. It is thus open to rational criticism, and most importantly it is through this criticism, which Popper sees as analogous in some ways to natural selection in organic evolution, that objective knowledge grows. Thus the argument is *not* that scientific knowledge has any absolute objectivity or truth by contrast with other forms of knowledge; indeed Popper strongly stresses the continuity of mythical and metaphysical thought with scientific. It is that 'objective knowledge' is knowledge—or speculation—laid open for inspection, for general scrutiny.

It is a criticism sometimes made of those who build computer and mathematical models, that they claim for those models a purported value-free and detached objectivity. This is a just criticism, if they make such a claim; and it is of course true that any model of some phenomenon is selective—otherwise it would not be a model—and those factors which the modeller selects for study must reflect his own interests, prejudices or biases. But the same criticism has all the more force against models or pictures of other kinds, whose assumptions or bias are not made clear in the way that the very explicitness of a mathematical formulation obliges. It is this property of openness to criticism, of testability, that Popper sees as the essential characteristic feature of *scientific* statements. Popper's theory places an emphasis on problems and problem-solving in the growth of knowledge, these problems being the ones presented by the clear failures of existing solutions to previous problems. The theory thus places emphasis on the importance of tradition and an understanding of the past of any subject. It is not by any means opposed to daring speculation in scientific hypothesis and in all creative work; but it counterposes to this a rigorous testing and critical analysis, in the light of existing knowledge and of practical experience.

References

1. Popper, Karl R. (1972) *Objective Knowledge: An Evolutionary Approach,* Clarendon, Oxford.
2. Magee, Brian (1973) *Popper,* Fontana, London p.60.
3. Popper, *op.cit.* p.116.
4. Craik, Kenneth J. W. (1943) *The Nature of Explanation,* Cambridge University Press.
5. Young, J. Z. (1964) *A Model of the Brain,* Clarendon, Oxford p.268.
6. *ibid.* p.269.
7. Alexander, C. (1964) *Notes on the Synthesis of Form,* Harvard University Press p.76.
8. Ashby, W. Ross (1952) *Design for a Brain,* Chapman and Hall, London.
9. Sturt, G. (1923) *The Wheelwright's Shop,* Cambridge University Press.   □

Environmental models—past, present and future

Dean Hawkes

In the simplest possible definition an environmental model, in the sense which is used in this paper, is some formal structure which relates a property of a built form to some physical quantity of heat, light or sound and some 'external' stimulus. For purposes of introduction three basic relationships which are familiar from conventional building science serve to illustrate the meaning.

First, the equation for the transfer of heat through a building element under steady-state conditions;

$$Q_f = UA\Delta t \qquad (1)$$

Here the thermal transmittance (U) of an area of material (A) together constitute a description of some property of the built form. The rate of heat transfer (Qf) is the physical quantity and the temperature difference between the two sides of the element (Δt) is the stimulus.

Turning from heat to light, consider the inverse square law of illumination;

$$E = \frac{I}{d^2} \qquad (2)$$

This is a particularly clear example of the structure. The distance (d) of the light source from the considered reference plane is a property of the built form. The illumination on the plane (E) is the physical quantity. The stimulus is the intensity of the source (I).

Thirdly, an example is taken from acoustics, Sabine's equation for the reverberation time of an enclosure;

$$T = \frac{0.16V}{A} \qquad (3)$$

This describes the relationship between the volume of a space (V) and the total quantity of absorption (A) which together describe the built form and the reverberation time (T). It apparently lacks the third element of our definition, the stimulus, until we appreciate that this is implicit in the definition of reverberation time itself. 'The reverberation time in an enclosed space is the length of time required for the sound pressure level to fall by 60 decibels, i.e. to one-millionth of its original intensity.'

Models which conform to this structure have been in existence and in use as aids to the design of buildings for at least one hundred years and the aim of this paper is to present a picture of the main trends in their evolution during that period. It is hoped that this will provide useful background for the later papers on recent developments and opinions in this field. The

opportunity has also been taken to indulge in a few speculations about future prospects.

The first example comes from the year 1865 and is concerned with the assessment of the effects of obstruction upon natural illumination. The British architect Robert Kerr (1865) proposed a *Table of Lighting (Figure 1)* which was a representation of one half of the sky vault as it would be visible from within a building. It was constructed by projecting lines from a quadripartite division of the hemisphere throught the jambs of an "average" window and calculating the relationships between the areas of the sky vault visible *(Figure 2)*. The "standard" of daylight which was proposed as being the minimum acceptable was represented by a table of related window widths and room dimensions;

Window width (feet)	room dimension (feet)
3	12 x 12½
4	16 x 12½
5	17 x 14½
6	20 x 15
8	20 x 20
10	25 x 20
12	30 x 20

When this was combined with an obstruction angle of forty-five degrees it was assumed that this represented the minimum quantity of natural illumination acceptable for domestic lighting. If the forty-five degree obstruction line is plotted onto the Table of Lighting *(Figure 3)* it can be seen that the minimum standard in terms of 'measures of lighting power' was sixty-eight for a room with a window of the dimensions given in the Table above. In using the Table it was possible to show that where a room had a window wider than that given as 'standard' a higher obstruction could be tolerated and where the window was narrower a lower obstruction was demanded.

In the present discussion there are three questions which this primitive model raises. First, does it tell us anything about the concerns in environmental design in 1865? Secondly, does it say anything about the architecture of that date. Thirdly, to what extent is its own form determined by both the environmental and architectural parameters?

The answer to the first question lies in the concern in Civil Law for the protection of 'Ancient Lights'. We might speculate in passing that the increased rate of construction in the large towns and cities in the middle of the nineteenth century drew particular attention to this problem and inspired Kerr, as a practising

TABLE OF LIGHTING FOR A WALL WINDOW.

		(Equal divisions of Quadrant.)			(Centre.) 61	58	53	18		Totals.
(Zenith)		Side.	S. diagonal.	F. diagonal.	Front.	Front.	F. diagonal.	S. diagonal.	Side.	
Vertical (6) 1		½	1	1	1½	1½	1	1	½	8
V. inclined (29½) 5		2	6	7	7	7	7	6	2	44
H. inclined (47½) 8		3	10	11	12	12	11	10	3	72
Horizontal (59) 10		4	13	14	15	15	14	13	4	92
(Horizon) Totals ...		9½	30	33	35½	35½	33	30	9½	216

(The left margin of the table is labelled vertically "Equal divisions of Quadrant.")

Figure 1   "Table of Lighting"   (After Kerr, 1865)

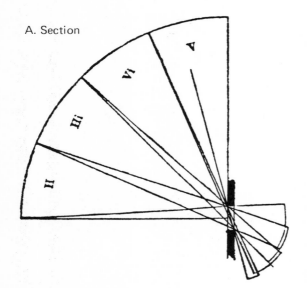

A. Section

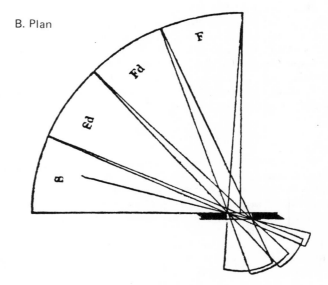

B. Plan

Figure 2   (After Kerr, 1865)

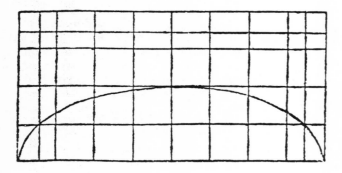

Figure 3   45° obstruction line

architect, to devise an 'objective' basis for analysis.

It is quite clear from the form of the model that buildings were seen to be primarily made-up of relatively small, side-lit rooms.

It is reasonable to suggest that Kerr's minimum standard of natural illumination was derived from direct experience of contemporary construction in which subjective impressions of the adequacy of illumination could easily be correlated with the geometry of the situation. Natural illumination in buildings is, of course, essentially a function of the geometry of room dimensions, window size and the magnitude of obstruction. Each of these is represented in the model, which thus embodies in its description of the architecture a statement of its environmental goal.

We have already discussed Sabine's equation at some length, but it merits further attention since the manner in which it was derived and first used is, on the one hand, entertaining, and, on the other, spells out the clear advantages of acquiring a quantitative grip on the problems of environmental design.

Writing at the turn of the century Sabine (1900) outlined at great length the manner in which he came to concern himself with the problems of architectural acoustics. In 1895 he was an Assistant Professor of Physics at Harvard, working in the fields of optics and electricity, when he was instructed by the Corporation of Harvard University to propose changes for remedying the acoustical difficulties in the Lecture-room of the Fogg Art Museum, a building that had just been completed. At that time the 'science' of architectural acoustics was, to say the least, primitive. There were many and conflicting recommendations for the ideal proportions of auditoria, 2:3:5 by some, 1:1:2 by others and 2:3:4 elsewhere (most of these, incidentally, without clear advice as to the exact points in the room to which the measurements should be taken). One writer, who had seen the Mormon Temple at Salt Lake City, recommended that *all* auditoria should be elliptical!

Into this confused situation Sabine brought his uncluttered mind and, as a start, made a clear statement of the objectives of acoustical design.

In order that hearing may be good in any auditorium, it is necessary that the sound should be sufficiently loud; that the simultaneous components of a complex sound should maintain their proper relative intensities: and that the successive sound in rapidly moving articulation, either of speech or music, should be clear and distinct, free from each other and from extraneous noises. These three are the necessary, as they are the entirely sufficient, conditions for good hearing.

Upon this analysis Sabine was able to structure his approach to the problems of the Fogg lecture theatre and to identify the physical factors which positively influence his criteria. This led him to the conclusion that the time which a sound takes to decay in an enclosed space is a fundamental determinant of acoustic quality. He discovered that this time in the Fogg lecture theatre was five and a half seconds.

During this time even a very deliberate speaker would have uttered the twelve or fifteen succeeding syllables. Thus the successive enunciations blended into a loud sound through which and above which it was necessary to hear and distinguish the orderly progression of the speech.

Moving on to the relationship between the properties of architectural form and reverberation time, Sabine pointed out that, "broadly considered, there are two, and only two, variables in a room—shape including size, and materials including furnishings." In a building, on the drawing board both of these may be varied, but when confronted by the problem of an existing room as he was, the only practical option was to explore the effects of materials.

In a remarkable experiment all the cushions from the seats of the Sanders Theatre in Cambridge were brought and stored in the lobby of the Fogg lecture theatre. They were then introduced, a few at a time, and their effect on reverberation time was measured.

This process was continued until all of the cushions—from a theatre seating fifteen hundred—were placed in the lecture room—seating capacity four hundred and thirty six. They were placed on all the seats, on the floor, against the rear wall up to the ceiling and on a scaffolding specially erected for the purpose. At this stage the reverberation time was measured at 1.14 seconds.

The next step was to compare the absorption of other materials with that of Sanders Theatre cushions so that realistic proposals could be made for corrective treatment of the Fogg theatre. In the end certain walls of the room were permanently covered with felt with the expected result of reducing the reverberation time and making the room in Sabine's own words, "not excellent, but entirely servicable."

On the strength of this success Sabine was asked in 1898 to act as acoustics consultant for the proposed Boston Music Hall (now Symphony Hall) the home of the Boston Symphony Orchestra. With commendable caution he decided to review his work before accepting the commission. The events which followed have been described by Frederick Hunt (1964) in his Introduction to the edition of Sabine's Collected Papers.

We find him then, on Saturday evening, 29 October 1898, quietly poring over his data on the duration of residual sound as a function of the running length of Sanders Theatre cushions he had brought into the Fogg lecture room. Suddenly he shouted triumphantly from his study, "Mother, its a hyperbola!"

The data from the Fogg experiments, when plotted as reverberation time (t) against length of cushions (x) fit the relationship.

$$(a+x)t=k \qquad (4)$$

with the constant 'a', the displacement of the origin of the hyperbola along the 'x' axis and representing here the absorption of the room surfaces minus the cushions given the value 146 and 'k' made equal to 813. This equation is the standard formula of a displaced rectangular hyperbola.

With the certainty of this discovery behind him Sabine accepted the Music Hall commission and set to work upon a further series of experiments designed to provide the data for the derivation of a generally applicable relationship. These involved the introduction of Sanders Theatre cushions into a series of rooms of differing sizes and properties *(Figure 4)*. In each room the effect of the cushions on reverberation time was measured and the results were plotted as before.

The generality of the hyperbolic law was demonstrated in this way, but the parameter 'k' remained unexplained until it was discovered that it had a constant relationship with the volume of the room of $k = 0.171V$. As first published and used Sabine's equation had the form:

$$t= \frac{0.171V}{A} \qquad (5)$$

and it was first used in the acoustic design of the Boston Music Hall. The intention was to reproduce as

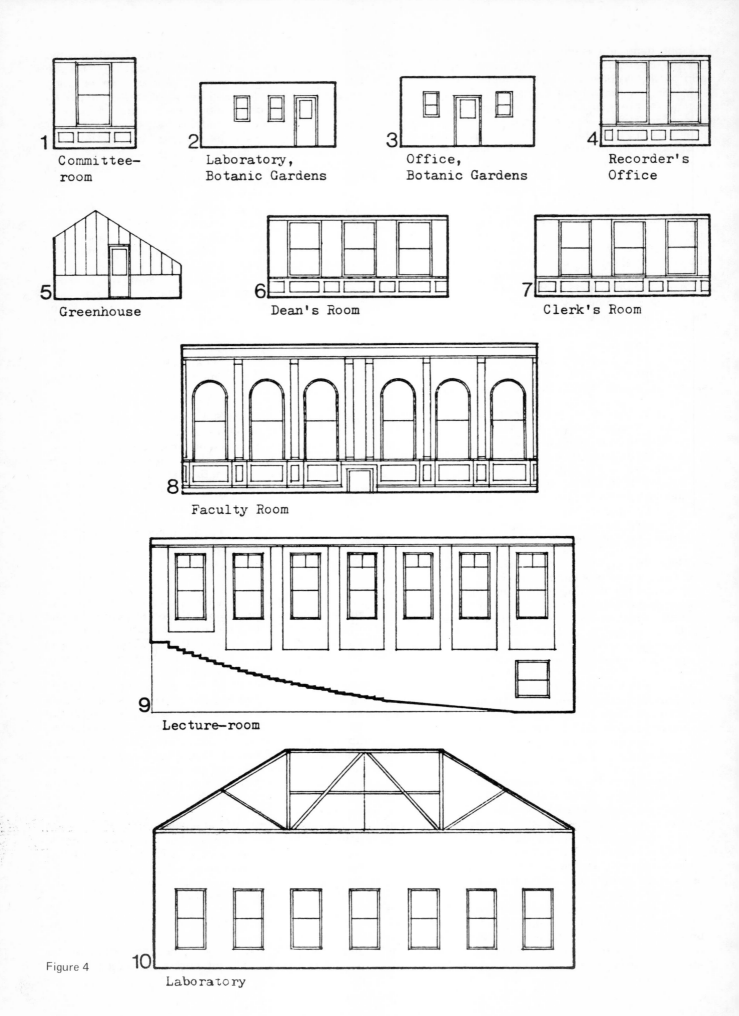

1 Committee-room

2 Laboratory, Botanic Gardens

3 Office, Botanic Gardens

4 Recorder's Office

5 Greenhouse

6 Dean's Room

7 Clerk's Room

8 Faculty Room

9 Lecture-room

10 Laboratory

Figure 4

nearly as possible, in a hall of different dimensions, the acoustic properties of the internationally regarded Gewandhaus at Leipzig. Sabine calculated from data that the Gewandhaus had a reverberation time of 2.30 seconds and his designed time for the Music Hall was 2.31 seconds. To complete the story it remains only to say that when the Music Hall was opened in 1900 it was acclaimed by both musicians and critics and it remains today amongst the best auditoria for music in the world.

Sabine's work is important in the context of the present discussion since it represents a major milestone on the road along which the bulk of the efforts of environmental studies have been directed ever since. It offered a clear understanding of the relationship between the properties of architectural form and a useful measure of a quality of the environment enclosed. Furthermore it presented that relationship in a form which could be quite readily used by a designer.

Moving on a little way in time, and changing from acoustics to lighting, we may look at a further model which serves to make some very important points about environmental models in general.

In order to overcome the extreme difficulties which follow from the application of the basic, inverse square law of illumination to the design of lighting installation the *Lumen Method* (Harrison and Anderson, 1920) was developed. This method has been the cornerstone of illumination engineering design for the past half century and it sets out to calculate the *average* illumination level on a horizontal working plane. It gives no information about the variation of illumination from *point to point* over that plane nor does it allow the *precise* level of illumination to be found at any specified point.

The method is based on the principle of the conservation of energy. If a room is considered where the floor is perfectly absorbing and where the walls and ceiling are perfectly reflecting it is clear that, no matter what the luminance distribution of the light fittings may be, or how many times the flux is reflected off the walls and the ceiling, all the flux must eventually reach the floor and be absorbed. The *average* illumination (E_{av}) on the floor must therefore be

$$E_{av} = \frac{F_1}{A} \qquad (6)$$

where F_1 is the total luminous flux emitted by the lamps and A is the floor area of the room.

In any "real" room light will be absorbed by the walls and ceiling and also by the light fittings themselves which will have the effect of reducing the value of E_{av}. The lumen method represents this effect by the introduction of a *coefficient of utilisation* (k_u). The equation can thus be rewritten

$$E_{av} = \frac{F_1}{A} k_u \qquad (7)$$

The coefficient of utilisation itself is a function of
a the shape of the room
b the properties of the light fitting
   (i) the proportion of light which it absorbs
   (ii) the distribution of the light from it
c the reflection factor of the walls (ρ_w)
d the reflection factor of the ceiling (ρ_c)

There are a number of alternative presentations of the lumen method, one of which is the *British Zonal Method* (IES 1960) in which the characteristics of all commercially available light fittings are incorporated into a classification system—the British Zonal (BZ) Classification—based upon their luminance distribution *(Figure 5)*. Description of the details of these methods is not essential here, but it is necessary to point out that they all incorporate some general descriptor of the geometry of the room. In most cases this is the *room index* (k_r) which is found from

$$k_r = \frac{jk}{(j+k)h_m} \qquad (8)$$

where j and k are the plan dimensions of the room and h_m is the mounting height of the fittings above the working plane.

As can be seen, this descriptor is concerned with the *shape,* but not with the *size* of a room and, to that extent, has the advantage of being applicable to any rectangular room.

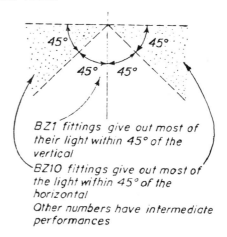

BZ1 fittings give out most of their light within 45° of the vertical
BZ10 fittings give out most of the light within 45° of the horizontal
Other numbers have intermediate performances

Figure 5

The fully presented versions of the lumen method have graphs or tables of experimentally derived coefficients of utilization where the values depend upon the index, some description of the light fitting characteristics—such as the BZ Classification—and the reflectances of the room surfaces.

The practical advantages of the lumen method are clear from this description. They are, however, obtained by sacrificing the ability to predict the variation of illumination over the working plane and the precise level at any specified point and also by restricting the design options to regular arrays of identical fittings in rectangular rooms. There are numerous situations in which these restrictions are of little significance, but the question must be raised of the likely effect of the nature of the method upon the objectives which designers set themselves.

The calculation of the average illumination on the horizontal working plane has, largely because of the existence of the lumen method, been the main concern in lighting design for almost half a century. More recently there has been a growth of interest in other approaches (for example, Lynes 1966), but the emphasis has been primarily upon the illumination of the "task" and it is arguable that the dreariness of many of the environments which modern buildings provide is a consequence of the methods by which they are designed. Lighting, even in utilitarian buildings, should do more than just put light on to the desk tops. When the flatness of the end is—via the design model—inevitably linked to uninspired means—a regular array of fittings—the criticism is compounded.

So far the discussion has not touched upon what is perhaps the major topic in environmental design, the maintenance of the condition of the air within a building within acceptable limits of temperature, freshness and cleanliness. Until quite recently the emphasis of research to aid the design of the thermal environment has been to devise usable techniques for the estimation of the demands which will be made upon the environmental control systems—heating, cooling or ventilating. This has, quite reasonably, meant that there has been a close relationship between the state of the systems technology and both the prediction methods used and the design objectives which are specified.

To give an example, if it is decided that the only environmental control in a particular building will be a supply of heat during the winter months sufficient to maintain a given internal air temperature, there is no point in making use of any prediction method more sophisticated than the steady-state equation. Provided a realistic allowance is made for losses due to ventilation, and after some factor has been allowed for heating-up the building, it is almost certain that the design will be seen to be "successful" since the building will always be adequately heated, except in the relatively unlikely event of freak weather conditions. It should not be imagined, however, that the design method describes in any way the interaction between a real building and the environment around it. It merely provides useful data for the design of adequate plant.

As the specification of user requirements becomes more precise, which must itself depend upon the availability of more sophisticated design skills, so the nature of the design stage is inevitably changed. The physiology of thermal comfort and the environmental factors upon which it depends have been the subject of a great deal of research and are well understood. A typical expression of the relationship between three major components of the environment, air temperature (t_a), the mean radiant temperature of the surfaces of an enclosure (t_r) and air velocity (v), is the dry resultant temperature (Missenard, 1935)

$$t_{res} = \frac{t_r + 3.17t_a\sqrt{v}}{1 + 3.17\sqrt{v}} \qquad (9)$$

Quite clearly from a relationship of this kind any given value of t_{res} can be achieved by numerous combinations of the three other variables. In practice "comfort" only exists within relatively narrow bounds since, for example, there should not be too large a difference between air and mean radiant temperatures and there are obvious practical reasons to limit the air velocity which is acceptable in a building. For normal design purposes the comfort zone for sedentary activities, expressed in terms of resultant temperature, lies within the range 19 °C–23 °C when the air velocity is 0.1 metres per second (Figure 6). This graph shows

two important facts. The first is that normal notions of comfort can be satisfied over quite a wide range of conditions. Secondly, that any one condition may be satisfactorily achieved in a number of ways.

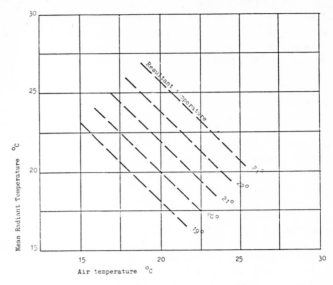

Comfort zone for sedentary occupation (v = 0.1 m/s)

Figure 6

Since the definition and specification of comfort is complex one must question the validity of design models which both simplify the specification and, in their formulation, imply a great deal about the method by which environmental control is achieved. Because of historical accident the design of the thermal environment within a building has been based upon the assumption that a designed building will have its environmental shortcomings made-up by the inputs of control plant of some kind. Banham (1969) has presented an extensive account of the evolution of this predominant attitude to environmental control. In brief, we have seen a progression from crude means of control such as the open fire, which do not, because of their nature, justify design consideration beyond rule-of-thumb type correlations between hearth size and room size; then we have passed through the introduction of centralised systems and the development of means of predicting the loads which they will have to meet and so on to the highly developed notions of "integrated" environmental control which exist today. These last require sophisticated analytical tools so that effects of all the environmental inputs can be taken into account in their design.

One feature of this potted history is that, even in the case of the "integrated" approach, there is the constant implication that environmental control depends *substantially* upon engineering installations. The effect is that the design of a building is subdivided into engineering and architectural components. Banham (op cit) makes eloquent protest on this very point.

In a world more humanely disposed, and more conscious of where the prime human responsibilities of architects lie, the chapters that follow would need no apology, and probably would never need to be written. It would have been apparent long ago that the art and business of creating buildings is not divisible into two intellectually separate parts—*structures* on the one hand, and on the other *mechanical services.* Even if industrial habit and contract law appear to impose such a division it remains false.

In recent years a significant shift in emphasis has occurred. As environments in buildings have become increasingly "artificial" with the demise of daylighting as an "adequate" source of working illumination and the widespread acceptance of the "benefits" of air-conditioning, even in temperate climates, so there has grown up a concern to "enjoy" these benefits at the least cost. Therefore any means by which the costs of highly serviced buildings may be reduced is clearly attractive both to the building owner and to the engineering industry. This more than any other cause has directed attention towards the nature of the architecture and the demands which are made upon the system from a new point-of-view. The emphasis has ceased to be on the direct calculation of the loads in a "pre-designed" building which would then be serviced. The objective is now to find an "economical" balance between all of the relevant variables, including the loads from the contents of the building—lighting, people and equipment. The argument is even extended to account for the visual and acoustical environments. Much of this effort has been directed towards the design of office buildings and the nature of the "end-product" is now familiar. Here the building envelope is arguably there primarily to protect the systems and it is these which have almost the entire responsibility for the environmental comfort of the occupants. The building has become primarily a product of engineering design.

A nice paradox lies here, however, in the fact that the analytical techniques which are necessary to design and support this style of building also offer the means to demonstrate that in many instances it is possible to provide entirely acceptable environments, some may say preferable environments, with minimal reliance on complex engineering systems!

As mentioned earlier, one of the basic requirements of a design model for a sophisticated modern building is that it should take into account the effects of periodic heat loads, particularly those due to solar radiation, but also of the variation in the inputs from the "contained" sources. In the latest edition of its Guide, the Institution of Heating and Ventilating Engineers (1970) has adopted the work which originated at the Building Research Station on the prediction of summertime temperatures in buildings (Loudon, 1968) as the basis for the calculation of cooling loads. This encompasses the principal responses of a building to the environment by taking account of time-lag effects due to the construction of the envelope, the effects of glazing types and blind systems on the solar gain through windows and the effect of the internal construction on the response to all the inputs.

The rate of heat flow into a building at any time is found by calculating the mean flow throughout the day and then the hourly deviation from this.

$$\left(\frac{Q_f}{A}\right)_\phi = \frac{Q_f'}{A} + \left(\frac{\widetilde{Q}_f}{A}\right)_\phi \qquad (10)$$

where

$\left(\dfrac{Q_f}{A}\right)_\phi$ = heat flow into room at time $\theta + \phi$

$\dfrac{Q_f'}{A}$ = $U(t_{eo}' + t_{ei}')$ = mean heat flow into room

$\left(\dfrac{\widetilde{Q}_f}{A}\right)_\phi$ = $fU(t_{eo} - t_{eo}')$ = deviation from the mean heat flow at time

θ = time lag *(Figure 7)*

t_{eo}' = daily mean sol-air temperature

t_{ei}' = constant or daily mean indoor environmental temperature

f = decrement factor *(Figure 8)*

The necessity of accounting for these effects with some precision is demonstrated by the example at *Figure 9.* This compares the flows through a concrete roof slab in the month of July when thermal capacity is ignored and when its effects are acknowledged.

Solar gain through windows is calculated from the following equations

$$Q_s' = S\,I'\,A_g = \text{mean solar gain} \qquad (11)$$

and

$$\widetilde{Q}_s = S_a\,A_g\,(I_p - I') = \text{swing in effective gain} \qquad (12)$$

The variables S and S_a are the solar gain factor and the *alternating* solar gain factor respectively, A_g is the area of glass which is insolated and I' and I_p are mean and peak solar intensities. Tabulated data gives values of S and S_a for many typical glazing and blind types.

The effects of the internal construction are accounted for by the *admittance* concept. This is a measure of the way in which a *surface* smooths out temperature variations. In general, lightweight constructions have low admittance and heavier elements have high. Admittance is reduced if a lightweight material is applied to the surface of a heavier piece of construction. For example, a carpet will substantially reduce the admittance of a concrete floor. The effect of admittance on temperature swing (t_{ei}) is formally expressed

$$\widetilde{t}_{ei} = \frac{\Sigma \widetilde{Q}_t}{\Sigma AY + C_v} \qquad (13)$$

where

$\Sigma \widetilde{Q}_t$ = the swing in the heat input

ΣAY = sum of all the admittances of the enclosing surfaces

C_v = ventilation loss

41

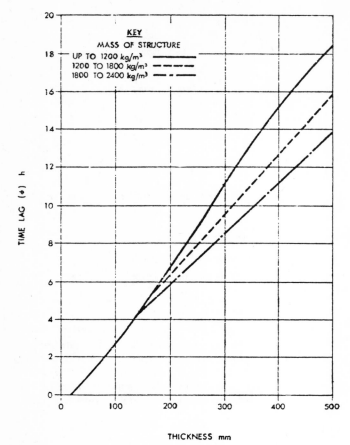

Figure 7

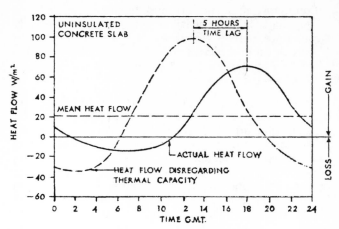

Figure 9

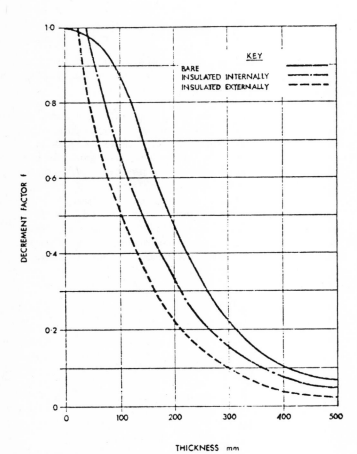

Figure 8

The effect of this variable on temperature swing is demonstrated in this simple example. A small room, 5m x 4m x 3m high has a peak swing in heat input $(\Sigma \widetilde{Q}_t)$ of 2500 watts and a ventilation loss (C_v) of 150 watts. If the admittance of the surfaces is taken as being 5.0 watts/m²/°C the temperature swing from the equation would be

$$\widetilde{t}_{ei} = \frac{2500}{(94 \times 5) + 150} = 4.0°C$$

If the average admittance were reduced to 2.5 watts/m²/°C the swing would then be

$$\widetilde{t}_{ei} = \frac{2500}{(94 \times 2.5) + 150} = 6.5°C$$

The environmental modelling work at Land Use and Built Form Studies (Hawkes and Stibbs, 1969, Hawkes, 1971) has been directed towards the representation of the *environmental system,* with heating, lighting and acoustic models brought together on the computer within a comprehensive descriptive model of built form. In this way it is possible to simulate the response of a building to both the external environment which surrounds it and to the environmental products of the activities which go on within it.

To illustrate one particular aspect of this work, the ability to calculate the overshadowing of one building upon another—or of the different parts of an individual building upon each other—brings a degree of precision to the calculation of solar effects which is otherwise impossible. This calculation is performed at close intervals on all facades of a building at hourly intervals throughout the day *(Figure 10).* The similar problem of calculating the shading on windows due to their reveals or overhangs is also incorporated.

The model calculates the daylight factor at specified points within the building and translates these figures into absolute illumination levels at hourly intervals throughout the day. This information is then taken to assess the likelihood of artificial lighting being in use. The heat produced by the occupants of the building and by the equipment which they use can have a considerable effect on the environment. The model allows alternative occupancy patterns to be input and can allow a variety of activities to be performed simultaneously in a single space so that these effects can be allowed for with ease.

Models of this kind become complex and inevitably make severe demands on the user in the business of data collection and input, which makes them unlikely to find a ready application as *generally* useful design aids. There are also likely to be problems at the output end where the designer is seldom looking for detailed analysis of *all* aspects of performance, but is rather trying to make a choice between limited options on the basis of their performance on one particular count.

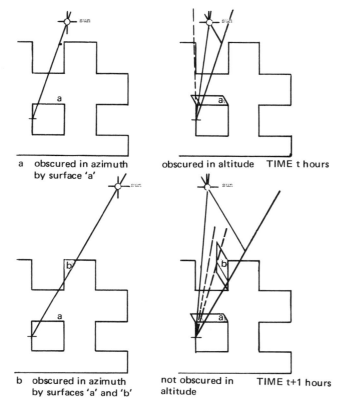

a obscured in azimuth by surface 'a'

obscured in altitude TIME t hours

b obscured in azimuth by surfaces 'a' and 'b'

not obscured in altitude TIME t+1 hours

Figure 10

The true value of a model of this kind lies in its use as a research tool. The study and subsequent discussion of environmental "topics" is probably the most promising way of improving the quality of design. For example, a recent study (Taylor, 1973) has explored the effects on environmental conditions in deep-plan buildings of alternative roof constructions. The "standard" response in the design of a building of this kind is to try to optimize the structural form, which usually suggests a lightweight roof. The roof is the largest single element and it is clear why it attracts this attention, but it is also the largest and most exposed element from an environmental viewpoint. On a sunny day the roof is almost certainly insolated for the whole of the period between sunrise and sunset. The results of the study showed substantial reductions in peak temperatures when heavy concrete roof constructions were compared with the more typical lightweight metal deck solution. The study has not yet compared the costs of the alternatives, but the benefits in either savings in plant costs or of more

acceptable environmental conditions suggest that the structural emphasis of much architectural design may be misplaced.

It is now necessary to draw together the threads. We established a formal definition of an environmental model and have seen that models conforming to this definition have a long history of development and use in the design of buildings.

Robert Kerr's "Table of Lighting" merits inclusion in any discussion of this subject on the strength of its early date alone, but its real importance to us is that it demonstrates how the problems of the model-builder are eased if it is possible to assume that the built forms with which he is dealing fall within strictly defined limits. In Kerr's case his model merely reflected the current practice in design and the simplification was thus justified but, as we have seen, there are potential dangers in making such simplifications in more sophisticated models.

Now to consider the contribution of Wallace Clement Sabine. The reason for the inclusion of his work is that it splendidly demonstrates the benefits which follow from the application of the clear-headedness of scientific methods to problems of design. It would be foolhardy to suggest that all the problems of auditorium acoustics were solved by Sabine at a stroke, but it cannot be denied that reverberation time is the crucial criterion and that by making use of Sabine's model—or nowadays of Eyring's recalibration of it—it is possible to predict what the reverberation time will be in an auditorium at all relevant frequencies. The determination of what the reverberation time *should* be for any particular auditorium is a separate issue. The existence of this very reliable model has brought a degree of confidence into this particular branch of architectural design which was previously completely absent, and in so doing has liberated the designer from his own uncertainty. If quantification of any aspect of design constrains the designer its merits are extremely dubious.

In looking critically at the work of the past it is all too easy to appear glibly negative. The Lumen Method has been used here to show how the production of a practical model may unwittingly impose severe restrictions upon the design solutions. The criticism is seriously made in the context of this discussion, but it should not be taken to apply to the quality of Harrison's and Anderson's original work which showed a high degree of technical originality. The point to be made is that, in practice, there is an understandable tendency for a design method to be selected because it is easy and convenient to use, rather than because it necessarily produces the best result.

Each of these examples is concerned with a single measure of the environment, but we have seen that the most recent developments in environmental modelling have attempted to take a more comprehensive view. At first this was in the service of the design of the engineering systems, but the same models, as we have shown, may be used to explore other approaches to control which make use of the capabilities of the building fabric more completely than has been the practice hitherto.

We can conclude then that model building has an

important part to play in the further development of environmental studies, particularly now that the potential of the computer can be utilised. We must, however, learn from the lessons of the past and be constantly on our guard to ensure that in this work we do not allow the excitement of the model-building activity itself, or fascination with particular technologies, to distract us from the real goal of satisfying the true environmental needs of the people who will use the buildings which we design.

References

1. Banham, R. (1969) *The architecture of the well-tempered environment.* London: The Architectural Press

2. Harrison, W. and Anderson, (1920) Coefficients of utilization. *I.E.S. Transactions* (New York) Vol. 15

3. Hawkes, D. and Stibbs, R. (1969) *The environmental evaluation of buildings: 1 a mathematical model* Working Paper 15, Cambridge: LUBFS.

4. Hawkes, D. (1971) *The development of an environmental model* Working Paper 55, Cambridge: LUBFS

5. Hunt, F. (1964) Introduction to *Collected Papers on Acoustics* New York: Dover.

6. Illuminating Engineering Society (1960) The calculation of coefficients of utilization. The British Zonal Method. *IES Technical Report No. 2* London: The Society.

7. Institution of Heating and Ventilating Engineers (1971) *IHVE Guide, Book A 1970* London: The Institution.

8. Kerr, R. (1865) *On ancient lights and the evidence of surveyors thereon* London: John Murray.

9. Loudon, A. (1968) *Summertime temperatures in buildings* BRS Current Paper 47/68 Watford: BRS.

10. Lynes, J. et al (1968) The flow of light into buildings *I.E.S. Transactions (London)* Vol. 49.

11. Missenard, A. (1935). Théorie simplifié du thermométre resultant *Chauffage et Ventilation* Vol. 12.

12. Sabine, W. C. (1900) Reverberation *The American Architect.*

13. Taylor, S. (1973) *The technical environment* Diploma dissertation (unpublished) University of Cambridge School of Architecture. □

Where can operational models of buildings get us?

E. M. Hoskins

Introduction

The concept of models as abstract representations of reality is well understood. It is possible to manipulate these representations to provide detailed information of the likely characteristics of reality, whether it be a prediction of the future or a representation of an existing situation. The problem facing us here is how these abstract representations of possible realities may be made useful to us in our day-to-day tasks, particularly in relation to problems of building. I hope to examine, albeit somewhat superficially, the overall characteristics of building models, their necessary constituents, and how they may be made operational in building design.

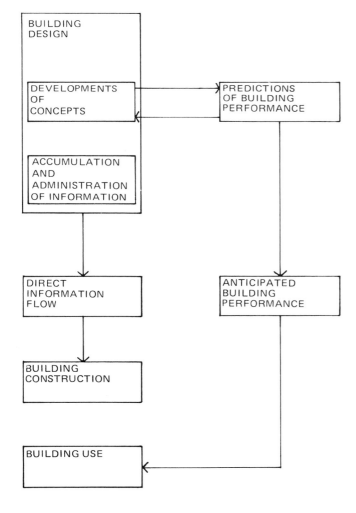

Figure 1

Information Flow in Building Design

The building design process can be seen as a continuum of information processing from the original assimilation of a brief through to the finalisation of contractual documentation. This process of information accretion and information flow is the area in which models in building design are required to operate.

Figure 1 outlines in a very simple form the types of information flow in the design process. This diagram demonstrates the information flow connections between the various periods of a building's life, i.e. design, construction and use. Three types of information processing occur at the design stage:

1. assembly of possible concepts
2. testing possible concepts
3. providing detailed production information on the finalised concept

The first two types of information processing can form a loop in the concept and design stage, 'an iterative design procedure', of which the outcome is hopefully a 'proven' complete concept acceptable in terms of the ultimate use of the building. The third stage of the concept and design is the assembly of production information for use by the contractor. It should be apparent that, although building production and building use are tied sequentially, the significant relationship is via the initial concept and design stage.

DESIGN

PRODUCTION

USE

In this light, it is possible to assess the impact of building design on these three stages. If the life of a project is viewed in terms of present value, one can estimate very crudely that the value of building construction is an order of magnitude greater than building design, and the value expended over the lifetime of the building may be an order of magnitude greater than construction costs. Even though accurate assessments of attributable in-use value are difficult to achieve, it can be seen that building design costs may well constitute less than 1% of the total building value.

Furthermore, when the fee scales for building design are broken down, the amounts expended on conceptual design, the seminal part of the design process, can be seen to diminish even further. This is because about 2/3rds of design fees are involved solely with the building production tasks of detailed design drawings, production documentation and site supervision.

The problems of building production are bound to become urgent at the design stage. They absorb a great deal of the effort expended, with attention devoted to project administration, cost-cutting to achieve a stipulated capital outlay, and the provision of contract information on time. The creation of the building concept can tend to remain a 'back of the envelope exercise' or perhaps a foray into the area of personal aesthetics, or social consciousness. Such an approach to building design is understandable, but in the light of the eventual expenditures of value and resources in the use of the building, it remains open to criticism.

I have tried to draw up a picture of the context in which building models have to operate. Quite clearly, it is possible to see them playing a role in the three areas already outlined, that is: assembly of possible concepts; testing of possible concepts; providing detailed production information on the finalised concept.

In other words, they should be able to aid the design team in developing plausible design solutions, in assessing the qualities of design solutions in a comparative manner and also in automating routine tasks for providing production documentation. If it were possible to achieve all these ends, the bias of the tasks in the design process would be likely to tip away from detailed design drawing and production documentation towards a much more careful and measured approach to the conceptual process of the design itself.

Systems providing these benefits are beginning to appear. When their operating contexts are examined, it is hardly surprising to find that they are generally being developed in relation to a systems approach to building problems; but more of that later.

Models and their Data Requirements

The idea of models as abstract representations of reality was mentioned earlier. Let us now go back to the model itself and establish that in general any model will consist of two parts:
1. given information on data
2. a method of manipulating that information, an algorithm

Methods of manipulating the information are several and often complex. The information employed during the design process, although a substantial amount for any single project, may be required in common by several algorithmic processes or may be specific to a single task.

By way of illustration of this point, let us look at a simple example, the insolation of a building facade partially obscured by an obstruction. Expressed in its simplest terms, the question to be answered is: "At what times on a certain day will the sun shine on point X of the facade of building A?". We have as data the location and size of building B, the location of point X in relation to it, and a table of attitude and azimuth of the sun at the particular latitude and season. All that data is required to carry out the calculation and to derive the result. The repetition of a series of straightforward trigonometrical calculations, i.e. the use of the algorithm for each given sun angle, will tell us the time of day when building B is obstructing point X on building A. The example is trivial, but it does serve to demonstrate that, although this calculation may be crucial to the prediction of the environmental

characteristics of point X in building A, the amount of actual information required about the subject, building A, is very small indeed; simply the location of point X in relation to building B. *(Figure 2)*

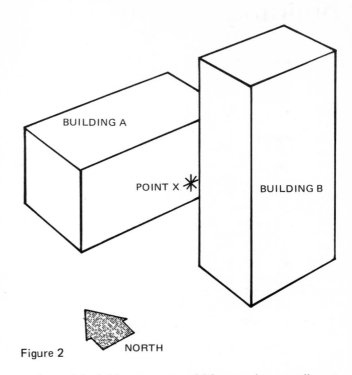

Figure 2 NORTH

A model of this nature would form only a small part of a larger system of environmental performance prediction for building A. Even so, the total information required for that complete task is still a small sub-set of total information required during the design and production of building A. In order to carry out wider-ranging environmental predictions, we may require more information about building A, for example, the reveal depth of the window at point X. However, we do not need to know whether it is bronze, aluminium or timber, nor the precise details of its cross-section. Similarly, one would require information on other qualities of building A, such as room outlines behind windows, 'U' values, densities and so on, all of which could apply to several construction methods. Further information of a completely different nature is required for the eventual construction of point X on building A.

The information about external obstructions and sun angles needed to carry out the insolation predictions we are using as an example is likely to be irrelevant for any other purposes in the building design process, unless other processes requiring its partial integration occur. Some do come to mind, for example, drawing perspectives calculating daylighting, and even taking the base levels of building B into consideration in calculating site works. However, none of these activities need necessarily be drawn into the scope of the design process of building A, and their integration should not be assumed.

It is possible to extrapolate from this example and say that any evaluative model of building performance, or any mechanism for manipulating design information for building *construction,* is likely to call only on a proportion of the total information required at the *design* stage of a building project. This can be

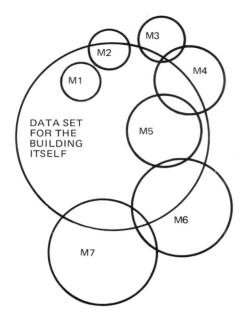

Figure 3

Figure 4

represented in a diagrammatic form where each set of information is specific to a particular model of the building's characteristics, and each examines it from a separate view-point.

The diagram shows that, when relating to total data set, the single building models or predictive methods may be able to call entirely on data relevant within the bounds of the building, may have data requirements in common with other models, and may also call on extraneous data, some of which may be common between techniques. *(Figure 3)*

It is an interesting aside that, by using a new technique developed by the CAD Group at the University Computer Laboratory here, one of the interpretations of the abstract model of a building can be a physical iconic model cut from hard plastic foam, using a computer-controlled model-making machine; the process has come full circle. *(Figure 4)*

Let us now also attempt to draw a distinction between various types of interpretation of building information. The first form of model, description insolation, is clearly an algorithm, since a series of manipulative calculations are performed to ascertain facts about the predictable building performance. However, other abstractions from the basic building data may be able to give other indicators of performance. For example, by identifying the number and cost of various items within the building, a comprehensive elemental cost picture could be built up. Such a process approaches much more to the straightforward task of examining bulk information and the selective sortation and accumulation of certain items from it.

Operational models of building for use in design are bound to contain both these characteristics. These are paralleled in computing terms as having elements both of scientific programming and conventional data processes.

The name Computer-Aided Building was coined some time ago, and can be taken to encompass systems which incorporate elements of automatic aids to design and automatic aids for production documentation. In general, aids in production documentation approach more closely to conventional data processing techniques, whereas aids to design tasks approach to more conventional scientific programming. As these different types of systems become more highly integrated, then a greater overlap occurs between the two techniques and they become increasingly interdependent. It is at this stage that the serious consideration of data structuring to access multi-dimensional and multi-facetted representations of buildings becomes important.

The Role of the Systems Approach

Using traditional contracting techniques, we see concept and design activities culminating in the tender. To achieve this, the bulk of design information is ordered and stereotyped within the formal contractual documents, the drawings, the bill of quantities and the ancillary schedules. The design is distilled to these formal items, and in the process much information employed in the design process can be lost. The reasoning behind this is well understood—it maintains the generalist nature of the contracting business. It is only when the traditional divisions in the building industry are broken down that it should be possible to take more advantage of a cooperative approach to building design and production; negotiated contracts, management contracting, the contractor-developer and the design-and-build package deal are all manifestations of approaches which should favour the bridging of the gap between designer and contractor. Theoretically, they should also be able to exploit a useful integration of information between the two.

As well as the various contracting arrangements already mentioned, a systematic approach to building problems and the use of building systems themselves can organise and increase the utility of information employed with the design process. At the same time, it is likely that the scope, but not necessarily the quantity, of information will be reduced. Within the defined extent of a building system, a preferred range of components should exist and the design solution's required conditions should be defined; in other words, either the detailed component designs themselves should exist, or the rules within which unique solutions are created should be defined. When one compares this situation in terms of information, quality and quantity to a one-off design approach, a remarkable contrast results. On the one hand the design team have open all the manufacturers' catalogues to choose from and thus have a continuous task of detailed design specification, probably based on little feedback of performance information, whereas, on the other hand, all items and specifications brought within the building system approach should be vetted and be known to be integrable within the system. The design and evaluation of the building system becomes a central support task.

Similarly, the systems approach to building can broaden to involve not just the construction techniques of the building, but also such items as standard briefing and room data information. As we will hear later, this systems approach in health building in particular can be taken even further by standardised detailed planning of large planning elements. Once again, in this case the design, up-dating and maintenance of the standard solutions becomes the major task, rather than the complete review of the detailed design as occurs in the one-off situation. Thus the project design team can manipulate a great deal of vetted information using only a shorthand notation, whether it be for a single building component or for a large predesigned section of a building complex. In most cases, their deliberations can apply to design decisions that involve overall building performance and quality.

Operational Models

Most of this paper has centred around the quantity and quality of information used in the design process. Much of this information is used to represent the design as it is developed and it forms an abstract model of the building as the design proceeds. It is possible to interpret from the model, or rather to make the model operational by carrying out algorithmic manipulations of the base data.

These are commonly carried out by simple manual techniques, but methods are also developed to carry out similar, or often more detailed, manipulations using the computer. In this way the repetitive process of multiple sequential calculations can be alleviated.

The sort of tasks which one might expect to carry out within the building design process include:

a. *Brief Making*
   1. preliminary financial feasibility
   2. room data processing
   3. activity data processing
b. *Outline Design and Various Spatial Planning Techniques*
c. *Building Performance Evaluation*
   1. environmental evaluation
   2. circulation evaluation
   3. capital cost evaluation
   4. running cost evaluation
d. *Building Element Design*
   1. standard calculations for superstructure and substructure
   2. site works analysis
e. *Building Element Selection*
   1. from catalogue according to performance characteristics
   2. from building system according to location requirements
f. *Building Services Design*
   1. element sizing
   2. element detailing
g. *Drafting*
h. *Element Listing*
   1. subcontractor schedules
   2. bill of quantities items

This list, though not exhaustive, does contain elements of the major CAB functions at the concept and design stage.

All these separate techniques require specific sets of information. As was shown earlier, in some cases there may be a significant overlap between tasks and the total information about the building, and in other cases there may be little common ground. There already exist computer techniques to carry out these processes as stand-alone tasks. Substantial benefits accrue if one can combine some of the tasks to produce an integrated approach to environmental analysis of building, for example, by the multiple re-use of dimensional information about the building. Although total data input sufficient for the whole set of analyses is greater than for a single one, some of the data is re-used time and again.

If it is possible to proceed further with integration, and retain information which is simultaneously adequate for all the processes already mentioned, further benefits result. One can use the computer to hold a completely operational building model, a 'building image', which is capable of replacing drawings as the definitive record of the design as it proceeds. In this way, any application program carrying out a specific task can access all the necessary information from the building image without the need for further data preparation. Further to this, it is also possible for the computer, under the direction of the user, to carry out routine design procedures, such as automatic selection of some components or automatic design of others. In this way, the machine itself can develop and enhance the building image held within the computer. In other words, it can carry out its own data input within the original framework set out by the design team. The use of the computer in this manner does assume that the building method itself is sufficiently organised to have routine procedures for the machines to follow slavishly. These are patently absent in traditional building techniques, but they are usually designed into any building system. The rigour with which this is achieved, however, is often open to question. The use of a unified model of a building can go further. It has other important qualities not contained within a conventional drawing. It can, for example, be 3-dimensional and can be interpreted in 3D. It retains a complete and continuous record of all the project team's influences on the building, and thus can act as a communicator between all members of the team. In this role it can prevent the clashes of interest which are so common between design professionals. It can be complete in that it contains and can access both such things as the locations of components and the disposition of rooms, and also abstract specifications for the elements of the building. The interpretations which can be put on it are diverse; it is equally reasonable to design a steel frame, schedule ironmongery, produce instructions for a bill of quantities, carry out elemental costing analysis, or decide on a summertime temperature prediction in a specific room.

The manner in which information is stored and handled to achieve these ends is a complex question of data structure design. In general terms, however, it appears to revolve around separable items of information, first, a store of component information describing such items as components and their properties, and second, briefing and activity data about planning elements of the building, and so on. This information concerning the scope of the building system and the building types involved is fairly general in nature and may normally be re-used on several building projects. The other complementary sets of information describe a single project and, in general, contain references to specific components and planning elements with a tag defining their location within the building. This "Project File" can be used both as the 3D description and referencing system for the building and also as the collation of briefing information independent of location before the layout of a building is finalised.

The problems encountered in the design of component data bases and project files will be discussed in papers later in the conference.

In Conclusion

Models of buildings are operational in many respects and are employed in many aspects of day-to-day traditional building design work. I have laid much emphasis on the role of a systems approach to building as being the key to the integration of these diverse activities, and crucial in the development of operational total models of buildings. The reason for this is simply that so much of the building information can be either taken as read, developed by means of predetermined automatable processes, or defined as data in a shorthand coded form. The present generation of computers and their allied software techniques do not have sufficient capacity to take up the challenge offered by traditional design and construction techniques. They are, however, playing a significant role when allied to systematic approaches to building problems. Experience is showing that academic developments that demonstrate the feasibility of an approach to this sort of problem are often a long way from the development of robust systems which will work reliably on a day-to-day basis. These present problems of technical development which both include substantial innovation and can build on academic experience and achievements but which, if ignored, are liable to cause much disappointment.

In this paper, I may appear to have been working against the interests of the designer; I do not believe this to be so. I believe most strongly that the sorts of tools that can be offered to the design team by these means can only increase his professional abilities, the predictability of his designs, and his standing amongst the public at large.

Having outlined the manner in which models of buildings can become operational in the case of system building, and having stressed the importance of the building image and its integrated qualities, it is important to examine how this image or model can be achieved in real life. I hope that some of the subsequent papers will dwell on these problems at greater length, both from the point of view of data processing for building and building evaluation procedures, and from the point of view of system building. ☐

Part 2

Description

Vitruvius Computatus

William Mitchell

There now exists an extensive body of theoretical and technical literature concerning computer-aided architectural design. Its principal (indeed almost exclusive) focus is the question of how computer-based techniques can facilitate the process of design. This paper is concerned with the different and ultimately much more interesting question of what the development of computer-aided design might imply for the character of architectural form. It argues that the notions of architectural form which, implicitly underlie much of the emergent theory of computer-aided design may be most usefully viewed as a direct continuation of the classical academic tradition of elementary composition. This tradition embodies an Aristotelian conception of form, and its evolution may be traced from antiquity.

Classical Conceptions of Architectural Form

The evolution of the classical ·tradition in architecture is a long and subtle story, and it is certainly not my intention to attempt to fully summarize it here. But to prepare the ground for the argument which follows, it is useful to recall some of the important stages and concepts.

In his well-known discussions of the forms of animals Aristotle developed a general systematic framework for comparative analysis of the forms of things:

If we were going to speak of the different species of animals, we should first of all determine the organs that are indispensable to every animal, as, for example, some organs of sense and instruments of receiving and digesting food, such as the mouth and the stomach, besides organs of locomotion. Assuming now that there are only so many kinds of organs, but that there are differences in them ... I mean different kinds of mouths, and stomachs, and perceptive and locomotive organs .... the possible combinations of these differences will necessarily furnish many varieties of animals. (For animals cannot be the same which have different kinds of mouths or ears.) And when all the combinations are exhausted there will be as many sorts of animals as there are combinations of the necessary organs[1]

In other words, forms were conceptualised combinatorially. They were seen as compositions constructed from limited sets of fundamental, elementary components.

Few records of the architectural theories of antiquity remain, but the one major treatise which has survived, Vitruvius' *De Architectura* (dating from the first century A.D.) utilised a similar procedure of dissecting complex forms into their elementary components, then discussing variations upon each type of component. In the third and fourth books of the ten-book work Vitruvius distinguished the alternative Ionic, Doric, and Corinthian "orders" of architecture. He discussed their constituent parts, described how these parts form the fundamental components from which designs for temples may be generated, and told in which circumstances each order could be considered appropriate. Fourteen hundred years later, in conscious imitation of Vitruvius, Alberti's *Ten Books on Architecture* developed a similar discussion, and in 1537 Sebastiano Serlio's book on *The Orders* presented the orders as canonical formulae from which all architectural forms were to be developed. The volume began with a plate *(Figure 1)* illustrating the Tuscan, Doric, Ionic, Corinthian and Composite orders, together with Serlio's explanation that just as ancient dramatists prefaced their plays with prologues, so he was introducing the major characters in his treatise on architecture. As Sir John Summerson has remarked, "He does it in a way which makes the orders seem as categorical in the grammar of architecture as, say, the four conjugations of verbs in the grammar of the Latin language."[2] The works of Serlio were to become a standard source book on architecture throughout Europe through the sixteenth and seventeenth centuries, and until the late eighteenth century most major theoretical treatises on architecture published in Europe (Vignola, Palladio and Scamozzi in Italy; De l'Orme, Freart, Perrault Cordemoy and Laugier in France; Blum, de Vries and Ditterlin in Germany and Flanders; Shute, Gibbs, Ware and Chambers in Britain) followed Serlio's lead in systematically structuring their discussion around the five orders and their properties.

In the early nineteenth century the highly influential works of J. N. L Durand, following a French classical tradition springing from Cordemoy and Laugier, carried neo-classical systemisation of the discussion of built form one step further. Durand, like his classicist predecessors, conceived of architectural form as being developed from a finite and well-defined vocabulary of elements. But in addition, the pages of his famous *Precis* explicitly demonstrated how wide ranges of alternative forms might be built up from systematic combinations of these elements, just as Aristotle had described how "the possible combinations of these differences will necessarily furnish many varieties of animals." *Figure 2* illustrates some examples.

This concept of elementary composition was

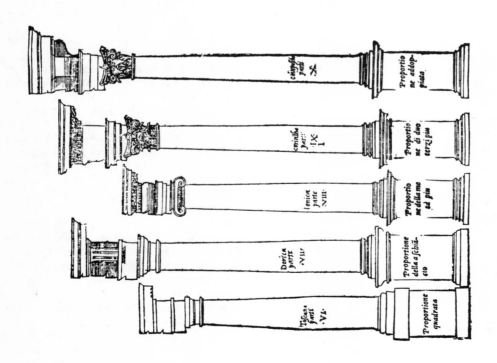

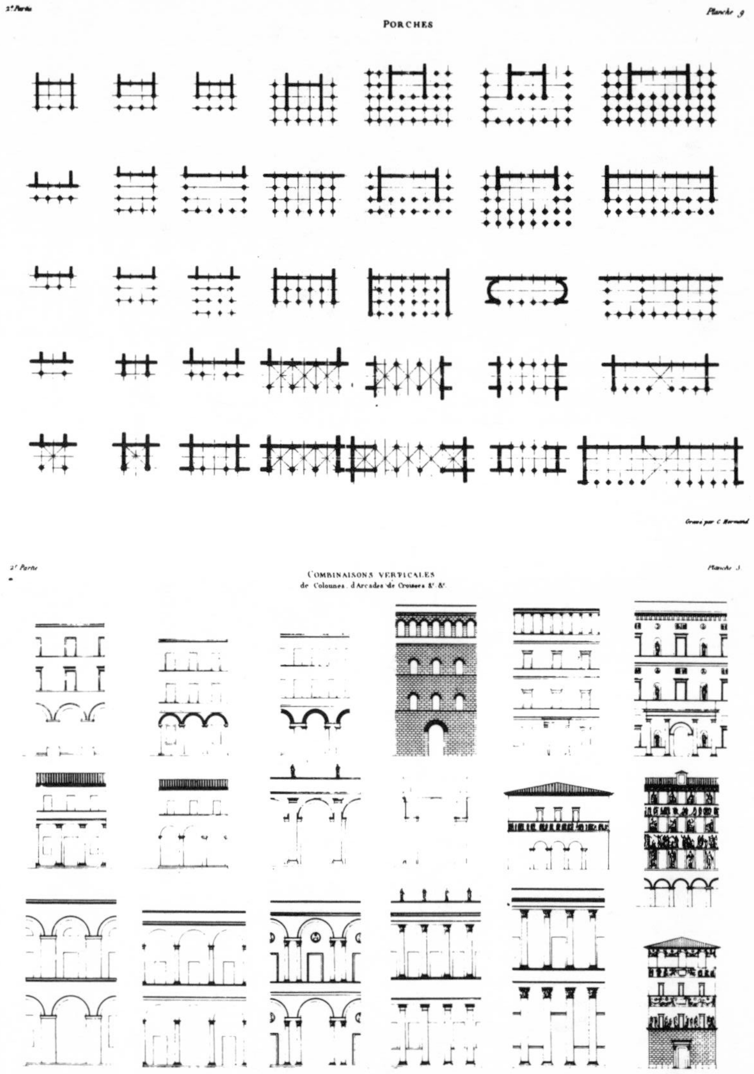

Figure 2:   Plates from Durand's Precis   (1802)

Figure 1:   The Orders of Serlio   (1540)

transmitted into the twentieth century largely by Julien Guadet's massive *Elements et Theories de l'Architecture* (Paris, 1902). Guadet like Durand was Professor at the Ecole des Beaux Arts, a position of immense influence. He was, as Reyner Banham has pointed out, the master of Auguste Perret and Tony Garnier, and his book "formed the mental climate in which perhaps half the architects of the twentieth century grew up." Banham has summarized the conception of built form upon which the *Elements* is based as follows:

> The approach is particulate; small structural and functional members (elements of architecture) are assembled to make functional volumes, and these (elements of composition) are assembled to make whole buildings. To do this is to compose in the literal and derivational sense of the word, to put together[3].

Conceptions of Form in Computer-Aided Design Systems

I suggest that the conceptions of built form which underlie most current approaches to computer-aided design are very much in the direct tradition of Durand and Guadet. This begins to be clear when we examine the role of representation techniques in design, and the particular techniques by which representations of buildings are stored in computer memory.

An architect normally generates a design for a building by operating upon some convenient representation or partial representation of that proposed building until the state of representation is judged to possess certain desired properties. Most commonly the representation consists of two-dimensional projections of edge-lines of three-dimensional forms, drawn in pencil on paper, and the operations performed upon it are making and erasing projected edge lines.

A computer-aided design system replaces this pencil and paper representation of the design with a systematic symbolic description (consisting of numbers and words) stored internally in the computer's memory, and the operations performed upon it are manipulations of symbols in accordance with the laws of logic and arithmetic. Unlike in a normal traditional design situation, the nature and sequence of these operations may not always be directly determined by the human designer, but may be wholly or partially under the control of some stored computer program. In other words, the design process may be wholly or partially automated.

In order to develop a method of symbolic description of a built form suitable for computer manipulation, it seems necessary to conceive of the form as divisible into a set of discrete and uniquely identifiable elements, and to develop some consistent systematic procedure for identifying and describing these elements.

Figure 3 illustrates a very simple built form, and *figure 4* a typical structure for its symbolic description by means of lists of numbers and keywords. The form is considered to be composed of orthogonally-arranged rectangular parallelepipeds. The first list, SPA, describes the properties of each parallelepiped. Each parallelepiped consists of twelve surfaces (six interior and six exterior), and the properties of these surfaces are described in SUR. Surfaces may be

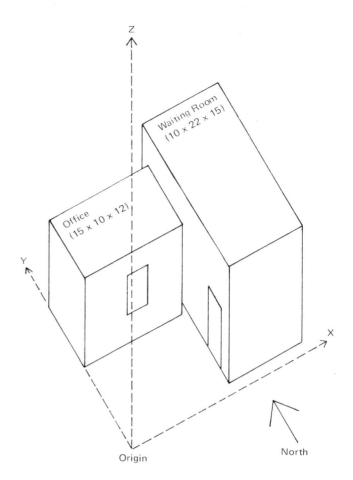

Figure 3:

pierced by rectangular openings, and the properties of these openings are described in OPE. By assigning particular numbers and keywords to locations in this structure, a description of one particular design utilising this particular limited vocabulary of form is built up as shown in *figure 5*. By manipulating these lists of symbols in the computer's memory the design is modified . . . just as, by manipulating lines on paper, an architect modifies designs in a traditional design process.

Now there is a very close conceptual relationship between data structure of this type and the classical academic treatises on design discussed earlier. In each case, the Aristotelian method of systematic analysis and descriptions of form is followed. A limited set of essential elements, for example the elements of the orders, the "elements of architecture" and "elements of composition" of Guadet, and the rectangular parallelepipeds, rectangular surfaces and rectangular openings of the data structure, are first defined. Each of these elements is allowed a certain range of variation of type and dimension, and by assembling combinations of variations on the elements widely varied architectural forms are generated. In this sense computer-aided design as it is currently approached may be seen as a direct extension of the academic classical tradition of elementary composition and particular computer-aided design systems as embodying particular theories of architectural form in much the same way as the treatises of Serlio, Durand and Guadet.

```
SPA ← LIST[ n]                      (1 list element for each space)
     SPA [ n] ← ARRAY[6]      (6 basic pieces of information stored for each space)
          [ n][ 1]:  space name
                [ 2]← ARRAY[3] (dimensions)
                [ 2][ 1]:  length
                   [ 2]:  width
                   [ 3]:  height
                [ 3] ← ARRAY[3]     (global location coordinates)
                [ 3][ 1]:  x-coordinate
                   [ 2]:  y-coordinate
                   [ 3]:  z-coordinate
                [ 4]:  floor area
                [ 5]:  volume
                [ 6] ← ARRAY[12]    (surface identifiers)
                [ 6][ 1]:  north face interior
                   [ 2]:  east face interior
                   [ 3]:  south face interior
                   [ 4]:  west face interior
                   [ 5]:  floor interior
                   [ 6]:  ceiling interior
                   [ 7]:  north face exterior
                   [ 8]:  east face exterior
                   [ 9]:  south face exterior
                   [10]:  west face exterior
                   [11]:  floor exterior
                   [12]:  ceiling exterior
     SPA [n+1] etc.
SUR ← LIST[ m]                      (1 list element for each type of surface)
     SUR [ m]← ARRAY[3]     (3 basic pieces of information per surface)
          [ m][ 1]← ARRAY[2]  (dimensions)
                [ 1][ 1]:  length
                   [ 2]:  width
                [ 2]:  identifier of material section
                [ 3]← LIST[p] (1 list element for each opening in the surface)
                [ 3][ p]   ARRAY[2] (2 pieces of information per opening in the surface)
                   [ p][ 1]:  identifier of opening
                         [ 2] ← ARRAY[2]  (location of opening in the surface)
                         [ 2][ 1]:  relative x-coordinate
                            [ 2]:  relative y-coordinate
     SUR [m+1] etc.
OPE ← LIST[ q]                      (1 list element for each type of opening)
     OPE [ q] ← ARRAY[ 3]    (3 pieces of information per opening)
          [ q][ 1]:  identifier of type of opening
                [ 2]← ARRAY[2] (dimensions)
                [ 2][ 1]:  length
                   [ 2]:  width
                [ 3]:  identifier of material section
     OPE [q+1] etc.
```

Figure 4:   Simple list structure for describing the geometry of a building

```
SPA[ 1][ 1]:  "OFFICE"
    [ 2][ 1]:  15
       [ 2]:  10
       [ 3]:  12
    [ 3][ 1]:   0
       [ 2]:  10
       [ 3]:   0
    [ 4]:      150
    [ 5]:     1800
    [ 6][ 1]:   1
       [ 2]:   2
       [ 3]:   3
       [ 4]:   4
       [ 5]:   5
       [ 6]:   6
       [ 7]:   7
       [ 8]:   8
       [ 9]:   9
      [10]:   "NONE"
      [11]:  10
      [12]:  11
   [ 2][ 1]:  "WAITING ROOM"
    [ 2][ 1]:  10
       [ 2]:  22
       [ 3]:  15
    [ 3][ 1]:  15
       [ 2]:   0
       [ 3]:   1.5
    [ 4]:      220
    [ 5]:     3300
    [ 6][ 1]:  12
       [ 2]:  13
       [ 3]:  12
       [ 4]:  14
       [ 5]:  15
       [ 6]:  16
       [ 7]:  17
       [ 8]:  18
       [ 9]:  17
      [10]:  19
      [11]:  20
      [12]:  21
SUR[ 1][ 1][ 1]:  15
          [ 2]:  12
    [ 2]:  "WALL SECTION A"
    [ 3]   LIST[ 0]
   [ 2][ 1][ 1]:  10
          [ 2]:  12
    [ 2]:  "WALL SECTION A"
    [ 3]:  LIST[ 0]          continued


SUR[ 3][ 1][ 1]:  15
          [ 2]:  12
    [ 2]:  "WALL SECTION A"
    [ 3][ 1][ 1]:  1
          [ 2][ 1]:  5
             [ 2]:  3
   [ 4][ 1][ 1]:  10
          [ 2]:  12
    [ 2]:  "WALL SECTION A"
    [ 3][ 1][ 1]:  2
          [ 2][ 1]:  5
             [ 2]:  0
   [ 5][ 1][ 1]:  15
          [ 2]:  10
    [ 2]:  "FLOOR SECTION A"
    [ 3]   LIST[ 0]
   [ 6][ 1][ 1]:  15
          [ 2]:  10
    [ 2]:  "CEILING SECTION A"
    [ 3]   LIST[ 0]
   [ 7][ 1][ 1]:  15
          [ 2]:  12
    [ 2]:  "WALL SECTION B"
    [ 3]   LIST[ 0]
   [ 8][ 1][ 1]:  10
          [ 2]:  12
    [ 2]:  "WALL SECTION B"
    [ 3]   LIST[ 0]
   [ 9][ 1][ 1]:  15
          [ 2]:  12
       [ 3][ 1][ 1]:  1
             [ 2][ 1]:  6
                [ 2]:  3
  [10][ 1][ 1]:  15
          [ 2]:  10
    [ 2]:  "FLOOR SECTION B"
    [ 3]   LIST[ 0]
  [11][ 1][ 1]:  15
          [ 2]:  10
    [ 2]:  "CEILING SECTION B"
    [ 3]   LIST[ 0]
  [12][ 1][ 1]:  10
          [ 2]:  15
    [ 2]:  "WALL SECTION A"
    [ 3]   LIST[ 0]
  [13][ 1][ 1]:  22
          [ 2]:  15
    [ 2]:  "WALL SECTION A"
    [ 3][ 1][ 1]:  2
          [ 2][ 1]:  14.3 continued
```

Figure 5:   Description of the building illustrated in Figure 3

```
SUR[13][ 3][ 1][ 2][ 2]:   0              OPE[ 1][ 2][ 2]:   7
          [ 2][ 1]:   3                        [ 3]   "DOUBLE HUNG GLASS"
                 [ 2][ 1]:   1              [ 2][ 1]:   "DOOR"
                        [ 2]:   0              [ 2][ 1]:   2.7
    [14][ 1][ 1]:   22                               [ 2]:   6.7
            [ 2]:   15                           [ 3]:   "1/2 HOUR DOOR"
      [ 2]:   "WALL SECTION A"            [ 3][ 1]:   "DOOR"
      [ 3][ 1][ 1]:   1                        [ 2][ 1]:   2.7
                 [ 2][ 1]:   12                      [ 2]:   6.7
                        [ 2]:   3              [ 3]:   "1 HOUR EXTERIOR DOOR"
    [15][ 1][ 1]:   10                    [ 4][ 1]:   "EXTERIOR"
            [ 2]:   22                          [ 2][ 1]:   10
      [ 2]:   "FLOOR SECTION A"                      [ 2]:   10.5
      [ 3]   LIST[ 0]                         [ 3]:   "VOID"
    [16][ 1][ 1]:   10
            [ 2]:   22
      [ 2]:   "CEILING SECTION A"
      [ 3]   LIST[ 0]
    [17][ 1][ 1]:   10
            [ 2]:   15
      [ 2]:   "WALL SECTION B"
      [ 3]   LIST[ 0]
    [18][ 1][ 1]:   22
            [ 2]:   15
      [ 2]:   "WALL SECTION B"
      [ 3][ 1][ 1]:   4
                 [ 2][ 1]:   2
                        [ 2]:   0
          [ 2][ 1]:   2
                 [ 2][ 1]:   5
                        [ 2]:   0
          [ 3][ 1]:   3
                 [ 2][ 1]:   4.7
                        [ 2]:   0
    [19][ 1][ 1]:   22
            [ 2]:   15
      [ 2]:   "WALL SECTION B"
      [ 3][ 1][ 1]:   1
                 [ 2][ 1]:   12
                        [ 2]:   0
    [20][ 1][ 1]:   10
            [ 2]:   22
      [ 2]:   "FLOOR SECTION B"
      [ 3]   LIST[ 0]
    [21][ 1][ 1]:   10
            [ 2]:   22
      [ 2]:   "CEILING SECTION B"
      [ 3]   LIST[ 0]
OPE[ 1][ 1]:   "WINDOW"
        [ 2][ 1]:   4              continued
```

Figure 5 (continued)

Is this continuity of the academic classical tradition of elementary composition in a rather unexpected way merely a historical curiosity of little practical consequence? I suggest not. It indicates that computer systems cannot be regarded as formally neutral tools in the design process. On the contrary, their use can be expected to demand acquiescence to particular formal disciplines. This implies several things. Firstly it becomes clear that the design and development of satisfactory computer-aided design systems is not simply a technical task to be left to systems analysts, engineers, and programmers. It demands a high level of *architectural* skill and capacity for rigorous analysis of built form. Secondly, as architects begin increasingly to work with such systems they will need to devote as much attention to understanding the vocabulary and syntax of form implied by the data structures of those systems as the classical architects of old devoted to study of the orders. Finally, if increasingly sophisticated systems become capable of automatically performing increasingly comprehensive design tasks, we can expect the designs which emerge from them to be characterised by particular stylistic traits. If computer systems become architects they may be academic classicists, heirs to Durand and Guadet.

References

1. *Politics,* 1290, trans. Jowett
2. John Summerson, *The Classical Language of Architecture,* M.I.T. Press, 1963
3. Reyner Banham, *Theory and Design in the First Machine Age,* Second Edition, Praeger, 1967

Acknowledgement

I wish to thank Jeffrey Hamer, UCLA graduate student, for his assistance in preparing the examples shown in figures 3, 4, and 5.   □

Computer representations of architectural problems

Janet Tomlinson

This paper is about the computer representations of architectural problems and how the programming language used for the representation affects the solution of the problems.

An architectural problem, in broad terms, involves asking questions about an object which exists or might exist and possibly modifying the object, depending on the answers to the questions. If the object does not yet exist, or is large, or contains information irrelevant to the questions to be answered, then dealing with a model of the object and not the object itself is certainly convenient and may be necessary. A computer representation is one type of model. The use of computers for modelling has both advantages and disadvantages which I do not want to go into here but other papers will discuss. As a brief illustration of the power of computer modelling, however, *Fig 1* shows a representation of one of the three-dimensional projections of a four-dimensional object, a hyper-cube. A computer model of a hyper-cube could represent all four dimensions and provide any projection in fewer dimensions as required: any other model or picture can only represent one projection in two or three dimensions.

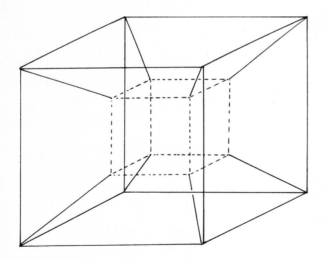

Figure 1   Representation of a hyper-cube

A drawing of an object probably needs a key to make the meaning of the drawing clear, but the key is small and only contains a little information. A computer representation of an object, on the other hand, is just a collection of bits and could be interpreted in an infinite number of ways. A lot of information is needed to define the correct interpretation of the rep-

resentation, and this information must be stored somewhere. A physical means of communication with the representation is also needed, and a program written to interrogate the representation fulfils both purposes, the information about the representation being implied by the program. In fact, a program was necessary to construct the representation in the first place, taking the information about the object from some external source and creating a structure which, when interrogated by the program, represents the original object.

The language in which the program is written becomes vitally important, as this language is the only means of communication between the architect and his model. If there were some information which simply could not be expressed in the language, then that information could not exist in the model. Fortunately, however, the required information can almost always exist in some form, the difference between programming languages lies in the ease of expression of information of various kinds and not in whether the information can be expressed at all.

Structures for the Computer Representation

I have said that a computer representation is a collection of bits, and that is true at the lowest level, but programming languages do not usually allow a structure in the computer's store to be regarded as a collection of bits. High-level languages in particular provide intrinsic structures of their own, and these intrinsic structures are different in the different languages. A representation created by a particular programming language will consist of structures allowed by the structuring facilities of the language used. The representation in terms of the intrinsic structures will still be translated into a representation in the computer's store when the program is run, but this is not relevant to the programmer who must write the program to build the structure with the structuring facilities his chosen programming language allows. To illustrate the sort of structuring facilities that are provided, I will give some examples of programming languages and their intrinsic structures. In Fortran, the basic structure is a collection of boxes for holding numbers, shown diagrammatically in *Fig. 2.* These boxes can be named individually, or they can be put together as rows, arrays or three-dimensional structures. The structures of boxes must be named, and each box within a structure can be addressed by quoting its coordinates in each dimension of the structure. In Standard Fortran, structures cannot have more than three dimensions, but many versions of Fortran allow structures with four or more dimensions;

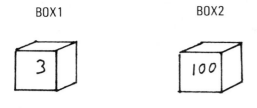

BOX1   BOX2

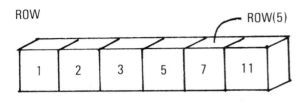

ROW   ROW(5)

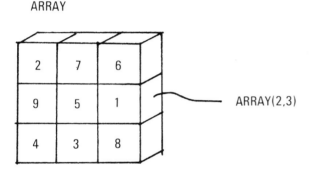

ARRAY

ARRAY(2,3)

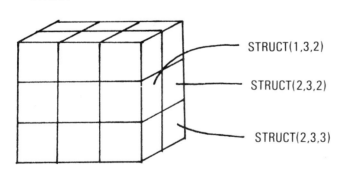

STRUCT

STRUCT(1,3,2)

STRUCT(2,3,2)

STRUCT(2,3,3)

Figure 2   Intrinsic structures in FORTRAN

this is an example of the structuring facilites being dependent on the particular version of the language in use, and not being common to all versions of the language. When writing in Fortran, a program to access each box in the structure is simple and concise. Starting from any one box, the neighbouring boxes in any direction can be found easily. This sort of structure might be convenient for representing the rooms in a building, for example, because the spatial relationships of the rooms are directly represented by the co-ordinates of the boxes.

In Cobol, the intrinsic structure is a tree with numbers or character strings held in the leaves at the ends of the branches *(Fig 3)*. A branch can either have a leaf at its ends or a node with any number of further branches. The branches are named, either individually or all the branches from a node may be named collectively with each branch identified by its position. In this structure it is easy to start from the root or a lower node and find all the leaves depending on the node. It is difficult to start from a leaf and find the nodes on which the leaf depends because each node must be tested to see if the required leaf depends on the node.

A structure of this sort could be used to represent a town as a number of zones each of which, for different stages in the town's development, has a number of parcels of land with a different land use. Some aspects of the way the town changes with time can thus be conveniently represented, but the geographical location of the zones is not implied by the structure. Each branch must be named, so a Cobol structure must have a predefined depth and cannot be extended once it is created. Also, no one type of node can occur at more than one level in the structure so a Cobol structure would not be suitable for representing a family tree, for example, because in a family tree each level should contain nodes of the same type, representing a person. A program to visit every leaf in the structure would be long, though not complicated, because each branch or collection of branches has to be named individually. The program would only work for a specific structure, and would have to be changed if the structure were changed.

The list-processing language LISP has an intrinsic structure which is a binary tree *(Fig. 4)*. That is, each node must have exactly two branches; numbers are again held in the leaves. Unlike the Cobol structure, the branches are not individually named. One can simply take the left or the right branch from any node, so each node can be teated as though it is the root of a smaller tree. Compact, powerful programs can be written to handle this type of structure, although the programs may take a relatively long time to run. A program to visit every leaf in the tree would be short to write, although longer in execution time than a Fortran program to visit a similar number of boxes. A LISP structure is often used to represent mathematical expressions, where parts of the expression may themselves be expressions.

Programming New Structures

We have already seen how, when using a high-level programming language, the programmer has to use the structuring facilities of the language to build representations of his objects. The programmer cannot use the computer's store except in ways allowed by these structuring facilities but he can write himself a program, or part of a program, to provide any structures which he can translate into the language's intrinsic structures using the facilities of the high level language *(Fig. 5)*. The structures the program is using may be very similar to the language's intrinsic structures (for example, if several words in a Fortran array are used to represent one entity), or the structures may be completely different. Fortran subroutines can be written to use a Fortran array as though it is a tree structure.

Some languages provide much better facilities than

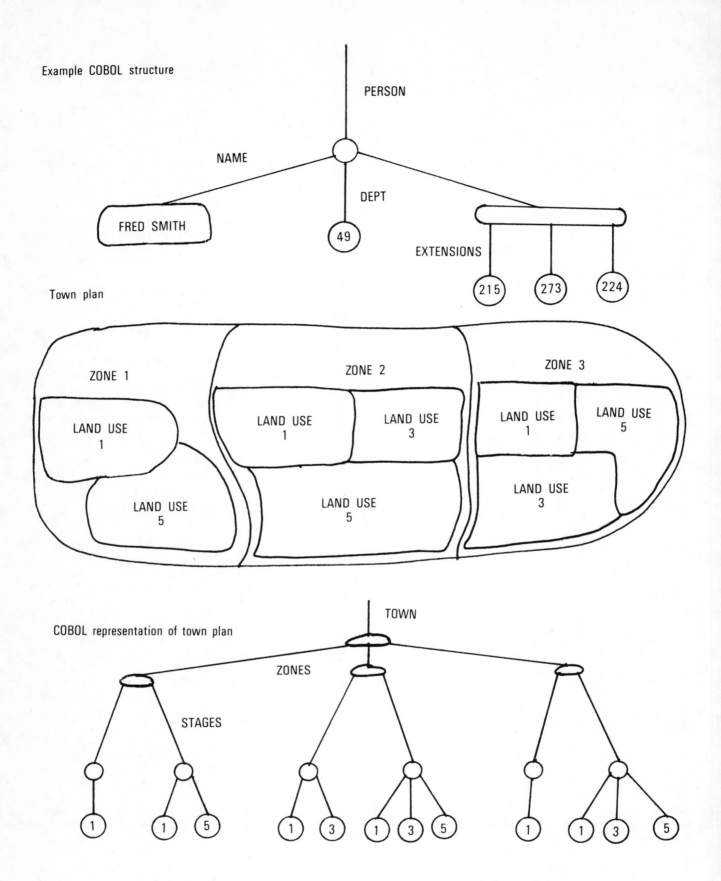

Example COBOL structure

PERSON

NAME

DEPT

FRED SMITH

49

EXTENSIONS

215   273   224

Town plan

ZONE 1

ZONE 2

ZONE 3

LAND USE
1

LAND USE
1

LAND USE
3

LAND USE
1

LAND USE
5

LAND USE
5

LAND USE
5

LAND USE
3

TOWN

COBOL representation of town plan

ZONES

STAGES

1   1   5   1   3   1   3   5   1   1   3   5

Figure 3   Intrinsic structures in COBOL

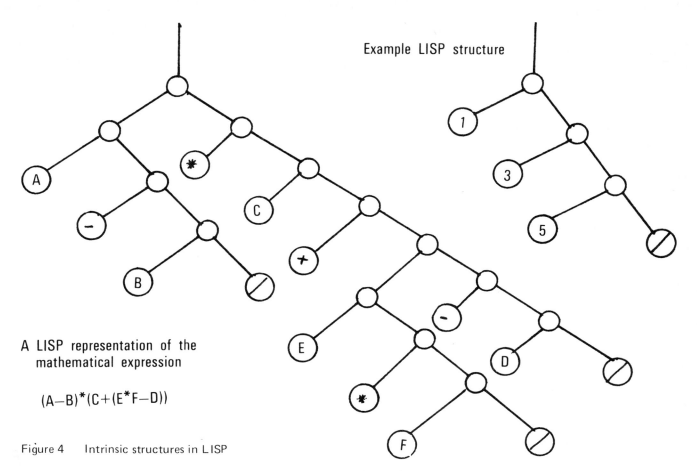

Example LISP structure

A LISP representation of the mathematical expression

$(A-B)^*(C+(E^*F-D))$

Figure 4   Intrinsic structures in LISP

others for programming new structures. In Cobol, for example, a Fortran-type structure can be programmed but not a LISP-type one, whereas in Fortran a Cobol or a LISP-type structure can be programmed.

A program involving structures very different from the intrinsic structures of the language in which the program is written involves more work for the programmer in the initial writing of the program, since the structure translation must be programmed. However, this is not the only penalty. The program will be more complex and so more difficult for another person or even for the author to understand; the structure manipulation of the final program will probably be in terms of function calls in the programming language which, although adequate for the job, may well be clumsy in expression and difficult to remember; the details of the resultant structures will not be explicit in the program but must be remembered by the programmer, and this again tends to lead to errors and difficulty in understanding the program. To sum up, while in general any structures can be provided in any language, the resulting program may be long, complex, error-prone and difficult to understand.

Special purpose languages, therefore, tend to concentrate on providing intrinsic structures which are suitable for the problems the language is designed to solve, and make the common operations on these structures easy and convenient. The languages for computer-aided design, for example, provide easy handling of ring structures; text-editing languages such as SNOBOL provide for handling strings of characters. Algol 68 is a general purpose language with a simple

intrinsic structure, but it provides convenient facilities for programming other structures. Thus Algol 68 attempts to reduce the penalties for working with a structure different from the language's intrinsic structures.

Programming Languages as Tools for Thought

To return to the architectural problem, the programmer has eventually to write a program which will build a representation of his object and answer questions about it. First, however, he must decide how to solve his problem and what the logic of the program should be. At this stage, he may resort to yet another representation of the object, for example by doodling on a piece of paper, and he may try to describe in English or by a flowchart what his program should do. Having achieved a conceptual solution, the programmer then translates it into a program and attempts to run the program (Fig. 6). The program may fail due to an error at any stage in the process. Errors in the translation phase are usually easy to find and correct, particularly if the logic of the conceptual solution was clear and readily comparable with the logic of the program, but an error in the conceptual solution may only become apparent as an error in the program and then the original solution must be modified and retranslated.

So far, the programming language has not helped the programmer to solve his problem at all, it has merely provided a tool for building and interrogating the computer representation. If, however, the programming language were a convenient means of expressing the conceptual solution, then not only would the translation phase be avoided altogether but

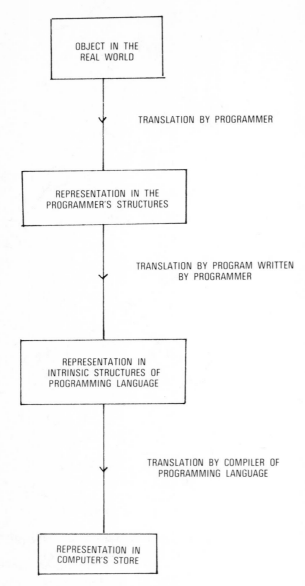

Figure 5   The successive translation of an object to its representation in the computer's store.

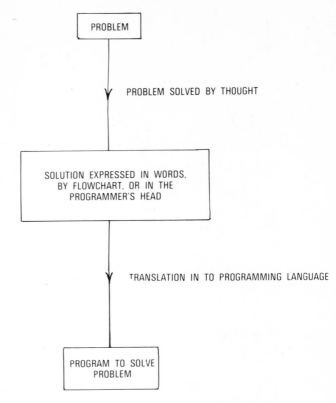

Figure 6   Diagram of the problem solving process.

powerful manipulations of these structures can be expressed economically and conveniently.

Characteristics of Architectural Problems

In representing architectural problems, we will want to represent objects about which we have several items of data. Some of this data will be numeric values or character strings, such as room dimensions, lengths of roads or areas of land. Other data may concern the relations between objects, for example rooms which are adjacent, roads which intersect or land parcels which contain sub-parcels. My examples of objects so far have all been tangible objects having some existence in the real world, but the only requirement for an object is that there is some information connected with it, the object does not have to be tangible. Thus, we could represent a marriage *(Fig 7)* as an object having a date, a duration and relations to the people concerned and to the children of the marriage.

Let us now consider the characteristics of the relations between objects, so that we can see how to represent them. A relation may be reciprocal (for example if room A is next to room B then that implies that room B is next to room A because the relation ' next to ' is reciprocal), or non-reciprocal (for example the relation between a parcel of land and a sub-parcel is not the same as the relation between the sub-parcel and the enclosing parcel) as illustrated in *Fig 8*. In addition, several objects may be related by sharing a property. For example, all the zones in a town are related by virtue of belonging to the same town, and all the offspring of one parent are related by having a parent in common.

The non-reciprocal relations between two objects can be combined into one-to-many relations (for example, one parcel can contain several sub-parcels),

the programmer would have a further tool available for the more difficult problem of designing and debugging the conceptual solution. In other words, if the programming language were also a tool for thought, then it would be of great assistance in solving the problem. In a field such as engineering, Fortran is found to be a clear and concise method of expressing the equations which have to be solved, and the process of solving them, while LISP is used as a tool for thought in research into Artificial Intelligence, among other topics.

When considering a tool for architectural thought, the intrinsic structures provided by the language will be particularly important, because the structure of architectural data is important and one of the aims of the language will be to provide an alternative to doodling on a piece of paper as a means of expressing the structure. We have seen that programming a new structure in a specific language tends to lead to clumsy, inelegant expressions which are not attractive for designing a solution to a problem, so we require a language with intrinsic structures which are convenient for representing architectural problems and in which

or into many-to-one relations (one beam in a building can be supported by several beams or columns). As a further level of complexity, there are many-to-many relations, such as the full parent-children relation which goes from two parents to all the children; this can be regarded as two one-to-many relations, one from each parent to all the children, or as a single binary relation between the parents and the children collectively *(Fig 9)*. The reciprocal relation can also be

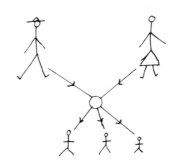

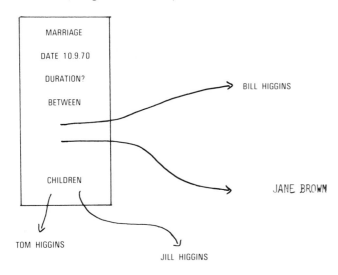

Figure 7   A representation of an intangible object

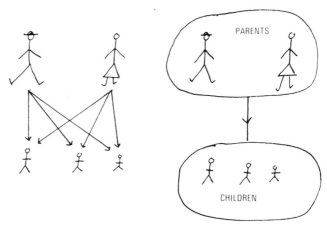

Figure 9   Representations of the parents–children relation

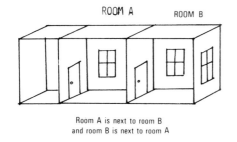

Room A is next to room B
and room B is next to room A

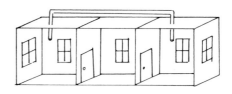

A structure which cannot be simply represented in the FORTRAN intrinsic structure

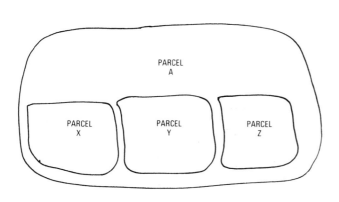

Parcel A contains parcel X;
parcel X is contained by parcel A

Figure 8   Reciprocal and non-reciprocal relations

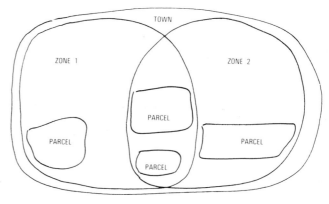

A structure which cannot be simply represented in the COBOL intrinsic structure

Figure 10   Illustrations of the limitations of two intrinsic structures

extended to more than two objects, though examples are not so common. The relation between all three poles in a wigwam, for example, is reciprocal as the poles all support each other, and this relation is similar to the common-property relation.

These various relations can conveniently be represented if we can collect objects together into a set and if we can represent a non-reciprocal binary relation. The common-property relation and reciprocal relations between two or more objects can be directly represented by forming a set of the related objects. One-to-many and many-to-one relations can be represented as a binary relation between an object and a set of objects. Many-to-many relations can either be represented as a binary relation between two sets, or decomposed into one-to-many relations and then represented as such. Reciprocal relations can be represented either as a set or, particularly for binary relations, as two non-reciprocal relations. Any one object may participate in a number of relations of these different types, and the representation of an object must allow for this.

Representing Architectural Problems

As an illustration of the complexity involved in representing objects and relations with these properties described earlier, I will show why the intrinsic structures described earlier are not adequate for the purpose without considerable modification.

The intrinsic Fortran structure has just one way of representing a relation, that is, by adjacency in some dimension of an array. This relation is strictly binary and non-reciprocal, but it can be used to represent binary reciprocal relations, and a number of these relations can represent a common-property relation. The representation cannot be used, however, for a one-to-many relation, nor a many-to-one, and no two objects can have more than one relation between them. The Fortran structure was adequate to represent the rooms in a building because adjacencies between the rooms could be represented by adjacency in the Fortran array, but if some of the rooms were connected by speaking tubes then these connections could not be represented in the Fortran structure *(Fig 10)*.

The Cobol structure also has one way of representing a relation; this relation is non-reciprocal and one-to-many. It cannot easily be used to represent reciprocal relations, and it cannot represent many-to-one relations. The Cobol structure could represent the zones in a town with their stages and parcels, but if any parcel belonged to more than one zone then the Cobol structure would not be adequate *(Fig 10)*.

LISP has facilities for representing a non-reciprocal one-to-two relation and this can be used to build up one-to-many relations or common-property relations in the usual way. The intrinsic LISP structure, like the Fortran structure, has no facilities for collecting together more than one piece of information about an object, so the connection between data referring to a single object would have to be by program.

The language L*, which I have been involved in

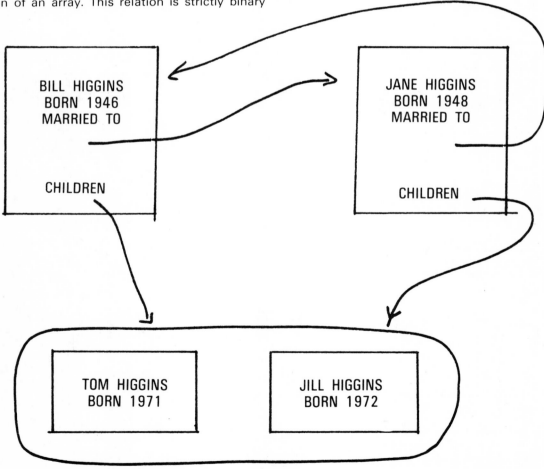

Figure 11   An example structure in L*

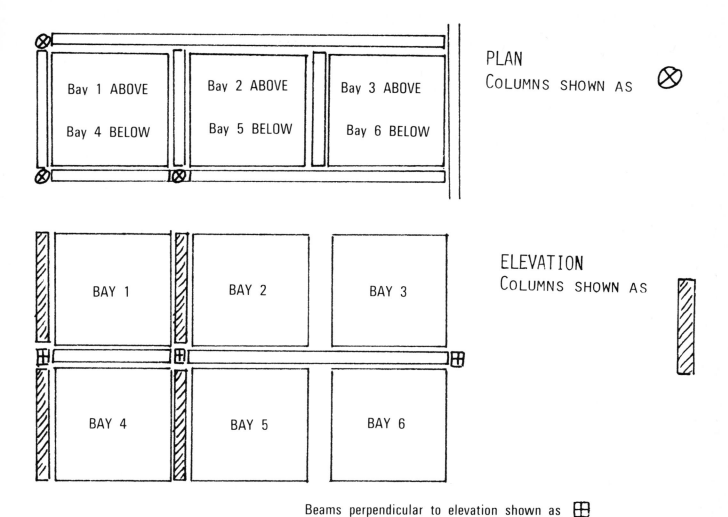

Figure 12   Part of the structure shown in plan and elevation

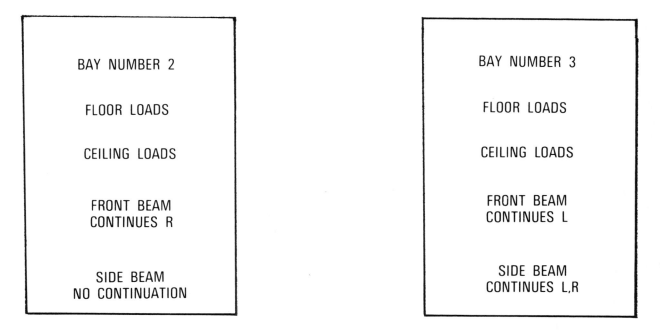

Figure 13   Part of the FORTRAN representation of the structure

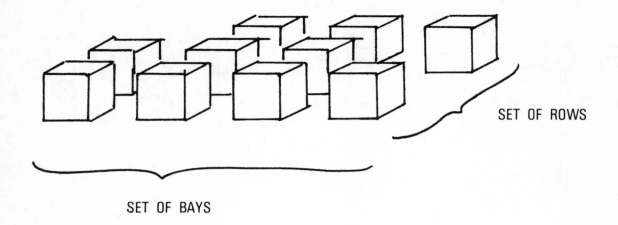

SET OF ROWS

SET OF BAYS

REPRESENTATION OF A FLOOR AS A SET OF ROWS

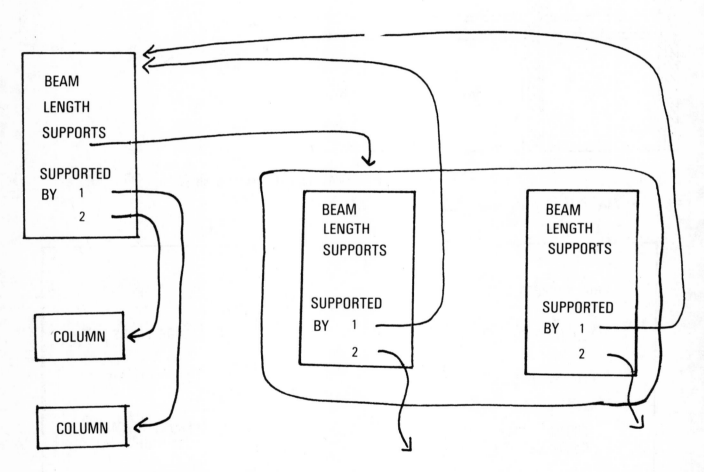

BEAM
LENGTH
SUPPORTS

SUPPORTED
BY   1
      2

COLUMN

COLUMN

BEAM
LENGTH
SUPPORTS

SUPPORTED
BY   1
      2

BEAM
LENGTH
SUPPORTS

SUPPORTED
BY   1
      2

Figure 14   Part of the L* representation of the structure

designing and implementing as a research project, has intrinsic structures which will represent objects with several pieces of data and taking part in several relations, sets of these objects and binary relations between objects or between an object and a set of objects *(Fig 11).* One of the aims of my research project is to see how effective this language is as a tool for thought about architectural problems.[1]

An Example

I would like to finish by giving an example of a problem which arose out of the Oxford system of building.[2] The solution to the problem has been programmed both in Fortran and in L* and different computer representations of the structure were used in

68

each case. I hope it will be apparent that the structure used in the Fortran solution, while convenient for the program, involves some considerable transformation from the original structure, whereas the L* structure is a natural and convenient representation of the structure involved in the problem.

The Fortran structure outlined here is not the main data structure of the system, which will be described by another speaker, but is a structure programmed for a specific problem.

The problem involves a building consisting of bays which form rooms with horizontal beams and vertical columns for support (Fig 12). The bays have both floor and ceiling loads and the beams may span up to four bays; both ends of a beam must be supported either by a column or by another beam. It was required to find the total load on each beam, made up of the floor and ceiling loads of bays adjoining the beam in appropriate directions and the total load on any other beam supported by the initial beam.

The Fortran structure uses a three-dimensional array to represent the bays, each bay has information about its floor and ceiling loads and also about beams which adjoin the bay and whether the beams are continued in the next bay in the relevant directions (Fig 13). Each bay is itself represented by a vector, to allow for all this information, so the whole Fortran structure is four-dimensional. A beam has no single representation, it is broken up into segments which are represented with the appropriate bays, so that in order to find the length of a beam, for example, several bays may have to be examined. To find the beams supported by a given beam, the bays with which the supported beams are associated must be found and the beams followed through as many bays as necessary.

In the L* structure, bays are represented as complete objects, and the three-dimensional structure of bays as a set of floors where each floor consists of a set of rows which is a set of bays (Fig 14). This has the advantage that if the building is an irregular shape, the shape can be allowed for, whereas in the Fortran structure enough dummy bays must be added to make the building a regular rectangular shape, and these dummy bays must be recognised as such by the program. A beam is also represented as an object, with relations "supported by" to the two beams or columns supporting the beam, and the relation "supports" to the set of beams supported by the original beam. A beam thus has a single representation and information about a beam can be found directly. The beams supported by a given beam are already formed into a set, so no further programming is required to find these beams.

References.
1.   Gray J. C. and Tomlinson J. C. (1973) 'The L* Data Language', Proceedings 28th National Conference of the ACM, 1973.
2.   Hoskins E. M., Richens P. and Hayward P. 'OXSYS. An Integrated Computer Aided Building System for the Oxford Method.'
     International Conference on Computers in Architecture, University of York, 20-22 September, 1972.   □

Computer design aids for large modular buildings

Jennifer Jacobsberg

Introduction

This paper describes an integrated design aid system which can assist architects, engineers and quantity surveyors concerned with the development, planning and construction of large buildings. Such a system is economically feasible where the building geometry is well-defined and coordinated, as in the Harness planning method and building system which has been developed by the Department of Health and Social Security in Gt. Britain (in association with the Regional Hospital Boards*) for the building and redevelopment of District General Hospitals which have in the region of six hundred to twelve hundred beds. The design aids to be described have been developed specifically for large hospitals and exploit the fact that Harness planning dimensions can readily be represented by a square grid. Deviations from the regular grid are represented and evaluated, but

*Now called Regional Health Authorities.

computation time and cost are thereby increased. Such deviations are therefore acceptable if they represent a relatively small part of the total scheme.

Building Description

Component parts

The basic grid for representing Harness hospitals is 5.4m square; the basic component parts are the departments and the harness zone, which gives the system its name. This zone is the main circulation and engineering services area, off which feed all wards, specialised functions, service and administrative units, collectively known as departments. A typical layout is shown in *Figure 1*.

From the information supplied by a design team, data is assembled on the size, shape and attributes of each department, the size and shape of the corridor area on each floor and the position of the departments with respect to the corridors.

Computer representation at general level

The assembled data is input to a computer. By program this information is converted to a form which provides a comprehensive picture of the building and

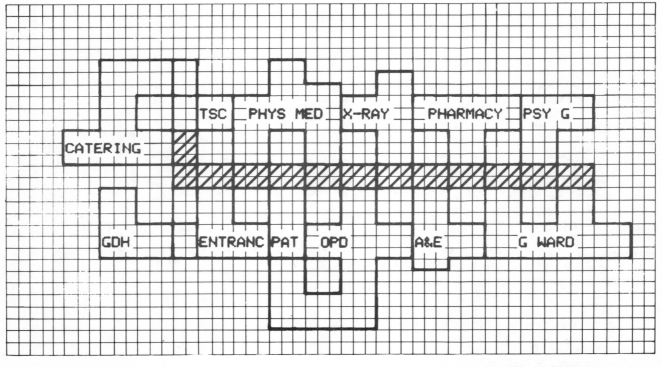

Figure 1

= 100 METRES

CIRCULATION ZONE.

70

is readily accessible by several evaluative programs.

Suppose the smallest unit of measurement for the building is 5.4m. If its maximum length is 54 units and its maximum width is 30 units, then a plan view of each level of the building can be represented in the computer as a two dimensional matrix. The matrix is 54 units long in the x direction and 30 units long in the y direction. Each entry in the matrix relates to an area approximately 5.4m square. In computer terms a unit of information is known as a "word" and this corresponds to each entry in the matrix. A "word" consists of 48 "bits" or binary digits, which can be thought of as the smallest identifiable part of a "word". In the example above, each floor of the building is represented by a plan matrix which consists of (54 x 30) "words". Each "word" may contain three categories of information as shown in *Figure 2*.

The contents code indicates whether the cell is department, corridor, courtyard, stilts or unspecified. Each department has a different code, as have distinctive sections of the circulation zone. The phase number associated with each built cell indicates the building phase. Cladding codes enable specification of cladding information in external wall situations. Each of these three categories of information can be referenced individually by computer programs. Another matrix, called the height matrix, has the same dimensions as the plan matrices but holds elevation details. Again there is provision for each "word" of the matrix to contain several categories of information, as shown in *Fig. 3*.

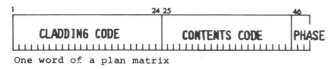

Figure 2

One word of a plan matrix

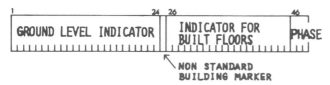

One word of a height matrix

Figure 3

Two indicators show presence or absence of building on each floor and ground level under built cells and elsewhere. There is a marker for building which does not conform to the standard construction and a phase number as before.

Computer representation at detailed level

The second part of the basic description held in the computer is mainly concerned with the corridor area and is held in a series of relatively small matrices. Each "word" merely contains information and no longer relates to a particular area. The circulation zone is considered as a number of units, usually 16.2m long and of varying width. A department is attached to one side of a unit, which is then known as its entrance slot.

Details of the entrance slot and of the phasing for each department are given in the first of the corridor matrices. The next three matrices hold a variety of information for each unit of the circulation zone, including its position in the plan matrix, a structure code, its length in 5.4m units and its phase. A final matrix gives details of position, phase, width for each 5.4m strip of corridor and also indicates whether it could be used as a lift site.

Comparison of detailed and general levels of computer representation

As the size of each rectangular plan matrix is determined by the maximum lengths of the building in the x and y directions, these matrices occupy relatively large amounts of computer storage. Inevitably a number of cells outside the walls of the building holds little information of value. By contrast several attributes of each built cell are recorded and the attributes of neighbouring cells are readily examined. Data in this generalised form may be used for several different applications. The corridor matrices holding detailed information on the circulation zone are more compact and use little computer storage. They tend, however, to be related to specific applications. This distinction between the plan matrices, which hold most of the required information on departments, and the corridor matrices underlines the difference between the well-defined structure and content of the departments and the more flexible nature of the circulation zone. This flexibility is acceptable because the corridor area is small in comparison with department area, of the order of one quarter.

Problems of non-aligned grids

To overcome one of the problems of representing a building on one rectangular grid, the concept of "site sectoring" was introduced. A building may be divided into three parts, and the surrounding rectangle for each is called a "site sector". Within each "site sector" the building is represented on a grid as before. *Figure 4* illustrates a situation where three "site sectors" are required.

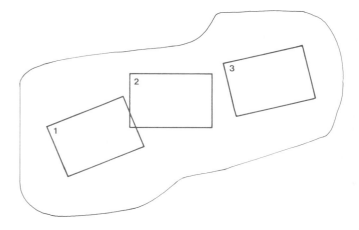

Figure 4

The computer representation described above is repeated for each "site sector" and information linking the "site sectors" is held with each representation.

In order to complete the description of a building it has to be positioned on a site and a means of representing the site devised.

Site Description

Site information recorded

On a contour map of the site are noted spot heights, bore-holes and building positions. Points are also marked at suitable intervals along the contours. The position of each of these points, relative to a selected origin, is recorded automatically using a digitiser. Additional data including the height of each contour and the depth of each substratum in the bore-holes is also recorded.

Computer representation of the site

A grid size of suitable dimensions for the site in question is selected, normally in the region of 5 to 16m square. The ground level at each point on this grid is deduced by interpolation from the digitised site data. A similar process is repeated for each of the substrata specified.

Relating the site description to the building description

An area of the site is selected which includes the entire "site sector" for the building and can be represented on a grid of the same dimensions. Using similar interpolation techniques the ground level before excavation is calculated for each grid square from data in the complete site matrix. If there are several soil types which might have to be excavated, this procedure is repeated for each substratum.

A building datum is chosen which is, for example, 300mm below the planned finished floor level of the lowest floor. It is then an easy matter to compare required site levels (held in the building description "height" matrix) with actual ground and substrata levels at equivalent points on the grids and to calculate the volume of excavation or fill required. Allowance is made for banking slopes at specified angles and for levelling areas outside the building. Required volumes of excavation and fill are rapidly recalculated for different building datum levels.

Structure description

Basic structural patterns

A well-defined modular building system is particularly suited to the use of standardized structural components. The Harness system uses a beam and column structure which, for departments, generally relates to modules 16.2m square. At present there are only three basic modules which are illustrated in plan view in *Figure 5*.

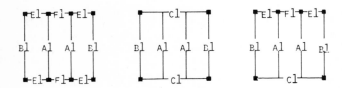

Figure 5

These modules, in different rotations, are used to make up four main patterns which describe the structure of most departments. A diagrammatic representation of these patterns is shown in *Figure 6*. Other patterns are available to cater for any non-standard departments.

Within the corridor area, the structure is more flexible and modules vary considerably in size.

However, a finite number of module shapes can be identified, each of which corresponds to a unit of the circulation zone.

Computer representation of beams and columns

Each beam is assigned a code which indicates its length, floor slab loading, internal or external position and vertical relationship with other floors. These are called beam "contexts" as they relate to a performance specification rather than an actual component. Similarly each column, or column "context", is assigned a code depending on the beams it supports and on whether it is at roof level. The entire computer representation and evaluation of structure is handled in terms of these "contexts". Only at the final stage, when the structure is being costed, are actual components selected and several "contexts" may be related to each component. This concept of "contexts" increases the flexibility of the structural system as the decision on which components to use may readily be changed without re-evaluatating the structure. The existing "contexts" may also be expanded or adapted to take account of different dimensional requirements.

When the basic structural patterns are input to the computer an ordered series of codes, identifying particular "contexts", is used. This applies to the beam configurations for the three basic department modules and to the beam and column configurations for all corridor area modules. As the structural data tends to be standard for several evaluations, it is held as a permanent computer file and not input for each building.

Relating the structure description to the building description

Each plan matrix of the building description is scanned for department codes. When a department is located its structural pattern code is extracted from a data file. The department shape is compared with the standard structural pattern and the appropriate beam "contexts" selected and inserted in a beam matrix, whose dimensions correspond to those of the plan matrix. As a maximum of four beam positions may surround one 5.4m square, each "word" of the beam matrix can hold up to four beam codes plus a phase number. In this way the structure for each department is rapidly and efficiently selected. Codes are changed to take account of external position and vertical relationships and to ensure that the structure is compatible from floor to floor. By reference to the beam matrix for each floor a corresponding set of matrices for department column "contexts" is assembled.

In the circulation zone, however, the structure has to be considered one unit at a time with reference to the corridor matrices in the building description. The structure code identifies the beam and column configurations to be used, modified where necessary by the length code. From these configurations beam and column "contexts" are selected and inserted in the appropriate matrix. By comparison with department structure the process is necessarily slower.

Deviations from the standard grid

Several of the possible corridor area modules are either narrower than 5.4m., or greater than 5.4m but less than 10.8m. They are represented as complete cells in a plan matrix but the structure programs use

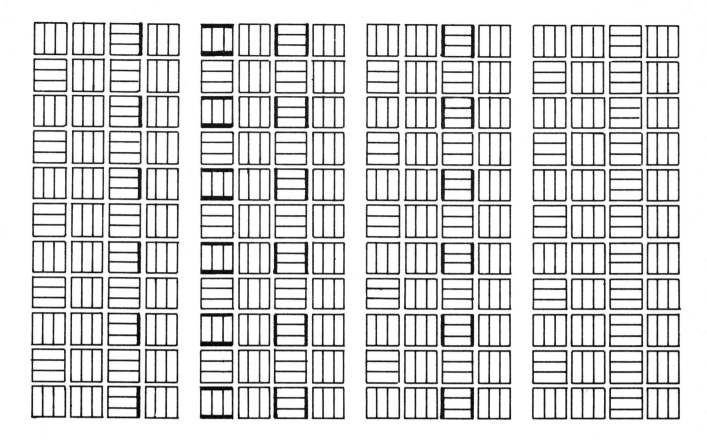

Figure 6

information in the corridor matrices to evaluate the narrow modules correctly.

Special beam codes are assigned to short beams and the appropriate beam and column configurations indicate displacement from the standard grid. Narrow modules are also held as complete cells in the beam and column matrices, but a displacement indicator enables correct alignment of modules in plan representations of the building structure, which are produced using these matrices. Part of a typical beam plan showing department modules, standard and narrow width corridor is shown in *Figure 7*.

Relating the structure and site descriptions

Foundation types may be selected with reference to structure and site data. At each grid point in the column matrix the area supported by a column is derived from the "context" code and the number of floors supported is totalled. From these figures a loading factor is calculated which is used in conjunction with the soil type at the equivalent grid point in the site description to determine a satisfactory foundation type.

Advantages of an integrated design aid system

One basic building description

Previous paragraphs have illustrated in detail how information is extracted from the same building description for use in different ways by the site and structural evaluations. Programs have already been developed to calculate heating loads and running costs, to measure site ratios, to place lift banks in optimum positions for minimal circulation and to draw perspective pictures of the completed building.

The heating programs rely heavily on the plan matrices from which the nature of adjacent cells and the position of the external walls of the building are readily determined. From the height matrix the perimeter of the building is established as the first stage in the site ratios program. The height matrix also supplies all the building information required by the perspective program. As the lifts program is concerned with the circulation zone it gains more information from the corridor matrices. Each of these programs requires a few lines of additional data, specific to the problem in hand. Their main data source is, however, the building description which is held in the computer as plan, height and corridor matrices. In other words, the basic building and site data is input once and converted to a standard, generalised format, which is used by a variety of programs with the minimum of extra information. Preparation and input of data is tedious and time-consuming but programs produce accurate results in a small fraction of the input time.

Extensions to an existing system

Once the basic data structure has been determined more evaluations can be added by increasing the number of programs without the overhead of large amounts of data input. A grid representation is particularly suitable for daylighting and solar gain programs which require information on the relative positions of built modules.

In addition to increasing the number of design aids a direct link to the production side could be established. The cost schedule of components, part of the present system, could be developed to meet production information needs.

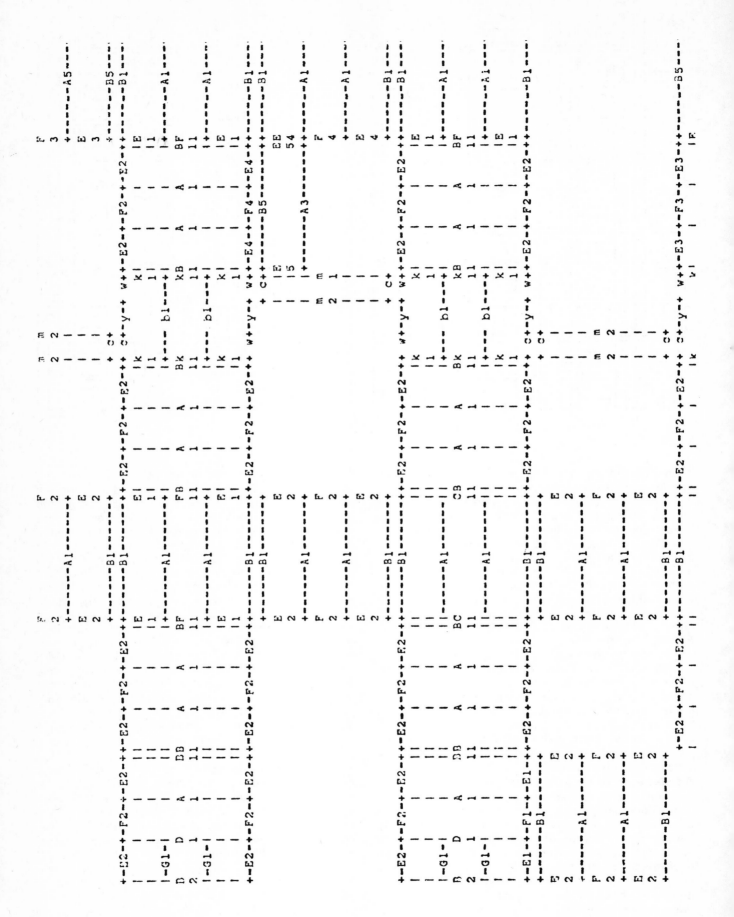

Figure 7

Conclusions

Most of the evaluative results that have been discussed could be calculated without the aid of a computer. For small schools, office blocks and similar buildings the required information could well be obtained by other means. Large buildings, on the other hand, necessitate long and tedious calculations, which can be effected more efficiently with computer aids.

The method of representation described requires a modular construction which can be represented on a regular grid of large dimensions. A one metre square grid, for instance, would tend to make the computation slow and cumbersome.

For a large modular building this system provides an efficient means of setting up one building description. This is used by different programs to supply several measures which can aid the decision making of the design team. Moreover the same results can be provided for a different design based on the same functional content with little additional manual input. In this way a design team may assess the comparative merits of several schemes well in advance of, and without the irrevocable cost of, the actual building. □

Building descriptions for data processing

Peter Hayward

Integrated Building Descriptions

For some time now a wide range of computer programs has existed to assist the designer in his task. These programs do things like rapid hidden line perspectives from any point, daylight, insolation and thermal analysis and the production of bills of quantity. These programs have tended to require time-consuming, and hence expensive, data preparation, and their use has been restricted to special situations where this cost can be justified.

Out of this situation has grown the notion that if computers are to have a wider role in producing either cheaper buildings, or better buildings for the same cost, then an integrated computer system is needed (Hoskins). This would consist of one building description for use by all design disciplines and all application programs. Once established such a description allows the use of any evaluation or design program without the need for specialised data preparation. Further, as a result of their calculations, these programs can directly modify the building image, avoiding further data preparation and input on the part of the user.

In computer terms a complete building description is usually contained in two separate files, one giving data about 'components' e.g. doors, cladding assemblies, etc., the other giving information about the spatial relationships of these components. Since a particular component may occur many times in one building, this separation of data saves a lot of space and appears a sensible thing to do. By analogy with the mathematical term 'highest common factor', this separation of repeated data items can be called factoring.

Data Factoring

This simple approach has two important implications that I would like to emphasise, but before I do this I must say a quick word about computers. Building descriptions tend to be very large and are stored on magnetic discs. The data is divided up into 'blocks' which form the natural unit of transfer into the computer's working, or core, store. The capacity of this core store is very small compared with the complete building description, and since reading and writing blocks are relatively slow processes, it is essential to minimise the number of transfers. The corollary of this is that as much related data as possible should be kept in one block.

To return to the implications of data factoring, it may be noted that the initial effect is to require two data transfers where only one would have been needed if the data had not been separated, i.e. if full details on the component had been stored in the same block as the location information. Thus, for random access of a single component in the building, factoring increases the number of transfers. However, if, as usually occurs, more than one component is wanted, as for example in drawing the partition layout of a room, the total number of transfers will be substantially reduced because the density of building components per block will be higher, fewer transfers being needed to access all the parts of the room. This assumes, as usually would be the case, that some attempt has been made to keep in one block components that are spatially close in the real building.

The other major advantage of factoring at this level is that changing the component data is very easy. Thus, if the price of a partition unit is increased, only one item of data in one block needs to be changed. However, if the component data were repeated many times throughout the geometrical description, changing the price of a partition unit would be a large and time-consuming job, because it would be necessary to search all through the building for occurrences of that component, and then change the price.

If I have, perhaps, laboured an obvious point, I apologise, but I wish to come back to factoring later in this paper.

Organisation of Building Component Data Bases

There are two extremes of file organisation that form the bounds of any particular implementation. The most straightforward, and probably the most common is the simple list file. In this type of file the data on one component is all stored in one place. Thus, if one knows the component's code or number, it is possible to find any of the details stored about it, e.g. its weight, size or price. However, with this type of file it is difficult to answer questions like 'Which cladding components are 2.4m high?', as it is necessary to search through all the blocks containing data on cladding panels in order to find suitable components.

At the other extreme of file organisation, all the data on size are grouped together and all the data on price are grouped somewhere else. This is called an inverted file, and it is easy to ask questions about specific properties because the considerably increased density of relevant data means that fewer disc transfers are needed to scan all the relevant data. However, with this type of file it is tedious to collect together different items of data on one component, as, for example, when doing a where-found catalogue or room-data printout.

Thus, as a first step in data base design, a decision is needed on whether data retrieval will be by component code number or by component attribute. The answer is usually both, but with access by code predominating so that list structures are the type most commonly used.

Indexing

An example of a list file is a telephone directory, and I would like to consider how we, as individuals, might access it to look up the phone number or address of a MR. GILBERT. Relying on the knowledge that the directory is in alphabetical order, we might open it a bit before the middle and then flip through the pages in the appropriate direction looking for GILBERT, perhaps reading 50 pages in the process. As I have explained, reading a page, or rather a block, of data into the computer takes a relatively long time so that reading 50 pages to recover one item would be unacceptable.

However, this problem can be overcome by indexing. Suppose the first page of the directory contains 26 lines, each one giving the page on which the names beginning with letter A, B etc. begin. By looking at page one it would be possible to go straight to the page containing the G's. If, instead of being a list of names, this page contained another 26 lines giving the pages where the GA, GB etc. started, it would be possible to go straight to the page for GI. If all the GI's fitted on one page, further indexing would not be worth while and one would search the GI's for GILBERT. Thus GILBERT would be found from reading only 3 pages.

If all the GI's did not fit on one page, one could introduce another level of indexing, but this would probably waste a page. A better solution would be a message at the bottom of the GI page saying something like 'turn to page n for more GIs'. This is called chaining information.

It should be noted that with indexing there is no longer any need for the directory to be in alphabetical order, except within the level of GI's. If more GI subscribers need to be put in the directory and a new page is needed, this page can be added on to the end of the directory without renumbering or altering any of the existing pages.

Similarly, in a computer, if the word 'block' is substituted for 'page' in the above example, it can be seen that indexing can be used to minimise the number of read transfers required to access any particular piece of information. The indexing system is usually tied to the component classification system used, and can be as detailed as one index entry per component. The component data is thus accessed in the minimum number of transfers and it is only at this level that data is actually stored, i.e. the address and telephone number is stored at the bottom of the index tree.

Self Describing Files

It was stated in an earlier section that integrated systems should provide all the data required for any required analysis. To sit down and decide, in advance of designing a data base, all the data items required would be a formidable and probably hopeless task. A much more satisfactory solution is to design a system sufficiently flexible to accommodate these inevitable changes in data requirements without alteration to the system.

In a conventional fixed format file, the structure of a component record is used to convey implied information and might look like *Fig. 1,* where it would be known that dimensions were the first item, that weight followed dimensions and price followed weight, and so on for all properties. This type of record structure lends itself to a COBOL implementation and is very heavily used in commercial data processing. However, it is not very good if different items of data about different components need to be stored. For example, the service requirements of a sink unit would be of interest but the service requirements of a chair would usually not be needed.

The solution is to make the record structure independent of the data stored, and this can be done by storing the implicit data of fixed format record explicitly. Thus *Fig 2* shows how each data item could be preceded by an identifier declaring its contents. The identifier can also contain a sub-record word count to allow for all fields being of variable length. Thus, the data stored on any one component can be tailored exactly to current requirements and new properties added at any time without altering the file structure.

Second Level Self Description

Using this sort of system, a second level of self description can be incorporated. If the data file also stores the external format of each of these properties *(Fig. 3),* for example, that dimensions are 3 real numbers, text is an arbitrary string of characters, a manufacturer's code is a letter followed by an integer and then another letter, it is possible to write programs that read data into the file that can be completely general and do not have to be changed when new properties are defined. For example, if data on dimensions is to be input and is preceded by the identifier DIMS, the program will know it should expect 3 real numbers and can fault illegal characters. Similarly the manufacturer's code mentioned above would only be acceptable if it were letter-integer-letter.

Typical fixed format record structure

CODE	Dimension data	Weight data	Price data	Text string	Service requirements

Figure 1

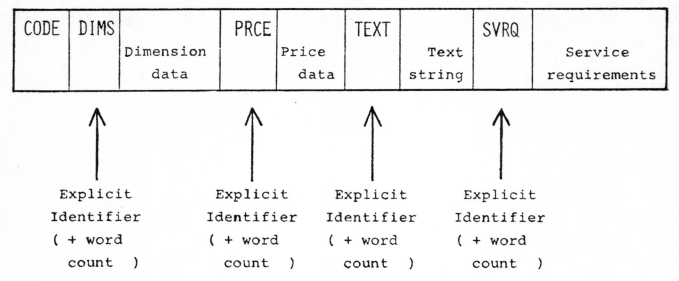

Figure 2

PROPERTY	IDENTIFIER	FORMAT
Beam code	BMCD	ILR
Dimensions	DIMS	3R
Manufacturer's code	MUCD	LIL
Price	PRCE	R

Figure 3

FACTORING AT THE LEVEL OF COMPONENT DATA

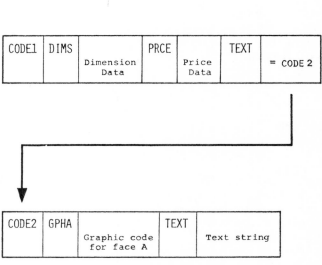

Figure 4

It is possible that such a system could be extended to handle further data verification based on values rather than types, e.g. a transmission factor is a real number less than one but greater than zero. Similar flexibility is possible in programs to printout the data base, since the format of any property is known and can be printed in a suitable manner. These programs need only be written *once* but can be used to read in, and print any as yet unknown and undefined item of data.

Data Factoring

Data factoring is another technique which is very useful at the component data level. For example, the text, thermal properties and graphic description of a whole range of cladding panels might be constant and could be usefully factored out. This may be done simply, as indicated in *Fig. 4,* where the character string of the identifier TEXT has been replaced by the code for another component, with the meaning that "the text for component code 1 is the same as the text for component 2 and is to be found with all the other data for component code 2".

Factoring at this level has exactly the same advantages and disadvantages as factoring at the building level. A decision needs to be made in each case to determine whether there are nett advantages or disadvantages. Our experience of a data base designed on these lines for Oxford Method components suggests that component level factoring produces considerable economies.

Assemblies

Another aspect of factoring occurs in the use of assemblies, by which I mean components whose major property (apart, possibly, from a text description) is a list of other components. Thus, a wash basin assembly might include the basin, taps, soap dispenser, a paper towel dispenser and waste bin.

There is nothing to stop the nesting of such assemblies to provide a building description without detailed locational information, which is nevertheless very useful for room data handling and scheduling. Thus, the first components *(Fig 5)* could represent the building, owning one component for each floor. Each floor would own one component for department, and so on down through rooms and assemblies to individual components. Such a system, called IBES,

PART LINKING AS USED IN THE IBES DATA STRUCTURE

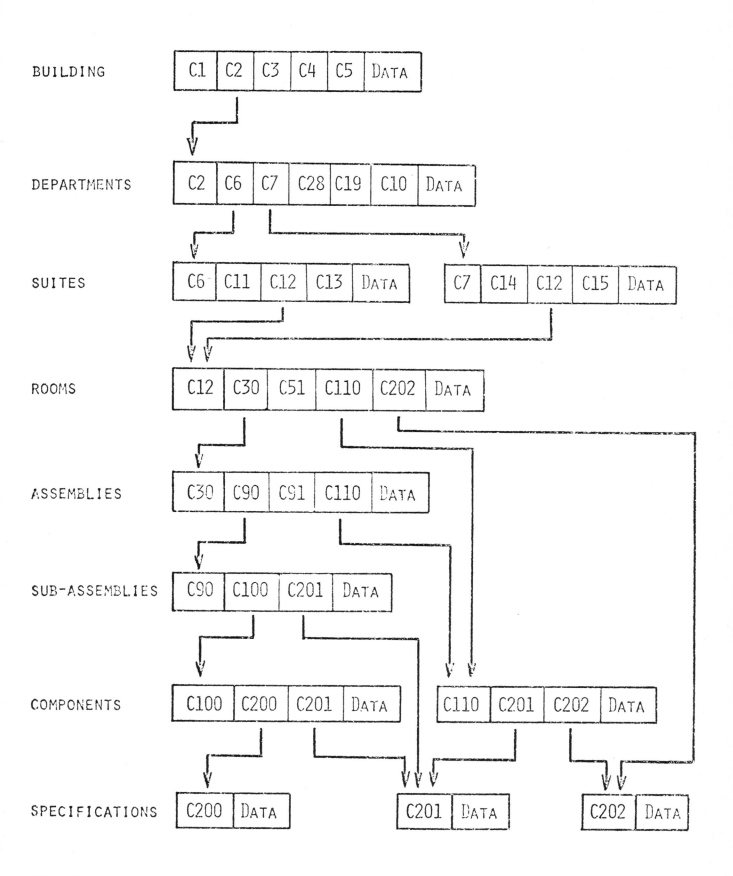

Figure 5

has been in use at the East Anglia Regional Hospital in Cambridge for 3 years.

Implementation

Time restrictions prevent any meaningful discussion of the other half of the problem—the spatial description of the building. This is not necessarily a bad thing because it is very much more difficult to generalise about the structure of this file, since it will reflect much of the individuality of the building system and also the eventual use that will be made of the computer system.

One thing that can be said is that the volumes of data involved are very large, say 5m characters for a hospital or 50m characters for a method building program. Such large file sizes and data volumes bring with them a whole range of problems of file integrity and security that can frequently be ignored when working with 'experimental' quantities of data. It is necessary to build upon and extend established techniques of data processing for use in computer-aided design of this type. It may be noted that the data structures discussed do not lend themselves to implementation in either of the commonest programming languages COBOL or FORTRAN. They evolved from a language-independent consideration of the problems of flexible data storage, and seem to be relevant to a large number of method building systems. □

Part 3

Environment

A new approach to predicting the thermal environment in buildings at the early stages of design *

Neil Milbank

Summary

This paper argues that existing thermal computer programs do not produce suitable information for architects, particularly at the early stages of design. Important building features which determine the thermal environment and the need for heating and cooling plant are reviewed and graphical design aids are proposed, with examples to show the summer conditions in naturally ventilated buildings. It is shown that it is not realistic to consider thermal conditions in isolation: the feasibility of achieving the desired natural ventilation rate and the use of artificial lighting are also important. Sample design aids are included for these aspects.

Introduction

One of the many requirements of good building is the provision of an acceptable thermal environment for the user. As living and working conditions have improved there has been a general rise in internal temperatures in winter and, more recently, a growth in the use of air-conditioning to restrict temperatures in summer. Whether their concern is with winter or summer temperatures, or with year-round energy consumption, designers must have methods of relating temperature and energy requirements to the building design, taking account of the needs and behaviour of the user and the prevailing climate.

This paper reviews the more recent developments in using computers to predict thermal conditions in buildings, and highlights the important parameters which decide the extent and quantity of services. As the theme develops it becomes clear that it is unrealistic to consider thermal design in isolation from other considerations, especially ventilation, lighting and structure. In addition it appears that the information needs of architects and engineers differ, not only at any one stage but also at different stages in the design process. For example, at the earliest stages the architect will be concerned with the general strategy of his design and therefore want to know in general terms what form the facade should take, and particularly its fenestration, whether for example natural ventilation will satisfy thermal comfort requirements, whether the building should be sealed, and whether internal or external shading devices are needed. Much later in the design process the engineer will want specific information on the capacity, energy consumption and costs of heating systems. Although both types of information are derived from the same

physical models it is probable that the presentation of material should be quite different for the two situations.

The present generation of thermal computer programs is best suited to evaluating or checking the performance of a given building design. This is ideal for the engineer to specify boiler capacity, for example, but does it suit the architect if he wants to assess the need for air-conditioning or the benefits of double glazing, before the design is well formulated. For his purposes alternative design material, which can be developed from the engineer's computer output, may be required. The paper contains examples of such architectural data concerned with the prediction of temperatures in summer, since one of the pressing needs is for guidance on the decision whether to air-condition or not. Finally, comment is made on the limitations of our present state of understanding of the way people use their buildings and the way this may limit the interpretation of the calculations.

Theoretical Considerations

Designers are familiar with the steady heat loss equation

$$\bar{q} = (\Sigma AU + C_v)(\bar{t_i} - \bar{t_o})$$

where	$\bar{q}$	=	heat requirement	W
	ΣAU	=	conduction loss through the fabric	W/°
	C_v	=	ventilation loss	W/°
	$\bar{t_i} - \bar{t_o}$	=	temperature difference between inside and outside environment	

This equation is valid in the situation where temperatures do not change significantly with time: it is ideally suited therefore for winter design conditions when we get long periods with low external temperature and little or no solar gain. The technique has its limitations when we want to explore the intermittent operation of plant, i.e. we permit the inside temperature to vary. To cope with this problem a number of empirical correction factors exist to allow for the larger boiler capacity needed in that event. This whole approach exhibits the usual compromise between the desire for speed and accuracy of calculation which must be set against the risk and cost of design errors. Usually the consequences of under-estimating boiler capacity are more serious than over-estimating.

It is the change in emphasis from winter to summer design, whether in the prediction of air-conditioning

*Copyright: Building Research Establishment, Department of the Environment.

loads or of internal temperatures, which has led to developments in the calculation procedures, since in summer the temperature and energy inputs are not constant and therefore the energy storage effects of the structure are more significant. The mechanisms of energy transfer, radiation, conduction and convection are sufficiently well understood to permit thermal models of the building behaviour to be developed, but it is only the introduction of computers which has made it feasible to do accurate calculations in a reasonable time and at acceptable costs.

Two types of model have been developed, each of which has proponents in different parts of the world. In their more sophisticated forms the two solutions give similar results to given design problems. One, which we call the 'finite difference' technique, treats storage effects by dividing the building structure into a number of layers and calculating the temperature/energy distributions at selected time intervals. The response factor' technique developed by Stephenson and Mitalas in Canada and adopted by the American Society of Heating Refrigeration and Air-Conditioning Engineers (ASHRAE)[1] is but one version of this approach. For use in design it is common to feed this type of program with the same sequence of weather data for several days until the model reaches a stable condition. In other words the hourly temperature and energy requirements are the same from day to day.

The second type of model may be called the 'harmonic' solution. This approach gives the temperature/energy pattern for a building assuming it has reached the stable, or equilibrium, state for some given cycle of weather and usage. The Admittance procedure, developed by Danter at BRS[2,3,4], and adopted by the IHVE[5] is typical of this type of solution. The Admittance procedure has the advantage that it can be used for simple manual calculations and it is used here to show the relative importance of the different factors which affect the thermal environment.

If we consider an energy input cycle q to a naturally ventilated building it will lead to an internal temperature cycle t, as shown in *figure 1*. We are concerned with the relationship between t and q. It can be considered in two parts, firstly the rise in the daily mean value of inside temperature above outside daily mean temperature and secondly the swing of internal temperature about its mean value. Dealing firstly with the rise in mean temperature, this is covered by the steady state heat loss equation,

i.e. over a period 24 hours, heat gains must equal heat losses, or:-

$$\bar{q} = (\Sigma AU + C_v)\ (\bar{t_i} - \bar{t_o})$$

where the terminology is unaltered from the previous equation.

From this one deduces that unless a building has an artificial cooling system, the mean inside temperature will be above the mean outside temperature. The precise rise in mean temperature depends on the magnitude of the gains in relation to the conduction losses and ventilation losses. Low U-values lead to higher temperatures whilst copious ventilation leads to lower temperatures for the same energy input.

Swings of temperature about the mean are related to swings in energy about its mean:

$$\tilde{q} = (\Sigma AY + C_v)\tilde{t}$$

where: $\tilde{q}$ = instantaneous variation of energy input from its mean value.

$\tilde{t}$ = instantaneous variation of temperature from its mean value

The term ΣAY is a measure of the energy going to storage. Y is called the admittance of the surface, its value lying in the range 0 to $6W/^{\circ}m^2$. High admittance values, characteristic of thick masonry materials, lead to small temperature swings for a given energy input. Low values, typified by suspended ceilings, carpeting, etc, lead to higher temperature swings. Values of admittance for a range of constructions are tabulated in the IHVE Guide.

The point of including these relationships is to give some feel for the problem and not to hope that you sit down and calculate. The calculation of hourly values of q, for instance, which covers the energy gains from sunshine and from occupants and lighting, is quite tedious and is a fit and proper task for computers to perform.

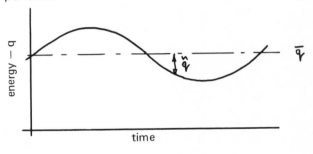

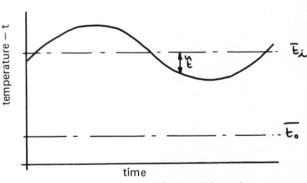

Figure 1   Under steady cyclic conditions the temperature and energy cycles repeat each day

Practical Aspects

As already mentioned, whichever theoretical model is adopted the calculation procedure, whether manual or computerised, is geared to stating the performance of a particular room or a particular building in particular circumstances. This suits the engineer if he wants to know the capacity of the boiler or the refrigerators—but what about the building designer? At the early stage of design he may well have insufficient information, in terms of firm design decisions, to do such sums and he would be daunted by the possibility of separate calculations for all the alternative design situations. In practice of course he

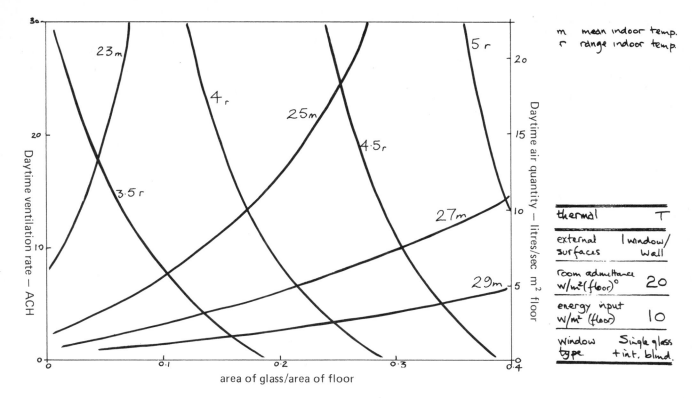

thermal	T
external surfaces	1 window/wall
room admittance w/m²(floor)°	20
energy input w/m² (floor)	10
Window type	Single glass + int. blind.

m mean indoor temp.
r range indoor temp.

Figure 2   Thermal design aid showing summer conditions in a two person office fitted with internal blinds

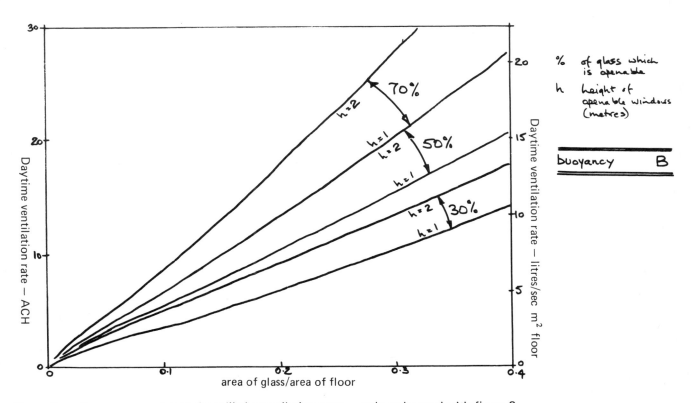

% of glass which is openable
h height of openable windows (metres)

buoyancy	B

Figure 3   Buoyancy overlay to show likely ventilation rates --- only to be used with figure 2

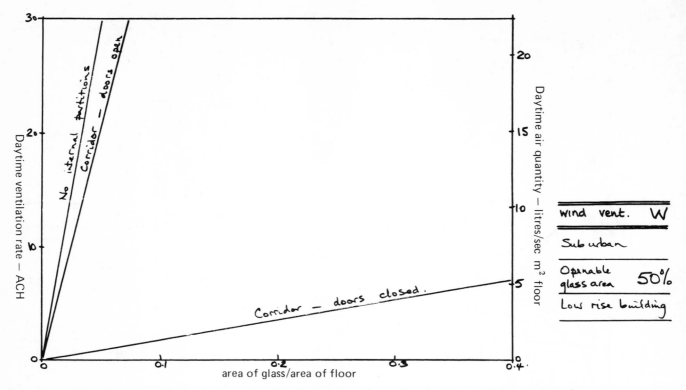

Figure 4   Wind forced ventilation is determined by the amount of opening glass area and the number of internal obstructions to air flow (based on wind speed coincident with air temperature and solar data used to calculate figure 2)

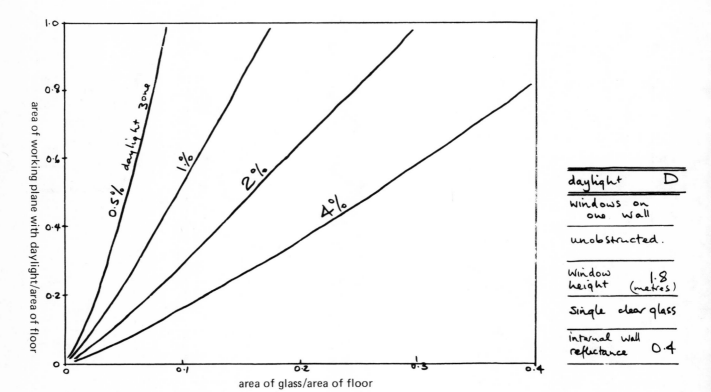

Figure 5   Daylighting can be expressed in terms of the proportion of floor area having the stated minimum intensity

relies on past experience to guide him towards acceptable solutions. But previous experience may not always help. A particular case in point is the design of buildings which do not get too hot in summer, yet do not require air conditioning. When buildings are required to satisfy these criteria most designers have little relevant experience, and they are in a quandary since there is often insufficient time to analyse many specific designs on a computer. In this situation there is scope for a design aid which shows desirable solutions, or trends, in general terms. One set of such aids is currently being developed at The Building Research Establishment in collaboration with the Department of the Environment and the Department of Education and Science.

The foregoing equations on thermal response support intuition and experience in establishing that in summer the important things controlling temperature in buildings are:

thermal insulation of the building
energy gain from the sun
heat gain from occupants and lights
the admittance of the structure
ventilation rate

With the exception of heat gain from the occupants—determined by the purpose of the building—the remaining items can be influenced by the designer. In buildings where the ratio of the areas of external surface to floor is low (as in most schools, offices, hospitals and flats) thermal insulation and solar gains will mainly be decided by the type and size of the windows and shading devices. By allocating values to energy input from occupants and lighting, and values for the thermal response, it is possible to establish relationships between inside temperature, ventilation and area of glazing for a given combination of glass and shading. Typical results are in *figure 2* which shows how the mean temperature and its range during occupied hours in summer vary in an office fitted with internal venetian blinds. These two measures of thermal performance are needed to evaluate thermal comfort[6].

These thermal aids only indicate desirable ventilation rates. It is necessary to check on the likelihood that they are achieved, by natural means, either by buoyancy or by wind forces. For this purpose, overlays *(figs 3 and 4)* are also available to indicate expected ventilation rates for the wind and temperature conditions experienced on hot sunny days. The ventilation diagrams introduce further variables such as the proportion of window that can be opened and, for buoyancy, the height of the window opening. Similarly, daylight predictors *(fig 5)* can be usd to establish in broad terms the relative distribution of daylight to give an insight into whether the lights will be used: if so, their energy consumption contributes to the internal gain.

These design aids have several advantages. One is that they reverse the computer output, since instead of defining the building and predicting its thermal performance we can define the thermal performance and see which, if any, building designs are likely to be satisfactory. The designer can then see where his options lie, and, sometimes of more importance, what is the benefit of relaxing a performance requirement.

Another advantage is the speed of assessment.

There is no need to go to a computer bureau or terminal or even to define the building in very precise terms.

A disadvantage is one shared with all such assessments, that of the assumptions made in the calculation—a point considered later. Another is the potential resistance to use by designers due to lack of familiarity with the terms admittance and energy input. This, I hope, is overcome by a short introductory guide to typical values. For example, in practice, the range of admittances will go from 8 W/$^\circ$m^2 floor for deep open-planned spaces with carpeted floors and suspended ceilings, to about 24 W/$^\circ$m^2 floor for smaller spaces with exposed masonry construction. Similarly energy inputs will range from about 10W/m^2 floor in general office areas where the lights are not in use in summer, to at least 100 W/m^2 floor in a heavily populated and well lit (1000 lux) department store.

We expect to issue a collection of these aids for trial, and, if satisfactory, it will be generally available from 1975.

Discussion

Whether design information is gathered from computer calculations or graphical aids, the user must always be aware of the assumptions behind the

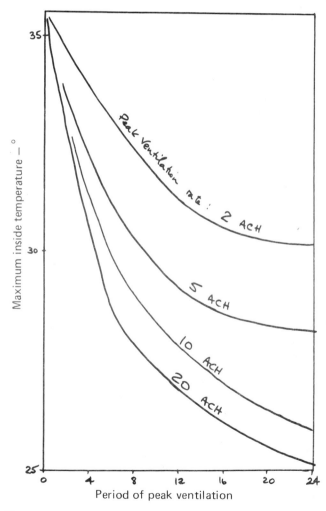

Figure 6   Calculated indoor temperatures are sensitive both to the rate of fresh air supply and the period of ventilation (background ventilation rate : 0.5 ACH) (room with 80% glass with internal blind)

calculations. Particularly where computers are used, there is a danger that the user is so bedazzled by temperature predictions to, say, one-hundredth of one degree Celsius that he loses sight of the likely accuracy of the calculation in any case. At the present time the theories of thermal response have been developed to such a stage that the validity of the prediction is more dependent on the assumptions than on the accuracy of the theory. For example, the admittance procedure will calculate temperatures to be within about one degree of the actual temperature when all the assumptions are satisfied[4]. However, changes in assumptions about the quantity and time period of the use of lights and the opening of windows for ventilation show how sensitive the calculation is to such variables. *Figure 6* shows the theoretical effect of varying the period and quantity of fresh air in a naturally ventilated office—an attempt to simulate different ways of using windows. It shows that with 80% glazing the peak summer temperature can be limited to 28° by a number of combinations of fresh air supply and ventilation period—4 air changes per hour (ACH) for continuous ventilation over 24 hours, 9 ACH for 12 hours, 30 ACH for 6 hours and about 50 ACH for 4 hours ventilation. There are clear advantages in prolonging the ventilation period. Similar studies can be developed to examine the use of sun blinds. Such considerations serve to emphasise the need for more information and research into the

way people use their buildings and facilities, rather than for further work into thermal response.

The idea of 'design-risk' in the terms of the period for which the building fails to meet some temperature requirement is also of interest. In certain circumstances, usually where the cost of halting a process (such as the manufacture of chocolates) can be assessed, cost-benefit studies show what risk can be justified. On this basis, for example, boilers might be sized to cope with external design temperatures of −1°, −5° or even lower, and air conditioning may be designed to cope with the highest temperatures ever experienced in a particular locality. For most buildings, however, it is not so easy to estimate the cost of occupants being either too cold or too warm and judgements may be made on other criteria.

The 1970 IHVE Guide contains information on the frequency and duration of cold spells, but rather less material on summer conditions. However, current investigations of meteorological data are yielding coincident hourly values of external dry bulb temperature, solar intensities and wind speeds and these will be particularly helpful in assessing the extent of overheating associated with any particular design risk. For example *fig 7* shows the probable daily mean solar intensities for the month of July. It is based on analysis of weather at Kew for the ten-year period 1959 to 1968. Averages are also given for two, three and four-day periods. The illustration shows that for the

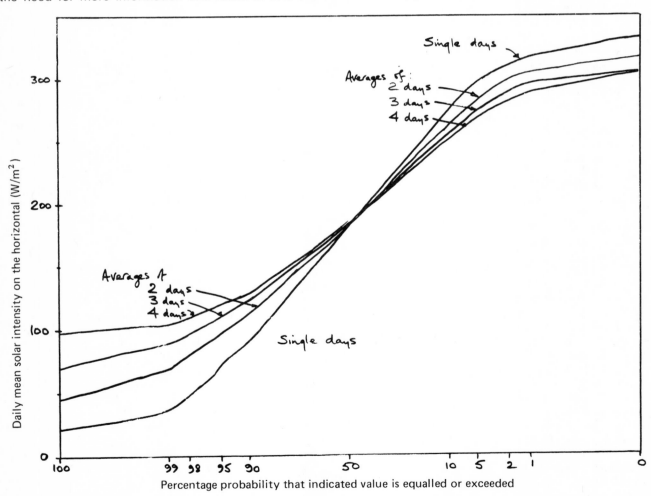

Figure 7   The choice of design weather data depends on the acceptable risk of failure

two-day average, which one would use for lightweight constructions, the average intensity will exceed 280 W/m² on 5% of occasions (or roughly one working day per month) whilst the highest recorded daily value was 325 W/m², some 15% higher.

Conclusions

This paper makes a number of propositions about the thermal design of buildings. Firstly it suggests that architects and engineers require rather different information about thermal performance at different stages of design work. These different needs reflect the different degrees of 'hardness' of information needed as the design progresses. At the earliest stage information should be qualitative and show broadly the extent of service needed for a particular building design—and in particular whether natural or mechanical ventilation, and even cooling, is necessary. Existing computer programs do not deal directly with this problem. Graphical design aids like those described here do so and have a useful role until such time that computers give the information directly. At the later design stages when firm decisions are made on plant capacity, computers will be used to a greater extent in future.

Secondly the prediction of thermal response has reached the stage where improvements in the theory have less importance than the bounding assumptions on the way people use their buildings—the window for ventilation, the blinds for protection from the sun, the artificial lighting. These user aspects are areas where further information and research would give most immediate benefit in design.

Thirdly there is the risk of failure associated with the choice of weather parameters for the design day. Current work on this subject will permit more serious study of this question, which must also be related to thermal comfort considerations.

The final point is that without computers it would not be practicable to assess the thermal performances of buildings in any great detail. The benefit is that it is now feasible to rationalise the decision on whether and when to air-condition for summer comfort. The technique described can be extended to cover winter conditions, energy consumption and costs-in-use. If pursued, then heating and cooling plant can be better matched to building energy requirements and it will be possible to think more systematically about control systems which better meet the users needs. Computer aided design is here to stay.

References

1. 1972 *'Handboook of Fundamentals'* American Society of Heating Refrigeration and Air-Conditioning Engineers, New York.
2. Danter, E (1973) 'Heat exchanges in a room and the definition of room temperature', *Symposium on Environmental Temperature*, 1973 (London, Institution of Heating and Ventilating Engineers).
3. Loudon A. G. (1968) 'Summertime temperatures in buildings without air-conditioning' *Symposium on Thermal Environment in Modern Buildings*, 1968 (London, Institution of Heating and Ventilating Engineers).
4. Milbank N. O. and Harrington-Lynn J. 1973 'Thermal response and admittance procedure' *Symposium on Environmental Temperature* 1973 (London, Institution of Heating and Ventilating Engineers).
5. *1970 The Guide*, Book A, The Institution of Heating and Ventilating Engineers, London.
6. Humphreys M. A. 'Comfortable temperatures for office workers in summertime'

Acknowledgements

This work is part of the research programme of the Building Research Establishment and is published by permission of the Director. The report covers the work of a team lead by the author. At the Building Research Establishment, Peter Petherbridge and Paul Mercer are developing the thermal and ventilation design aids, using computer programs developed here by John Harrington-Lynn and Richard Jones; Jim Godfrey leads the daylighting work. Obviously we draw information from other areas of the Station and are grateful for the co-operation received from our many colleagues. □

Traffic-noise prediction techniques for use in environmental planning

M. E. Delany

Introduction

Designers of roads need to predict noise levels arising from road traffic; they must evaluate the environmental impact of any proposed roadbuilding schemes to optimise both route and configuration. Planners and developers also need to predict the effect of road traffic if they are to make maximum use of land alongside major roads. Administrators require reliable data for strategic planning; for example they need to know the effect of speed limits on traffic noise, and the relative contribution to the overall noise level made by the various classes of vehicle, so that the potential effects of vehicle noise legislation can be predicted.

In this paper some of the techniques available for predicting traffic noise will be reviewed, with particular emphasis on environmental planning.

Empirical Techniques

Ultimately the validity of all prediction data should be established by systematically comparing predicted levels with measured noise levels. There are, however, certain data which must of necessity be derived from field measurements and these only are considered in this section.

The physical problem of predicting levels of traffic noise at a particular location can be divided into two components:

(a) predicting the noise level at a reference distance in terms of the traffic parameters (the intrinsic noise level)

(b) predicting the sound field in terms of the road configuration, the intervening ground cover and the complex urban fabric (propagation).

Now clearly prediction of the intrinsic noise level must be largely based on analysis of field data and, in view of the obvious importance of the result, surprisingly few studies have been reported.

Freely-flowing traffic

Freely-flowing traffic on substantially straight and level roads is the most important case for which predictions are required and has figured as part of the NPL research programme.[1] Field studies at various sites were carried out yielding nearly 100 samples of noise each of 15 minutes duration, measured at a height of 1.2 m above ground and at a specified distance from the centre of traffic flow on the nearside carriageway; simultaneously traffic flow rate, vehicle speeds and traffic composition on both carriageways were recorded. Statistical analysis of the noise

---

*Note L_{10} is the noise level in dB(A) exceeded for just 10% of the time, with corresponding definitions for L_{50} and L_{90}.

samples gave corresponding values of L_{10},* L_{50}, L_{90} and in each case the noise levels and the traffic parameters were subjected to multiple regression analysis. Best correlation was obtained by using as parameters the total rate of traffic flow Q (both carriageways combined), the mean traffic speed v (arithmetic mean of all vehicles on both carriageways), and the percentage of heavy vehicles p (the percentage exceeding 1500 kg). In this case the following linear regression equation for the unobstructed noise level in dB(A) at a distance of 10m from the centre of flow on the nearside carriageway was obtained:

$$L_{10} = 18.1 + 16.2 \log v + 8.9 \log Q + 0.117 p \qquad (1)$$

with similar equations for L_{50} and L_{90}. This expression should remain valid over the interpolating range of the variables

$$50 \leqslant v \leqslant 100 \text{ km/h}$$
$$800 \leqslant Q \leqslant 4500 \text{ veh/h}$$
$$5 \leqslant p \leqslant 50\% \text{ heavy vehicles}$$

and implies an increase of 2.7 dB(A) for a doubling of traffic flow, an increase of 4.9 dB(A) for a doubling of mean traffic speed, and an increase of 4.7 dB(A) for a change from 10% to 50% of heavy vehicles. These results were published early in 1972 and differed significantly from the design guide then in widespread use throughout the United Kingdom[2]; recently new or revised design guides have been issued [3,4] and in these respects are in reasonably close accord with the NPL data.

Comparing measured field data with corresponding predictions from Equation 1 shows excellent agreement *(Fig. 1)*. The root-mean-square error amounts to only 1.4 dB(A) and 85% of measured results fall within ± 2 dB(A) of the predictions .Such precision is as good as could be expected from an empirical relation depending on only three traffic parameters and is quite adequate for environmental planning purposes. However, it must be emphasized that for any given road configuration the input parameters are often highly interdependent; correlation coefficients between log Q, log v and p as high as 0.8 have been reported. Thus, on any given road, increasing the flow rate or the percentage of heavy vehicles will frequently cause a reduction in mean traffic speed so that the net increase in noise level may be very small.[1] When predicting noise levels for existing roads no problems due to this interdependence will be encountered provided that simultaneous observations are made to obtain appropriate values of p, Q, and v; when estimating noise levels for projected road schemes, however, care must be taken to ensure that the traffic parameters used in the regression equation for intrin-

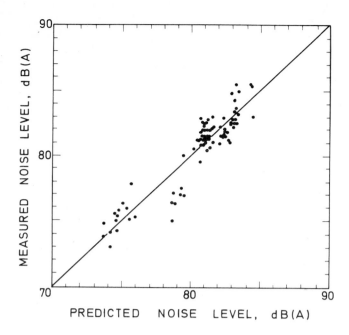

Figure 1

sic noise level are compatible with real-life traffic flow considerations.

Stop-start conditions

The above results apply only to continuous freely-flowing traffic. Minor modulation of traffic flow, it has been found, has negligible effect on the value of L_{10} provided that the observation point is not immediately adjacent to the traffic control or junction causing the flow modulation: on the other hand, L_{50} and, more especially, L_{90} may be greatly affected.

Stop-start conditions as found in some urban areas have been studied by Gilbert and Crompton[5]. Broadly their results indicate an increase of 2.8 dB(A) for a doubling of flow and that a typical heavy vehicle has a noise equivalent of approximately ten cars (values in good agreement with the results of previous section for freely-flowing traffic) and, as might be expected under these conditions, they found very little dependence on mean traffic speed. However, they report the degree of "platooning" of vehicles appears to affect the noise level to some extent although the precise mechanism has not been established.

Gradient

Estimates by different workers for the increase in intrinsic noise level with gradient have varied from 1-2 dB(A) for typical motorway gradients [2] up to 12dB(A) for a gradient of 1:8.[6] The latter value appears to be anomalously high, probably due to the procedure used to normalise data to a constant traffic speed of 64 km/h. From preliminary analysis of unpublished NPL field data, supported by data from 20 urban sites reported by Gilbert[7], a linear increase in intrinsic noise level of order 0.4 dB(A) per one degree of gradient would appear to hold up to nearly 10° (i.e. for gradients not steeper than 1:6). However, the increase in noise nuisance associated with gradients may not be entirely reflected by the rather small increase in A-weighted sound level indicated here. Spectrum analysis clearly shows that the character of the noise changes markedly as the gradient increases, with increased prominence of low-frequency components.

Effect of ground cover on sound propagation.

A final example of a configuration best tackled by a proper analysis of field data is the effect of ground cover on the propagation of noise away from a road. Due to interference effects between the direct wave travelling from source to receiver and the ground-reflected ray, a frequency-dependent attenuation is observed in excess of the normal level decrease due to spreading in free-space (the latter amounting to 6 dB per double distance for spherical spreading from a stationary point source and 3 dB per double distance for cylindrical spreading from a line source). The magnitude of this excess attenuation depends on the height of the source and receiver above the ground and on their separation, also on the complex acoustical impedance of the surface layers of the intervening ground.

Systematic data on traffic noise propagating over different types of ground cover taken at a fixed height of 1.2m above ground have been subjected to regression analysis[1]. In each case the data can be well approximated by a linear function of the logarithm of distance from the traffic stream, the attenuation being characterized by the slope of the regression line. Over a hard concrete surface the level decrease is close to the 3 dB per double distance associated with loss-free cylindrical spreading from a line source; for propagation over typical grassland the attenuation rate is increased to 4.5 dB/double distance whilst in the case of growing wheat the attenuation rate reaches 6.6 dB/double distance. Thus serious errors can be introduced when extrapolating results from one site to another unless differences in ground cover are taken into account.

Computer simulation

Computer simulation of noise from freely-flowing traffic has been developed by several workers in recent years using random "snapshot" techniques to estimate the time/level noise distribution[8]. In a recent development of this (unpublished NPL work) a whole traffic stream has been simulated producing sequential samples from a true time history.

In this computer model two classes of vehicle have been used, cars and heavy vehicles, each with its own characteristic octave-band noise spectrum, but up to nine categories can be accommodated when the requisite input noise data become available. The probability distribution for vehicle spacing can be varied; so far results have been obtained using both Poisson and negative exponential distribution functions. Any width of road can be simulated with up to six lanes of traffic, each with its own mean speed, mean flow rate and percentage of heavy vehicles. Randomly apportioned increments and decrements are made to account for the fact that some vehicles may be travelling faster or slower than the mean of their particular traffic stream or for the fact that individual vehicles may be intrinsically noisier or quieter than the mean of their class. When appropriate, ground absorption effects can be included and it is also possible to make allowances for shielding due to interposed barriers or for simple modulation of traffic flow.

At each instant of time the noise contributions from all the individual vehicles within range are summed. Then the traffic stream moves along for $\frac{1}{2}$-second and

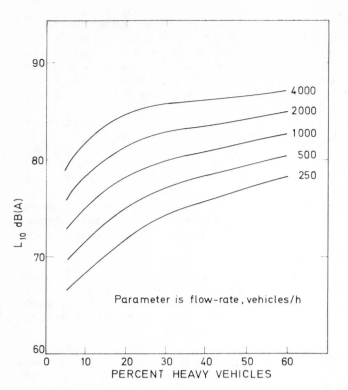

Figure 2

the level is recalculated. After 1000 such computations of overall noise level the cumulative distribution curve is constructed, leading to the appropriate values of L_{10}, L_{50} and L_{90}. Using typical results obtained from simulation studies it was found that results for L could well be approximated by a relation of the form

$$L_{10} = \alpha + \beta \log v + \gamma \log Q \qquad (2)$$

where v is again the mean speed and the Q the flow rate (the total rate on 2/3 lane roads but flow-rate on the nearside carriageway only when there are more than three lanes or a dual carriageway). Now, however, instead of a simple linear dependence on percentage of heavy vehicles derived from regression analysis of field data, the coefficients α, β, γ depend on p. This can be seen clearly in *Fig. 2* which shows

typical results for a speed of 64 km/h. For the range of variables most frequently encountered, this non-linear dependence on p is not very significant and generally there is good agreement between the results of computer simulation and field data, leading to added confidence in both results.

For normal planning purposes the computer model is rather too sophisticated—the detailed input data are generally not available at the design stage and can only be obtained for actual cases of special interest. However, the technique can prove invaluable in providing quantitative data for longer-term strategic planning. For example, the basic noise levels associated with the different classes of vehicle can be readily changed and recently predictions have been produced for the changes in L_{10} to be expected from imposing stricter vehicle noise criteria. Another result to emanate from the simulation studies is the way that the variation in L_{10} with flow rate is different for low than for high flow rates; over the range 1000-4000 vehicles/h the noise level increases by approximately 2.5 dB(A) per doubling of flow but at the very low flow rates commonly encountered during the night (50-200 vehicles/h) the increase for doubling of flow is nearer 6 dB(A).

However, the results of computer simulation can be no better than the basic data which are input and at the moment this is a weak link. Moreover, it has not yet been possible to take into account the varied driving conditions adopted by drivers of motor vehicles when on a real road. Undoubtedly the technique is capable of considerable development and future computer models should include the effects of acceleration associated with intersections, gradients, etc.

Theoretical calculation

In predicting propagation of noise away from the road, relatively simple and well-defined configurations are often encountered which are amenable to theoretical calculation. The shielding associated with a noise barrier erected parallel to a traffic stream is one example.

From fundamental theory supported by numerous scale studies[9] it has been established that the shielding of a point source due to an interposed semi-

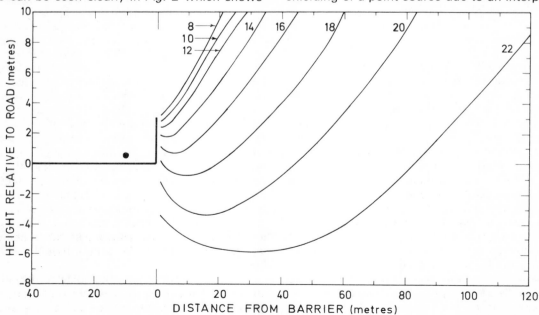

Figure 3

infinite barrier can be expressed in normalised form simply in terms of the path difference in wavelengths between the direct sound and the diffracted sound; this gives the shielding in excess of the 6 dB per double distance expected for simple spherical spreading from a point source and is frequency dependent. This has been extended to the traffic noise situation as follows [10]. Using a typical traffic noise spectrum and considering an array of spaced sources representing a traffic stream, a new normalized curve was obtained giving the shielding in dB(A) in excess of the cylindrical spreading rate of 3 dB/double distance. The new curve is simply in terms of the path difference, d, in metres and can be readily approximated by polynomial functions in log d, enabling noise fields behind a barrier to be readily predicted using desk calculator or computer. By way of example *Fig. 3* shows the noise field for a 3m high barrier at a distance of 10m from the traffic stream; the number against each contour gives the attenuation in dB(A) relative to the unobstructed noise level at a distance of 10m from the centre of flow on the nearside carriageway (which, in turn, is obtained from equation 1). As shown, the contours relate to an elevated road with parapet but by extension the same contours can be used for a road at grade with a noise barrier or even to estimate results for a road in partial cut. Using one set of contours for a number of different but related configurations necessarily involves a loss of accuracy, for ground absorption is neglected, but this is not too important once a barrier is present to obstruct the wave which would otherwise have grazed the ground. It certainly provides a broad visual impression of the resulting noise field and some 50 sets of such contours have been published covering a range of conditions commonly met with in practice [10].

Another example is predicting the effect of a gap in an otherwise continuous noise barrier, as might be required for vehicular or pedestrian access. Here there are two components of noise to be considered—the energy diffracted over the barrier and the energy penetrating the gap. Now if the observation point is actually at the aperture, the whole traffic stream is visible and is effective in contributing to the overall noise level whereas some way back from the aperture only a very small segment of the traffic stream is visible and the noise energy is correspondingly much reduced; thus the noise level due to sound penetrating the gap falls off much more rapidly than over open ground. In fact, the noise contribution due to the gap can be readily calculated from simple line-source theory whilst the diffracted contribution can be estimated from the normalized shielding curve referred to above. Summing these two components on an energy basis gives the resulting noise level. The agreement between theory and experiment has been found to be good and it is a simple matter to produce graphs summarising results of noise level as a function of distance behind the barrier for a range of gap widths [11].

There is another application of simple geometry allied with line-source theory in what at first may appear to be a very different problem—propagation of noise from a major road along side-roads leading into it. Evidence from field and model studies indicates that multiple reflections between facades of houses flanking a side road do not signigicantly affect L_{10},

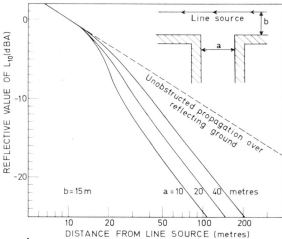

Figure 4

although they certainly do affect L_{90}. Again the principal parameters are the effective aperture at the main road and the distance of the aperture from the traffic stream; sets of design curves are readiliy prepared and an example is shown in *Fig. 4*.

Scale model techniques

The fourth and final technique available for predicting traffic noise involves the use of scale models. Basically, scaling consists of maintaining as constant the ratio of the size of the obstacles involved to the wavelength of sound, but an additional requirement is that the acoustical properties of all surfaces should also be scaled and it is this which can present difficulties in practice. Moreover, account has to be taken of the rapid increase in the rate of attenuation of sound in air as the scaling factor, and hence the sound frequency, increases.

The model developed at NPL for investigating the propagation of noise away from major roads has a scaling factor of 30:1 and involves working over the frequency range 2-80 kHz [12]. The source, representing a single motor vehicle, is a small air jet and the system is electronically equalized to produce an A-weighted vehicle noise spectrum. Road surface and other reflecting surfaces are simulated by sheet aluminium, grassland by specially selected fibreboard covered with coarse nylon cloth, and houses by plywood boxes covered with hardboard rough side exposed. The area covered by the model is approximately 5m square and the whole model is contained within a free-field room lined with polyurethane foam wedges. In use the source travels along a slot in the main road and every 10 cm, corresponding to every 3m full scale, a $\frac{1}{4}$-inch diameter condenser microphone at the observation point is used to digitally record the noise level. In this way the noise history of the drive-by of a single motor vehicle is obtained. It was found that merely summing the total energy of the drive-by produced a quantity which correlated reasonably well with the corresponding value of L_{10}, and this was used to derive provisional prediction data. Recent developments have included the use of an on-line computer system which has permitted the drive-by data obtained from the model to be combined with a simplified version of the computer simulation procedure to produce values of L_{10}.

To validate the technique detailed measurements were made in the field and on the scale model for 10

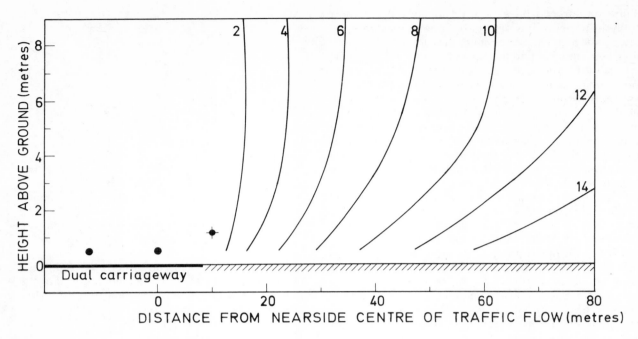

Figure 5

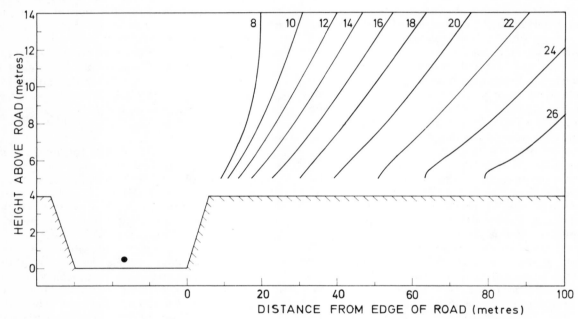

Figure 6

different site configurations; good correlation between these data was found. For instance, considering propagation up to 60m from the roadway over open grassland, the standard deviation of the error in predicting attenuation amounted to only 1.3 dB(A) so nearly 90% of the predicted values should fall within ±2 dB(A) of the measured field data. With simple barriers the standard deviation of the error amounted to approximately 1.7 dB(A) and even for the more complex urban sites reached only 2.5 dB(A).

Basically the model gives results for a single traffic stream, but, when required, it is relatively easy to combine results obtained with two separated traffic streams to produce data for actual road conditions although seldom is this degree of sophistication justified. By way of example, *Fig 5* shows contours of noise level relative to the unobstructed 10m value for propagation over typical open flat grassland.

However, the real value of the modelling technique is shown when situations such as a road in cut are under consideration, for systematic evaluation can be readily effected. *Figure 6* shows contours for a road in natural cut, not only conveying the general noise picture but also allowing adequate precision for interpolation. An interesting case is that of a road in retained vertical-sided cut, a configuration advocated for use in view of the reduced land requirements. Here it has been found that with highly-reflecting walls the resulting multiple reflections of sound considerably reduce the effective attenuation, adverse effects which can often be largely eliminated by sloping the walls at some 10-20° to the vertical.

Other studies which have been, or are being, made using the model facility include the build-up of noise in streets flanked by very tall buildings (canyon effect), propagation of noise along curved side-streets, and the penetration of noise through the gaps between buildings. The method has considerable potential and it appears that comparable facilities are being set up in France, Germany, Holland, Scandinavia and the USA. The most serious drawback of the technique is that meteorological effects are necessarily ignored but this should present little difficulty so far as environmental planning is concerned as neutral conditions would seem appropriate. In any case, refraction due to wind and temperature gradient is not usually a significant factor within the first 60m or so of a roadway where the greatest noise pollution occurs.

Conclusions

For simple and well-defined road configurations and for freely-flowing traffic the intrinsic noise level at, say, 10m from the road can be predicted in terms of the traffic parameters within reasonable precision—the standard deviation of the error between predicted and observed values of L_{10} being of order 1.5 dB(A). However, with more complex road configurations such as gradients, intersections, changing speed limits, this will increase to at least 2 dB(A). Moreover on top of this there is the additional error involved in predicting the propagation of noise away from the road; even for the simplest case of largely unobstructed flat grassland the standard deviation of the error is likely to be of order 1.5 dB(A) and with a complex urban environment will probably exceed 2.5 dB(A), the error tending to increase the further the observation point is from the road. Overall it is concluded that, at best, at least 30% of current noise level predictions will be in error by at least 2 dB(A) and the general situation is significantly worse. True, given sufficient information about any given site and the relevant details of traffic flow it would in principle be possible to achieve greater precision, but in practice the requisite input data are just not available. In fact, the precision achieved at present is probably adequate for most environmental planning purposes and the remaining task is merely to increase the range of configurations for which prediction data are available. The inherent limitations of current noise prediction guides must, however, be carefully considered when laying down criterion levels and establishing related legislation.

References

1. Delany, M. E. (1972), "Prediction of traffic noise levels", *National Physical Laboratory Report Ac 56.*
2. "Motorway noise and dwellings" (1971), *Building Research Station Digest* 135.
3. "Motorway noise and dwellings" (1973), *Building Research Establishment Digest* 153
4. Dickinson, J. (1972), *New housing and road traffic,* (London: H.M.S.O.)
5. Gilbert, D. and Crompton, D. H. (1971 & 1972), "Prediction of L_{10} noise levels", Unpublished reports, Civil Engineering Dept., Imperial College of Science & Technology, London.
6. Johnson, D. R. and Saunders E. G. (1968), "The evaluation of noise from freely-flowing traffic", *J. Sound Vib. 7, 287.*
7. Gilbert, D. (1971), "L_{10} noise levels and road gradients", Unpublished report, Civil Engineering Dept., Imperial College of Science & Technology, London.
8. Galloway, W. J., Clarke, W. E. and Kerrick, J.S. (1969), *Highway noise: measurement, simulation and mixed reaction,* (National Cooperative Highway Res. Prog. Report 78).
9. Maekawa, Z. (1968), "Noise reduction by screens", *Applied Acoustics,* 1, 157.
10. Delany, M. E. (1972), "A practical scheme for predicting noise levels (L_{10}) arising from road traffic", *National Physical Laboratory Report* Ac 57.
11. Delany, M. E., Copeland, W. C. and Payne, R. C. (1971), "Propagation of traffic noise in typical urban situations", *National Physical Laboratory Report* Ac 54.
12. Delany, M. E., Rennie, A. J. and Collins, K. M. (1972), "Scale model investigations of traffic noise propagation", *National Physical Laboratory Report* Ac 58. □

Models, mathematics and megalomania

Richard Stibbs

The purpose of this paper is to present some work on the solution of the problem of natural light illumination in a highly obstructed space by means of a computer model, and to use the example of this work to describe some of the dangers and benefits attendant on the use of computer models both within the academic and the professional environments.

The main contention is that the most valid and useful application of these models is within the academic sphere where they can be used as a tool in the study of methods of description of the built environment and in the study of the interrelation of environmental factors. Where the danger lies is in any attempt to use these computer models as direct design tools, a danger which arises mainly from the problem of the area of applicability, a concept which is discussed in more detail later.

Let us consider two examples of the benefit and dangers of models; one admittedly outside the direct field of environmental models. It is clear that a wider understanding and use of models to simulate heat flow through glazing would have been of immense benefit in curbing the enthusiasm for large areas of south-west facing glazing. The History faculty building in Cambridge, England, is a notorious example. On the other hand, overreliance on the results of computer models may have had an effect in pushing engineering techniques to their limit in the box girder bridge failures.

Types of Model

Let us define our terms of reference. A model is a homomorphic representation of some external object; that is to say that the model can be a representation of more than one external object. Outside pure mathematics the only isomorphic or faithful representation of a physical object is the object itself. This is important because it implies that the model must necessarily have a lesser informational content than the object at any particular instant in time. But a model, if it is to be useful, has an important property in that it is easier to modify than the object. Note that the above definition of a model implies a purely descriptive function and it is as well to keep distinct the two uses of the term model which are especially confused in the environmental field. These two uses are the descriptive one and the analytic one, the latter normally encompassing the former.

Models may be quantitative or non-quantitative. The field of non-quantitative models I will leave to the psychologists and the design methodologists but it is interesting to note that there is a constant movement of factors into the quantitative field from the non-quantitative. For example, the definition of visual privacy and environmental temperature. Although dismissing the non-quantitative model in the context of this paper, I would stress that in my opinion it is, and should be, in this field that the true design process takes place influenced and not determined by quantitative models.

Quantitative models, in turn, may be divided into geometric models and numerical ones. The geometric models include scale models, plans and projections, all of which can be mapped from the object by means of a purely geometric transformation, while numerical models are self-evidently stated in terms of numbers, as in the specification of points on a plan in terms of Cartesian co-ordinates. It is interesting to note that any use of a geometric model normally involves an implicit mapping into a corresponding algebraic model; for example, the use of a ruler to measure a distance on a plan. Indeed, any geometric model may be mapped into an algebraic one although in some cases this will lead to inefficiency in representation, as in the numerical mapping of an arbitrary three dimensional surface to high precision.

The Uses of Models

I will now restrict my remarks to numerical models, especially as all environmental models are involved with properties of materials which are conveniently defined numerically rather than geometrically. Let us examine a particular environmental model which is the most highly developed in the country, is used more often than any other, utilises the country's largest computer, and whose results are very easily checked by anyone. I refer to the Meteorological Office's model of half the northern hemisphere which it runs on an IBM 360/195 computer several times daily. Why does this model not always give correct results? Among the answers may be wrong data, a paucity of data, inadequate theory and errors in calculation. If this most sophisticated of models is prone to error, what are the chances for other environmental models? To consider this, take the different elements of an analytic environmental model. These are input data, description (or data structure), calculation and results. The error proneness of these elements is somewhat dependent on exterior influences. In the case of data, data collection. Description depends on a conceptual model, calculation on theory, and results (or answer) on the question asked. Let us look at these elements and relationships individually. Data collection is a well known problem in environmental models. Either data is not available or cannot be found, or it is available in a form not easily convertible to the requirements of the model, usually because of bad model design. Data verification is an important technique to be used either in the form of self consistency and limit checks. or in the visual output of geometric information in the form of plans and perspectives with numeric data superimposed.

Next comes the problem of description. This should be dependent only on the conceptual model of the external object and not constrained by particular data structure limitations. There is a classic example of a descriptive model constrained by a data structure, where a particular worker in this field was intoxicated with the virtues of ring structures (which can be a very efficient method of describing two-dimensional relationships). His particular model of a room for environmental calculations omitted both the ceiling and the floor because only the walls fitted nicely into a single ring. That is an extreme example, and clearly a real implementation of a model depends on the computer tools available, but convenience of implementation must be carefully balanced against consequent loss of information.

What exactly is meant by the conceptual model? This is needed because a decision has to be made about both the individual elements of the description and about the generality of the description. The more general the description is, the larger it is, and except in the case of system building or in a building with an extreme amount of repetition the amount of data becomes uncollectable and unmanageable. There is another important point about generality and the need for a particular conceptual model, and that is in the description of a built form; the correct elements to use are very dependent on the analysis needed. This may appear obvious, but there have been attempts to synthesize models for use in both structural and environmental calculations. This is misguided because the elements of interest for a structural calculation are contained in the framework and cladding, while the environmental calculation is concerned with spaces as elements surrounded by surfaces which define boundaries and which have certain environmental properties. The old definitions of a net give a good simile, either a series of strings knotted in two dimensions or a series of holes kept together with a string. The structural and the environmental descriptions are complementary and in consequence it is difficult to transform the one to the other or to synthesize a joint description. Nevertheless, care must be taken when avoiding the Scylla of generality to avoid also the Charybdis of specificity, because, as I stated earlier, probably the most important result of using an environmental model is to enable the study of the interrelation of properties, rather than the study of one property alone, to take place.

We now move on to the next element of the model, that of calculation or analysis. The possibility of error owing to failure in the computer is small and very much less important than errors in theory and errors in translating the theory into calculation. I would contend that it is in this area that the greatest danger lies when the model is being used by the architectural profession, because when both the theory and implementation are released from their academic birthplace there is the probability that the limits of applicability will not be made clear. The creators of the theory or the authors of the implementation may be clear in their own minds about the limits, but this knowledge is usually not passed on because of forgetfulness, lack of documentation or because of commercial interests. A good test of any computer environmental model is to see if it ever put out a message saying that 'the theory is not applicable with this data', or if limits of confidence are ever printed after output values. This problem is especially acute with environmental models because they tend not to be based directly on the first principles. At first sight this is surprising, for, after all, the classical physics of heat, light and sound was fairly well understood and documented in the nineteenth century, but the reason that most models are based on approximations is because the sheer complexity of the built form makes calculation from first principles daunting, both with regard to data collection and time and cost of implementation. So approximative models with limited applicability are created.

Evaluating the Results

Finally the results (or answers) have to be considered, and the main problem here is whether the results are the answers to the right question. The classic example is daylight factor. This is not a measure of the absolute illumination in a space due to natural light but a measure of the geometric properties of the space. If it is used as a relative measure of the response of two spaces to the same sky conditions then it is an immensely valuable tool but any standard which claims that 2.001% is good and 1.999% is bad gives an artificial importance to the concept.

A related danger is that the results from an environmental model may mean that other important questions are not being asked. There is a possibility of inflating the importance of the easily calculable, although this is no reason for not calculating the easily calculable.

So how well does the work that I am now going to present measure up to the criteria implicit in the foregoing discussion? Not well at all; but in my own defence I would state that it is an unfinished piece of academic work, interesting in the techniques used but unusable at the moment by anyone other than myself. A full description of the mathematics involved in the work may be found in my paper 'The prediction of surface luminance in architectural space'.[1]

Algorithms for Daylighting Calculations

Most authorities on daylighting, and in particular Hopkinson[2] consider that the approximate methods of calculating the internally reflected component are accurate enough for normal usage. These methods are usually based on the theory of the integrating sphere and are taken to the limit of usefulness by the BRS split-flux formula. The main disadvantages of all these methods is that they given an average value for the internally reflected component of daylight. This normally is of no significance because the sky and externally reflected components tend to overwhelm the value of the IRC, but in highly obstructed or in deep plan situations there comes a point where the magnitude of the IRC is the same or larger than that of the other two components and in this case one clearly wants the IRC as a function of room position. Secondary disadvantages of the split flux method are the assumptions of uniform height, infinite obstructions, and obstruction and ground luminance assumed to be 0.1 of the average sky luminance.

Earlier work on the exact solution for multiple reflections of light, for example that by Spencer and Stakutis,[3] produces formulations of the problem in terms of integral equations which are insoluble analytically except in very constrained situations such as between parallel walls.

The aim of this work is to take the integral equation formulation of the problem for planes at any angle and any reflectance, and to use appropriate numerical techniques to produce algorithms suitable for the computer solution of the problem.

The physics of the problem can be divided into five stages. The first is the determination of the initial flux received from a CIE sky (or any other sky luminance distribution which can be mathematically defined or tabulated) on all external planes, taking account of obstructions by other external planes. The next stage is to find the final luminance of the external planes due to this initial flux and to multiple interreflections between these planes.

The third stage is to find the initial flux received on all planes in the object room through the window or rooflight due to the sky luminance and the outside obstructing planes. The fourth stage is to find the final luminance of the inner planes due to multiple interreflections and the last stage is to use these final luminances of inner and outer planes to find the illumination at any specified reference point.

Application of the Algorithms

As any useful application of daylighting algorithms will need to consider a reasonably large number of planes, it is clearly important to be able to handle the properties in a fast, efficient way. This is achieved by having a certain amount of redundant information.

Surfaces including windows are described as a series of rectangular planes. A rectangular plane can be fully described by specifying the co-ordinates of three of its four corners. The only other geometric information we require is the sense of the plane, that is which side is the light-reflected side. This can be uniquely specified by describing the three corners in a consistent order which we choose to be clockwise looking at the light reflecting side. From this basic information we derive the centre of the plane, the unit perpendicular, the side vectors and the area. The following section briefly describes the vector algebra that is needed to accomplish this:

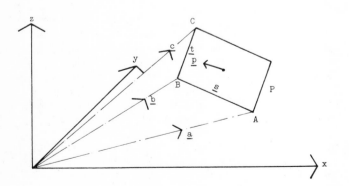

Figure 1

Consider the plane P defined by corner co-ordinated A, B, C, and therefore by corner vectors $\underline{a}$, $\underline{b}$ and $\underline{c}$, then the side vectors s and t are immediately defined by

$$\underline{s} = \underline{a} - \underline{b} \qquad \underline{t} = \underline{c} - \underline{b}$$

and the centre vector $\underline{d}$ by $\underline{d} = \dfrac{\underline{c} + \underline{a}}{2}$

The perpendicular $\underline{p}$ is perpendicular to $\underline{t}$ and $\underline{s}$ and is therefore given by $\underline{p} = \underline{s} \wedge \underline{t}$ which can be immediately normalised to give the perpendicular $\underline{p} = \dfrac{p}{|p|}$

The area is clearly $\underline{t} \cdot \underline{s}$.
Any point on the plane is described by $\underline{q}$.

where $\underline{q} = \underline{d} + m\,\underline{s} + n\,\underline{t}$, $-\frac{1}{2} \leqslant m \leqslant \frac{1}{2}$ and $-\frac{1}{2} \leqslant n < \frac{1}{2}$ (1)

We now move from the consideration of one plane to considering two or more. For each plan we wish to know whether light can be received on it from any of the other planes or, in other words, whether they can see each other. To solve this problem let us look at the following cases.

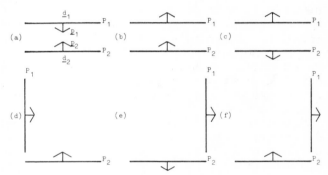

Figure 2

If the point defined by a perpendicular is given by $\underline{u} = \underline{d} + \underline{p}$ then for all cases except (f) planes are facing if $|u_1 - u_2| < |d_1 - d_2|$. This condition only breaks down for (f) in a very restricted set of circumstances.

We now consider the problem of subplane definition. It is clear that certain properties of the plane are common to all subplanes, including the physical properties and the value of the perpendicular. If we divided any plane symmetrically so that all its subplanes are similar to the plane then any subplane is fully defined by its centre and its area. Now its centre, as it is a point on the full plane, can be defined by values of n and m in equation (1). Thus the only information needed for the subplanes is a set of three numbers giving n, m and the area.

Although it is easy to define the subplanes, it is very important to sub-divide the planes a minimum number of times. This is because we are dealing with a quadratic problem in that as we are concerned about the interaction between planes, the amount of calculation is proportional to the square of the total number of subplanes. Also, as our original planes are of differing size it would not be a good idea to divide all the planes into the same number of subplanes, so for the optimum subdivision we use the following recursive algorithm.

The criterion for the size of a subplane is that $s/R^2 < 0.01$ where S is area of subplane and R is the distance to object point.

R is chosen to be the distance to the nearest corner of the nearest plane. We take a plane, test to see if it satisfies the relationship above, and if it does we have subdivided enough; if not, we divide the plane into four and repeat the process for each subplane. This is clearly a recursive procedure which will not stop if we have two adjacent planes, because the subdivision will continue into the join as the ratio will not change, so some arbitrary limit on the depth of subdivision is chosen. This limit is usually such that the computation time is kept within bounds, as an extra level of depth could increase computation time by 16 times. The most useful depths are such that subdivision is up to 16 or 64 subplanes.

The first program takes the description of planes as sets of 3 sets of Cartesian co-ordinates, along with the reflectivities of each of them, and produces an interal representation of the extended data for each plane and also a representation of all subplanes produced by the algorithm described in the preceding section. In effect this algorithm produces a tree structure of subplanes and then interrogates it to give the list of subplanes.

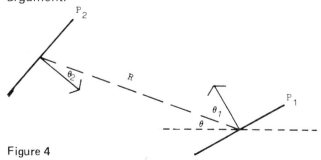

Figure 3

The transformed data is then output on to a backing store device for later use. It must be run for both the external and internal set of planes.

The next program takes this geometrically manipulated data for the outside planes and works out the luminance level for each plane. The initial luminance is calculated from the table produced earlier for a CIE sky of illumination normal to a plane as a function of orientation of the plane. This must be modified owing to the shading effects of the other planes which obstruct the sky. Clearly this effect will vary across each plane, but it will not vary significantly across the subplanes. The effect of obstructions is measured at each subplane centre and the value assumed to be constant across the subplanes. To find this obstructing effect we divide the obstructing planes into their subplanes and calculate the obstructing effect of each of these using the following argument.

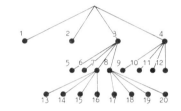

Figure 4

The true obstructing effect of P_2 at d_1 is

$$I = \int_{P_2} d\theta d\phi \; \frac{9}{7\pi} \; \frac{(1+2\sin\theta)}{3} \; \frac{\cos\theta_1 \; \cos\theta_2}{R^2} \quad (2)$$

but the condition $S/R = < 0.01$ holds so that we may effectively approximate this integral to

$$I = \frac{9}{7\pi} \; \frac{(1+2\sin\theta)}{3} \; S_2 \frac{\cos\theta_1 \; \cos\theta_2}{R_{12}^2} \quad (3)$$

We have the luminances of the outer planes due to direct illumination from the sky, which must be used to find the final luminances due to the direct illumination plus the multiple reflected indirect illumination.

Now if L is the luminance then $L_i = A_{ij} L_j'$ where the A_{ij} are functions of configuration factors and reflectivities and areas. If the initial luminance is L_i^1 and the luminance after the nth reflection is L_i^n we know that $L_i^n - L_i^{n-1} = B_{ij} L_j^{n-1}$. We also know that $L_i^n - L_i^{n-1} < L_i^{n-1}$ and therefore we have a reasonable convergent equation which should iterate to a solution. We can use this iterative scheme in two ways. The B_{ij} are constant for each iteration so we could set up a table of B_{ij} and access this table. Unfortunately we are liable to have, say, 150 subplanes and therefore 150 x 75 entries in the table. As one of the design aims of the implementation is to keep the individual program small it was decided to recalculate the coefficients B_{ij} each time round the iteration. In practice a maximum of three iterations is necessary to achieve convergence within 0.01% so the time penalty is not too extreme. The program outputs to a backing store device the final luminances of the outer planes.

We now have stored these luminances and the geometry of the inner and outer planes. It remains to connect these different bits of information. For each inner plane we wish to know the initial luminance due to the sky and the outer planes, then we can iterate as above to find the final luminances. The process is of course complicated by the presence of the windows of the inner space which are the only connection between the inner and outer planes, indeed the windows are the only planes common to both sets of planes. Clearly the only inner planes which are directly affected by the outside are the ones that can be seen by the inner window planes, and the only outer planes that may be seen are those seen by the outer window planes.

For each inner subplane we need both the illumination due to unobstructed sky which can be seen through the window planes and the illumination from the visible outer planes. To do this accurately would entail an integration of the sky luminance across the window opening which in general would be very sordid; add the problem of taking into account the obstructing planes and it becomes impossible to contemplate for the large number of evaluations needed here. Yet again we look for approximations.

The algorithm we choose is as follows. For each inner subplane we look at each window subplane and calculate, using the approximation described above, the illumination from the unobstructed sky. From this we must subtract the sky illumination obstructed by the outer planes and add the illumination from these same outer planes. We make a further approximation that the subplane of the outer planes can be either fully seen or not seen at all through the window subplane. To test whether it can be seen, we calculate the solid angle subtended by the window subplane from the centre of the inner subplane and compare it with the angle subtended by the line joining the centre of the window subplane and the centre of the outer subplane. This is equivalent to considering the window subplane aperture as a cone of the same solid angle and testing whether the centre of the outer subplane lies within this cone. Having found whether it is approximately seen, we can do the requisite additions and subtractions in the usual way. Clearly this requires a large number of tests as for each inner subplane and we must test all outer subplanes against all window subplanes. To cut down these tests we make an initial test of complete outer planes by testing all four corners to see if any of them lies within the cone of visibility.

This algorithm will leave us with the initial luminances of all the inner subplanes, which we can use to iterate in the usual way to the final solution for the luminances of the inner planes.

It will be remembered that an early assumption in the work is that both the inner and outer planes define convex spaces, so that we can have no plane obstructing another. For the outer planes in any realistic situation this is clearly a valid assumption. It would be a strange geometry of obstructions which made more than a negligible effect from part-seen planes.

For inner planes this will not be true. We might be concerned with L or T shaped spaces. Allowances for this can be made by using an extra non-implemented program which could take the expanded geometric data for the inner planes and produce for each subplane a list of other subplanes which are hidden. Keeping to the usual philosophy, part-hidden subplanes would be neglected.

The luminances produced by the algorithms described above can be used for daylight or glare analysis. Glare analysis is straightforward. We can choose a reference point and we can immediately calculate the solid angles subtended by any of the planes whose luminance distribution we have already calculated.

For daylight factor evaluation we no longer need to use crude approximations for sky component and externally reflected component, and we have the inner plane luminances for an accurate evaluation of the internally reflected component.

For the sky and the externally reflected component we can proceed in either of two ways. In the first we can numerically integrate over the visible sky and the obstructions, taking into account part-hidden obstructions. For a few evaluations this can be contemplated. For the second method we divide the window planes into a large number (up to 10,000) subplanes and use the same algorithms as presented in previous sections. Clearly the larger the number of subplanes the better the accuracy.

Conclusion

This work awaits further development, but one point is clear. Even using the power of a very large computer the time needed to reach a solution makes this program useful only in a research context or as a tool to check illumination in a highly critical architectural design. For day to day work either the traditional tables or cheap computer models based on them are the best cost effective methods.

In conclusion, my contention is that computer environmental models are not, and should not, be sweeping the architectural practices of the country. They have their place, usually an expensive place, as research tools to explore new concepts of environmental relationships.

References
1. Stibbs, R. J. (1971). 'The prediction of surface luminances in architectural space'. Working Paper 54 Land Use and Built Form Studies.
2. Hopkinson, R., Petherbridge P. and Longmore, J. (1966) *Day Lighting* (London: Heinemann)
3. Spencer, D. E. and Stakutis, V. S. (1951). 'The integral equation solution of the daylighting problem'. *Journal of the Franklin Institute* **252,** 225.

□

Fundamental studies of wind flow near buildings

J. Hunt

Introduction

The wind flow around a building affects people in or near the building in the following ways, some of which are facetiously illustrated in *Figure 1*.

Comfort of Pedestrians

High winds and gusty winds are regarded as unpleasant by most people, and sufficiently high winds have blown pedestrians over. Since buildings produce the largest relative increases or decreases in wind speed at ground level, pedestrians feel the full extent of these changes in wind speed. For this reason, the effect of buildings on the comfort of people near the building can range from dangerous, when people can even be knocked over and fatally injured (Penwarden, 1973) and inconvenient, when clothes are blown about and eyes irritated (Hunt & Poulton, 1972), to beneficial, when people are sheltered from the approaching wind (Jensen 1954). A difficulty for the designer when he is concerned with pedestrian comfort in windy conditions is that there is no systematic data on people's response to the wind. Nevertheless, casual observations have led to some criteria being proposed. A wind of 5m/sec is considered to be annoying, and 10m/sec to be disagreeable (Penwarden, 1973). Lawson (1973) suggests that a site should be regarded as intolerable if 10m/sec. is exceeded more than about 2% of the time. This uncertainty will partly be resolved by the results of experiments sponsored by the Building Research Establishment (B R E, 1974) which I am undertaking with Dr. E. C. Poulton of the Medical Research Council with about 500 subjects in a large wind tunnel at the National Physical Laboratory.

It is worth noting that in other countries criteria may be quite different. In Southern Russia high winds near buildings are regarded as pleasantly cooling, and in the north they usefully blow away the snow. It has been proposed that in Australia winds are acceptable if they only blow people over (about 20m/sec is required) once a year! (Melbourne and Joubert, 1971).

Dispersion of Smoke and Fumes

Most buildings produce their own pollution in the form of exhausts from heating and ventilation plants, kitchen, and incinerators, They also experience air

Figure 1.   The wind environment problem.

pollution which is created elsewhere, e.g. by traffic. The wind around the building can help or hinder the dispersion of these airborne pollutants and therefore is crucially important in determining the concentrations of air pollution experienced by people in or near the buildings (Halitsky, 1968). Adequate dispersion of smoke is also vitally important for reducing fire risks. In general, high winds at ground level help the dispersion of air pollution produced by vehicles, so that, if vehicles and pedestrians have to use the same thoroughfare, the need to reduce air pollution and the need to improve pedestrian comfort can conflict.

Wind-created Noise

Certain types of building, for example the library at the University of Warwick, enable the wind to produce an unacceptably loud noise inside the building.

Landing of Aircraft and Helicopters

In the lee of a building the wind speed is reduced and the gustiness increased. This makes the landing of aircraft and helicopters near buildings difficult and dangerous, which is why pilots and civil aviation authorities are becoming concerned about buildings around airports. *(Nancoo, 1974).*

Note that the pressure on the building is related to the wind flow round it, and the distribution of pressure on the building determines its overall structural load and the load on individual cladding elements, and affects the performance of heating and ventilating systems. The wind flow near a building affects the surface movement of rain, which in turn affects the penetration of rain into the building and the discolouring of the building's exterior surfaces. These problems are outside the scope of this paper.

The importance of these effects of the wind round a building shows that the way in which the shape and size of a building or group of buildings forces the wind to flow round it or through it is as much a part of the functioning of the building as its heating, ventilating or lighting. Consequently, it may be as important for the architect and planner to be able to predict the wind flow near buildings, as to predict any other aspect of its performance.

The Study of Architectural Aerodynamics

Architectural aerodynamics is the study of wind flow around and wind loads on buildings with the object of understanding and eventually predicting these flows. With regard to the wind flow, the first practical object of this study, both theoretically and experimentally, should be to develop simple models of the flow round a single building and groups of buildings which will enable the architect to estimate the wind condition around his proposed building. It is essential that these models be intelligible and that the predictions of the model be easy to apply. This requires presenting the models by means of diagrams of the flow streamlines and physical concepts such as pressure, and presenting the predictions in brief tables or simple mathematical formulae which can be evaluated by slide rule or desk calculator. Only if such models are developed are wind conditions likely always to be incorporated at an early stage by all architects.

At present, guide-lines do exist (Lawson, 1968, and BRE 1973) which, although incomplete, should, if followed, eliminate some of the designs which produce poor wind conditions. Examples of buildings which have been erected in the last 10 years which produce unpleasant ground level wind conditions have been described in a Building Research Station Digest (1972). In some cases architects have been careful to investigate by means of wind tunnel tests the wind conditions in a number of possible designs before deciding which to choose (White, 1968; Taylor, 1971).

However, such experimental investigations are costly and, if they became widespread, or worse still mandatory, there would soon be an acute shortage of wind tunnels and aerodynamicists. For this reason what is needed are simple prediction methods and 'alarm signals' to tell the architect when he should seek aerodynamic advice.

The second practical objective of architectural aerodynamics is to enable the architect to obtain detailed and sufficiently accurate predictions about any proposed design. This may be necessary for the final detailed design, especially for tall buildings; for example, the best kind of door opening is determined by local pressures, or the position of heating plant exhausts can best be chosen when the wind flow is known. This may in future be possible with the use of computers alone. But the results of attempts that have been made so far in the USA by Djuric & Thomas (1971) and Hirt & Cook (1972) using the largest available computers to compute flow round tall rectangular buildings are not at all representative of actual wind conditions. For some years to come the second stage in the analysis of wind conditions, if it is necessary, must be experimental using wind tunnel tests.

As well as describing the aims of the study of architectural aerodynamics, a brief description of the *methods* is also appropriate. The basis of the theoretical approach is the dynamical equations of fluid motion. Because these consist of three non-linear partial differential equations of second order, a type of equation to which there are no general solutions, these equations can only be solved analytically for a few idealised situations. In principle, there is no reason why computers should not solve these equations. But at the moment there are no computers large enough to use these equations to solve a problem of any practical relevance. In fact, no direct computer solution has even been developed for any turbulent flow, such as the natural wind. Consequently, in turbulent flows simplifying assumptions have to be made. Then some useful progress is possible, which will be described in the next section.

To obtain detailed information even about a uniform steady flow round a building, or indeed round an ideal shape such as a circular cylinder, then experiments are needed which are usually performed in wind tunnels. To simulate in a wind tunnel the natural wind flowing round a building, the approaching wind also has to be simulated correctly, i.e. both the increase of the wind speed with height and the turbulence must be modelled correctly. *(A recent meeting was held to discuss the available techniques and the limitations of wind tunnel simulations (Fernholz and Hunt, 1975)).* Two simulation methods in use in the UK are those developed by Counihan (1969) and Cook (1973). There is a problem in deciding in how much detail the wind need be simulated when so little is known about the sensitivity of people to wind conditions. To help in understanding the complex flows round buildings, research experiments have been and are being undertaken, variously in steady uniform flows, uniform flows with turbulence added, and shear flow with small amounts of turbulence. In conjunction with theory, such basic experiments have enabled conceptual models to be developed for flows round basic building shapes.

Some Results of Fundamental Studies

Application

When a specialist in building aerodynamics attempts to predict the wind conditions near a building or a group of buildings, he usually compares the building or the group to some simple building shape or group of buildings the flow round which has been studied before. Taking into account the differences between these paradigm flows and the actual flow, an approximate prediction can be made. As already mentioned, it is to be hoped that this approach can eventually be systematised sufficiently to enable architects to use it.

In this section, we describe flows round a few of these simple building shapes or groups of building shapes for various conditions of the approaching flow. Where space does not permit a full description, references are given.

The Two-dimensional Cylinder

The best understood flow around an obstacle in the study of fluid mechanics is probably that around a cylinder in the shape of an aerofoil cross section, but this knowledge has little application to building aerodynamics. The next best understood external flows are the flows round cylinders with cross sectional shapes such as circles, rectangles or octagons. This is of some use because these flows are similar in many important respects to those round tall buildings. Such flows are best described by dividing them into two main regions shown diagrammatically in *Figure 2a*.

These regions are distinguished by the pattern of the 'mean stream-lines' of the flow, which at any point are parallel to the average velocity and which approximate to the average path of a particle, for example, the path of a piece of waste paper or airborne pollutant. In the external flow region (E), all these streamlines emanate from the flow upwind, and consequently the flow in this region is sensitive to conditions upwind, for example, to the level of the turbulence or the presence of sources of air pollution.

The flow downwind and close to the sides of the building is usually described as its wake (W). For about 10 to 13 widths downstream, the mean flow recirculates and the average streamlines form loops; this part of the wake is often called the 'bubble'. Down-wind of the 'bubble' the streamlines are all pointing forwards, but the wind speed remains markedly less than upwind. The crosswind variation in the wind speeds at various positions in front of and behind the building are shown in *Figure 2b*.

The most significant feature of the wake is that, whether or not the approaching flow is steady, the

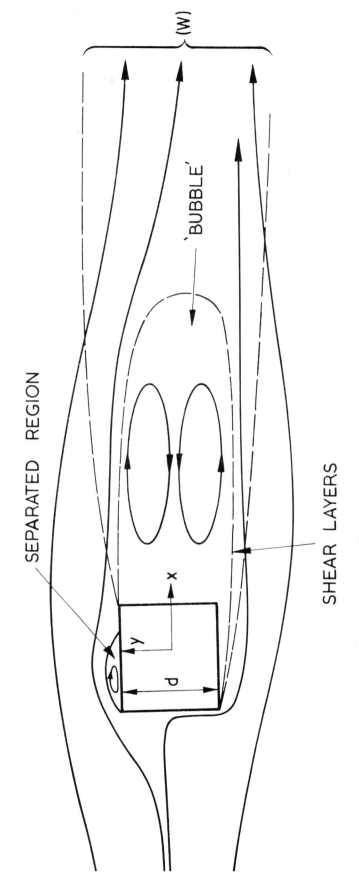

Figure 2(a).   Flow round a two-dimensional rectangular cylinder. Pattern of mean streamlines and the postulated flow regions.

flow in this region is very unsteady, with the unsteady component of the wind being of the same magnitude as the steady component. In the natural wind, even in a city, the unsteady component of the wind is less than 30% of the steady component. Thus the flow in the external region, except very close to the ground, is not as turbulent as in the wake.

In *Figure 3* a typical instantaneous picture of streamlines is sketched. This shows how the edge of the wake region has an irregular shape and that the flows in regions (E) and (W) are more inter-connected than appears from the average picture shown in *Figure 2(a)*.

Having divided the flow into these regions, it becomes possible to devise theories to describe the flow. In the external flow, assuming the upstream flow is uniform, the mean velocities in the x and y directions u, v are given by the solution to Laplace's equation

$$\nabla^2 \phi = 0$$

The solution to this equation can often be found analytically, but otherwise it can be computed straightforwardly. The solution is determined by the boundary conditions, which are that the velocity must

be parallel to the surface of the body and the wake. Since the wake has such an irregular boundary, this condition is somewhat artificial, and a suitable hypothesis has to be made. Two well-known methods which compare well with experimental results for flow round circular and rectangular cylinders are those of Parkinson and Jandali (1970) and Roshko (1954), the more recent method being simpler to apply. These calculations enable the distribution of average velocity around the cylinder and the average surface pressure to be predicted; they are not applicable to flow round three-dimensional obstacles in a shearflow.

In the highly unsteady wake region close to the body, any realistic calculation of velocity must begin by predicting the unsteady flow, especially the vortices shed from the sides of the cylinder, which were shown diagrammatically in *Figure 3*. Complete numerical solutions of two-dimensional flow round cylindrical bodies, including all the effects of viscosity close to the surface have been obtained by Harlow & Fromm (1963) and other workers. However, such calculations require enormous computing time because the minute details of the flow close to the surface cannot be

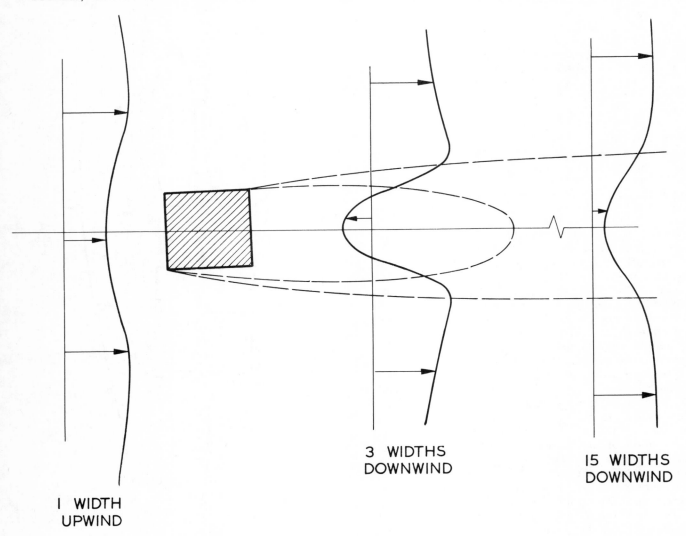

1 WIDTH
UPWIND

3 WIDTHS
DOWNWIND

15 WIDTHS
DOWNWIND

Figure 2(b).   Flow round a two-dimensional rectangular cylinder. Variation with y of the x - component of mean velocity at various downstream positions.

104

neglected. But simpler calculations based on assumptions about the generation of vortices at the surface of the body also seem to predict these wake flows adequately. A recent model is that of Clements (1973), but even this probably needs more computer time than might ever be possible for a design calculation. It also probably produces too much information. Usually all that is needed is to know the frequency of vortices (n) and the average value ($\bar{u}$) and fluctuations in velocity u', which can most simply be obtained experimentally. Typically, for a rectangular cylinder with thickness d, in a windspeed $\bar{u}_\infty$, $nd/\bar{u}_\infty \simeq 0.1$ and on the centre line at a point 4 diameters downstream $\bar{u} \simeq 0.5\,\bar{u}_\infty$, $u' \simeq 0.3\,\bar{u}_\infty$ so that fluctuating velocity is of the same order as the mean velocity.

Further downstream, beyond the 'bubble', the average velocity is positive, but the turbulence remains high for over thirty diameters downstream.

Now consider the case of a cylinder placed in a flow which is turbulent but which everywhere upstream has the same *average* velocity. This is a useful idealisation of a tall building in the wind, and it accurately describes the situation of a cylinder placed in a wind tunnel with a grid of bars fixed at the entrance of the tunnel. The changes in the turbulence in the flow round the cylinder can be described theoretically (Hunt, 1973). Two effects occur. Firstly, the obstacle blocks the turbulence, i.e. the eddies must pass round the body. Secondly, the eddies are stretched and distorted by the mean flow, so that their velocities are changed. As an example consider the turbulent velocities on the centre line of a square cylinder. The former effect tends to reduce the turbulent velocities in the flow direction u_x' and amplify those in the perpendicular direction u_y', while the latter effect amplifies u_x' and reduces u_y'. Which effect dominates depends on the relative scale of the building to the

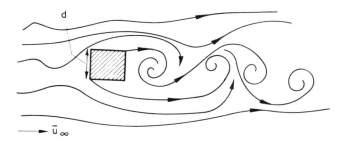

Figure 3. Instantaneous pattern of streamlines showing the formation of vortices.

turbulence—the larger the building the larger the latter effect. Confirmation of these theoretical predictions is provided by the experimental measurements taken on the centre line of a square cylinder in a wind tunnel placed with its front face perpendicular y and at 45 degrees to the wind. See *Figure 4(a), (b)*.

In the case of a tall building these results are useful for calculating the dispersion of air pollution, for calculating fluctuating pressures on the building, and indirectly for calculating the turbulence near the ground.

Groups of Two-dimensional Cylinders

Tall slender buildings are sometimes placed close together, for example the World Trade Centre in New York, or power station cooling towers. When the direction of the wind is such that the buildings are not in each other's wake, then similar methods as for a single cylinder, based on potential flow theory, can be used to predict the increase in wind speed between the cylinders. A typical value to be expected between two cylinders is about $2.0\,u_\infty$ as compared with $1.4\,u_\infty$ at the sides of a two-dimensional cylinder. A simple but effective mathematical model of the flow between a bank of cooling towers was developed by Owen, 1967, which showed that the resistance of the whole group of cooling towers slowed down the flow by almost as much as the velocity between them was increased. When cylinders lie in each other's wake, the turbulence behind those up-wind can be amplified and diffused by those downwind. This is a similar situation to that between the tubes of a heat exchanger (Owen, 1965).

Roof Vortices

When the wind flows over pitched or flat roofs, strong vortices often occur. The vortices on the top of a cube-shaped building are shown in *Figure 5 (c)*, which is taken from a review by Ackeret (1965).

Figures 5(a), 5 (b), also from that review, show the pressure distributions over a cube and a delta-shaped aircraft wing, which suggests that flow over a delta wing is a useful model for the more complex flows that occur over flat roofs.

The practical importance of developing a model for such flows is that this may enable us to predict the high suction forces that occur on roofs and also to show how the roof vortices will disperse the exhaust from any proposed chimney on the roof. (See Halitsky, 1968). Lawson (1968) describes the roof vortices which occur on roofs with more irregular shapes than on pitched roofs.

Cylinder in a Shear Flow on a Plane

One difference has already been mentioned between a uniform steady flow and the natural wind, namely, the latter's turbulence. The other two main differences are that the velocity of the wind varies with height (the wind shear), and that the atmosphere is bounded by the ground. The effect of these differences is felt by every pedestrian approaching a tall building, namely, a reversal and an increase of the ground level wind speed on the upwind side, violent fluctuations in wind speed on the downstream side, and high winds near the sides, as shown in *Figure 6*.

A measure of this increase in average wind speed at a height a from the ground is the amplification ratio introduced by Wise (1971). $R = \bar{u}(a)/\bar{u}_\infty(a)$, where $\bar{u}_\infty(a)$ is the wind speed upwind at the same height a. A simple but incomplete estimate of these amplification effects can be given in terms of the wind speed $\bar{u}_\infty(h)$ approaching the top of the building, height h. This wind produces a pressure $p_s(h)$ on the upwind face of $p_s(h) \simeq \tfrac{1}{2}\,\rho\,\bar{u}_\infty^2(h)$ where ρ is the density of air. For a tall building (h>3b), the pressure at the bottom is not zero but may be a half or a quarter of $p_s(h)$. Therefore, there must be a flow down the face of the building, w, which can be no greater than $\sqrt{2p_s/\rho} \simeq \bar{u}_\infty(h)$ This should be an upper limit for the downflow velocity. On low buildings (h<b) the pressure over the front face is nearly the same at all heights, and the down flow velocities are small compared with $\bar{u}_\infty(h)$.

Figure 4. The change along the centre line in the root mean square of the x — component of turbulent wind, u'_x, upwind of a square cylinder placed in a turbulent wind. Upwind u'_x is equal to $u'_{x\infty}$. Results are given when the upwind face is perpendicular to the flow ($\alpha = 0$) and is at 45 degrees ($\alpha = 45$). Also shown are the effects of a change in the ratio, a/L_x, of the size of the body to the scale of the turbulence.

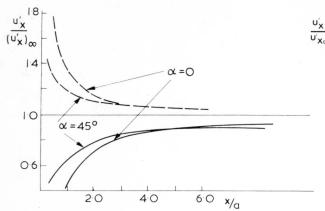

(a) Theoretical predictions when a/L_x is zero and infinitely large.

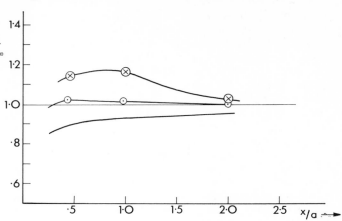

(b) Experimental results:
— a/L_x = 0.19 Bearman's experiments
⊗ a/L_x = 1.25 Cambridge experiments $\}$ $\alpha = 0$
⊙ a/L_x = 1.8 Cambridge experiment $\alpha = 45°$
(taken from Hunt, 1972).

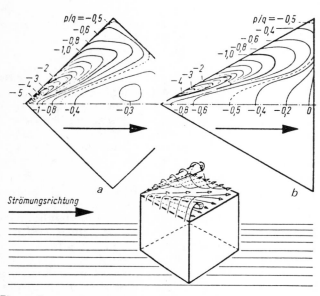

Figure 5. Roof vortices on a cube-shaped building.
(a) Pressure distributions measured on a model cube in a wind tunnel.
(b) Pressure distributions on a delta shaped aircraft wing — showing the similarity with (a).
(c) Streamlines showing the roof vortices which cause the low pressures.
Note that p is pressure and $q = \frac{1}{2}\rho\,\overline{u}_\infty^{\,2}$ where $\overline{u}_\infty$ is the upstream velocity. This diagram is taken from the review by Ackeret (1965).

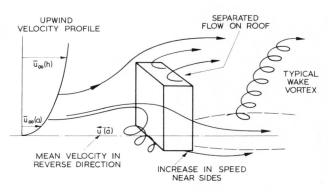

Figure 6. Effects of wind shear on the flow round a building.

See, for example, the experiments of Good & Joubert (1968). When the down flow reaches the ground, then it tends to produce a forward flow which, at a height a, we can estimate from the pressure on the building at the ground $p_s(0)$ to be less than $(\overline{u}_\infty^{\,2}(h) - \overline{u}_\infty^{\,2}(a))^{\frac{1}{2}}$

Thus, we can crudely estimate the amplification ratio R to be less than $(\overline{u}_\infty^{\,2}(h)/\overline{u}_\infty^{\,2}(a) - 1)^{\frac{1}{2}}$

This estimate of R agrees with the measurements in front of a building made by Sexton (1971).

In the wake behind the building, the pressure is lower than on the upstream face and tends at all heights to be approximately equal to its value near the top.

Thus, the pressure in the wake on the ground $p_w(0) \simeq \frac{1}{2}C_{pb}u^2(h)$, where C_{pb} is the base pressure coefficient for the relevant cylinder shape. These values of $p_w(0)$ and $p_s(0)$ result in a flow round the base of the cylinder approximately equal to that near the top. This, of course, is *greater* than the velocity near the ground upstream, and at the sides. An upper limit for R is $\overline{u}_\infty(h)/\overline{u}_\infty(a)$.

The effect of wind shear on the unsteady flow in the wake behind cylinders is not understood (Maull & Young, 1972), but experiments do show that vortex shedding is changed, not eliminated. Physical reasoning also shows why vortices in the shear flow

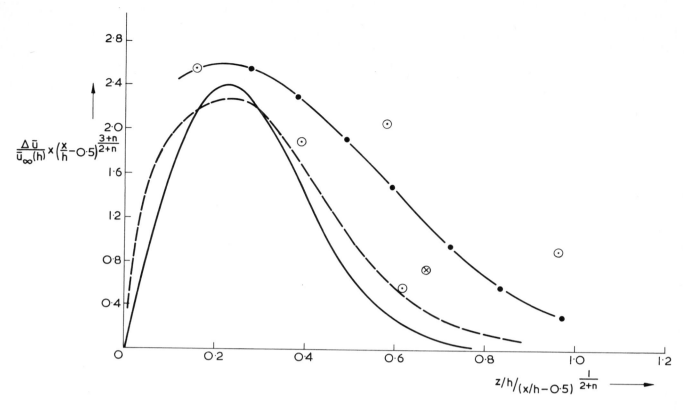

Figure 7. The reduction in velocity $\Delta\overline{u}$ downwind of a cube-shaped building as a function of the distance downwind x, the distance from the ground y, the height of the building h, and n the exponent of the wind's velocity profile ($n \simeq 0.15$ in the country). The theoretical line — is compared with wind tunnel experiments of Counihan — — — and with full scale measurements behind a hangar by Colmer:
x   x/h = 2.4 — · — · — best curve through experimental points. (taken from Hunt, 1972).

should produce swirling upward flows, which are often found in the lee of tall buildings.

Flows Round Low Buildings

The wind near low buildings was first studied in Denmark by Jensen with a view to studying how buildings could most effectively provide shelter from the biting winds of Jutland. In general, low buildings do provide shelter from the wind, unlike most tall buildings.

But how low is low? Flow in the lee is always sheltered on average even if more turbulence is created. The flow at the sides always show some increase, i.e. R >1. The big difference between low and high buildings is in the upwind flow. If $R \lesssim [\overline{u}^2_\infty (h) / \overline{u}^2_\infty (a) - 1]^{1/2}$ then taking $a \simeq 2m$ and a typical wind profile, we find R<1 if h<8m. Thus, a building below about 8m. should always provide shelter upwind, but above this height some amplification may be expected. A simple theory has been developed to estimate the shelter, or the reduction in velocity Δu (z), at a height z behind buildings with approximately square shape (Hunt, 1971, 1972, Counihan, Hunt and Jackson, 1974). The theory indicates that Δu decreases in proportion to the distance downwind x as $(x/h)^{-3/2}$, as compared with $(x/h)^1$ for a long low building. In practical terms, this means that the shelter lasts for about 10-13 building heights downwind, whereas for a long, low building it can be felt 20 building heights downwind. Results of the theory are compared in

Figure 7 with wind tunnel and full-scale measurements. There are many applications of such simple formulae in the planning of playgrounds, parks and other sheltered areas, and in assessing the effect of one building or row of buildings on another downwind.

Groups of Buildings of Different Sizes

A common situation in shopping centres, groups of office blocks, or city streets is where a building (A) is upwind of another much taller building (B). (See *Figure 8*).

Two main effects occur. Since the wind speed increases with height, for the reasons explained earlier, there is a flow down the upwind face of (B) in the same way as if the upwind building were not present. This downflow again leads to an upwind flow near the ground. If (A) is close enough, it inhibits the back flow. The second effect is caused by the wake flow of (A) impinging on (B), and producing a high stagnation pressure on (B) above the wake boundary and a low pressure below. This difference in pressure produces a strong downflow on (B) and a reverse flow at the ground. This is the familiar vortex photographed in wind tunnel models at the Building Research Station (Wise, 1971). If the buildings are too close, or too far away, this effect is weak.

Two tall buildings placed close together can also induce high wind speeds at ground level. At La Défense outside Paris, where two blocks 80m. tall are only 8m. apart at one corner, wind measurements have given a value of R=3. This

107

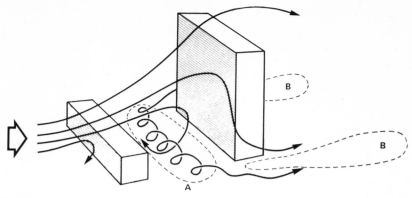

Figure 8.   Flow around two buildings of different
sizes (taken from B.R.E. Digest 141, 1972)

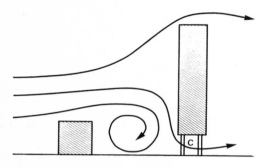

Figure 9.   Flow under a tall building on Pilotis
(taken from B.R.E. Digest 141, 1972)

is greater than an estimate for R based on the formula $\overline{u}_\infty$ (h) / $\overline{u}_\infty$ (a) which is 2.8. Thus in quite exceptional circumstances our upper limit may be exceeded.

Tall Buildings on Pilotis

This architectural device of placing a tall building on pilotis, shown in *Figure 9*, or of having an open passage way underneath the building often produces an excellent but unwanted wind tunnel at ground level. A simple physical argument suggest that the wind underneath is only a little less than $\overline{u}_\infty$ (h), the wind approaching the top of the building. Consequently, as an upper limit, $R \simeq \overline{u}_\infty$ (h) / $\overline{u}_\infty$ (a) $\simeq$ (h/a)$^{0.28}$, if we take the usual formula for the increase with height of wind speed. Thence for a 75m building, taking a = 2.0m, the amplification ratio $R \simeq 2.7$. Halving the height of the building would still produce a value of R = 2.4. Values of R as high as these have been observed by the Building Research Station at a number of sites (B.R.S., 1972), all of which have had to have expensive modifications made to them after the buildings were completed. Ways in which these undesirable winds can be avoided are described in the B.R.S. Digest.

Conclusions

1. The role of computers in predicting the wind round buildings is likely to remain limited to research investigations for several years to come.

2. Fundamental theoretical and experimental studies are beginning to throw up simple descriptive and mathematical models of flows round buildings. These should enable designers to predict the general features of wind round a proposed building or group of buildings at an early stage in the design. Some examples of these models have been given in section three of this paper.

3. To obtain *detailed* information about any new design, wind tunnel studies are necessary. However while criteria for wind conditions which are acceptable to people remain so vague, wind tunnel tests do tend to produce more information than can be used by the architect.   □

References

1. Ackeret J. (1965) 'Anwendungen der Aerodynamik im Bauwesen'. Zeit fur Flugwiss *13*, 109

2. Building Research Establishment (1974) An ill wind B.R.E. News p.6, no.26.

3. Building Research Station (1972) Wind environment around tall buildings, Digest 141.

4. Clements R. R. (1973) An inviscid model of two-dimensional vortex shedding, *57*, 321.

5. Cook, N (1973) On simulating the lower third of the urban adiabatic boundary layer in a wind tunnel. Atmospheric Environment *7*, 691

6. Counihan J. (1969) An improved method of simulating an atmospheric boundary layer in a wind tunnel. Atmospheric Environment *3*, 197

7. Counihan, J., Hunt, J.C.R., Jackson, P.S. (1974) Wakes behind two-dimensional surface obstacles in turbulent boundary layers. J. Fluid Mech. *64*, 529.

8. Djuric, D. and Thomas, J.C. (1971) A numerical study of convective transport of a gaseous air pollutant in the vicinity of tall buildings Proc. Symp. on *Air Pollution, Turbulence and Diffusion*, New Mexico, December, 1971.

9. Fernholz, H.H. & Hunt, J.C.R. (1975) Wind tunnel simulation of the atmospheric boundary layer: a report of Euromech 50. To be published in J. Fluid Mech.

10. Good, M.C. and Joubert, P.N. (1968) The form drag of two-dimensional bluff plates immersed in turbulent boundary layers. J. Fluid Mech. *31*, 547.

11. Halitsky J. (1968) Gas diffusion near buildings 'Meteorology and Atomic Energy' p.221, Published by U.S. Atom En. Comm.

12. Hirt, C.W. and Cook, J.L. (1972) Calculating three dimensional flows around structures and over rough terrains. J. Comp. Phys. *10*, 324.

13. Hunt J. C. R. (1971) The effect of single buildings and structures. Phil. Trans. Roy. Soc. *A, 269*, 457.

14. Hunt J. C. R. (1972) 'Some theories for the mean and turbulent velocity distributions in flows around bluff bodies' Symp. on *External Flows* at Bristol University, July 1972

15. Hunt, J.C.R. (1973) A theory of turbulent flow

round two-dimensional bluff bodies. J. Fluid Mech. *61,* 625.

16. Hunt, J.C.R. and Poulton, E.C. (1972) 'Some effects of wind on people' Symp. on *External Flows* at Bristol University, July 1972.

17. Jensen M. (1954) Shelter effect. Danish Technical Press. Copenhagen.

18. Lawson T. V. (1968) Air movement and natural ventilation Architects Journal Handbook on Building Environment. Section 3.

19. Lawson T. V. (1973) The wind environment of buildings: a logical approach to the establishment of criteria Univ. Bristol Dept. Aeron. Eng. Dep. TVL/7301.

20. Maull, D.J. and Young, R.A. (1972) The wake of a bluff body in a non-uniform flow. Symp. on *External Flows,* Bristol University, July 1972.

21. Melbourne, W.H. and Joubert, P.N. (1971) Problems of wind flow at the base of tall buildings, p. 105, Proc. 3rd. Int. Conf. on *'Wind effects on buildings and structures'.* Tokyo Saikon 6 (1971).

22. Nancoo, M.E. (1974) A status report on low level turbulence and wind shear effects on aircraft. The Log (publ. by British Airline Pilots Association) *35,* 211.

23. Parkinson, G.V. and Jandali, T. (1970) A wake source model for bluff body potential flow. J. Fluid Mech. *40,* 577.

24. Penwarden A. D. (1973) Acceptable wind speeds in towns Build Sci. *8,* 259.

25. Owen P. R. (1965) Buffeting excitation of boiler tube vibration. J. Mech. Eng. Sci. *7,* 431

26. Owen P. R. (1967) Some aerodynamic problems of grouped cooling towers p. 73 Proc. conf. *'Natural Draught Cooling Towers-Ferrybridge and after'* Inst. Civil Engineers.

27. Roshko A. (1954) A new hodograph for free streamline theory. N.A.C.A. technical note 3168, 1954.

28. Sexton, D. E. (1971) Discussion on 'Effects due to groups of buildings' Phil. Trans. Roy. Soc. *269,* 483

29. Taylor J. R. B. (1971) Liverpool Civic and Social Centre: preliminary wind tunnel testing to determine environmental conditions Phil. Trans Roy. Soc. *269,* 487

30. White K. C. (1968) Wind tunnel testing to determine the environmental wind conditions for the proposed town centre development at Corby. Paper 34 *'Wind effects on Buildings and Structures'.* Loughborough Univ. of Technology, 1968.

31. Wise A. F. E. (1971) Effects due to groups of buildings Phil. Trans. Roy. Soc. *269,* 469.

Acknowledgements

I am indebted to Alan Wise and Alan Penwarden at B.R.E. and Dr. David Maull at Cambridge for many helpful discussions.   □

Part 4

Space
and activities

Activity modelling in hospitals

Keith Ray

Introduction

The hospital study described in this paper has been concerned with the patterns of daily activity in a hospital, and in particular with the amount and type of traffic between the wards and departments and the way this traffic is distributed throughout the day and night. The primary concern has been to establish how the activity patterns are influenced both by the operational policies and by the physical layout of the hospital, and the aim has been to develop a model which takes these policies and the layout as input and which may be used to make predictions about what each person is doing and what his location is throughout his working hours.

In developing such a model, the main factor we have taken into account is the need in hospital planning for a more sophisticated technique to bring together the physical planning of the buildings and the operational policies which are to be applied to each of the wards and departments. At the present time, in planning the physical relationships between the different parts of a new hospital, a matrix is constructed, such as the one shown in *Figure 1,* which is intended to reflect the strength of association or 'link' between the various wards and departments. The hospital buildings are then planned in such a way that, wherever possible, the wards and departments which are shown by this matrix to be most closely related are placed next to each other. The numerical values in this matrix are determined by a number of factors, and amongst these are assumptions about the amount and type of traffic flowing between the wards and departments. Although this matrix is adequate as a reflection of a preliminary estimate of the amounts of traffic involved, it is clear that the numerical values shown in the matrix must be subject to changes resulting from the particular set of operational policies adopted for a specific hospital. Not only will different operational policies be preferred in different hospitals, but also within the life of a single hospital policies may well be revised or replaced by others within the same overall physical framework. As a result, we suggest that in different hospitals the numerical values shown in the matrix may be quite different, and we hope that the models described in this paper may go some way towards indicating how the matrix should be changed in specific cases.

Of course, computer modelling of activity patterns is by no means new to hospital planning. A number of models already exists for simulating the results of different decisions concerning, for example, admissions policies, bed allocation policies, and operating-theatre schedules, but whilst these models are clearly valuable for the purposes for which they were designed, they are in practice of little use in the physical planning of a whole hospital. The reason for this is that these models are all concerned with one specific small part of a hospital, and whilst they are of value for finding optimum solutions to their own particular problems, the effects on the hospital as a whole due to changes in one of its parts tends to be outside their scope. Also, these models have in general been developed for administrative purposes rather than for planning purposes, whereas we have set out here to take a much broader view of the hospital and to combine these two areas.

Many problems arose in developing a suitable model to meet our requirements and the most serious of these resulted from the fact that a hospital is an exceedingly complex organisation. *Figure 2* shows the plan of Newmarket General Hospital and we may see from this diagram that even a very small hospital such as this consists of a large number of quite different sections, and although these may be physically self-contained and even geographically quite isolated from each other they are nonetheless constantly interacting with each other throughout the day and night and, on the face of it, our task in setting out to model the detailed activity patterns in a whole hospital is prohibitively large. In practice we are left with the choice of either taking a rather superficial view of the whole hospital or, alternatively, taking a much more detailed view of each of a number of different wards and departments in turn, but neither approach is very satisfactory on its own. If we only take an overall superficial view of the hospital, then the results will inevitably lack detail, whereas if we only followed the more detailed approach by looking at each ward and department in turn then we would risk making insufficient allowance for the close inter-relationships between these wards and departments. In view of this we decided to look at each of the two possible approaches in turn, and we developed two quite different types of model which reflect the different levels of detail.

In the first place, we developed a simple model for predicting the total amounts and the types of daily traffic between the wards and departments in the hope that this information would give us at least a very rough overall view of the activity patterns in the whole hospital. In developing this model we were only interested in the movements of people around the hospital and it was not necessary at this stage to know anything in detail about the activity patterns within the

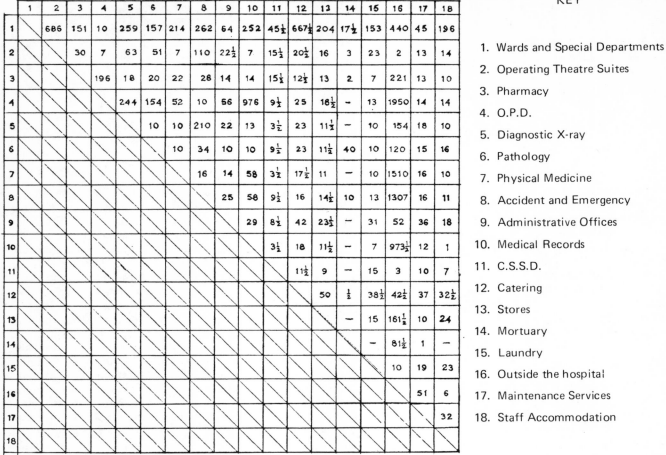

	1	2	3	4	5	6	7	8	9	10	11	12	13	14	15	16	17	18
1		686	151	10	259	157	214	262	64	252	45½	667½	204	17½	153	440	45	196
2			30	7	63	51	7	110	22½	7	15½	20½	16	3	23	2	13	14
3				196	18	20	22	28	14	14	15½	12½	13	2	7	221	13	10
4					244	154	52	10	56	976	9½	25	18½	–	13	1950	14	14
5						10	10	210	22	13	3½	23	11½	–	10	154	18	10
6							10	34	10	10	9½	23	11½	40	10	120	15	16
7								16	14	58	3½	17½	11	–	10	1510	16	10
8									25	58	9½	16	14½	10	13	1307	16	11
9										29	8½	42	23½	–	31	52	36	18
10											3½	18	11½	–	7	973½	12	1
11												11½	9	–	15	3	10	7
12													50	½	38½	42½	37	32½
13														–	15	161½	10	24
14															–	81½	1	–
15																10	19	23
16																	51	6
17																		32
18																		

KEY

1. Wards and Special Departments
2. Operating Theatre Suites
3. Pharmacy
4. O.P.D.
5. Diagnostic X-ray
6. Pathology
7. Physical Medicine
8. Accident and Emergency
9. Administrative Offices
10. Medical Records
11. C.S.S.D.
12. Catering
13. Stores
14. Mortuary
15. Laundry
16. Outside the hospital
17. Maintenance Services
18. Staff Accommodation

Figure 1. Matrix showing the assumed strength of association between wards and departments.

wards and departments. As a result, the model is capable of handling hospitals considerably larger than the one shown in *Figure 2* without becoming unmanageable. The output from this first model gives us the sort of information we could get by placing a man at the entrance to each ward and department with instructions to record the total numbers and the types of people arriving and leaving throughout the day and night. In the case of a specific hospital we could indeed carry out a survey of this sort to establish the patterns of daily traffic but, of course, the model has the advantage over a survey in that it allows us to examine the results of applying very many different operational policies without having to interfere with the day-to-day running of the hospital. In addition, the model allows us to speculate about the patterns of daily traffic in hospitals which have yet to be built.

Having established a rough overall view of the activity patterns in the hospital, our next step was to develop a series of models for predicting the detailed patterns of daily activity within each ward and department in turn. In terms of the plan of Newmarket General Hospital shown in *Figure 2,* this means that, whereas in the first model we were thinking of each ward and department as being a closed box which we could not look into, we are now thinking in terms of lifting the lid off each of these boxes in turn in order to see exactly what is going on inside. In practice, this required considerable care since the activity patterns within different wards and departments are related,

and, for example, it is clear that the daily routine in each of the surgical wards in a hospital is governed partly by the operating theatre schedules. As a result, these various more detailed models are closely interactive as we shall see later on, and the output from one model may be part of the input to the next, but we have found in practice that these interactions may be handled without too much difficulty. The output from one of these more detailed models is a set of timetables which show exactly what each person in the ward or department concerned is doing throughout his working hours, and one of the main uses of this information is that it allows us to deduce details about the timing and distribution of the daily traffic in the hospital which in the output from the first model was dealt with on a simple aggregated basis. In this paper, we shall describe these two different types of model in turn, and attempt to show how each one might contribute significantly to improvements in the methods used in hospital planning.

A model for predicting the patterns of daily traffic in a hospital
An Overall View of the Hospital

We shall describe first the development of a simple model for predicting the overall pattern of daily traffic in a hospital. The output from this model is a set of matrices showing the total number of journeys of various different types made on a particular day between any pair of locations in the hospital, and we have found in practice that this information gives us at

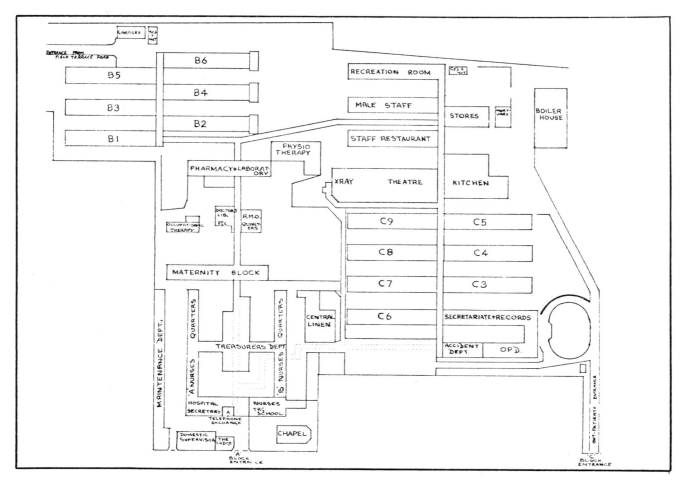

Figure 2.   Plan of Newmarket General Hospital.

least a very rough picture of the daily activity patterns in the hospital as a whole. We shall discuss very briefly how the use of the model may lead to improvements in planning the design of new hospitals by showing how the matrix in *Figure 1* should be changed in specific cases, and also how it may be used to plan limited amounts of reorganisation within existing hospitals.

Characteristics of the Daily Traffic Patterns in a Hospital

Hospital Traffic

The first step in developing the model is to decide exactly what sort of traffic we are dealing with, and how we might best set about describing it. We are thinking here in terms of the movements of people and equipment between the wards and departments, and as examples we might consider a doctor visiting each of a number of different wards on his daily 'round' or a porter taking a patient in a wheelchair from a ward to the X-ray department. This traffic may be divided into that which is essential, and that which is not essential; broadly speaking, the first category of traffic covers all journeys directly related in some way to the treatment and care of the patients, whereas the second category of traffic consists largely of journeys of a more social nature. The model we have developed in fact predicts only the essential traffic, but this is not a serious drawback since the work described in this paper is aimed at improving the design and organisation of hospitals, and it seems not unreasonable to suggest

that hospitals should be planned primarily around the treatment and care of the patients.

The essential traffic may be divided further into that which is predictable, and that which is unpredictable. From discussions with hospital staff it became clear to us that nearly all the essential traffic is predictable at least on a daily basis, and it was with this idea of predictability in mind that we developed the model. Of course, there are journeys which are essential but unpredictable (for example, we might think of the journeys which result from the death of a patient) but these are relatively few, and since our model is basically a stochastic model we may in any case allow for journeys of this type in a probabilistic way.

The essential, predictable traffic which we are interested in consists of a very large number of individual journeys, and to describe each of these journeys fully we need to specify the following three parameters:

a.   the type of person and equipment involved

b.   the place where the journey started

c.   the destination of the journey

We will now discuss these three journey parameters in turn.

Types of Journey

In our model we divided the daily traffic in the hospital into the nine categories shown in *Figure 3*, and we have labelled these v = 1, 2, 3, . . . 9. This division is, of course, quite arbitrary and we could if we wished add or remove categories according to the

```
v = 1 :   Patient on foot.

v = 2 :   Patient in wheelchair or on stretcher trolley.

v = 3 :   Nurse.

v = 4 :   Doctor.

v = 5 :   Other medical or technical staff.

v = 6 :   Porter.

v = 7 :   Porter with bulky goods or equipment, (e.g. trolley).

v = 8 :   Other ancilliary staff.

v = 9 :   Visitors, (i.e. friends and relatives).
```

Figure 3.   The categories of essential traffic.

sort of output we would like from the model. However, we have tried here to choose categories which reflect different degrees of inconvenience, or cost, for the hospital and its staff, since this will be important later when we show how the model may lead to improvements in the matrix reflecting the strength of association or link between the various wards and departments.

The Starting Points and Destinations of Journeys

To complete the description of each journey we must also specify where it began and where it will finish. Returning to the plan of Newmarket General Hospital which we gave in *Figure 2,* we first identify all the different sections, or locations, and these are listed in *Figure 4.* We have labelled these locations d = 1, 2, 3, . . . 38, and we notice in particular the importance of locations d = 37 and d = 38. These are the two entrances to the hospital and they are included as 'dummy' locations in order that we may make provision for journeys which begin or end outside the hospital.

At present we are only concerned with the movements of people around the hospital, and what actually goes on within each ward and department is not of immediate interest. In other words, it is only when a person has passed through the entrance to one of the wards or departments and out into one of the corridors that he appears in the output from the model, and as a result we may simplify the plan of the hospital and present it in the schematic form shown at the bottom of *Figure 4.* This schematic plan shows just the corridor system forming the skeleton of the hospital, and the position of the 'front door' to each ward and department, and what we are interested in now is the total number of journeys of each of the nine types discussed earlier between each pair of numbers shown on the schematic plan.

We should point out that although in this example the corridor system is very simple, so that there is rarely a question of choosing between alternative routes, this need not always be the case. In larger hospitals there may frequently be many possible routes for a journey, but we would then assume that, other things being equal, the shortest possible route is always taken.

The Technique for Recording the Traffic Patterns

Having described the three parameters used to identify the individual journeys made within the hospital, we are now in a position to record the daily traffic patterns as a matrix of the form:

$n(d_1, d_2, v)$ = the number of journeys of type v which start at location d_1 and end at location d_2 where, in the case of Newmarket General Hospital, v = 1, 2, ... 9, d_1 = 1, 2, ... 38 and d_2 = 1, 2, ... 38

This matrix is clearly very large even for quite a small hospital, and in the case of Newmarket General Hospital nearly 13,000 different types of journey are possible, at least in theory. The model in fact presents the results in the form of nine 38 x 38 matrices, with each matrix showing the number of journeys of one distinct type. So, for example, we obtain one matrix giving the journeys made by patients on foot, another one showing the journeys made by patients in a wheelchair or on a stretcher trolley, and so on. Of course, we could present the results in any alternative form we wished by rearranging the matrices, and in practice this allows us to condense the large amounts of detailed output into something more tangible. For example, we may in practice be interested in the total numbers and types of journeys beginning or ending at one particular ward or department, or we might consider the traffic passing a particular point in one of the corridors. In all cases, however, this aggregation will take place after the model has been calculated.

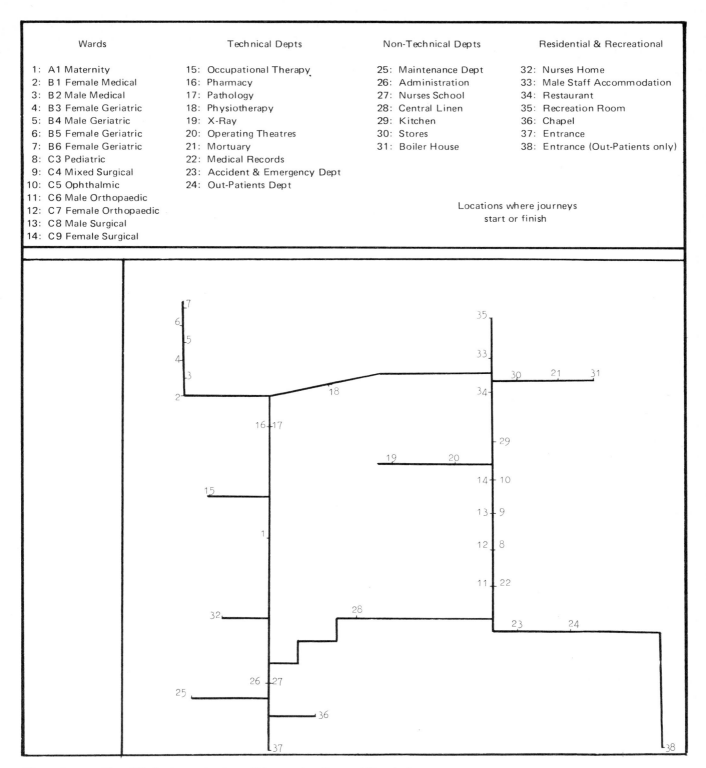

Wards	Technical Depts	Non-Technical Depts	Residential & Recreational
1: A1 Maternity	15: Occupational Therapy	25: Maintenance Dept	32: Nurses Home
2: B1 Female Medical	16: Pharmacy	26: Administration	33: Male Staff Accommodation
3: B2 Male Medical	17: Pathology	27: Nurses School	34: Restaurant
4: B3 Female Geriatric	18: Physiotherapy	28: Central Linen	35: Recreation Room
5: B4 Male Geriatric	19: X-Ray	29: Kitchen	36: Chapel
6: B5 Female Geriatric	20: Operating Theatres	30: Stores	37: Entrance
7: B6 Female Geriatric	21: Mortuary	31: Boiler House	38: Entrance (Out-Patients only)
8: C3 Pediatric	22: Medical Records		
9: C4 Mixed Surgical	23: Accident & Emergency Dept		
10: C5 Ophthalmic	24: Out-Patients Dept		
11: C6 Male Orthopaedic		Locations where journeys	
12: C7 Female Orthopaedic		start or finish	
13: C8 Male Surgical			
14: C9 Female Surgical			

Figure 4.   Simplified schematic plan of Newmarket General Hospital.

The Prediction of the Daily Traffic Patterns in the Hospital

The Principles behind the Model

The model we have developed for predicting the numerical entries in the matrix $n(d_1, d_2, v)$, in other words the total number of journeys of type v made on a particular day starting from location d_1 and finishing at location d_2, is based on two main principles which are as follows:

a.   Firstly, we have assumed that all the essential activities going on in a hospital arise directly from the needs of the members of one or other of the five classes of 'activity generating agents' listed in *Figure 5*. Provided our interest is confined to the essential activities only, then this assumption seems not unreasonable.

b.   The members of each of the five classes of 'activity generating agents' give rise to very many different individual activities, but, of course, by no means all of these result in traffic of the sort

117

g = 1 :   THE IN-PATIENTS

g = 2 :   THE OUT-PATIENTS

g = 3 :   THE ACCIDENT AND EMERGENCY CASES

g = 4 :   THE STAFF

g = 5 :   THE WARDS AND DEPARTMENTS AS 'HOTEL-TYPE ROOMS'

THE ACTIVITIES WHICH RESULT IN TRAFFIC

IN-PATIENTS	OUT-PATIENTS	ACCIDENT AND EMERGENCY CASES	STAFF	WARDS AND DEPARTMENTS AS 'HOTEL ROOMS'
1: SURGERY	13: X-RAY	20: SURGERY	29: STAFF ON-DUTY	32: CLEARING RUBBISH
2: X-RAY	14: PATHOLOGY	21: X-RAY	30: STAFF OFF-DUTY	33: DELIVERY OF STORES
3: PATHOLOGY	15: PHARMACY	22: PATHOLOGY	31: STAFF TO MEALS	34: MEALS FOR PATIENTS
4: PHYSIOTHERAPY	16: PHYSIOTHERAPY	23: PHARMACY		35: LAUNDRY
5: OCCUPATIONAL THERAPY	17: SEEING DOCTORS	24: ADMISSION		36: CLEANING
6: PHARMACY	18: ARRIVAL	25: SEEING DOCTOR		37: MAINTENANCE
7: ADMISSION	19: DEPARTURE	26: DEATH		38: ADMINISTRATION
8: DISCHARGE		27: ARRIVAL		
9: TRANSFER		28: DEPARTURE		
10: SEEING DOCTORS				
11: DEATH				
12: SEEING VISITORS				

Figure 5.   Traffic-generating activities

which concerns us here. For instance, the in-patients in a hospital generate many activities which take place wholly within a ward. The second main assumption behind our model is that for each of the five classes of 'activity-generating agents' in turn we can draw up a list of all those activities which result in the sort of traffic we are interested in. In the case of Newmarket General Hospital, the activity lists we have used in developing the model are shown in *Figure 5*.

We see that in this case there are 38 relevant activities, and we have labelled these serially from a = 1 up to a = 38. Of course, when applying the same model to a larger hospital we may have to extend this list of activities to allow, for example, for journeys made to highly special-ised departments, such as radiotherapy, which are absent from Newmarket General Hospital, but this is purely a matter of detail and it does not affect the principle behind the model.

Our use of the word 'activity' in the context of this model calls for some explanation. We are using the word 'activity' here in a very broad sense, and, for example, under the heading a = 2, or 'X-ray' we include all journeys and tasks which are related directly to the processes of taking patients to the X-ray department, taking X-ray photographs, returning the patients to the wards and also delivering the final developed pictures as required. As a result, the activity we have labelled 'X-ray' under the general heading of in-patients may encompass not only journeys made by the in-patients and X-ray department staff, but also journeys made by porters and nurses. We have defined the activities in this very broad way in order that each of the essential journeys we are interested in predicting should be the direct result of just one of the 38 activities listed in *Figure 5*. The great advantage of this is that in the model it is then possible to work through the complete list of 38 activities and calculate in turn the individual contribution each one on its own makes towards the daily traffic patterns in the hospital. The overall pattern of daily traffic may then be found by adding together the individual contributions of all 38 activities in the list.

The model, in fact, consists of five parts, each of which deals with one of the five classes of 'activity generating agents'. We will describe firstly how the model predicts the traffic generated by the in-patients, and then we will discuss very briefly how the calculations for the other four classes differ.

Calculating the Traffic Generated by the In-Patients

The technique for calculating the contribution made by the in-patients towards the overall traffic patterns in a hospital is represented in *Figure 6* in the form of a simple flow diagram. There are six main steps involved in these calculations, and they may be sum-marised in the following way:

a.   Firstly, we identify the different types of in-patient found in the hospital. In the case of Newmarket General Hospital there are ten main types, and these are listed in *Figure 7*. However, we could easily subdivide each of these 10 categories to allow, for example, for the different physical conditions of certain patients without upsetting the principles behind the model.

b.   The second step is to look at the distribution of the 10 types of in-patient within the hospital. In other words, we find out exactly whereabouts on the plan of the hospital shown in *Figure 4* the members of this first class of 'activity generating agents' are located. Of course, the in-patient population within the hospital will often change from one day to the next, and as a result the traffic patterns themselves will vary and this will be reflected in the output from the model.

c.   The next step is to return to the list of activities generated by the in-patients and define a 'unit quantity' for each one in turn. Earlier we identified 12 activities generated by the in-patients which result in movements round the hospital, and these are shown again in *Figure 7* alongside the corresponding 'units'. To a large extent the choice of units is obvious and straightforward, although we might make special note here of the choice of a non-singular 'unit' for activity number 12.

d.   We must then derive the probability that, on a typical day, an in-patient of each of the 10 different types identified earlier generates a unit, or more than one unit, of each of the 12 relevant activities which result in traffic round the hospital. This sort of information is largely of a medical nature, and although we will not go into details here, the information is not particularly difficult to find in practice.

e.   Once we know the probability that an individual in-patient of each type generates a unit of one or other of the 12 relevant activities, and already we know the in-patient population within each ward, then we are in a position to estimate the total numbers of units of these activities generated on a particular day in the various parts of the hospital, and we have denoted this in *Figure 6* by the values of N(d,a).

f.   The final, and perhaps the most important, step in the model is to relate the number of units of an activity generated in different parts of the hospital to the resulting journeys between the wards and departments, and we do this by defining the 'operational policy' for the activity which, broadly speaking, describes 'how the activity gets done' in that specific hospital. To demonstrate more clearly what we mean here the operational policy governing the activity 'surgery' may state for example that patients must be taken individually from ward to theatre by a theatre porter, and that at all time during transit they must be accompanied by a nurse; in this case, each 'unit' of the activity 'surgery' will result in 10 distinct journeys, which are as follows:

  1.   Theatre porter travels from the theatre to the ward.
  2.   Theatre porter returns to the theatre with . . .
  3.   The patient on a stretcher trolley, and accompanied by . . .

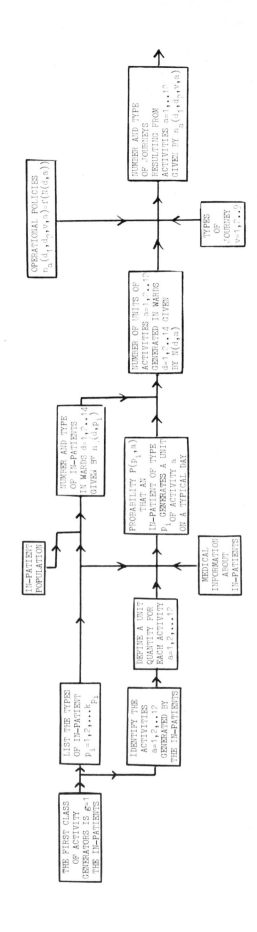

Figure 6.   Flow chart for calculating the traffic generated by the in-patients

4. A nurse.
5. The nurse then returns to her ward.
6. After the operation the nurse travels to the theatre suite.
7. The theatre porter then transports . . .
8. The patient back to the ward accompanied again by . . .
9. The nurse.
10. Finally the theatre porter returns to the theatre suite.

Once we have specified the ward where this 'unit' of surgery was generated then we may interpret these 10 distinct journeys in terms of the entries in the traffic matrix $n(d_1, d_2, v)$. For example if the patient came from the male surgical ward identified in *Figure 4* as location 13, then the first of the 10 journeys would add one to the entry for $n(20,13,6)$ in the matrix produced as output from the model. Clearly a different operational policy, such as a policy of using general porters rather than special theatre porters to transport patients, would result in a different set of journeys, but in all cases the operational policy may be expressed in the following quite general form:

$$n_a (d_1, d_2, v) = f N (d, a)$$

Where $N(d,a)$ is the number of units of activity a generated at location d, and $n(d_1, d_2, v)$ is the resulting number of journeys of type v which start at location d_1 and end at location d_2. The way in which this general equation arises may be seen from the example given earlier.

These calculations, which are portrayed in *Figure 6* by the flow diagram, must be carried out for each of the 12 relevant activities in turn, and then by combining the results together we may deduce the total contribution made by the in-patients towards the traffic patterns in the hospital.

Of course the in-patients are responsible for only part of the daily traffic within the hospital, and the remainder of the model is concerned with the corresponding contributions made by each of the other four classes of 'activity generating agents'. In fact the calculations for the other four classes are very similar to those for the in-patients, and we shall only briefly mention the more important differences in each case.

Calculating the Traffic Generated by the Out-patients

The technique involved in calculating the traffic generated by the out-patients is very similar to that portrayed in *Figure 6,* although we see from *Figure 5* that in the case of Newmarket General Hospital there are only 7 activities to consider in contrast to the 12 for the in-patients. Furthermore all the 'units' of these seven activities are generated in the same place, that is the out-patients' department, and so in this case the pattern of the resulting journeys is somewhat more straightforward.

Calculating the Traffic Generated by the Accident and Emergency Cases

The calculations for the accident and emergency cases are virtually identical to those for the outpatients, except that we see from *Figure 5* that two further activities are included, namely 'death' and 'admission', neither of which affects the outpatients. Otherwise the only difference is that the 'units' of these activities are generated in the accident and emergency department, which we have labelled as location 23 in *Figure 4*.

Calculating the Traffic Generated by the Staff

We see from *Figure 5* that in our model we only attach three activites to the members of staff which result in traffic within the hospital. The reason for this is that although the staff clearly engage in many other activites involving journeys around the hospital, these in general are related directly to the needs of the patients and have, therefore, been dealt with in the earlier calculations. The only journeys not covered by the other calculations are the journeys on- and off-duty and to meals, but the method for predicting these movements is similar to that shown in *Figure 6*.

TYPES OF IN-PATIENT

$p_i = 1, 2, \ldots k_{p_i}$

p_i = 1 : SURGICAL

p_i = 2 : MEDICAL

p_i = 3 : CHESTS

p_i = 4 : GERIATRIC

p_i = 5 : E.N.T.

p_i = 6 : ORTHOPAEDIC

p_i = 7 : OPHTHALMIC

p_i = 8 : GYNAECOLOGICAL

p_i = 9 : MATERNITY

p_i = 10 : PEDIATRIC

a=1 : SURGERY	:	THE PERFORMANCE OF ONE OPERATION
a=2 : X-RAY	:	THE TAKING OF ONE PATIENT'S PHOTOGRAPHS
a=3 : PATHOLOGY	:	THE ANALYSIS OF ONE PATIENT'S SPECIMEN
a=4 : PHYSIOTHERAPY	:	ONE PATIENT'S TREATMENT BY PHYSIOTHERAPIST
a=5 : OCCUPATIONAL THERAPY	:	ONE PATIENT'S TREATMENT BY OCCUPATIONAL THERAPIST
a=6 : PHARMACY	:	THE PROVISION OF ONE PATIENT'S DRUGS
a=7 : ADMISSION	:	THE ADMISSION OF ONE PATIENT
a=8 : DISCHARGE	:	THE DISCHARGE OF ONE PATIENT
a=9 : TRANSFER	:	THE TRANSFER OF ONE PATIENT
a=10: SEEING DOCTORS	:	THE EXAMINATION OF ONE PATIENT
a=11: DEATH	:	THE DEATH OF ONE PATIENT
a=12: SEEING VISITORS	:	ONE PATIENT SEEING TWO FRIENDS OR RELATIVES

Figure 7.   In-patients and their activities.

Calculating the Traffic Generated by the Wards and Departments as 'Hotel Rooms'

The final group of 'activity generating agents' are the wards and departments considered as 'hotel rooms'. Under this heading we deal with all the remaining essential domestic and administrative activities which result in journeys within the hospital, and in the case of Newmarket General Hospital we found that there are 7 such activities to be considered. These are the activities which we cannot relate directly to the needs of specific patients, but rather contribute towards providing 'hotel' facilities within the hospital. The method used to predict the traffic resulting from these final 7 activities is, however, similar to that shown in *Figure 6*.

The Complete Model

For each of the five classes of 'activity generating agents' we may produce a flow diagram similar to the one for the in-patients shown in *Figure 6*. Now we defined the 38 activities listed in *Figure 5* in such a way that each essential journey made within the hospital was accounted for under just one of these activities, and so to deduce the overall traffic patterns we simply need to add together the contributions made by each individual activity on its own. The flow diagram for the whole model, which is shown in *Figure 8*, therefore consists of five parts each of which, taken on its own, resembles *Figure 6*. The top part of *Figure 8* is of course identical to the earlier diagram and deals with activities 1, 2, 3, . . . 12, whilst the other four parts correspond to the outpatients, the accident and emergency cases, the staff, and the wards and departments as 'hotel rooms', and deal with activities 12 to 19, 20 to 28, 29 to 31 and 32 to 38 respectively. The final output from the model, in the shape of the overall traffic matrix $n(d_1, d_2, v)$, is produced by amalgamation at the point marked 'A' in the diagram.

In this paper we have described the model in terms of Newmarket General Hospital which is of course rather small by modern standards. However, it is important to point out here that this choice of hospital was quite arbitrary, and that by revising or extending the list of activities given in *Figure 5* we may apply the same model to quite different, or much larger, hospitals without having to revise the basic principles described earlier.

The Uses of the Model

Many of the journeys made in a hospital are in some sense undesirable. For example, journeys involving the movement of very ill patients introduce a risk of a setback in their recovery, whereas the movement of bulky goods or equipment clearly hinders the rest of the traffic in the hospital. As a result, there are certain types of journey which may appear in the output from our simple traffic model which should as far as possible be avoided, or failing this at least kept as short and brief as possible. Now an important lesson we have learned from using the model shown in *Figure 8* is that different operational policies may give rise to quite different patterns of daily traffic in a hospital, and since we recognise that some journeys are less desirable than others this suggests that in specific cases there may be considerable scope for improving the compatibility of the operational policies and the physical layout of the various wards and departments. Our approach has been to put a 'cost' per unit distance on each of the different types of journey which may occur within the hospital and then use the model to determine the total 'cost' of the essential daily traffic patterns. The additional calculations involved in this operation are shown on the extreme right of *Figure 8*. If the total 'cost' of the essential daily traffic patterns is found upon calculation to be high then the operational policies and the physical layouts of the wards and departments are badly suited, and if possible one or other should be changed accordingly. Our suggestion is that, other things being equal, the operational policies and the physical layout of the hospital should be chosen in such a way that the total cost of the essential daily traffic patterns is kept as low as possible.

In practice these ideas may be equally well applied both to the design of a new hospital and to planning certain improvements within an existing hospital. In an existing hospital the physical layout will probably be fixed so that any optimisation of the traffic patterns must be achieved through changes in the operational policies applied to the wards and departments. In this case we may feed different sets of operational policies into our model at the point marked 'B' in *Figure 8*, and then finally select the set of policies which result in the lowest overall 'cost'. On the other hand, when designing a completely new hospital the physical layout is highly flexible and may be chosen in order to suit some predetermined set of journeys predicted by the model, since although the predetermined policies remain fixed the spatial relationship between the wards and departments may be changed at will. Then by feeding in different alternative physical plans, or by using a standard algorithm, we may search for the particular layout of the wards and departments which best suits the choice of policies. In addition there are intermediate cases where, for example, new buildings are being erected on an existing site, or existing buildings may be put to different uses, but these are handled in more or less the same manner.

Discussion on the First Model

The first half of this paper has described a simple model for predicting the overall patterns of daily traffic in a hospital, and the last section discussed very briefly how this model may be used as an aid in hospital planning. Many objections may be raised against a simple method of this sort and perhaps the most serious of these are, firstly, that it is excessively 'mechanical' and, secondly, that it makes certain assumptions which are patently unrealistic; for example, the model assumes that the journeys associated with each individual surgical operation are unrelated, whereas in practice a theatre porter may in certain cases collect a new patient at the same time as he returns the previous one to the ward. However, it is important to remember that any hospital is an exceedingly complex organisation, and that to obtain any useful results at all we have to simplify its behaviour to such an extent that it does obey a set of 'mechanical' rules. The most critical step in building an activity model of the sort described in this paper is deciding which simplifications are reasonable and which are not, and thereby arriving at the set of 'mechanical' rules which are appropriate in a particular case.

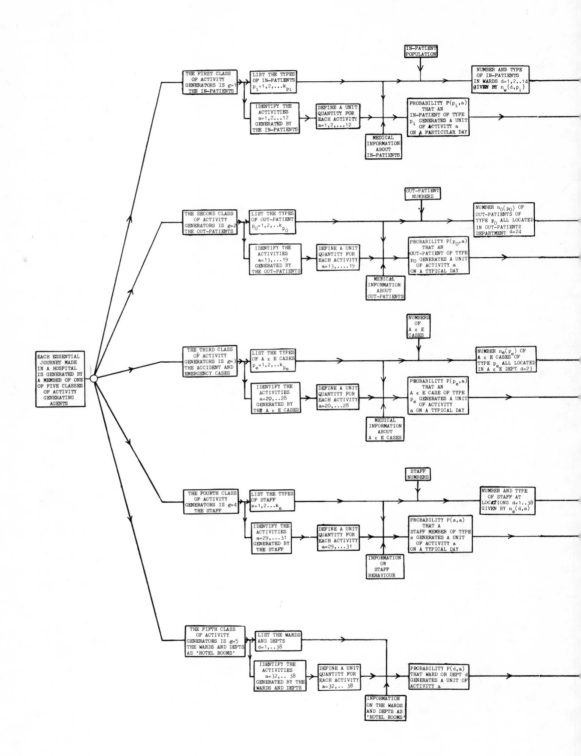

Figure 8.   Flow chart for calculating the essential daily traffic.

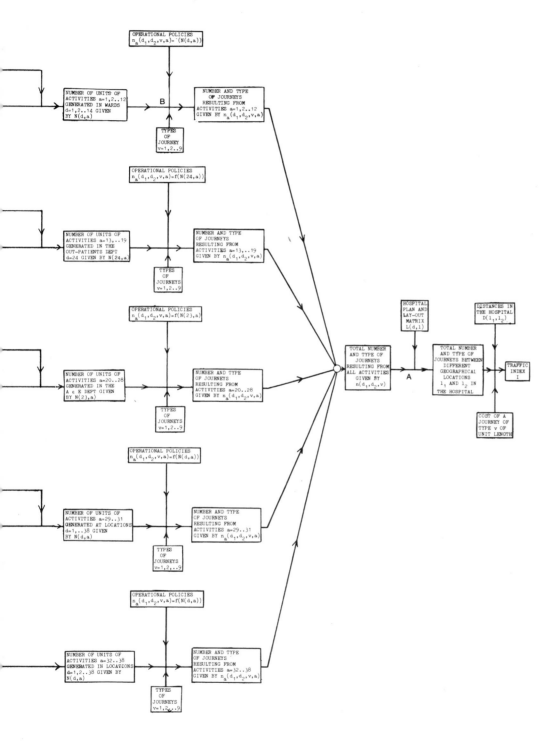

A further objection to the model is that it only gives the aggregated traffic patterns, whereas in some cases it would be useful to find out how this traffic is distributed throughout the day and night. However, this objection is not serious since we saw earlier that in many areas of planning it is the aggregated traffic patterns which are important, and in any case the models described in the second half of this paper will give us the distribution of the daily traffic if we find we need to know it.

In practice we have found that our simple 'mechanical' model has given us valuable insights into the working of a hospital, and that it has provided us with a useful and sensible framework on which to construct our more detailed investigations into the activity patterns within specific wards or departments.

Models for predicting the patterns of daily activity within the wards and departments

A Detailed View of the Hospital

Having established a rough overall view of the activity patterns in the whole hospital, the next step in the study was to develop a series of models for predicting the detailed patterns of daily activity within each ward and department in turn. In terms of the plan of Newmarket Hospital shown in *Figure 2*, this means that we now take the lid off each of the 'closed boxes' in turn and see exactly what is going on inside. Our object now is to predict what each person in one of these wards or departments is doing at various points in time throughout his working day.

There are two main reasons for our taking this more detailed view of the hospital. Firstly, the earlier model predicted just the total numbers and types of journeys made on a particular day between different parts of the hospital, but we find that by looking in more detail at exactly what goes on within the wards and departments we may now go on to deduce how this traffic is distributed throughout the day and night. This type of information could be very important if, for example, congestion on the staircases or in the lifts were a problem.

Secondly, these more detailed models allow us to carry out simple experiments to test the effects of different policy decisions affecting the daily routines in the wards and departments. Clearly it is important to ensure that a particular choice of operational policies does not impose an impossible workload or an undesirable routine on any member of staff.

The output produced by these more detailed models is a set of timetables and we show an example of one of these in *Figure 9*. These timetables show the exact location of the staff throughout their working hours and the various activities they become

involved in, and equipped with this information we may deduce details about the time at which the different journeys round the hospital take place.

We started this more detailed part of the study by developing a model for predicting the daily activity pattern within one of the wards. We chose the wards as the starting point because they are the most prominent feature in the hospital and also because of the important part the in-patients play in determining the activity patterns in the rest of the hospital. However, the models for the different departments are very similar in concept.

We mentioned at the outset that the activities in the various wards and departments are related, and the overall traffic patterns predicted by the first model go some way towards indicating the nature of the relationship involved. Clearly, in order to construct a model for predicting the daily activity patterns within a single ward on its own, we must recognise these interrelationships and find some way of allowing for them.

Firstly, we must look in some detail at the form these relationships take. What we find is that the various journeys into and out of the ward impose certain constraints on the times at which some activities may take place, and, for example, the journey of a patient to the operating theatre imposes quite a rigid constraint on the time at which this patient is given his premedication. Clearly, in this case it is the actual timing of the journey rather than merely its occurrence which is all important. In *Figure 10* we outline briefly how these constraints arise, and how the model for predicting the daily routine in the operating theatres also plays a part in determining the activity patterns in the various different surgical wards. In a very similar way we show in *Figure 11* how the staff 'rounds' link the activity patterns in several different wards.

The next step is to decide how we may allow for these interrelationships. What we do is to take the constraints imposed on the ward routine by the different journeys as part of the input to the ward model, and we assume that this is given beforehand. The more detailed models are obviously closely interactive and the output from one may form part of the input to the next.

Characteristics of the Daily Activity Patterns in the Wards

The Data Required to Predict the Activity Patterns

The object of the ward model is to assign particular activities to each member of the ward staff and thereby arrive at a timetable for the day in the ward. We assume that these activities result from the needs

TIME	9am	10am	11am	12am	1pm	2pm	3pm	4pm	5pm	
LOCATION		Office	Ward 1	Ward 2	Ward 3	Can-teen	Clinic		Mess	
ACTIVITY		Plan theatre lists	Ward rounds			Lunch	Out-patients visits		Tea	

Figure 9.   A Consultant's daily activity.

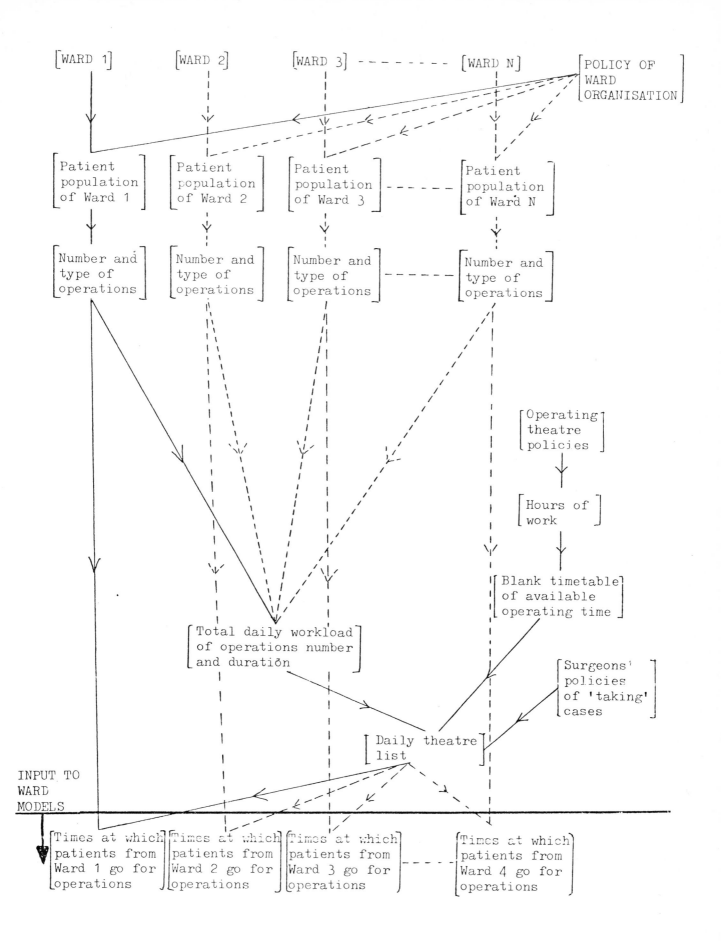

Figure 10.   Operating theatre routines.

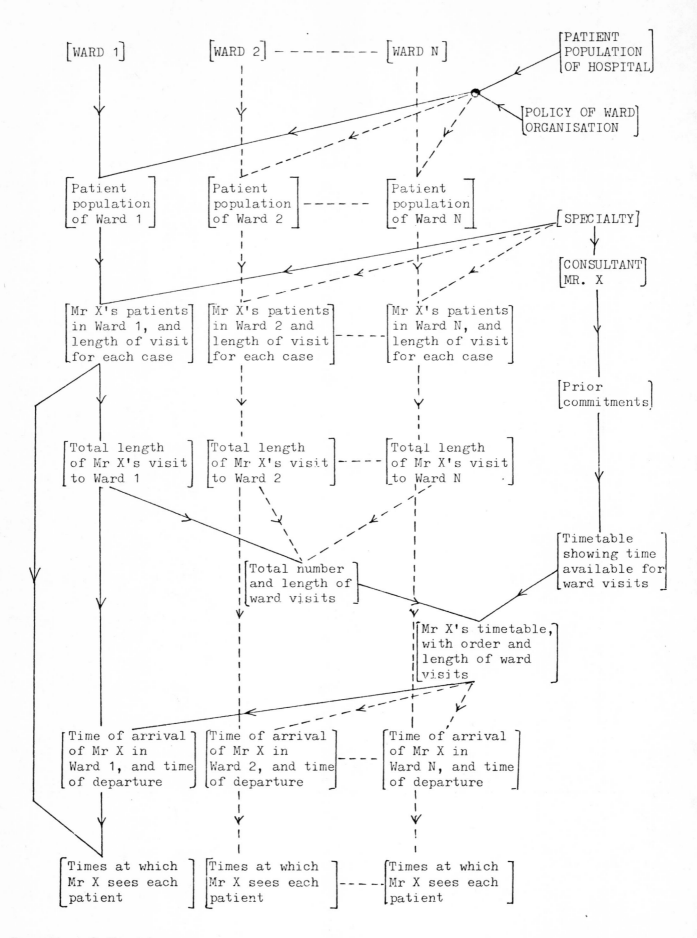

Figure 11.   Staff rounds.

of the in-patients, and so the first lot of data we require is concerned with the patient population of the ward.

We need to know the number of patients of different types at the various stages in their illness, since these are the factors which govern the amount of work to be accomplished on any particular day. The patient population in a ward generally changes from one day to the next, and these changes will be reflected in the corresponding sets of time-tables. In fact one useful function of the ward model is to assess how serious these changes are, and to arrive at a policy to allow for the fluctuations in the workload. We have constructed a simple 'sub-model' for generating the patient population in a ward on successive days, but will not go into this detail here.

The next lot of data we require are details about the numbers and types of staff working in the ward, in other words the number of people available to engage in the various daily activities. On the reasonable basis that the nursing activities always take priority in the ward, we consider here just the nursing staff and omit from the discussion, for the time being, the remaining domestic and auxiliary staff. In practice the staffing levels, for the nurses in particular, reflect the average workload expected in the wards, and on this basis we have developed a simple formula for calculating the number of nurses who should be assigned to any specific ward as a function of the typical patient population in the ward. However, as with the in-patient population sub-model, we will not go into the details of this formula here, but merely draw attention to its existence.

The Essential Daily Activities

Having dealt with the patients who generate the activities in the ward, and the nursing staff who carry out the various tasks which arise, the next step is to consider exactly what activities are involved in relating the needs of the in-patients to the nurses' daily routine. In contrast to the first half of this paper, where we were thinking of activities in a very broad sense, we are now using the word 'activity' to refer to one of a large number of highly specific 'tasks'. For the purposes of outlining the principles behind the ward model we shall confine our attention here to the nursing activities or 'tasks'.

We notice firstly that the activites within a ward may be broadly classified as either 'essential' or 'non-essential' according to whether their absence from the daily routine would, or would not, jeopardise the patients' treatment and recovery. For example, the medicine rounds are clearly essential activities, whereas cutting the patients' hair and fingernails is one activity which may be excluded from the daily routine without causing any undue hardship. A basic assumption behind the model is that essential activities always have priority over non-essential activities.

We also assume that the essential activities are predictable at least on a day-to-day basis, and although this may at first glance seem to be a gross oversimplification it is not too unreasonable in practice. Of course, some totally unpredictable activities do occur (such as, for instance, the death of a patient) but, in fact, activities of this type fill only a very small proportion of the daily timetable for a ward.

On the basis that the vast majority of the essential activities are predictable we now compile a list of all the essential nursing 'tasks' which arise at some time throughout the day and night, and we show the first part of this list in *Figure 12*. The whole list extends to some 95 nursing tasks, and we assume that any additional taks not included in this total must be non-essential. We should point out that, whilst *Figure 12* may reflect the typical routine in certain wards, the order of the tasks shown here is quite arbitrary and in no way influences or constrains the output from the model.

The Extent of each Essential Activity

The object of the ward model is to arrange the essential tasks listed in *Figure 12* into a particular pattern on a timetable, but before we can start considering how to do this we must decide on the extent of each task, that is the total amount of nurses' time each one occupies. This is clearly a function of the number, type and condition of the patients, and since we have already dealt with the patient population it is now a simple matter to work through all 95 activities in turn and calculate the total number of nurse-minutes each one will occupy on the particular day being considered There is in practice no shortage of the basic medical information required for these calculations.

The Constraints on the Daily Activities

The final step before describing the actual model is to consider the constraints which govern how we place each of the 95 essential nursing tasks on a timetable. We have found that for each activity there may be up to four basic constraints, which are as follows:

a. A constraint on the number of nurses involved in the activity, and on whether one nurse can take over from another.

b. A constraint on whether the activity is continuous or split up into several parts. In other words, once the activity has been started must it be carried through to completion without a break? Also, related to tnis, will the activity be started if, in fact, it is clear that it cannot be completed without a break?

c. A constraint on the time at which the activity is started.

d. A constraint on the time at which the activity is completed.

The first two constraints govern the shape of the space allocated to the activity on the timetable, whereas the other two govern its actual position. It is through the second pair of constraints that we take care of the interrelationships between the activity patterns in different wards and departments which we discussed earlier.

The constraints show up a clear subdivision of the 95 essential activities into those which are 'scheduled', such as meals, and those which are 'un-scheduled' such as bedmaking. Scheduled activities take place at a predetermined time each day, although it is important to bear in mind that this need not be the same time each day; for example, although helping the consultant with his round is clearly a scheduled activity, the time at which it occurs may be quite different from one day to the next depending upon

TIME	STAFF	NURSING DUTIES	ORDERLY'S DUTIES	DOMESTIC DUTIES	VISITORS
6.00 a.m.	2 night nurses	N(1) Patients awakened N(2) Temperatures taken now or later N(3) Special 6 or 8 hourly medicines N(4) Cups of tea and early breakfasts N(5) Fluids charted N(6) Sanitary round and outputs charted N(7) Urine specimens collected and tested for diabetics and new patients N(8) Patients prepared for operations (early) N(9) Special treatments, e.g. rectal irrigation for morning X-ray N(10) Test meals commenced N(11) Dressing if required early N(12) I.V. infusions maintained N(13) Bathe seriously ill patients with special attention to the mouth			V(1) Night sister on her final round
7.00 a.m.		N(14) Some beds made now N(15) Bowls given out to patients capable of washing themselves N(16) Attention to pressure areas N(17) Mouth washes given N(18) Bowls and mouth washes cleared N(14) General bedmaking begins N(19) Accept stores from porters		(Maid comes on duty) D(1) Collects glassware and crockery from lockers, washes up and puts on trolley for later use D(2) Cleans ward floor with suction cleaner D(3) Dusts furniture D(4) Cleans lockers and table tops	V(2) Porters in and out with refuse V(3) Porters with stores
7.30 a.m.	6 day nurses and staff nurse come on duty	N(20) Reports from night nurses N(14) Beds made, if not earlier N(21) Patients prepared for theatre list N(2) Temperatures taken now if not earlier N(22) Fresh water jugs and glasses given out N(23) Medicines and special drugs such as insulin and premedication N(24) Night nurses give written reports			
8.00 a.m.	Sister comes on duty, 2 night nurses go off duty	N(25) Night nurses report to sister and go off duty N(26) Breakfast and special diets served	(Orderly comes on duty) O(1) Dusts and cleans lockers O(2) Cleans sterilizer and instruments		
8.45 a.m.	4 nurses and sister go to coffee	N(27) Seriously ill patients fed N(28) Fluids charted N(29) Sanitary round and outputs charted N(30) Give and clear handbowls	O(3) Prepares sterilizer for morning use O(4) Scrubs mackintoshes O(5) Attends to flowers	D(5) Clear breakfast and washes up	V(4) Newsagent

Time	Nursing (N)	Orderly (O)	Maid (D)	Visitors (V)
		(Orderly goes to coffee)	(Maid goes to coffee)	(Ward open)
9.00 a.m.	N(31) Medicine round			V(5) House officers
	N(32) Prepare trolleys for dressings			V(6) Physiotherapist
	N(33) Accompany patients to theatre and X-ray etc.			V(7) Lab. technician collects specimens
9.15 a.m. Sister and 4 nurses return, 2 nurses and staff nurse go to coffee	N(34) Sister does round of patients, kitchen and other ancilliary rooms			V(8) Dietician
	(Nursing treatments start)	(Orderly returns)	(Maid returns)	V(9) Consultants
9.30 a.m.	N(35) Dressings	O(6) Cleans hand bowls	D(6) Cleans hand-basins in ward	V(10) Registrar
	N(36) Attention to the seriously ill	O(7) Puts out clean linen in ancillary rooms and at ward hand basins	D(7) Clean all ancillary rooms, sinks, toilet articles, w.c's etc.	V(11) Nursing admin. staff
	N(37) Bathing patients in bathroom			
9.45 a.m. 2 nurses and staff nurse return	N(38) Special treatments, e.g. dermatological	O(8) Takes messages to and from other departments	D(8) Scrubs floors	
	N(39) 4-hourly charts at 10 or 12	O(9) Receives and checks stores, hardware and linen	D(9) Cleans cupboards refrigerator and kitchen equipment	
	(Help with medical staff rounds)			
	N(40) House officers rounds			
	N(41) Physiotherapist visit	O(10) Prepares mid-morning drinks and gives these under supervision	D(10) Prepares kitchen for lunch	
	N(42) Helps lab. technician			
	N(43) Dietician's round			
	N(44) Consultants			
	N(45) Registrars			
	N(46) Nursing admin staff round	O(11) Strips beds of discharged patients		
	N(47) Admission of new patients	O(12) Makes up clean beds		
	N(48) Collection and testing of urine specimens	O(13) Cleans lockers		
	N(49) Special medicines and injections given prior to lunch	O(14) Cleans thermometers and containers		
	N(96) Discharge patients			
12.00 noon	N(50) Serves lunch	O(15) Scrubs mackintoshes		(Ward closed)
	N(51) Seriously ill patients fed	O(16) Cleans lunch		
	N(52) Fluids charted	O(17) Cleans handbowls	D(11) Washes crockery and tidies kitchen	
	N(53) Sanitary round and outputs			
	N(54) Handbowls given and cleared			
12.30 p.m. Sister and 4 nurses to lunch	N(55) Medicine round			

Figure 12. Essential tasks.

how the consultant organises his daily work, and in this context it is useful to refer back to *Figure 11.* The distinction between scheduled and unscheduled activities plays an important role in the ward model since we assume that the scheduled activities are accommodated in the timetable first, and that the unscheduled activities are then fitted in wherever time is still available, subject, of course, to the four constraints discussed earlier.

Assuming we have determined the appropriate set of constraints for each of the 95 essential nursing tasks, then we are finally in a position to start allocating these tasks to a specific position on a daily timetable according to our simple model.

The Prediction of the Daily Activity Patterns in the Wards

The Four Steps in the Ward model

The ward model fills up the daily timetable for the nurses in four distinct and serial steps, which are briefly as follows:

a. Firstly, the nurses' shift system is superimposed on the blank timetable.
b. Secondly, the scheduled essential activities are placed in their predetermined positions.
c. Thirdly, the unscheduled essential activities are allocated to those nurses who still have free time in such a way that all the constraints are satisfied.
d. Finally, any remaining nurses' time is allocated to some non-essential activities.

We shall now discuss each of these four steps in the model in turn and show how each one contributes to the final timetable of activities in the ward.

Step 1: The Shift System

The starting point for the model is a completely blank timetable which has an entry for each individual nurse and which extends over the 24 hours of both day and night. Since none of the nurses works all of the time, the first step in the model is to specify the shift system and thereby fill in those parts of the timetable where nurses are off-duty or at meals. Under a system of 'split-duties' we might typically end up with the diagram shown in *Figure 13.* This diagram shows the available nurses' time, and the purpose of the rest of the model is to fill up all this available time with essential and non-essential nursing activities.

Under a different shift system *Figure 13* could appear totally changed. In particular the system of 'split-duties' is unpopular with nurses and in many hospitals this has now been dropped in favour of simple early and late shifts. One use of the ward model is to see what effect a change of this type is likely to have on the daily routine in the wards.

Step 2: The Scheduled Activities

Once we know the number of nurses available at each point in time on the timetable then we may begin placing all the scheduled activities in their predetermined positions on the diagram shown in *Figure 13.*

We notice first that there are certain groups of scheduled activities which always occur in sequence, and in addition invariably occupy all the available nurses. Because of these special characteristics we refer to each of these groups of activities as being a 'routine', and, for example, the 'early morning routine' comprises the following seven activities:

	N (1) : Patients woken up
Early	N (2) : Temperatures taken
Morning =	N (3) : Special 6-hourly medicines given
Routine	N (4) : Cups of tea and early breakfasts

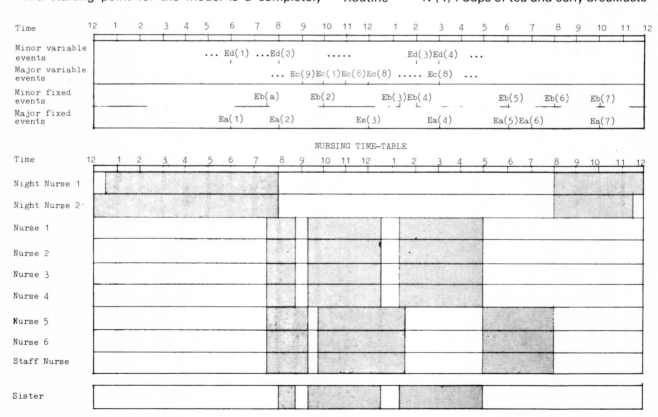

Figure 13.   The input to the model.

N (5) : Fluids charted

N (6) : Sanitary round and output charted

N (7) : Urine specimens collected and tested.

The second 'routine' during the day is the 'breakfast routine' which consists of the following five activities:

		N (26) : Breakfast and special diets
Break-		N (27) : Seriously ill patients fed
fast	=	N (28) : Fluids charted
Routine		N (29) : Sanitary round and output charted
		N (30) : Give and clear handbowls

In a similar way there are corresponding groups of activities making up the lunch, tea and supper routines' and these, together with the visiting time and late evening routines, are shown superimposed on the timetable of activities in *Figure 14.* Since each one of these routines occupies all the available staff we find that the day in the ward has now been divided up into six quite different periods of time.

We now place the remaining scheduled activities in their predetermined positions on the timetable, and, for example, we see in *Figure 14* that on this particular day the activity of helping the consultant on his round occupies a block of time in the late morning. When we have dealt with all of the scheduled essential activities then the timetable might typically appear as shown in *Figure 15.* We notice that on any particular day the corresponding framework of scheduled activities, such as the one shown in *Figure 15,* is unique and deterministic. By contrast the rest of the model is concerned with the unscheduled activities and since it is therefore non-deterministic, we must fall back on the technique of simulation.

Step 3: The Unscheduled Activities

Not all the 95 essential activities are accounted for in *Figure 15,* since many of them are unscheduled and have up to now been left out, so the next step is to accommodate the remaining essential activities into the spaces still vacant in the diagram in such a way that the four sets of constraints which we discussed earlier are satisfied. We have developed a simple sampling technique for predicting a series of feasible timetables for the unscheduled activities, but will not go into details about techniques here.

When all 95 essential tasks have been allocated to the nurses then the timetable might typically appear as shown in *Figure 16.* It is clear from the diagram that on this particular day the essential work is insufficient to keep all the nurses fully occupied, and so in this case there are times during the day when some of the nursing staff will engage in non-essential work. This brings us to the final part of the model.

Step 4: The Non-Essential Activities

To fill up the remaining blank spaces in *Figure 16* and thereby complete the timetable for the ward we adopted a simple 'time-budget' approach. We first drew up a list of all the non-essential activities which we thought were relevant in the particular ward we were looking at. We then divided the day into a series of periods, and for each period we specified the probability that a nurse who is free from any essential work will engage in one particular non-essential

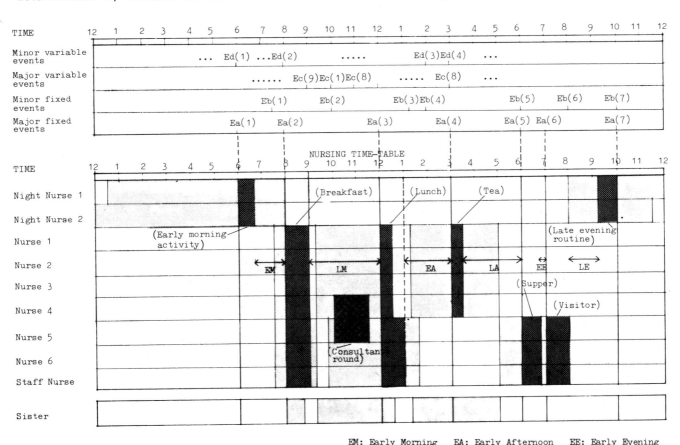

Figure 14.   Stage (1) in the model.

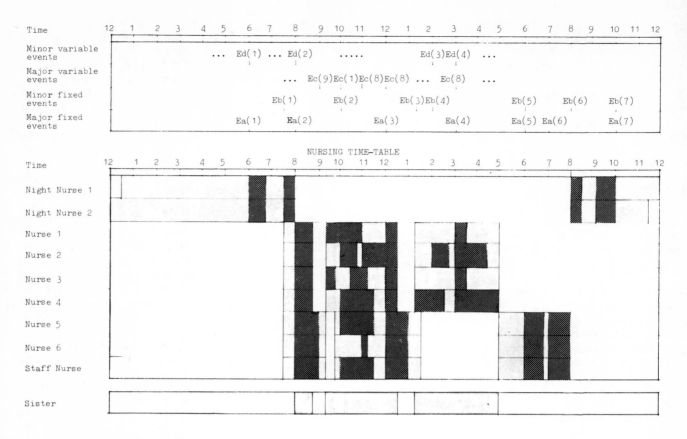

Figure 15.   Stage (2) in the model.

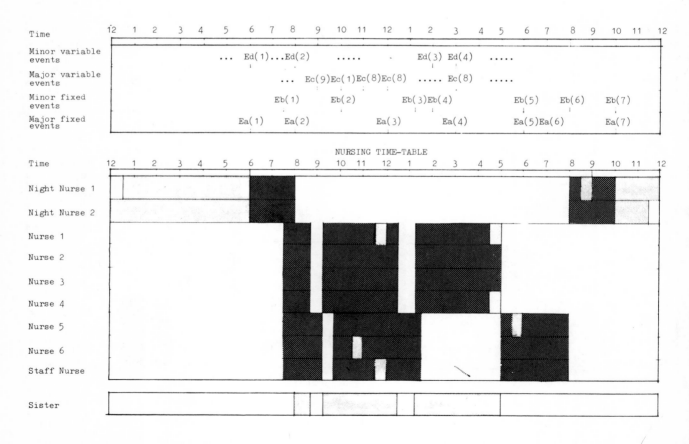

Figure 16.   Stage (3) in the model.

activity from our list. In this way we built up the table of probabilities representing the 'time-budget', part of which is shown in *Figure 17*.

The final step in the model consists of working through all the remaining blank spaces in *Figure 16*, and for each space in turn sampling from the appropriate row in the 'time-budget' shown in *Figure 17*. The timetable for the daily activities in the ward is then finally completed.

	Tidying cupboards	Getting patients up	Tidying lockers	Extra patient care	...
Early morning (6.00—8.00)	0.2	0.0	0.2	0.0	...
Late morning (8.00—12.00)	0.05	0.5	0.05	0.2	...
Early afternoon (12.00—3.00)	0.1	0.5	0.1	0.2	...
Late afternoon (3.00—6.00)	0.1	0.2	0.2	0.3	...
Early evening (6.00—8.00)	0.2	0.0	0.2	0.2	...
Late evening (8.00—10.00)	0.3	0.0	0.1	0.0	...

Figure 17.   Non-essential work.
Probability of free time being devoted to a particular non-essential activity.

The Use of Simulation

Although the sequence of scheduled activities shown in *Figure 15* will be unique on any particular day, the final timetable of activities in the ward is the product of a stochastic sampling technique and is, consequently, just one from a large number of possible timetables. To devise any useful results from the model we must, therefore, follow the usual procedure of producing a series of simulated timetables for each particular day, and only by examining the whole series of possible timetables can we then reach any useful conclusions about the effects of any choice of operational policies for the ward.

The Uses of the Model

The ward model we have outlined in this paper allows us to examine the consequences of changing the conditions or operational policies affecting a ward without having to implement these changes in practice. This is obviously quite a valuable facility, and we shall now mention very briefly the types of experiment we might conduct using the model.

The first type of experiment concerns the policy of allocating patients to wards. At present most hospitals organise their wards by specialities, but there is a growing movement towards policies of progressive patient care in which equally ill patients of many different types are nursed together. Clearly this type of change will have a profound effect on the nursing routine in the wards, and we could use the model to predict the timetable of events under the new system.

We might also consider changing the nurses' shift system. We mentioned earlier that the system of 'split-duties' portrayed in *Figure 13* is unpopular and that there is pressure to replace this by a series of straightforward early and late shifts. This would result in a higher staffing level in the afternoon at the expense of having fewer nurses on duty in the evening, and we could use the model to examine the consequence of such changes.

Thirdly, we might examine the effects of introducing an extra visiting time in the early afternoon. The arrival of visitors usually brings all the nursing duties to a standstill, and so this change would result in increased workload for nurses on duty in the late afternoon and evening. We could use the ward model to test whether or not these changes are reasonable.

Finally there are numerous detailed policy changes which we could test. For example, we might try changing the waking-up time, the patients' meal times, or the hours during which the ward is 'open' to the doctors. The real value of having a model of this type is that not only may we test the effects of changes in one policy, but in addition we may examine the accumulative effects of many simultaneous policy changes which may be difficult or impossible to determine by mere speculation or discussion.

Discussion on the Second Model

The second half of this paper has described a model for predicting the patterns of daily activities within a hospital ward, and we have outlined briefly some of the uses to which this model might be put. With only minor modifications this same approach may be adopted in developing further models for predicting the activity patterns within the various hospital departments.

Similar objections to those discussed in relation to the first model may be raised against the ward model, although again we may defend the model on the grounds that some assumptions must be made in constructing any model, and it is whether or not these assumptions are appropriate which is important Fortunately the ward model is sufficiently flexible to accommodate many different sets of assumptions without having to be totally reconceived or restructed.

Finally, the ward model should be seen as being complementary to the work described in the first half of the paper, for whereas the first model provides an overall perspective of the hospital's activity patterns, the ward model and the models for the various departments fill in the important detailed features in this picture.   □

An interrogation language for building descriptions

Charles Eastman

Introduction

At some time in the not too distant future, I expect to find the original record of a building design not in architectural drawings, but in a computer readable and storable form. The economic and organizational advantages of this change are very large. After a design is complete, contractors, building inspectors, clients, financing institutions and other users of design information would be able to apply their particular evaluation or analysis more quickly and in greater detail than is now allowed with a design recorded in drawings. If an instantly updatable common record of the design description were available to each consultant and member of the design team during design, management and design coordination could be greatly improved. As examples, the location and routeing of mechanical equipment could be more easily checked; quantity surveys and the ordering of materials could be automated; dimensional coordination would be automatically accomplished by the "bookkeeping" within the computer. The point of view taken here is not so much one of computer-aided design as one of a management information system for design control. Of course, a translation program would be able to generate drawings from the computer's description, whenever they were needed.

This general conception is very appealing and I am confident that such systems will exist for the building professions sometime in the future. In order for this development to be realised, a common data base must be designed, capable of storing the complete description of a building in convenient formats. Furthermore, procedures must be created that allow designers and others involved in design and construction to easily interrogate, analyse, and modify the design description. For purposes of discussion, I shall be calling such a system *A Building Description System.*

Many issues remain to be resolved before a general Building Description System can be realised. Specifically, the capabilities of such a model must include:

a) a means to store a "complete" description of any building element, including, minimally, its spatial description, materials, weight, cost, and source of supply;

b) a means to spatially organise the elements into a configuration representing a building; e.g. apply the geometric transformations to their spatial description;

c) means to directly interrogate the data base in order to answer directly a limited range of questions;

d) analytic routines that allow answers to more complex questions, such as structural integrity, thermal properties, lighting levels, and capital and operating costs;

e) means to display and output portions of the resulting data base in particularly meaningful formats for visual inspection.

All of these capabilities must be able to be efficiently operable within a data base capable of dealing with all the separate parts of a building, e.g. on a database of from one to ten million elements. Thus the development of efficient methods of sorting and searching will play a crucial role in the practical development of such a system.

A project at Carnegie-Mellon University has been initiated to design and implement the various parts of a computer based Building Description System, and in this paper some central concepts underlying the (ongoing) design of that system are presented. Rather than attempt a general overview of the system, I focus on a particular set of capabilities that seem of great importance in the practical design of a building description system. These are the capabilities required to interrogate the data base regarding simple spatial relationships (capability c).

Interrogation of a building description is easily exemplified, currently, by the draftsman's ability to read architectural drawings. If asked, a draftsman can organise information describing parts of a building, check them for consistency, and derive inferences regarding a much broader range of questions than were explicit in the information given to him in the first place. This inferential capability suggests that architectural drawings involve a logic or language that allows deductions according to well defined, though inarticulated, rules. In logic, given a set of propositions it is possible to infer from these a large number of other propositions. In the same way a draftsman may derive information not originally input, answering such questions as, "What is the minimum width of this corridor", "What is the length of this pipe run?", "What is the area of room A14?", "Can a twelve inch duct be run between the ceiling and girder in room 18F?".

It is clear that some of these interrogations of architectural drawings are not trivial. Drawings are limited in their ability to directly represent three dimensions, and a draftsman may have to spatially integrate information from several drawings to answer such questions. It is our hope, in fact, that interrogation can be greatly simplified in a computer based system.

In order to develop an interrogation capability for building descriptions, we shall also need to know the data structure being operated on. In fact, aspects of the building element descriptions should be tailored to facilitate its efficient interrogation. Thus we shall be reviewing in this paper capability (a) along with (c), but in a more cursory form.

In ignoring the other capabilities, I assume that some of them are straightforward. Capability (b) for example, would build upon common and well-defined procedures that are part of most computer graphic languages.[1] Capabilities (d) and (e) are also crucial to the successful operation of a building description system and are receiving serious consideration in our research effort. Discussion of them here would greatly expand what will prove to be an already complicated set of capabilities. They will, therefore, be treated separately later.

The boundary between direct interrogation of drawings (capability c) and analyses derived from them (capability d) may not be clear. Consider such questions as, "At what point in room 18F is the lighting level lowest and what is that level?", "What is the maximum heat load on room 14A?", "What are the expected construction costs of this building?". Each of these questions requires specialised knowledge regarding lighting, thermodynamics or costs, in addition to the spatial logic inherent in the drawings. Currently, lighting, thermodynamics or costs are also treated as specialised analysis routines in which a fixed analysis is possible, (with the possibilities of a finite number of options or branches). A language, on the other hand, is a modular symbolic system allowing a very large or infinite number of interrogations or analyses to be formed from a small set of primitives. Our focus will be on a language for interrogating the spatial properties of a building system. The boundary between linguistic interrogation and analytic procedures is ultimately an empirical one, in terms of the power and generality that can be incorporated into a finite logical system.

Current approaches to the interrogation of graphical descriptions have taken a limited form. While it is true that syntactically organised languages have been implemented for constructing pictures and designs[2], I am not aware of any language of inquiry having been developed for any applications-oriented graphic system. Rather, each relation or property of potential interest has been defined as a subroutine or boolean function that can be called with variable **arguments**.[3] The effect in practice is a predefined and limited set of simple analysis routines.

I should emphasise at this point that what follows has not been implemented. The interrogation language to be described is a first pass effort in the development of a system and I am positive that significant refinements will follow. Furthermore, all details are not resolved. At best, I hope this discussion clarifies the problems of such a system and provides a foundation on which others can quickly build.

Notes on the general system

We envisage a building description system oriented towards man-machine problem solving, using time-sharing computer facilities. Hardware will consist of a graphic terminal, with limited local processing

capabilities. The data base for storing the building description will be on a memory device connected to the terminal, such as a disc drive. Thus different building descriptions may be selected at the terminal, as designers move from one project to another. Hard copy graphic and alpha-numeric output would also be available. The central time-share system would act as the control system allocating tasks to the local data base. Several graphic terminals could be interlinked to the same local computing and memory capability. A general outline of the proposal system design is shown in *Figure 1*.

Design work may or may not take place directly at the terminal, depending on the nature of the work. Work emphasising formal analyses probably would be, while visual and material design decisions probably would not. As decisions were made, these would be given to the machine, which would then update the building description. At various times, summary output in the form of drawings and quantity listings could be generated, for easy circulation and review by the design staff, clients, and users.

The availability of such a system guarantees that drawings are consistent and current at the time of their output. The design of laboratories, hospitals, factories, and other complex buildings especially would benefit from the coordination available through the terminals with the common building description. Each special field would also have at its disposal the range of analytic procedures currently available. I would expect that such a common data base would justify the development of many other forms of analysis also.

The Building element model

In order to deal with the naturally arising breadth of concerns in a building's design, several constructs of that design must be available to be operated upon. The building element model must respond to *all* assessing requirements, not only those of interrogation. For example, structural analyses, quantity surveys and other analyses of the physical properties of a building require a detailed description and explicit referencing to the physical elements making up the building. For architectural and behavioral considerations, it is equally important to be able to directly access and analyse the spaces enclosed by the physical elements. Moreover, the spaces and the physical components may require various groupings and organizations for different analyses, depending upon which of their functions are being considered at the time. The building element model is designed with these issues in mind.

Definition of a Building Element

A building element is defined as a domain within Cartesian space, making up part of a building and possessing homogeneous properties. Solid physical elements, such as walls or structural members, satisfy these definitions as they occupy defined volumes of space inside which we may assume homogeneous properties. A room also satisfies these criteria and may be defined as a building element. Clearly, what properties are homogeneous depends upon which properties of space are to be distinguished. With regard to the system design, physical properties are open-ended. The user is required to define which properties of objects or space he wishes to distinguish.

135

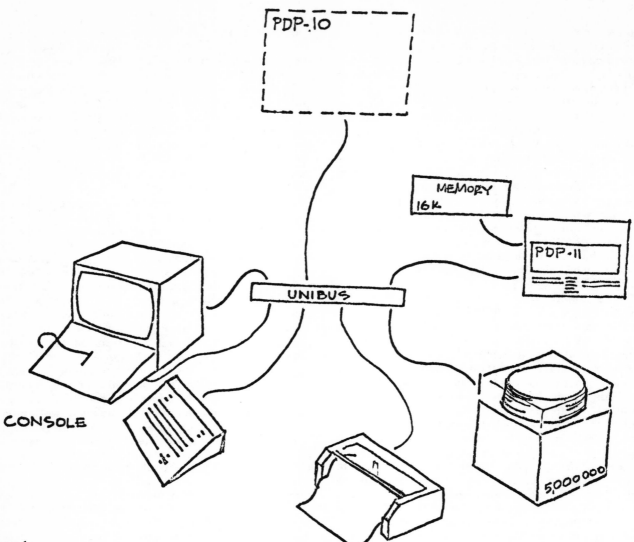

Figure 1

At the minimum, we would expect these to include material, cost, and density, but others may be added.

For the user, each element is named, either as a simple variable or as a subscripted variable. An element is named by a character string in the standard way and collections of elements defined as array entries may have up to four dimensions. Possible element names might be:

W   SILL (4)   GIRDER (3,4,17)
DOOR (2,3,17,6)

An element array has special properties. The array will be considered a *model* and its entries as *instances* of that model. That is, associated with the array name will be structural definition of a class of elements, with certain variables in this definition defined as variables. The instances will include values for these variables. At the minimum, each instance will separately define a location. In addition, a limited number of other variables may be associated with an element instance. These may be used to define the varying dimensions of instances of elements, their materials, costs, weight etc. All other aspects are assumed to be homogeneous across the instances of the array.

The collection of elements within an element array can be referred to and operated on all together. Thus SILL refers to all elements in the element array SILL. An operand which is applied to an array is applied to every element in the array. An example of an element array will be presented shortly.

The elements and element arrays constitute the basic definition of a design. In addition to the above elements the sytem provides two other elements which are reversed definitions and always defined. One of these is ∀, the universal set of all elements currently defined. When designated, it treats all elements concatenated one after the other. The other is ∅, the null set. The use of the universal null sets will be shown later.

It is often desirable to refer to elements in a variety of ways and these references may involve elements from several element arrays. For instance, a user may wish to refer to the plenum above the ceiling on a certain floor of a high-rise office, or the north wall of a space. The collections of elements defining these entities may involve, in the first case, certain fixtures, ducts, pipes, and ceiling panels that were originally defined as part of a variety of element arrays and in the second case a collection of walls, windows, and structural elements. Rather than demand that all references to elements be organized into a single hierarchical set notation, the user is provided with the facility for defining collections of elements in a way that overlaps the element arrays. These collections are called Sets and denoted as S. < name >. This facility for naming collections of elements is distinguished in this discussion by capitalisation. Arrays of Sets are also possible. Examples of Set names might be:

S.WALL (13)   S.MECHANICALS(3,17)
S. ENTRANCE

A Set consists of the names of its constitutent elements. These elements may be simple elements, instances of an element array or the collection of elements included in an element array or any combination of the above.

An element's spatial and geometric definition is not open-ended and requires a precise definition. An element shape is depicted as a three dimensional spatial domain. We represent such a domain by a set of closed curves which delineate it. Each curve is approximated by a point vector (an ordered set of points), and will be represented as $C^k = (P^k_0, P^k_1, \ldots, P^k_i, \ldots, P^k_n, P^k_0)$. k is the identifying label or level of the curve, i the index of the points in the curve and each $P^k_i = (x_i, z_i)$, where x and z are standard Cartesian coordinates. P^k_0, the point listed twice is called the *closing point* of curve C^k. Each curve depicts the intersection of the element with a plane perpendicular to the y axis. The level k of the curve is the real valued y coordinate of the plane on which the curve lies.

Each closed curve partitions a plane into two disjoint domains, one being finite and the other infinite. Either one can be designated as the curve's *inner* space and the other as its *outer* space. A curve's inner space is precisely the domain the curve delineates and represents. The ordering of the point

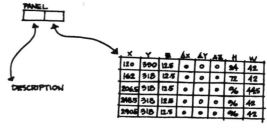

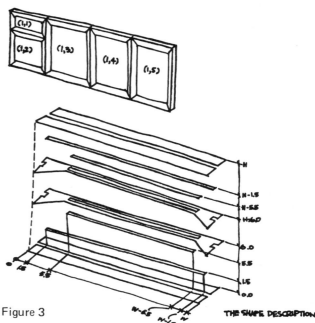

Figure 3   THE SHAPE DESCRIPTION

vector shall always be with the inner space to the right of the vector.

The curves characterising a shape are spaced in the y-coordinate at irregular intervals corresponding to the y-values at which changes occur in the shape description. An example of how such curves might depict a precast concrete wall panel is shown in *Figure two*. The set of curves depicting an element comprise a curve set. This set is the definition used by the system to depict the shape of an element. A set of such curve sets defines the arrangement of elements.

Clearly, many conventions may be applied to the point vectors to derive different curves from them. Several of these have been reviewed, for example, by Forrest.[4] For ease of initial implementation, we expect to restruct shapes to those made up of planar surfaces. This restriction leads to many initial processing simplifications, which may be removed later if our other concepts prove feasible.

An example of how the shape model shown in *Figure 2* may be used to specify a set of different panels is shown in *Figure 3*. Panels of different widths and heights, as desired, are efficiently defined with the model-instance capability.

Definition of Points

As element shape definitions are composed of point vectors, an efficient method is needed for inputting and referring to points in space. The general definition of a point is .(y,x,z). A curve or point vector is made up of a sequence of points, all with the same y dimension. Thus the input of a curve is $(y_1, x_1 z_1, x_2 z_2, x_3 z_3, \ldots x_m, z_m, x_1 z_1; y_2, x_{m+1}, z_{m+1} \ldots)$. That is, the y value of a curve is input first, followed by a set of x, z points.

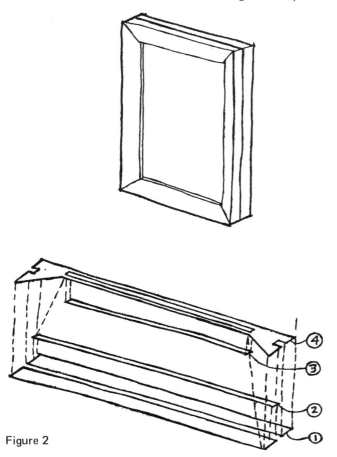

Figure 2

A precast concrete panel and the four sets of curves that define the shape of the bottom half.

Each pair of points is separated by commas. A colon introduces a new y value. Multiple domains are easily accommodated within a sequence of x and z values. If the first x,z combination is repeated, this is immediately recognized as a closed curve and the next point is treated not as a continuation of the vector, but as the start of a new curve. This places a small restriction on the form of input allowed.

Seldom will it be convenient to input points through a keyboard; more often a digitiser or tablet will be the desired input device. In these cases a point may be entered as

$$\cdot (y' < \text{digitised input} > '),$$

where the quote indicates that an alternative designated peripheral will be generating the input. For inputting a curve, this same method is used.
That is

$$\cdot (y_1' < \text{digitised set of x, z points} > '; y_2' < \text{digitised set of x, z points} >' \text{ etc.})$$

is the form proposed, where the y values (followed by quotes) are input from a keyboard and the x,z points input from a tablet.

With this brief and admittedly sketchy introduction, I leave the building element description. In what follows, we will assume that collections of elements can be input and that these have had their spatial properties defined in such a way that they form a meaningful building arrangement stored in the system's data base. Associated with the instances and/or element definitions are material, weight and cost information. We wish to derive spatial information from this data base, with performances parallel to those of a draftsman reading a drawing.

Operators for the Interrogation Language

The goal is the development of a general interrogation language for building description systems. By a language we mean, more precisely, a set of primitive operators and the syntax for combining them into large numbers of combinations. A formal language which serves similar purposes in a different field of application is algebra. The primitive operators in that case are $+$, $-$, $\div$, x, $\sqrt{}$, which operate on elements or pairs of elements. In the case of algebra, the elements operated on are variables designating a single number (or in complex arithmetic, a pair of numbers). In our case, the elements operated on will be element shapes, stored as a set of point vectors.

The required capabilities of such a language seem derivable from two different classes of performances. In fact, almost any interrogation seems analysable into these two parts. The most obvious is the analysis of the shape or properties of a spatial domain. We may wish to know its width, height or volume, or the area of different sections or the distance between two points on its surface. We may also wish to know its weight, cost, material or other property. We shall call those operators which interrogate information about a domain *Domain Analysing Operators*. A less obvious but equally important capability is the means to derive new domains that are functions of the building elements. We may wish to analyse, for example, the domain made up of all walls or the domain which represents the corridor system. By being able to regroup and derive new temporary domains for interrogation, the user is provided with great flexibility in specifying the parts of the design. This second

capability is provided by operators I shall call *Domain Generating Operators*. These two classes of operators will provide the principal capability for the design interrogation language to be described. We have already given some indication of input capabilities, as provided by the point and curve input capabilities, but in addition we shall also need output defining commands.

Operators will be defined in the conventional infix notation form. In general, operators will have as operands one or two entities. That is, they will be unary or binary only. Operators may have as operands specified subsets of the data types defined earlier. Some operands may be *points,* and when these are required I shall denote the class of all points as a subscripted p. Operators may also have as operands *an element or Set.* This class of operand shall be denoted as a capatalised A or B which stands for a simple element or Set, an entry in an element array, or Set array or whole Set or element arrays. A third class of operand is the *expression.* An expression is a sequence of operators and operands that may be syntactically interpreted to result in the definition of one or more domains. An expression may also result in a point. An expression shall be denoted by f. Also needed will be simple variables which may be directly specified, that is, *a constant* or a variable name which has received an assignment. These shall be denoted with a subscripted C.

Let us consider first the domain generating operators.
Domain Generating Operators.

The Domain Generating Operators provide a means of grouping building elements or spaces and of defining these groups as single domains so they may be analysed. A reasonable basis for deriving such operators is the set operations of union, complement, and intersection. The union provides a means of aggregating many elements together and eliminating common edges within a set of elements. The complement provides means of defining the negation of elements, which is important in many interrogations. The intersection also provides an important function. If the intersection of two solid elements is not ϕ, then they overlap. The intersection, then, provides the important capability of identifying spatial conflicts. Because we recognised early that the set operations would play a crucial role in realising a design interrogation language, we were tempted to call our computer system a "Venn diagram machine". But as the needed capability of the system became apparent, operators much beyond the set theoretic ones were employed for generating domains.

The currently proposed set of domains defining operators are described in *Figure 4,* along with a graphic example of their operation (in two dimensions). They consist of three' general subclasses. The first are the definitional operators for naming or referencing particular elements or domains. These are the *assignment,* which corresponds to its algebraic counterpart, and the *pointer* which allows graphic or spatial accessing of an element by pointing to it. The two pointers are particularly important in facilitating graphic man-machine interaction. Without the ability of pointing, users of the system would be required to know the names of each element. In general, the two-dimensional property of the display will give one of the

DEFINITION OF BUILDING DESCRIPTION INTERROGATION LANGUAGE
DOMAIN GENERATING OPERATORS

Symbols & operands	Name	Description of Transformation	Treatment of attributes	Graphic Example Before / After	Comments
DEFINITIONAL OPERATORS
$B = f$	assignment	assigns a domain to an element name	attributes are transferred	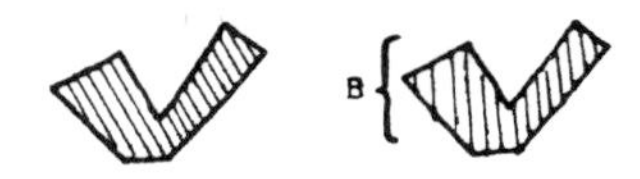	B may refer to only one element. B may not be an array name.
$p \, ! \, f$	pointer	defines the element in domain f which includes point p.	attributes are transferred		
$p \, !! \, f$	pointer	defines the region in f which incorporates point p.	attributes are proportionally transferred		
RELATIONAL OPERATORS
$- f$	complement	defines the domain of all space not belonging to f.	no attributes are transferred	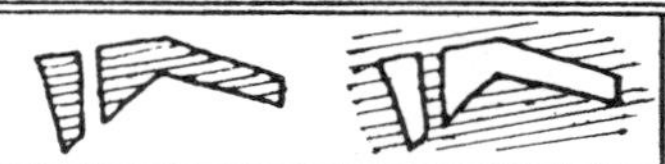	
$f_1 \cup f_2$	union	defines the domain of all space belonging to f_1 or f_2 or both.	adds all attributes which are interval scales	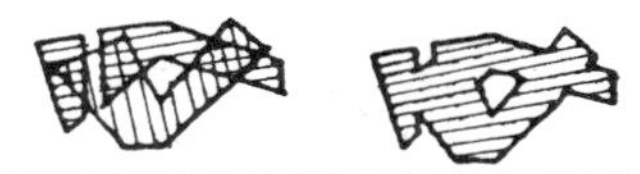	
$\cup(s)$ or $\cup(f_1, f_2, f_3)$	union	defines the one or more domains which are the union of the set S.	adds all attributes which are interval scales.		
$f_1 \cap f_2$	intersection	defines the domain of all space belonging to both f_1 and f_2. $(f_1 \cap f_2 = -(-f_1 \cup -f_2))$	computes all interval scale values as proportional to volume. If proportional allocations from f_1 and f_2 agree, attributes are passed		the set theoretic difference operation is $f_1 \cap (-f_2)$
$@ \, f$	enclosure	defines the domain enclosed by f	no attributes are transferred		the y dimension must be enclosed or limited by level.
PROJECTIVE OPERATORS
$f_1 \leftarrow f_2$	connector	defines a cone projected from f_1 that covers f_2 $(f_1 \leftarrow f_2 \neq f_2 \leftarrow f_1)$	no attributes are transferred		
$f > C$	increaser	defines a domain that is the shape of f but extended C units in size	no attributes are transferred	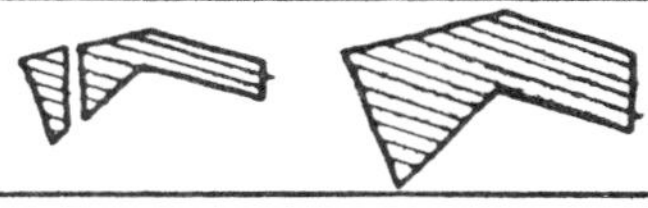	does not increase the y dimension
$f < C$	decreaser	defines a domain that is the shape of f but decreased C units in size. $(f < C \equiv -(-f > C))$	no attributes are transferred		does not decrease the y dimension
$\uparrow C_1, C_2 \uparrow$	level	defines the domain of all spaces $\geq C_1$ and C_2.	no attributes		
POINT GENERATING OPERATORS
$f_1 * f_2$	contact	defines a point that is the center of the common area of the two domains.	no attributes		
maxx f minx f maxy f miny f maxz f minz f	max x min x max y min y max z min z	defines that point which is the external point on f	no attributes		notifies user if more than one point is defined

Figure 4

dimensions implicitly. The location of cursor or light pen will provide the other two.

The second subclass of domain generating operators might be called the relational operators. The boundaries of the domains defined by the relational operators are already existent and the new domains are simply a reclassification, in a sense, of inside and outside. These consist of the *complement,* the *enclosure, the union,* and *intersection.* The only operator in this subclass that is unfamiliar is the enclosure, which defines the spaces enclosed by another domain. See *Figure 4* for a description of their operation.

The third and fourth subclasses of domain generating operators are called the domain projective operators and the point generating operators. The domain projective operators, in contrast to the relational operators, generate new domains within newly projected boundaries. The first of these operators is the *connector,* which projects a cone from the broadest extent of one element so that it engulfs the other defined element. It is followed by the *increaser* and *decreaser,* which define a domain by moving all x and z boundaries the distance specified by the variable either outside or inside their original definition. The distance moved is perpendicular to the

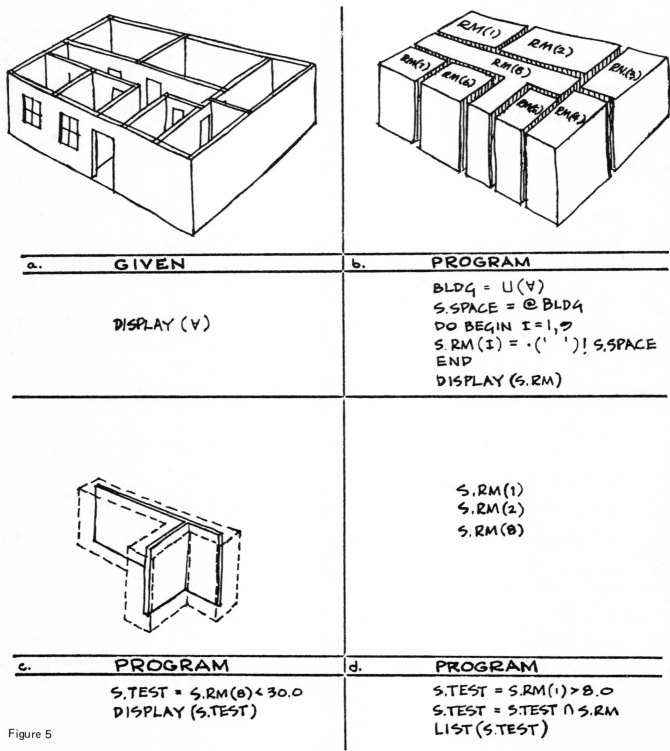

a. GIVEN	b. PROGRAM
DISPLAY (∀)	BLDG = U(∀) S.SPACE = @ BLDG DO BEGIN I=1,9 S.RM(I) = ·(' ')! S.SPACE END DISPLAY (S.RM)
	S.RM(1) S.RM(2) S.RM(8)

c. PROGRAM	d. PROGRAM
S.TEST = S.RM(8) < 30.0 DISPLAY (S.TEST)	S.TEST = S.RM(1) > 8.0 S.TEST = S.TEST ∩ S.RM LIST (S.TEST)

Figure 5

140

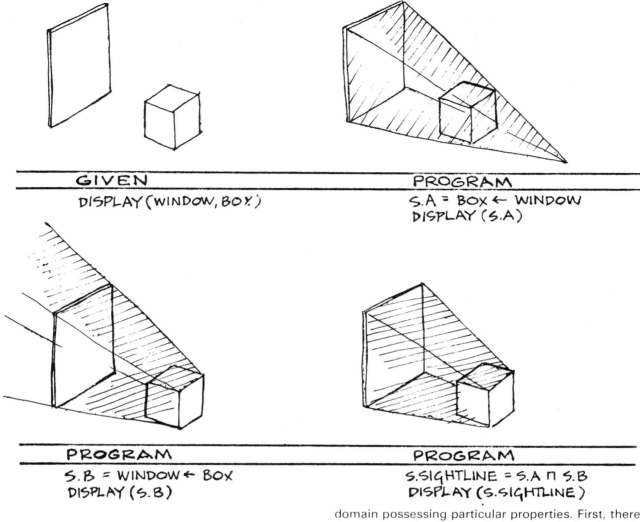

GIVEN

DISPLAY (WINDOW, BOX)

PROGRAM

S.A = BOX ← WINDOW
DISPLAY (S.A)

PROGRAM

S.B = WINDOW ← BOX
DISPLAY (S.B)

PROGRAM

S.SIGHTLINE = S.A ∩ S.B
DISPLAY (S.SIGHTLINE)

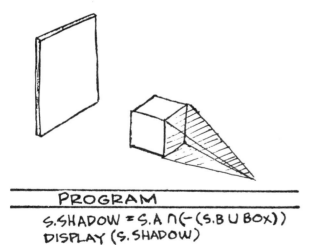

PROGRAM

S.SHADOW = S.A ∩ (¬(S.B ∪ BOX))
DISPLAY (S.SHADOW)

Figure 6

domain possessing particular properties. First, there is the *contact*. It defines the centre of the boundary between two domains. Then there are the extremal operators *min x, max x, min y, max y, min z, and max z,* which define the points satisfying the given property.

These may seem a large number of operators to gain an understanding of in a short amount of time. A feeling for the utility of these particular operators may be gained, though, in examples of their application. In order to obtain some performance, we need some minimal capabilities for defining the form of output of information. Finally, let me simply propose two other commands. These are LIST and DISPLAY. LIST provides alphanumeric output, listing each of the elements which intersects with the defined domain(s). DISPLAY provides graphic output, a picture of the derived domain in a useful form (which will not be elaborated here).

Figures 5, 6, and *7* give scenarios showing the use of the domain generating operators. *Figure 5* shows how the element descriptions can be easily extended to include the spaces. In *Figure 5(b)* each room is pointed to with a pen in sequence and it is entered and named. In *Figure 5(c)* the hallway is tested for its width. As it must be ⩾ 60 inches wide (because of, say, building codes) we subtract 30 inches from each side. By inspection it is then possible to see if it is too narrow and by how much. In *Figure 5(d)* the system is asked to list those rooms adjacent to Room (1).

original surface. The y dimensions are not altered. The last of the domain projective operators is the *level,* which defines the universal domain between two y values.

Last, we have a set of point generating operators. These are operators which define that point on a

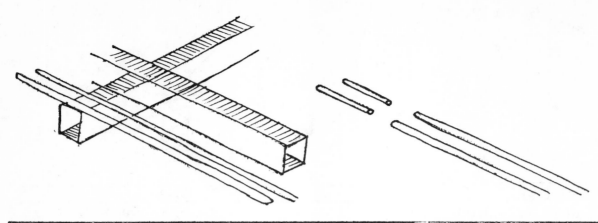

GIVEN

DISPLAY (PIPES, DUCT)

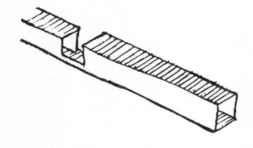

PROGRAM

DUCT(2) = DUCT(2) ∩ (−DUCT(1))
DISPLAY (DUCT(2)

Figure 7

Figure 6 shows how the connector may be used to define sightlines and shadows. *Figure 7* shows how the layout of ducts and piping can be examined for spatial interference. Of course, many other expressions are possible. The requirement of any expression is that the result is a domain (possibly null). Attributes are transferred in each operation in a logically consistent way.

Domain Analysis Operators

In each of the examples just given, the output was a listing of domains or its graphical representation. In many cases these forms are not satisfactory, for we wish to derive a specific distance or value from an element or derived domain. This is the purpose of the Domain Analysis Operators, which in general are combined with the point generating operators. Only a few analysis operators are defined here. They are shown in *Figure 8*. Others could be added if they were found to be needed. The three that are specified are the straight distance, internal distance, and volume operators. The *straight distance* operator computes

PROGRAM

S.PIPES = PIPES ∩ (− (DUCT(1) > 6))
DISPLAY (S.PIPES)

the straightline distance between a point and a domain. The *internal distance* operator, on the other hand, takes as points two that are on or within the same domain. It computes the shortest path within the domain between the two points. If the points are not associated with a common domain, the result is ϕ. The last domain analysing operator is the volume, which returns the volume of the specified domain.

Examples of how the domain analysing operators can be combined with the others to determine a variety of relationships are shown in *Figures 9 and 10*.

An important and straightforward extension of these capabilities is to combine them with the operators of boolean logic, for example those found in FORTRAN. With this extension, we can ask not only the walking distance from a room to fire stairway, but also if that distance is less than some limit. This provides means for specifying building code checks on spatial relationships. Most important, these tests could be defined in a general way prior to the evaluation of a particular plan. Thus general evaluation procedures for the spatial aspects of building and fire codes are possible.

Discussion

I have outlined the structure of a language and data base that begins to incorporate the capabilities of a draftsman reading architectural drawings. It must be emphasised that the approach taken has *not* been to store descriptions of architectural drawings within a computer, but rather to store a description of a building. As can be evidenced from the few examples, the interrogation performance holds the promise of being quite powerful, if response times can be made reasonably fast.

Thus far, I have dealt with only the operators and operands available to the user. I have not discussed how the operators would be translated and the resulting transformations on the domains executed. This is not to say that these issues have not been addressed. The conception for such an interrogation language, in fact, grew out of the development of algorithms for the set theoretic operations that were first developed for two dimensions and with our data structure are easily extensible to three dimensions.[5]

General strategies (as yet not formally defined) have been outlined for most (but not all) of the

Figure 8

SYMBOL & OPERANDS	NAME	DESCRIPTION OF TRANSFORMATION	TREATMENT OF ATTRIBUTES	GRAPHIC EXAMPLE BEFORE	GRAPHIC EXAMPLE AFTER	COMMENTS
DOMAIN ANALYZING OPERATORS						
$P_1 \# f_1$	straight distance	computes the straight line distance between two points	no attributes			
$[P_1, P_2]$	internal distance	computes the shortest path connecting two points that are within a single domain	no attributes			
$\%f$	volume	computes the volume of domain f				

operators. In several cases, alternative methods exist and we are deliberating on the best procedure with which to proceed. An important additional capability required for realising such a system is the ability to sort elements spatially so as to answer the question, "What occupies this space?" A very efficient sorting procedure is needed to generate answers to this question and we have recently gained some insights that may lead to a solution. To summarise, the system I have outlined is somewhere between a gleam in my eye and a reality.

The problem I have explored is the design of a language, which in itself is a challenging intellectual problem. Few methodologies exist for designing languages. My own approach has been to collect protocols on my own interrogation performance on a set of working drawings. This has provided a rough repertoire of performances to be incorporated within the language. Next were derived a set of operators and a syntax for their combination that achieves the performances collected earlier. This part of the effort has been completely intuitive. An early hypothesis growing out of previous work was that the set theoretic operations would play a vital role in expressing relations between the elements of a design. The effort described here was built upon that one initial assumption. As in all linguistic models, Occam's razor and performance have been the sole criteria. The parsimony to be achieved is of two sorts: (1) surface parsimony, in the ease of expressing the most common forms of interrogations. That is, are the most common statements easy to make? (2) implementational parsimony, in computer execution of the transformation on the domains.

The building description system developed here requires many extensions before a practical system is implementable. I shall list only a few of the unresolved issues.

The language developed here focuses on interrogation only; methods for permanently updating the data base were not considered. In reality interrogation and updating are likely to proceed in an intermixed mode. Thus the capabilities laid out here require expansion and modification to allow alterations to the permanent building description. A similar problem is the separation of elements or domains, temporarily defined for purposes of interrogation, from those that are to be permanently defined. Particular corridors, runs of pipes or other parts of buildings may be grouped for particular interrogations. It would be undesirable, though, to retain these permanently in the system. It is very desirable to retain a single grouping of all solid elements currently defined, with each element included only once. From this grouping would come cost analyses, working drawing output, and other records of the design. The point is that overlapping groupings of physical elements should be defined using the set elements, as shown in the examples, to maintain the basic building description in a non-redundant form. Also, I propose that most overlapping groupings be deleted at the end of any terminal conversation.

Another important issue is the convenience of the man-machine language. Many aspects seem awkward and "formalistic". Slight modifications in the

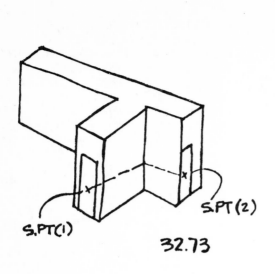

S.PT(1)

S.PT(2)

32.73

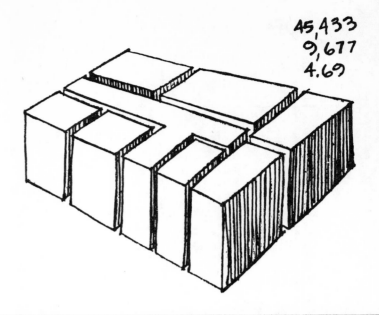

45,433
9,677
4.69

PROGRAM

S. PT(1) = DOOR (1) * RM (8)
S. PT(2) = DOOR (12) * RM (8)
LIST ([S.PT(1), S.PT(2)])

PROGRAM

C1 = % RM (8)
DO BEGIN I = 1, 7
C2 = % RM (I) + C2 END
LIST (C1, C2, C1/C2)

Figure 9

The first interrogation derives the distance between the entrance and Room 8. The second computes the volume of circulation and assigned space, then the circulation-assigned ratio.

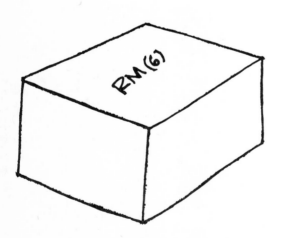

RM(6)

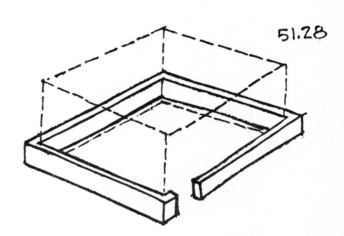

51.28

PROGRAM

S. PERI = (RM(6) > 1.0) ∩ ↑1.2, 2.6↑
S. PERI = S.PERI ∩ (-RM(6))

PROGRAM

S. PERI = S PERI ∩ (-DOOR (6))
LIST([MINX DOOR(6), MAX X
DOOR(6)])

Figure 10

This interrogation determines the perimeter of the space. Notice that these operations are dependent on only two variables, room number and door. It could easily be made a subroutine.

definitions of the operators may allow significant simplifications in the interrogations most commonly desired.

Central to eventual implementation is the efficient execution of each operator. Each is an algorithm requiring efficient execution. Definition of efficient codes for each of them is our major current concern.

The value of such a building description system has, I trust, been made apparent. The challenge of realising the capabilities of such a system is great indeed. This paper outlines a first crude plan for realising parts of a system. Hopefully, we and others will quickly add to this beginning.

References

1. Newman, William and Sproul, R. F. (1973) *Principles of Interactive Computer Graphics,* McGraw-Hill, New York; Gray, J. C. (1967) "Compound Data Structures for Computer aided Design" Proceedings ACM National Conference, August, 1967, pp. 355-365.

2. Yessios, C. (1973) "Syntactic Structures and Procedures for Computable Site Planning" unpublished Ph.D. thesis, School of Urban and Public Affairs, Carnegie-Mellon University, Pittsburgh, May, 1973; Rosenfeld, A. (1969) *Picture Processing by Computer,* Academic Press, New York, Chapter 10.

3. Eastman, C. M. (1973) "Automated Space Planning" *Journal of Artificial Intelligence* 4, pp. 41-64; Weinzapfel, Guy (1971) "IMAGE: An Interactive Graphics Based Computer System for Multi-constrained Spatial Synthesis" *Proceedings. Eighth Annual Design Automation Workshop* June, 1971.

4. Forrest A. R. (1969) "Curves for Computer Graphics" *Pertinent Concepts In Computer Graphics,* M. Faiman and J. Meiergett (eds.) University of Illinois Press, Urbana, Illinois; Forrest, A. R. (1972) "On Coons and Other Methods for the Representation of Curved Surfaces" *Computer Graphics and Image Processing,* 1:4, December, 1972, pp. 341-359.

5. Eastman, E. M. and Yessios C. I. (1972) "An Efficient Algorithm for Finding the Union, Intersection and Differences of Spatial Domains" Institute of Physical Planning Research Report No. 32, Carnegie-Mellon University, Pittsbu h PA, September 1972. ☐

Understanding building plans with computer aids

Tom Willoughby

Introduction

For this paper much of computer aided building planning work is taken as read. A full bibliography is given for reference.

We discuss why 'additive' methods fail and the reasons for the success of the simpler 'permutational' method.

Two simple examples are given of effective circulation planning with a permutational algorithm.

The possibility of planning buildings on a purely rational basis has interested architects for some time. Building design was, in the past, a product of preconceived ideas, function preference, and judgement. It was hoped that systematic methods would provide a strategy or direction for the plan, which was derived from the impartial interaction of functional demands. To an extent the strategy was intended to replace the dominance of an initial concept in defining the overall form of a building.

Various methods were suggested, at different planning scales from the graph theoretic approaches of Levin (1964), Buffa (1963), Steadman (1970) and Christofides and Viola (1971) to the heuristic algorithms of Armour and Buffa (1963), Whitehead and Eldars (1964), Beaumont (1967), and Willoughby (1970-71). These methods concentrated on generating a good or optimum plan from a set of pre-defined criteria.

The development of automatic planning mechanisms coincided in part with the movement towards design method. The attempts at automatic building planning are not unreasonable at first sight, for they searched for a logical method of finding an overall building plan. Alexander (1964) suggested a relational approach to the planning of a village community in India. He decomposed the problem into small parts, each of which was studied in detail. These were then diagrammatically reassembled. The theory held that if the method of assembly were good and each small part were exactly fitted into its context the resultant whole diagram would indicate a good form.

To compare Alexander's problem and solution to building planning can be misleading because the scale is reduced and he does not translate diagram directly to form. However, additive methods, such as those of Whitehead and Eldars, propose that the piecing together of a series of small parts with a sequence of partially optimizing decisions will produce a near optimum whole. They argue that the order of placing is dependent on the degree of connectivity and that it seems reasonable that the most connected units should be at the centre of the plan.

Unfortunately this is unsupported theoretically and practically. A series of optimized parts rarely produces an optimum whole, for the whole may well require a modification of the parts from the various optima found in isolation from each other. The whole becomes only a local optimum dependent on the rules of assembly of the parts.

Achieving quality in planning

How good was a plan found by an additive method? The question is not considered by most methods, and few attempts are made to see if the result can be improved. Only in methods such as those of Bernholtz and Fosberg or Seehof et al is a series of sample results taken and the best selected. Whitehead and Eldars, Beaumont, Willoughby, and Lee and Moore all used a deterministic algorithm to produce a single solution, which they hoped would be good.

Permutational algorithms, to be discussed later, produce local optima with a 25% variation in quality. The quality of a single local optimum from an additive method is completely undetermined even within the limited criteria used to generate a solution. In addition nearly all multi-sample additive methods make no attempt to keep the size of the sample within reasonable bounds or to draw conclusions about the quality of the best plan they find. Computational mechanisms require that the criteria be defined numerically. This is always difficult in designing, for the language of numbers is not amenable to the shades of opinion and compromise used by the architect. After initial set-backs illustrated in most of the plans produced by additive methods the direction forward seemed to be by increasing the number of criteria considered. Plans that were concentric when only direct distance circulation was considered might be made more realistic by specifying other factors. Thus Beaumont includes natural light and a coherent though uncontrolled circulation space, and Willoughby adds orientation, departmental shape, and site conditions.

Not only does the addition of more criteria fail to improve the realism of the solutions, it further confuses an already uncertain situation. More elaborate algorithms require intricate counterweights for a range of criteria. As more criteria are added it becomes increasingly difficult to control their interrelation and progressively less clear how their relative strengths affect the final plan. It may well be possible to express in numerical terms a limited number of criteria, but only when the relationship is readily understandable.

One method of understanding the complex

relationships among many criteria is to take many samples of local optima, adjusting the weightings on each computer run and examining the effect on the plan. Few of the multi-criteria additive methods adopt: this course, because of greatly increased computer costs. Computational resources are part of the problem.

The generative algorithms depend on a limited number of constraints, yet the object is to give an overall strategy to contain all criteria. No allowance is made for structure, aesthetics, or economics, and thus the results are 'good' only in the very limited framework of minimum circulation and a few other constraints. The guiding strategy for a design is not a direct product of independently solved sub-problems, and from the start it is a misconception to suppose that the general framework for all criteria can be produced from very few.

A general difficulty is the need to specify all criteria before starting on the design. The 'if, then' situation is completely missed where decisions become hard only within the developing context of a design. For example, departmental sizes or shapes may be fixed in additive algorithms. In many design situations these would be known only as approximate areas, which become a fixed shape and proportion at a late stage in the initial planning process. The connectivities too may only be fixed in general terms and might be mutually compromised as the design develops to achieve an overall goal.

It is simpler to define criteria if the context is carefully constrained. For example, if departments are all of a given modular size for structural reasons, then the problems of change can be avoided to an.extent. However, this implies that important overall decisions have been made. As indicated in the methods of Seehof and Willoughby (1971) this is essential to ensure a reasonable result.

The mechanism used to generate plans depended upon a series of arithmetic steps that calculated the order of the departments to be placed and their positions relative to each other. A small alteration in one of the criteria, say changing a connectivity value from 8 to 7, could change the order of location and the whole nature of the solution. The instability of the plans raises doubts about the usefulness of a plan based on a particular set of numerical criteria.

If a plan produced by an additive algorithm is taken as giving a general indication of the direction of a solution, it follows that slightly different organisation structures should have building forms of completely different shapes. The object of the additive method is to give an overall strategy, yet no consistent general direction emerges. In its use of buildings an organisation is essentially dynamic, always attempting to change to a form that better satisfies the goal of the enterprise.

Flexibility of plans

Weeks (1969) argues that although specific activities may have very definite environmental requirements, provision for these is not incompatible with a general framework. The object should be to have a built-in potential beyond immediate need. This implies incorporating redundancy to increase a system's ability to cope with the unpredictable. An analogy is the ability of a species to adapt non-genetically to a changing situation. The building should have a reservoir of resilience based on a non-specific physical framework. A general theory for planning buildings must allow for elements of plan that will remain valid throughout a period of change, and the physical expression of such flexibility should be as non-abrasive as possible to the changing function of an organisation. A reasonable approach is to attempt not to form buildings entirely around circulation patterns or around any single set of criteria, but to see how various built forms broadly accommodate a range of organisations.

Clearly no building can be all things to all men. An open plan may be splendid for an office and appalling for a hospital. However, the degree of fit and misfit will be broad, generally implying a range of geometries that provides choice in a given organisational situation. Thus the inference is that the building form, even if it were possible, should not be entirely the product of one circulation pattern. Quite the reverse, it should be of a form to allow change in many ways.

Comparison of additive and approximate permutational algorithms

All additive algorithms with the exception of methods such as those of Bernholtz and Fosberg and Seehof et al. try to follow a closely guided path to a single near optimum solution. Whitehead and Eldars (1965), Willoughby (1970)1) Beaumont (1967) attempt to stimulate automatically their version of a rational approach to design. They use the computer as an inquisitive mind looking for a single good solution through a series of carefully worked out sequential steps. Unfortunately the computer is singularly unsuitable either for simulating human thinking, which is partially nonsequential, or making a set of complex sequential decisions which might represent a design process. So additive methods soon encounter serious computational and theoretical difficulties.

Approximate permutational algorithms permute the activities within a building shell until no arrangement can be found with a lower circulation distance. This is a local optimum. For successful use of approximate permutational algorithms the building plan is defined, and activity units organised within it. The search systematically trudges through thousands of worthless complete solutions, on the conviction that by so doing the chances of finding a good solution are high. This is unlike the human design process, where an overall strategy guides towards a single solution or small group of solutions.

The computer is particulary suitable for this type of mindless task, where many variants are examined to find a single good result. Experience in permutational research suggests that for a given amount of computer time, this method produces a better quality of result than the deterministic heuristics used in additive methods.

Permutational algorithms carefully limit the problem to be tackled. For example Armour and Buffa define a perimeter but leave unspecified the internal partitions, whereas the permutational method of Vollmann et al. specifies the whole plan and in doing so increases the usefulness of the results. When the building form is limited, permutational possibilities are reduced, and there is a guarantee that the results are at least understandable. Further permutational

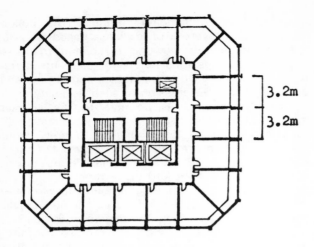

Services are in the centre of the plan. Lighting is natural, and each office is large enough for two persons. The horizontal module is 3.2 metres.

Figure 1   Plan of a Floor of the Economist Building

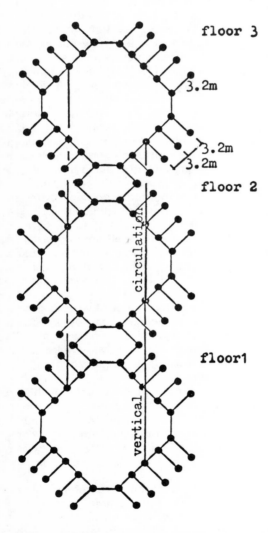

Each module of the network has a length of 3.2 metres. Vertical circulation speed is one-third of horizontal travel speed.

Figure 2   Schematic Network of Communication

methods use only circulation as a criterion, avoiding the theoretical and practical complications of counterweighting many factors.

The majority of additive algorithms place elements sequentially, and forbid any fluidity in the order of placing. By making one irrevocable step at a time no feedback is permitted, and if a disadvantageous direction develops there is no way of correction. On the other hand the permutational method always manipulates a complete plan and maintains the fluidity of all activity units which may be moved several times before a local optimum is reached. In addition, the cheapness of the approximate permutational algorithm allows many samples of local optima to be taken, making it probable that the best solution will be better than that of a single attempt additive algorithm.

Application of a program

We now look at a permutational program used with two existing building plans: first, part of the Economist building in St. James's, London, designed by Allison and Peter Smithson in the early sixties; secondly, the experimental open plan office at Kew built for the Home Office in 1968–69 by the Ministry of Public Building and Works.

The Economist Building

The Economist building has fourteen floors and is rented to several organisations. The Economist organisation occupies the tenth to fourteenth floors, and we examine a segment of three storeys. The organisation placed departments or groups of departments so as to minimise inter-floor traffic. Lifts tend to be used for going to and coming from work, and the stairs are used for trips to local floors. *The Architects' Journal* comments that considerable rearrangement of partitions took place in the first year but that after this little change occurred. The partitions can be moved, but they are not of the easily clipped-in type.

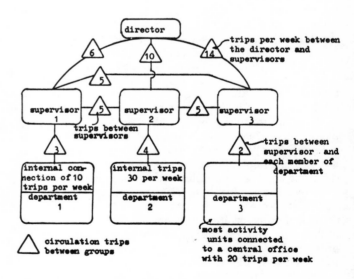

The figure shows the number of trips per week between each member of the hierarchy. For example, on the left the supervisor of department 1 makes three trips to each member of department 1.

Figure 3   Trips Between Groups of the Hierarchy of Organisation and Circulation

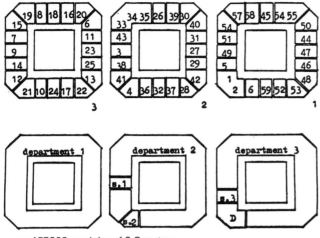

score 155902 modules of 3.2 metres
s.1 = the supervisor to department 1
D = the director

Departments are coherently placed on each floor. The director is placed in a corner on the lowest floor without destroying the integrity of the other departments. The director has the highest contact with supervisor 3. All the supervisors are near the stairs, and therefore contact among them is efficient.

Figure 4   A Plan of the Building Derived by the Permutational Algorithm

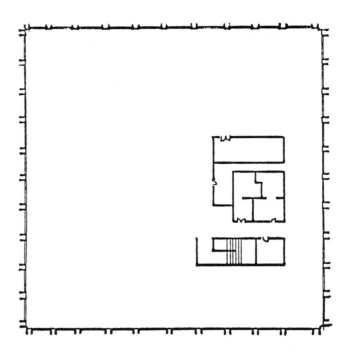

The floor is open except for the service core.

Figure 5   Main Floor Plan for the Experimental Open Plan Office at Kew

For computer application the plan is described as a simple network of communication: horizontal distances between adjacent rooms on the same floor are assumed to be equal. The circulation pattern, resulting from a simple structure of organisation, is a combination of circulation for control and for completion of the work task. Circulation flow is greatest within the departments. Next comes contact by each supervisor with each member of his department. Supervisors make contact among themselves and with the director as seen in *Figure 3*.

Results

The plan shown in *Figure 4* is the best of a group of samples taken with the computer. Each plan took $4\frac{1}{2}$ minutes on a Titan ICL computer. To reduce the computation cost to a minimum we use a limiting formula derived by Willoughby (1972) (Doctoral thesis),

$$n = \sqrt{\frac{RK}{C}}$$

where n = the optimum sample size
    R = the range of the total circulation distances of the local optima
    K = the cost of one unit of the range and
    C = the cost of taking one local optimum on the computer

The value of n is the number of samples at which the cost of continuing to sample will be greater than any advantage found in the plans so obtained. After 20 local optima are sampled we find that the range is approximately 40,000 units or 128,000 metres. If it

cost 75p in computer time to take one sample, and circulation cost of one metre of movement is 0.01p and the organisation remains in the building for 100 weeks, then the optimum sample size is

$$n = \sqrt{\frac{128,000 \times .01 \times 100}{75}}$$

or $n \doteq 42.$

If the cost per sample is £1.50 the optimum sample size is reduced to about 30.

An open plan office building at Kew.

The second example is of an open plan office building at Kew. The plan is divided into 73 equal size modules and planned with another circulation pattern. Access is from underneath, allowing a central entrance. The plan is shown in *Figure 5*.

Results

The best plan found with the algorithm, shown in *Figure 8* places the main office in the centre of the plan. Part 3 clusters around the centre of the plan, and most of part one is pushed behind the service core.

The characteristics of the local optima found differ from those of the Economist building. The range was found to be only 10,320 metres after 20 samples. In other words, there is far less to be gained or lost in the single-floor open plan, where many local optimum plans are a good average standard. The small range affects the optimum sample size so that despite the size of the permutational problem having increased from 60! to 73!, the optimum number of samples is small. Each local optimum costs 50 per cent more to

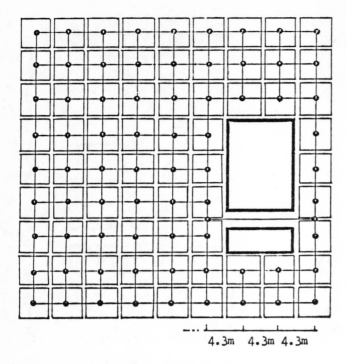

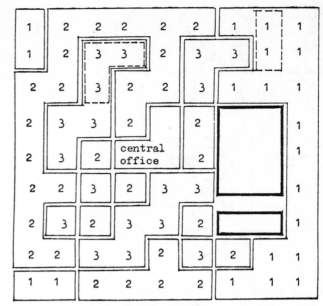

Score 222196 modules of 4.3 metres

Figure 8   The Best Local Optimum of the Open Plan

Schematic plan for the open plan office with 73 modules 4.3m x 4.3m. Circulation is assumed to be from node to node by the links shown.

Figure 6   Schematic Communications Network

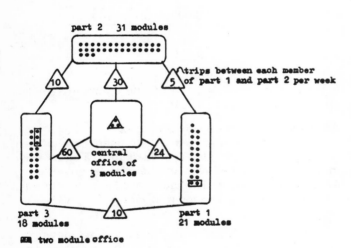

The circulation pattern includes a central office that concentrates work and control. The activities are split into three parts, which do not represent departments. Each activity has no circulation to members of its own part, only to the other parts. The division into parts is used only for descriptive convenience. The control office occupies three modules, there is a two-module office in part 1 and a three-module office in part 3.

Figure 7   Basic Circulation Pattern

take in computational terms, so let each cost £1.25. Then if the organisation remains in the building for 100 weeks and the cost of movement is 0.01 per metre, the optimum sample size n is

$$n = \sqrt{\frac{10320 \times .01 \times 100}{125}}$$

or $n \simeq 10$.

The plans are considered only in terms of circulatory efficiency, and the results should be seen as diagrams which influence planning, not as complete solutions.

References

1. Agin, N. (1966). Optimum seeking with branch and bound. *Management Science,* Vol. 13.
2. Aigner, D. J. (1968). *Principles of Statistical Decision Making.* New York: Macmillan.
3. Alexander, C. (1964). *Notes on the Synthesis of Form.* Cambridge, Mass.: Harvard University Press.
4. Almonde, M. (1966). An algorithm for constructing university timetables. *Computer Journal,* Vol. 8.
5. Archer, B. L. (1965). *Systematic Method for Designers,* reprinted from *Design.* London: Council of Industrial Design.
6. Armour, G. C. and Buffa, E. S. (1963). A heuristic algorithm and simulation approach to relative location of facilities. *Management Science,* Vol. 9.
7. Arthurs, A. M. (1967). *Probability Theory.* London: Routledge and Kegan Paul.
8. Bartless, M S., ed. (1966). *Sequential Methods of Statistics.* London: Methuen.

9. Beaumont, M. J. S. (1967). *Computer Aided Techniques for the Synthesis of Layouts and Form with Respect to Circulation.* Ph.D. Thesis. University of Bristol: Department of Engineering.

10. Bellman, R., Cooke, L. and Lockett, A. J. (1970). *Algorithms Graphs and Computers.* York: Academic Press.

11. Bellmore, M. and Nemhauser, G. C. (1966). The travelling salesman problem: a survey. *Operations Research,* Vol. 14.

12. Bernholtz, A. and Fosberg, S. (1969) *A Generalised Program for Transforming Relationship Values into Plan Layouts.* Unpublished paper. Harvard Graduate School of Design.

13. Broadbent, G. H. (1968). A plain man's guide to systematic design methods. *RIBA Journal* (May).

14. Buffa, E. S. (1963) *Models for Production and Operations Management.* New York: Wiley.

15. Buffa, E. S., Armour, G. C. and Vollmann, T. E. (1964). Allocating facilities with CRAFT. *Harvard Business Review* (March-April).

16. Bulmer, M. G. (1965). *Principles of Statistics.* London: Oliver and Boyd.

17. Bullock, N., Dickens, P. and Steadman, P. (1968). *A Theoretical Basis for University Planning.* Report No. 1. Cambridge: LUBFS.

18. Carson, C. B. (1959). *Production Handbook.* New York: Ronald Press.

19. Cemach, H. P. (1965). *Work Study in the Office.* London: Maclaren and Son.

20. Christofides, N. and Viola, P. (1971). The optimum location of multi-centres on a graph. *Operational Research Quarterly,* Vol. 22.

21. Computer Aided Circuit Design (1968). *Proceedings of Conference on CACD,* March 26th-28th, Sheffield University.

22. Conway, R. W. and Maxwell, W. L. (1961). A note on the assignment of facility location. *Journal of Industrial Engineering* (January-February).

23. Croes, G. A. (1958). A method for solving travelling salesman problems. *Operations Research,* Vol. 6.

24. Dale, E. (1953). *Planning and Developing the Company Organization Structure.* Research Report No. 20. New York: American Management Association.

25. Dantzig, G. B., Fulkerson, D. R. and Johnson, S. M. (1954). Solution of a large scale travelling salesman problem. *Operations Research,* Vol. 2.

26. Duffy, F. (1968). *The Office is More Than a Network of Communications.* Unpublished Paper. Berkeley: Department of Architecture, College of Environmental Design.

27. Economist Building Re-Visited (1969). *Architects' Journal Information Library* (3 September).

28. England, R. (1971). Planning complex building systems, *Nature,* Vol. 229 (January).

29. Facey, M. and Smith, G. (1966). Offices in a regional centre: a study of office location in Leeds, *Location of Offices Review.*

30. Fairweather, L. and Sliwa, J. A. (1969). *Architects' Journal Metric Handbook.* London: Architectural Press.

31. Flood, M. (1937) in Dantzig, Fulkerson and Johnson (1959).

32. Freeman, H. (1948). ed. *Sampling Inspection.* Statistical Research Group Columbia University, Applied Mathematics Panel, Office of Scientific Research and Development.

33. Gaskell, T. J. (1967). Bases for vehicle scheduling. *Operational Research Quarterly,* Vol. 18.

34. Gass, S. I. (1958). *Linear Programming; Methods and Applications.* New York: McGraw-Hill Book Company.

35. Gavett, J. W. and Plyter, N. V. (1966). The optimal assignment of facilities to locations by branch and bound. *Operations Research,* Vol. 14.

36. Gerard, G. L., Meyer, and Polake, E. (1971). Abstract models for the synthesis of optimization algorithms. *SIAM Journal of Control* (November).

37. Gilmore, P. C. and Gomory, R. E. (1964). Sequencing a one state-variable machine: a soluble case of the travelling salesman problem. *Operations Research,* Vol. 12.

38. Golomb, S. W. and Baumert, L. D. (1965). Backtracking programming. *Journal of the Association for Computer Machines,* Vol. 12.

39. Haberstroth, C. J. (1961). Organization structure: social and technical elements. *Industrial Management Review* (Autumn).

40. Haggett, P. and Chorley, R. J. (1969). *Network Analysis in Geography.* London: Edward Arnold Ltd.

41. Haire, M., ed. (1959). *Modern Organization Theory.* New York: Wiley.

42. Harvey, W. S., Nicholson, T. A. J., Pullen, R. D. and Quas, D. P. (1969). Optimization of paper machine scheduling. *Operational Research Quarterly,* Vol. 20.

43. Hawkes, D. (1970). *Factors Affecting Bulk and Separation of Buildings.* Ph.D. Thesis. University of Cambridge: LUBFS.

44. Held, M. and Karp, R. M. (1962). A dynamic programming approach to sequencing problems. *Journal of the Society of Industrial and Applied Mathematics,* Vol. 10.

45. Hillier, F. S. (1963). Quantitative tools for plant layout analysis. *Journal of Industrial Engineering* (January-February).

46. Hillier, F. S. and Connors, M. M. (1966). Quadratic assignment problem algorithms and the location of indivisible facilities. *Management Science* (September).

47. Home Office Building at Kew (1971). *Architects' Journal Information Library* (6 January).

48. Ingham, C. K. (1970). *Size of Industrial Organization and Worker Behaviour.* Cambridge Papers in Sociology, 1. Cambridge University Press.

49. Ingoll, E. and Shrage, L. (1965). Application of the branch and bound technique to some flow shop scheduling problems. *Operations Research* Vol. 13.

50. International Labour Office (1958). *Introduc-*

tion to Work Study. Geneva: I.L.O.

51. Jackson, D. M. and Steadman, P. (1965). *An Application of the Theory of 'Clumps' to Problems of Communications and Circulation in Office Buildings.* Unpublished paper.

52. Jones, J. and Thornley, D. G. eds. (1962). *Conference on Design Methods.* London: Pergamon.

53. Kendall, M. G. and Stuart, A. (1962). *The Advanced Theory of Statistics,* Vol. 1 and 2. London: Charles Griffin and Company.

54. Krag, R. L. and Thompson, G. L. (1964). A heuristic approach to solving travelling salesman problems. *Management Science,* Vol. 10.

55. Langdon, F. J. (1966). *Modern Offices: A User Survey.* National Building Studies Research Paper 41. London: HMSO.

56. Lawler, E. L. and Wood, D. E. (1966). Branch and bound methods: a survey. *Operations Research,* Vol. 14.

57. Le Corbusier (1924). *The City of Tomorrow.* London: Architectural Press.

58. Le Corbusier (1927). *Towards a New Architecture.* London: Architectural Press.

59. Lee, R. and Moore, J. M. (1967). Corelap: computerized relationship layout planning. *Journal of Industrial Engineering* (March).

60. Levin, P. H. (1964). The use of graphs to decide the optimum layout of buildings. *Architects Journal* (7 October).

61. Lin, S. (1965). Computer solutions of the travelling salesman problem. *Bell System Technical Journal,* Vol. 44.

62. Lindley, D. V. C. (1971). *Making Decisions.* London: Wiley Interscience

63. Litteler, J. A. (1969). *Organizations Structure and Behaviour.* New York: Wiley.

64. Little, J. D. C., Murty, K. G., Sweeney, D. W. and Karel, C. (1963). An algorithm for the travelling salesman problem. *Operations Research,* Vol. 11.

65. McCausland, (1969). *Introduction to Optimal Control.* New York: Wiley.

66. Makower, M. S. and Williamson, E. (1967). *Teach Yourself Operational Research.* London: English University Press Ltd.

67. Manasseh, L. and Cunliffe, R. (1962). *Office Buildings.* London: Batsford.

68. March, L. and Steadman, P. (1971). *The Geometry of Environment.* London: R.I.B.A. Publications Ltd.

69. Martin, L. (1965). *Whitehall: A Plan for the National and Government Centre.* London: HMSO.

70. Martin, L. and March, L., Eds. (1972). *Urban Space and Structures.* Cambridge University Press.

71. Marples, D. L. (1968). Roles in manufacturing organizations. *Journal of Management Studies* (May).

72. Medd, D. (1968). 'People in Schools: and an Attitude of Design'. *R.I.B.A. Journal,* June.

73. Meyer, P. L. (1970). *Introductory Probability and Statistical Applications.* Reading, Mass.: Addison-Wesley.

74. Milward, G. E., ed. (1962). *Organizations and Methods.* London: Macmillan.

75. Moseley, L. (1963). A rational design theory for planning buildings based on the analysis and solution of layout problems. *Architects Journal* (11 September).

76. Nicholson, T. A. J. (1971). A method for optimizing permutation problems and its industrial applications. In Welch, D. J. A., ed., *Combinational Mathematics and its Applications.* London: Academic Press.

77. Nugent, C. E., Vollmann, T. E. and Ruml, J. (1968). An experimental comparison of techniques for assignment of facilities to locations. *Operations Research,* Vol. 16.

78. Pilkington Research Unit (1965). *Office Design: A Study of Environment.* University of Liverpool: Department of Building Science

79. Reiter, S. and Sherman, G. T. (1965). Discrete optimizing. *Journal of the Society of Industrial Applications and Mathematics,* Vol. 13.

80. Riggs, J. L. (1970). *Production Systems Planning Analysis and Control.* New York: Wiley.

81. Ritzman, L. P. (1972). The efficiency of computer algorithms for plant layout. *Management Science,* Vol. 18.

82. Rudolfsky, B. (1964). *Architecture without Architects.* London: Academy Editions.

83. Russell, L. and Ackoff, R. L. (1961). *Meaning, Scope and Methods of Operations Research.* New York: Wiley.

84. Scott, A. J. (1971). *Combinatorial Programming, Spatial Analysis and Planning.* London: Methuen.

85. Seehof, J. H., Evans, W. O., Friedricks, J. W. and Quigley, J. H. (1966). Automated facilities layout programs. In *Proceedings of the Association for Computing Machinery, 21st National Conference, 1966.* Washington, D.C.: Thompson.

86. Standard Telecommunications Laboratories, *Placement of Circuit Units on Board,* Harlow, Essex. C.A.D.E. Study Paper No. 13 and 18.

87. Steadman, P. (1970). *The Automatic Generation of Minimum-Standard House Plans.* Working Paper 23. Cambridge: LUBFS.

88. Steinberg, L. (1961). The blackboard wiring problems: a placement algorithm. *Society of Industrial and Applied Mathematics Review,* Vol. 3.

89. Tabor, P. (1970). *Traffic in buildings.* Ph.D. thesis. University of Cambridge: LUBFS.

90. Vollmann, T. E. and Buffa, E. S. (1966). The facilities layout problem in perspective. *Management Science,* Vol. 12.

91. Vollmann, T. E., Bugent, C. E. and Zartler, R. L. (1968). A computerized model for office layouts. *Journal of Industrial Engineering,* Vol. 19.

92. Walker, R. S. (1960). An enumerative technique for a class of combinatorial problems. In *American Mathematical Society Proceedings of Symposia in Applied Mathematics.* Vol. 10.

93. Weeks, J. (1969). Multi strategy buildings. *Architectural Design,* Vol. 10.

94. Whitehead, B. and Eldars, M. Z. (1964). An approach to the optimum layout of single

storey buildings. *Architects' Journal* (17 June).

95. Whitehead, B. and Eldars, M. Z. (1965). The planning of single storey layouts. In Hendry, A. W., ed., *Building Science,* Vol. 1, No. 2. London: Pergamon.

96. Williams, H. J. (1968). *Computer Graphics in Architecture.* Unpublished paper. Boston, Massachusetts: ICG Systems.

97. Willoughby, T. (1970). Computer aided building plans, a generative approach. *Official Architecture and Planning* (September).

98. Willoughby, T. (1970). A rational approach to design. *Architectural Association Quarterly* (October).

99. Willoughby, T. (1970). *A Generative Approach to Computer Aided Planning.* Working Paper 42. Cambridge: LUBFS.

100. Willoughby, T. (1971). Computer use: a direction for computer aided planning methods. *Building* (February).

101. Willoughby, T. (1971). Evaluation of circulation performance. *Architectural Design* (May).

102. Willoughby, T., Paterson, W. and Drummond, G. (1970). Computer aided architectural planning. *Operations Research Quarterly,* Vol. 21. □

Automatic hospital layout

J. C. Gray

HAPA, the automatic assembly program for Harness hospitals, is a complementary system to the evaluative system. Its purpose is to attempt to automate the positioning of hospital departments around a pre-defined circulation route, the Harness, under the control of user directives. Its major role is to accept the design team's requirements of the scheme and then, taking full acount of these, to locate the unconstrained departments in such a way as to reduce the total circulation in the hospital to a minimal value. Although it is possible for the system to make up hospital layouts in an unconstrained situation, it is not likely that such a pursuit would be fruitful. I regard HAPA as being a tool to be used to aid the exploration of design ideas rather than one that effectively generates solutions *de novo*.

HAPA is an interesting example of the automatic assembly process which is tuned specifically to a single building method and which therefore can avoid some of the pitfalls of more generalised research techniques for automatic assembly. The major simplifying feature that Harness provides is that the hospital departments are preplanned, so that it is possible to assemble them around the circulation zone into cohesive whole buildings.

The assembly or placement mechanism functions in two separate stages. The first stage examines the possible general locations for departments, and the second makes definitive decisions about their absolute location within separate zones of the layout. The resulting layout is a recognisable Harness hospital and not just a tangled agglomeration of building elements, as is often produced by generalised automatic assembly techniques.

The system is highly interactive, and the user can modify any of his constraints at will (the brief, the profiles, the hospital shape, and so on), so that he can both experiment with differing design concepts and explore the effects of minor changes in constraints.

It would be useful to explain quite carefully the manner in which the system is used, both to demonstrate the operation of the system in creating hospital layouts and also to give some idea of what is involved in using an interactive computer-aided design system. The employment of HAPA requires a certain amount of previous data preparation, and also the use of commands which direct the system housekeeping, in addition to those which control the automatic layout process. The user communicates his requirements to the machine using any of about 30 presently available commands, and the computer responds by carrying out his instructions and producing appropriate messages and pictures. Although a logical order of steps is set out, the system is very flexible. The user can retrace at any time and change previous assumptions in order to explore alternative strategies.

STEP		COMMAND
1	Setting up the Data Profiles Traffic information Brief Execute file	EXECUTE
2	Entering the System Hospital name	VERSION
3	Reading and Confirming Data	DEPS PROFS
4	Defining the Hospital Shape	LEVELS HSTREET CORNERS BLOCK
5	Superimposing Constraints on the Location of Departments	PUTDEPS LINK RELEASE CLEAR CLEAR A CLEAR M
6	Clustering Departments	CLUSTER A CLUSTER B CLUSTER M RANK
7	Positioning Departments	POSITION POSITION M
8	Displaying the Layout	DISPLAY
9	Making Manual Adjustments	PUTDEPS
10	Evaluating the Layout	EVALUATE PRUNE
11	Storing the Resulting Layout	DUMP LOAD
OTHER FACILITIES		? PRINT FILE TIMELEFT QUIT

Figure 1

STEP 1
Setting up Data
Standard Profiles

The shapes of departments in Harness hospitals are to a large extent predetermined. It is therefore possible to set up a library of standard profiles which are used again and again. The profiles are set up in computer terms by representing each 16.2m square module in the plan of a department by a single character. Thus, by typing the department configuration and attaching an identifying code to it, it can be inserted and stored in a library of standard department profiles. A department's configuration and its equivalent representation would be stored as in *Figure 2* where 'X' represents solid buildings, ' ' represents a courtyard, and 'E' represents the location of the department entrance.

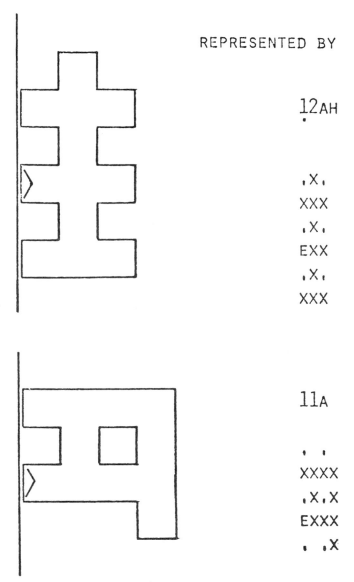

REPRESENTED BY

12AH

,X,
XXX
,X,
EXX
,X,
XXX

11A

, ,
XXXX
,X,X
EXXX
, ,X

Figure 2

Additional or modified department profiles can be included in the course of a run by using the same command as is used to read the library data

The Program

The program employs the same standard traffic information as is used by the other Harness development planning programs for circulation assessment and lift location. It is in the form of the weighted numbers of trips in 24 hours between pairs of department types of standard sizes, and is modified in accordance with the operational policies laid down for Harness by the Department of Health and Social

Security. When the program receives the brief, it can generate a unique traffic matrix for the scheme.

The Brief

Each Harness hospital has a unique brief of departments depending on local hospital requirements. Each brief can be prepared before the use of HAPA, but amendments can be made interactively. The brief can contain both information about the departments and also some generalised constraints. The scope of brief information is as follows:—

(i)   Department name
(ii)   Traffic data and the type and size of departments which are used in the automatic generation of the unique traffic matrix.
(iii)   Profile name referring to the library of profiles or to new profiles input for specific situations.
(iv)   Absolute restrictions which include ground floor only, top floor only, restrictions to specified levels, automatic handing not permitted, and ignoring the department in automatic placing procedures.

An 'Execute' File

It is possible to set up a file of HAPA commands which can be read and acted on sequentially by the program using the EXECUTE command, thus avoiding interactive working when it is not required.

When this data has been set up, the user is in a

```
LEVELS 1
HSTREET 2 0 0 0 0 0
LEVELS 2
HSTREET 19 12 0 0 0 5 6
LEVELS 3 4
HSTREET 19 0 0 0 0 3 6
CORNERS
5 6 6
6 7 6
/
BLOCK
C 2 1 4 11
/
INTERACT STFK1

DEPS F /JJ/STFK D
PROFS F /ME/PROFLIB
PROFS F /ME/STF.P

PUTDEPS
STORES: E2 -7 6 H
/

LINK
ENTRANCE: NEXT: OPD+FR
X-RAY: NEAR: OPD+FR
THEATRES: ABOVE: OPD+FR
MORTUARY: NEAR: PATH 1
PHARMACY: NEAR: OPD+FR
ITU: NEAR: THEATRES
EDUC'N PG: NEAR: EDUCATN
MAT WARD: NEXT: MAT+SCBU
/
INTERACT STFK2
```

Figure 3

position to start working with the system. It is quite likely that he will only need to create a brief, and possibly an execute file, the other data being basically standard from scheme to scheme.

STEP 2
Entering the System

On entering the system, the program asks for the current hospital name. It can also receive a version identifier via the VERSION command. This information can be appended to all significant ouput from the system so that it can be identified at a later date. Having received the hospital name, the system returns to command reading status.

```
HARNESS/HAPA/*(X20888)

HAPA AT YOUR SERVICE
HOSPITAL NAME?  -  OXBRIDGE

*VERSION AUG73
```

Figure 4

STEP 3
Reading and Confirming Data

The system automatically reads the standard traffic data from a file when this is required but it has to be instructed to read specific files containing the department's brief and then the profile library. Using the same commands, DEPS and PROFS, it is possible both to interrogate, amend and output the program's current profile and department information.

STEP 4
Defining the Hospital Shape

The maximum permissible outline of hospital shape is a double cruciform arrangement of Harness street.

These limbs are defined to exist or not using the HSTREET command in combination with the LEVELS command, which permits repetition of the same configuration on several layers. Each limb that is defined automatically prescribes a clustering zone in which the departments themselves may be located. Departments may only access the Harness street from one direction, and a default configuration of clustering zones is assumed unless countermanded by the CORNERS command. The BLOCK command can be used to prevent sections of the defined Harness street from having departments attached to them.

A typical arrangement of Harness Street might appear as in *Figure 6.*

STEP 5
Superimposing Constraints on the Location of Departments

(a)   The PUTDEPS command allows the user manually to locate departments either absolutely or generally within the layout. The following alternatives are available:

(i)   location within a clustering zone, i.e. anywhere on a specified limb at a defined level
(ii)   location within a planning zone, i.e. on a specific side of a clustering zone
(iii)   absolute location at a specific entrance slot on a limb at a defined level
(iv)   the fourth option allows the user to move the department from its existing position along a limb by a specified number of entrance locations.

(b)   The LINK command allows for the setting up of qualitative positional relationships, 'QPRs', between departments. These include ABOVE, BELOW, NEXT, OPP, NEAR, FAR, RTOF AND LTOF.

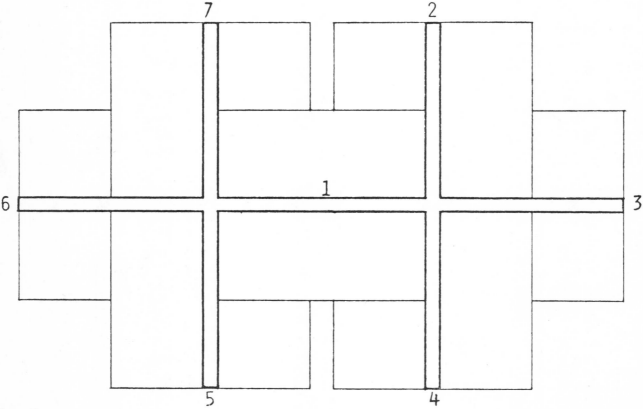

Figure 5

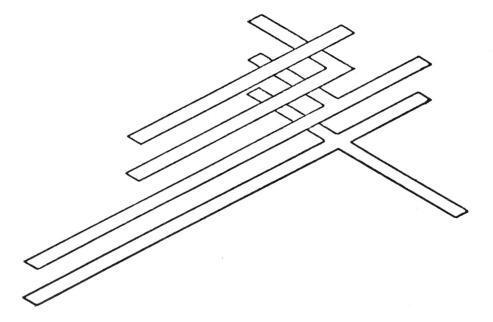

Figure 6

```
LINK
ENTRANCE : NEXT : OPS+FR
X-RAY : NEAR : OPD+FR
THEATRES : ABOVE : OPD+FR
MORTUARY : NEAR : PATH 1
PHARMACY : NEAR : OPD+FR
ITU : NEAR : THEATRES
EDUC'N PG : NEAR : EDUCATN
MAT WARD : NEXT : MAT+SCBU
```

Figure 7

The system takes account of these constraints whenever locating departments within the layout. It is quite common to have important departments constrained by a complex series of QPRs which are often difficult to achieve. QPRs are countermanded by the UNLINK command.

(c)   Other countermanding commands include: RELEASE, release a specific department from its position in the layout; CLEAR, remove all departments from the layout or from a specific level; and CLEAR A and CLEAR M which, respectively, release all automatically or manually positioned departments.

When conflicting constraints occur, the system mormally checks and informs the user so that he can rectify the situation. The user can always DISPLAY the layout as it stands to review the situation.

STEP 6
Clustering Departments

The purpose of this step is to allocate the departments which are not already located to suitable zones within the layout. These clustering zones are prescribed automatically when the Harness street is defined as in Step 4.

At this point, the system takes account of all departmental constraints imposed by PUTDEPS, LINK and the original brief. The system acting on the known size of limbs also assessses the likelihood of departments of various sizes fitting along the currently considered limb. It is quite clear that the order in which departments are clustered into zones is important. There are three alternative mechanisms for assessing this:

(a)   CLUSTER A and CLUSTER B attempt different mechanisms for automatic ordering.
(b)   CLUSTER M takes a manually defined order for clustering. The default is the original order of departments within the brief, but this can be adjusted using the RANK command.

All clustering alternatives have a manipulating parameter which effectively reduces the apparent size of the zone and thus the amount of building allowed to fit into it. This slack is necessary when POSITIONING departments at the next stage. The outcome of the step is the allocation of all available departments to clustering zones within the layout. The algorithms used in CLUSTER are described in more detail later.

STEP 7
Positioning Departments

This POSITION command examines each clustering zone in turn and places departments at specific entrance slots, taking into account any outstanding constraints, for example, NEXT, ABOVE, OPPOSITE.

It automatically maintains the courtyard pattern that is defined by the Harness system and also tries 'handing' departments where permissible to attempt to compact the layout. The departments are placed either in order of decreasing connectivity to other departments in other clustering zones, or in order of manual ranking if so requested.

STEP 8
Displaying the Layout

The DISPLAY command can be used to show position of located departments on one level at a time on the storage tube screen.

It contains several options which include:
(a)   level required
(b)   blocked entrances (confirmation of BLOCK command)

```
? T C

HOSPITAL - EDWARD , VERSION - B1

DEPT CLUSTERS

UNCLUSTERED -

PATH 2
LINEN
MANG IND
CHPL+LIB
STORES
WORKS
BOILER


CZ: 1,1


CZ: 1,3


CZ: 2,1

E  -  14  Y CHR W
E  -  02  A+E
E  +  06  OPD+FR
E  +  02  ENTRANCE
E  +  12  PHYS MED
E  -  06  G WARD
E  -  12  PHARMACY
E  +  10  X-RAY


CZ: 2,3
```

```
E  +  06  MORTUARY
E  +  10  PATH 1
E  +  02  HSSU
E  -  10  ISOL'N
E  -  06  MANAGEMT
E  -  02  EDUCATN
E  +  04  EDUC'N PG


CZ: 3,1

E  -  12  ITU
E  +  02  PAT SERV
E  -  04  A WARD 2
E  -  14  DAY WARD
E  +  06  THEATRES
E  +  12  A WARD 1


CZ: 3,3

E  +  02  CATERING
E  -  04  A WARD 3
E  +  10  PAED W


CZ: 4,1


CZ: 4,3

E  -  04  MAT WARD
E  +  04  MAT+SOSU


✱
```

Figure 8 (Step 6)

(c) positioned departments
(d) clustering zones
(e) entrance slot locations
(f) sending output to the plotter instead of the screen

STEP 9
Making Manual Adjustment

The layout resulting from the two-stage automatic placement process can always be modified by manual adjustment using the PUTDEPS command already described in Step 5 to locate departments specifically, to move departments, or to hand them.

STEP 10
Evaluating the Results

The EVALUATE command carries out some very simple analyses of the layout. These include:
(a) the calculation of current circulation
(b) the summation of Harness street area, department area, roof surface area, and wall surface area
(c) the calculation of department/Harness ratio, average building height, wall to floor area ratio and total surface area to floor area ratio

It often happens that the originally defined Harness street is in excess of the requirements of the layout.

The PRUNE command deletes all portions of the Harness which are superfluous and would markedly affect the evaluation.

STEP 11
Storing the Resulting Layout

The progress made in any run of HAPA can be stored on computer file for future use by means of the DUMP command, and the specific layout can be reinstated by the LOAD command for further adjustment or manipulation.

Other facilities

The system contains several other facilities as yet not mentioned which aid the user in his operation of the program. They are necessary house-keeping, and include:
(a) ? this command gives various diagnostic textual output, which includes information on:
   (i)   the Harness street dimensions
   (ii)   the clustering zone contents and parameters
   (iii) pictorial maps of specific clustering zones
   (iv)   department positions
   (v)   the unique traffic matrix
   (vi)   links between departments, QPRs
(b) PRINT Output may be sent to the line printer if too voluminous for output on the screen.
(c) FILE Any output on screen or teletype may be

```
*POSITION
CZONE 1,01 DONE

POSITIONING FAILURE
QPR 'A+E NEXT OPD+FR' UNSATISFIABLE

*UNLINK
A+E:OPD+FR
/

*LINK
A+E:OPP:OPD+FR
/


*

POSITION
CZONE 1,01 DONE
CZONE 2,01 DONE
CZONE 2,02 DONE
CZONE 2,06 DONE
CZONE 2,07 DONE
CZONE 3,01 DONE
CZONE 3,06 DONE
CZONE 3,07 DONE
CZONE 4,01 DONE
CZONE 4,06 DONE
CZONE 4,07 DONE

LAYOUT COMPLETE

*DUMP /ME/20-1802
```

Figure 9 (Step 7)

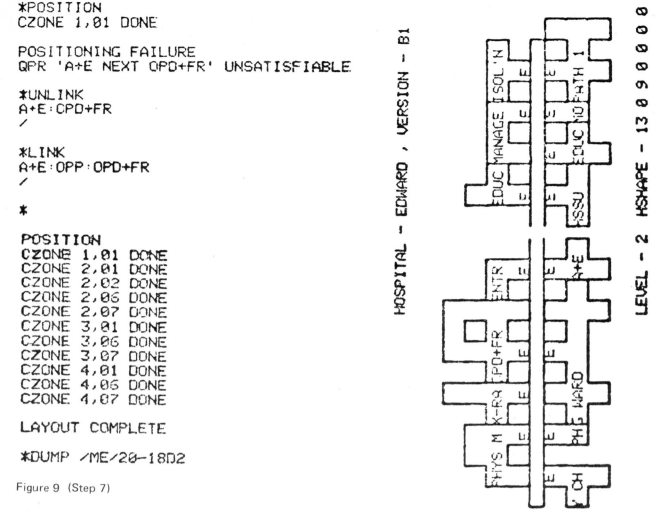

Figure 10 (Step 8)

(d) TIME LEFT The system indicates amount of computation time remaining of original requested allocation.

(e) QUIT Finishes off a HAPA session and reports on the amount of computation time used.

Systems and Design of HAPA

Having given an outline of the facilities offered in the HAPA system, it is worth discussing in general terms the systems design approach used in HAPA. The program has been designed in a modular fashion, i.e. segments can be extracted and amended independently. Segments often correspond precisely with the commands used in the system. A substantial amount of background work has been carried out on the problems of manipulating and describing the hospital itself, not only the locational arrangement and the avoidance of clashes of departments, but also the complex structure of constraints which are built up by the user to suit a particular scheme.

The automatic sections of the program for Clustering and Positioning are written as separate modules. Three Clustering and two Positioning alternatives already exist in the system. As ideas for enhancement and development of these sensitive sections occur they can be included as further optional modules, and earlier versions can be phased out as they become obsolete.

Clustering and Positioning

The Clustering process first of all satisfies all absolute constraints, including appropriate QPRs, constraints to certain levels and constraints to various clustering zones or sides of clustering zones. The departments are either continually re-ranked for order of importance in automatic clustering or inserted in clustering zones in a manually predefined order. The best clustering zone for any department is assumed to be that in which the department can still fit, and where it causes the smallest increase in the total circulation between clustering zones with respect to the already clustered departments. A fixed allowance is made for changes in level. The ranking of departments can either be in order of total traffic with other departments or, as in the CLUSTER B command, in order of normalised traffic to already clustered departments. This ensures that small departments with significant traffic to only a small number of already clustered departments tend to be grouped with those larger departments, rather than excluded until the end of the process when they may be situated far from the only departments with which they have significant traffic. At present, this latter algorithm appears to give the most plausible layouts.

Currently the positioning process works one clustering zone at a time. It first accepts the location of all manually positioned departments in setting up a description of the zone, and then ranks the departments in the cluster in an order of importance with regard to other clustering zones in the hospital. It can assume manual ranking if the POSITION M command is used. Departments are then tried for fit in the zone in that order. The system obeys the constraints of space available in the zone and QPRs such as Next, Left of, Right of and Opposite, and sets up "above" constraints for the zone above. The system can attempt handling of departments, when permissible, for a more compact fit of departments within a zone.

```
CURRENT CIRCULATION=239647

H=544 D=1539 R=937 W=1362


DEPTS:HSTREET = 282
AVGE # LEVELS = 222
WALLS:FLOOR = 54
ROOF+WALLS:FLOOR = 98

*
```

Figure 11 (Step 10)

The system does have short-comings. These include:
1. It is not very sensible about vertical stacking
2. In placing departments it gives preference to the right-hand end of the central limb of the Harness street rather than treating both ends equally.
3. Its ability to pack departments into zones is not as ingenious as that of project teams used to Harness development planning. This is a function of the mix of profiles within a brief for a particular scheme.

However, with more development alongside project design teams and further modifications of the various crucial placement modules, it is possible to envisage improvements within the overall structure of the system.

Conclusion

HAPA, in comparison with more generalised mechanisms for automating the layout problem, is significant in several ways, mainly because it is tuned to the problem of a specifc systems approach to building i.e. Harness.

It includes the following characteristics:
1. It manipulates the predefined spatial elements, departments which are capable of forming a compact and cohesive building.
2. It operates by placement around a circulation route, the configuration of which is provided and manipulated by the user.
3. It operates in three dimensions.
4. It employs detailed traffic data for all automatic location procedures, founded on operational policies of live hospital projects.
5. Its placement mechanism is two-stage.
6. The system is modular and the crucial placement algorithms are capable of being developed separately from the system as a whole.
7. It contains facilities for setting up a wide range of constraints and controls for the user, from the restriction of departments to certain levels, limbs or locations, to the creation of qualitative positional restraints.

In other words, it can perform useful tasks of automatic layout within the specific environment of the Harness system of hospital development planning. □

Part 5

Building systems

Systems as a species

Geoffrey Hutton

In this paper I propose to tilt at a few windmills and stand back a little from the immediate application of computers to building problems, a subject in which I am certainly interested as my firm owns one of the beasts and also uses bureau machines extensively. My commitment in this field is essentially practical. I nearly said 'commercial' for, in terms of survival, the two words are synonymous.

Definitions

The word 'systems' is prominent in the title of the conference and when we speak of 'building systems' this expression worries me, as I believe it does many others, because of its general imprecision and the assumptions it contains. Incidentally, 'industrialised building' is another such expression.

The word 'system' is widely applied in many fields, and general definitions are:
1) a complex whole, a set of connected things, an organised body of material or immaterial things or
2) a method or organisation, or considered principles of procedure.

These definitions are commonly understood but they have become subjected to many specialist nuances. To some extent the word has lost precision and for this reason, in coding texts for retrieval purposes, it has been found useful to regard 'system', 'method', 'procedure' and 'theory' as synonymous. Thus the title of the session "Theory of building systems" could be expressed equally well as "System of building theories". 'Industrialised building', on the other hand, is coded with the ideas of 'manufacture' and 'assembly'. Incidentally, it is also considered that, for the purpose of retrieval, 'design' and calculation' are also synonymous. Clearly, it is necessary to define the contexts in which the expression 'system' is used and consider the ways in which it is applied in the building industry.

The term 'system' is used in many contexts. For example, there are the following systems:

    Administrative
    Assembly
    Classification
    Communication
    Computer
    Control
    Disposal and collection
    Exchange
    Expression
    Hierarchical
    Identification
    Knowledge
    Management
    Political
    Production
    Social
    Solar
    Supply and distribution
    Weapon

Clearly, there are patterns of interdependent influences governing the form and performance of all things and these are the systems which are postulated or established as a means of making life comprehensible. These systems are the basis of design and require data in order to be tested.

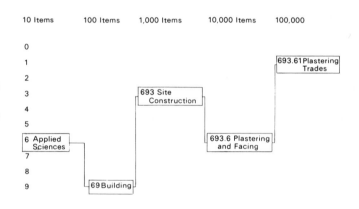

Figure 1 The UDC, a hierarchical system

There is a danger that the word 'system', when attached to a particular field, can be taken to indicate a certainty of performance which may not be justified. Systems can be constructed to include only convenient facts and can be proved in artificial circumstances. For a long time, for example, the Piltdown man was accommodated in theories of human descent and many hypotheses of prehistory fail to account for the technical knowledge needed, not to build, but to brief, Stonehenge.

It is tempting to become involved in a semantic analysis of the term and, by definition, restrict or elaborate its meaning. Bruce Martin, in his stimulating book on standards in building, concludes that a system is a 'physical whole, especially one made up of a number of units arranged in a complex way, some of which are movable'. I do not find this helps very much and when one tries to define a 'whole', or what at any given moment may be regarded as a 'whole',

163

we are forced to conclude that, like meat and poison, one man's 'whole' is another man's 'part'. Indeed, Bruce Martin concluded that the 'whole' was beyond analysis and only the units of which it was made could be investigated.

Systems in Building

When we talk about buildings, we are discussing the combination and interaction of a variety of explicit and implicit systems. For example, the classical orders could be used to define a building explicitly or implicitly.

It is invidious to try to establish a priority of systems out of a random list applying to building but, I think, necessary, if only to ensure that decisions are taken in the right sequence and with a real appreciation of the factors involved.

A building is the outcome of, at least, the following systems:—

> Administrative
> Assembly
> Communication
> Control
> Disposal and collection
> Exchange
> Expression
> Management
> Political
> Production
> Social
> Supply and distribution

In this context, the use of the expression 'building systems' becomes so loose as to be meaningless and, I think, even dangerous. When the nature of the 'system' is investigated, it almost invariably proves to be a method of production or assembly, usually of the structural frames or carcass. Any structure becomes a system of forces and materials merely by the process of erection. All buildings contain many other systems to achieve a variety of objectives. These may, or may not, be consciously related but, nevertheless, act together to give a performance which is more or less desirable. The classification of any particular way of building as a 'building system' is a completely arbitrary matter and implies that other methods are in some way less systematic. The men who built Stonehenge had a good system, two uprights and a beam, but their organisation, tools and incentives were no doubt different from ours. Building is only a means to an end, not an end in itself: the end must be demonstrated in terms of cost and performance.

It is suggested that, at this point, the expression 'building system' as descriptive of any particular level of prefabrication or as having any special meaning beyond common usage to indicate the existence of interdependence in an organisational or material context, should be abandoned. Our concern should primarily be with the sequences expressed by the words force/effect, activity/event, process/product, perception/pleasure or pain (in the body or the wallet).

There is some doubt whether the merely physical structure and envelope of a building is the most significant factor in terms of overall performance. To many architects, this might seem to be beyond question and this is reinforced by the fact that the initial realisation of their schemes is principally on paper.

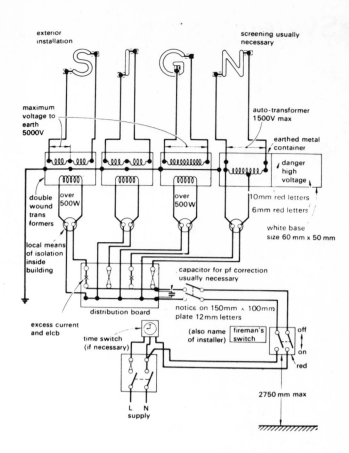

Figure 2 The system for an illuminated sign represented by its circuitry (Electrics 72/73)

Adaptability of a Building

Planning is still mainly the arrangement of space dimensionally rather than in time. The system of inputs and outputs, processes and controls in the use of buildings is generally imperfectly understood and, in accepting this, designers prefer indeterminate solutions capable of extension and change (less often, replacement and renewal). The prediction of change, however, is not well developed nor has its incidence in the past been extensively investigated. Establishing the frequency and cost of extension, internal rearrangement and renewal would enable the priority of this aspect of building performance to be assessed. It is interesting that many old buildings appear to have been altered and extended without difficulty and without initial investment in facilities for this purpose. This has been normally motivated by social and economic circumstances not envisaged by the original designer. What is adaptability worth? The ability to dismantle and re-erect buildings is obviously valuable for some military buildings, emergency housing, exhibitions, temporary wards and so on.

Evolutionary Development

In the past, there has been a strong force of vernacular, unselfconscious, incremental decision-making in the evolution of building. This appears to have been influenced and perpetuated by builders rather than professional designers. I think this vernacular force still exits and prospers, and has much to offer, and I want to introduce the idea of evolutionary development in products we use, considering how, if at all, the computer might influence this development.

The basic proposition is quite a simple one: that artifacts (and organisations) are the product of man (the toolmaker) in place and time, that a natural balance exists only for a moment and that design can exist and develop only with the making of products where the human, technical and material resources of manufacture and marketing are concentrated.

An independent design profession could not have produced one of the lower animals, still less a mammal. Although the camel is reputed to be a horse designed by a committee, its adaptation to its own circumstances is precise, otherwise no camel would survive. Design, technology and the market are inextricably intertwined. The alternatives are buyer/specifier or designer/builder: the designer/specifier is no longer a runner, except for prestige building. For me, the division is between the investigation of requirements and evaluation of results (building-owner responsibility) and the provision of products and buildings (a competitive service by industry).

The concept of the 'building system' too easily assumes hierarchy of components and elements, just as the rectilinear plan is determined by graphical techniques. The hierarchy is, of course, very convenient for computing. From the point of view of construction, modular economy and appearance, it might be less than desirable.

Units of Pre-fabrication

Buildings, obviously, have to be erected and the size and volume of units should be governed by considerations of convenience in assembly rather than multiplicity of arrangement. The prefabrication of volumes whenever possible, rather than frameworks, seems to me to offer much greater opportunity for the integration of services, equipment and finishes off site. Ideally, these volumes should be carefully tailored to their proposed use and not compromised by generalisation between activities, although such generalisation is inevitable in structurally based prefabrication. Perhaps the structural engineer should not be consulted until late in the design process! The larger the generalised unit of prefabrication, the more likely is the activity contained to be compromised or waste incurred, as the increment for design purposes is a coarse one.

The advantages of structurally based prefabrication have been difficult to establish except when the structure forms the major part of the cost of the finished building (very often in long-span types). When high standards of finish or complex service installations are required, conventional building methods are still competitive and much more adaptable. It seems that the incremental building kit has got to be demonstrated as having more than a marginal advantage over conventional building techniques.

Advantages of Repetition

Repetition is the acknowledged basis of production and is recognised in nature. For example, within limits, people are all the same and this applies to all organisms which have become adapted to particular circumstances. Reproduction of satisfactory solutions to problems larger than those occasioned by the individual part or element seems to me the most fruitful basis for building design. A complete building lends

itself to study and development as an organism, and can be evolved through successive variants to achieve a precise match with the users' activities. That in any given period there might be a demand for ten, one hundred or a thousand such buildings is merely a matter of production of the design, for which suitable techniques and materials would be used. Repetition of standard designs makes optimum use of the learning curve in any technique (in the factory or on the site) and has the advantage that the use of a particular model of building is familiar to staff and maintenance workers wherever it may be built. Information gathered on such designs is directly comparable and is readily used in new models.

The effect of the site and locality on building form is too easily exaggerated, though constricted and irregular sites probably need special treatment. It does not seem to me that there is any particular size or type of building which cannot be repeated with advantage if the use is not unique.

The computer, like any other tool, will affect the product. However, it would be wrong to favour designs because they can be readily processed on a computer. The machine can certainly be used to assemble lists of generalised components in a preconceived Baykostyle building kit, but it can as readily be used to smooth curves and prepare data for numerically controlled machines with coordinates spaced at less than five-metres.

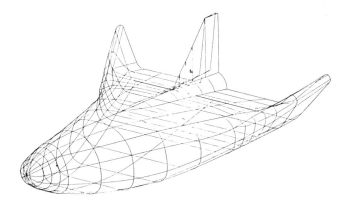

Figure 3 A computable form which is yet an integrated unit

If replication of buildings as specific objects or functional assemblies is accepted, what is the aesthetic effect of repetition? Variety would be time-based (model 1, model 2 etc) related to the size, purpose, life and quantity of particular building types required, with all the design capital going into the type building rather than a generalised kit-type solution. The repetition of individual buildings is likely to be less soporific visually than the proliferation of curtain walling.

The Effects of Competition

Variety, of course, implies choice, invites comparisons, provides competition which ensures efficiency, in turn (political pressures apart) providing for survival and benefiting the user. This is nature's method of optimisation which, I suggest, is at present beyond computation.

There is a tendency for competitors to become alike, often even working to agreed standards. Thus, choice is concentrated on significant variables out of an apparently vast range. These characteristics for selection are important in forming data banks. Natural selection works on fine distinctions which are irreversible, as time is involved, a hierarchy of development which nevertheless implies matching to circumstances. This pattern holds true in commerce, where it can be as disastrous to be too far ahead of a market as to be left behind.

Darwin's grandfather expressed the evolutionary idea in verse,

> "First, forms minute, unseen by spheric glass,
> Move on the mud, or pierce the watery mass.
> These, as successive generations bloom.
> New powers acquire and larger limbs assume".

Darwin, in his conclusion to 'The Origin of Species', set out the laws governing change in nature as "Growth with Reproduction; Inheritance which is almost implied by reproduction; Variability from the indirect and direct action of the external conditions of life, and from use and disuse; a Ratio of Increase so high as to lead to a struggle for Life, and as a consequence to Natural Selection, entailing Divergence of Character and the Extinction of less-improved forms. Thus, from the war of nature, from famine and death, the most exalted object which we are capable of conceiving, namely, the production of the higher animals, directly follows." I consider that this exposition of the forces of nature is no less applicable to the shells and lodges of man than it is to those of the nautilus or the beaver. To vary Darwin's last sentence: 'Thus from the competition of techniques, from shortage and failure, the most magnificent structure we are capable of conceiving directly follows'.

User Requirements

The balance of user requirements with available resources is a function of competition in a market (natural selection). Man in place and time, exercising skill with tools and materials, is capable of supplying the appropriate product if the buyer can discriminate, and the wider the choice the better for him.

Natural selection in building is taking place constantly and should be encouraged. The market for building products is like a pond, heaving with technical and commercial competitors at all levels. A domesticated fish could be said to survive in this environment if protected by a plastic bag; a sponsored product only thrives while protected by its sponsor. Centrally developed building products and processes for a protected market are of this nature, frequently have an unrecorded demise and offer few advantages over individually designed buildings, which seem to be preferred by users.

Such products and processes are motivated by considerations of special use, economy and independence of source of supply. The first is rarely valid, the second rarely achieved and the third illusory. It is significant that, in wartime, the forces of natural selection were sufficiently strong to ensure the rapid adoption of many building methods now thought substandard, but at the time found acceptable by users.

Simple proprietary buildings, evolved for industrial and commercial use, are virtually unnoticed in the field of more monumental building, yet, given the urgency and right market, could be evolved for other purposes. Many adults spend their working lives in well-lit and insulated sheds: is it inconceivable that similar buildings might be suitable for schools? Perhaps too high a price is paid for architecture, when buildings over 100 years old are still in use for many social purposes.

The building industry suffers from interruptions in economic policy and the monopoly purchasing effect of large public programmes. Only in housing are whole building designs purchased by public authorities on any scale, whereas this practice is common in the private sector for houses, offices and factories. Confidence in this sector is indicated by speculative building (in effect, for stock). This can give real choice to the user not having time or money to commission a bespoke building. Greater production is required to allow more rapid turn-over of land and to permit users to change premises with altering circumstances.

The protection of some old buildings (like that of some animals) is desirable for social, historic or economic reasons. This also means the perpetuation of the skills, tools and materials necessary for their maintenance and reproduction.

Data Collection

Models of buildings and situations have been the major subject of this conference. With these, one endeavours to predict. My own interest is in the data base to be derived from real situations. It seems to me that such data bases are the prerequisite for decision-making models of situations and that valuable deductions may be drawn from acquired data subjected to analysis. The best 'models' are complete buildings on which data may be gathered, capable of specific analysis, rather than general deductions about performances over extended periods, based on assumptions.

From this, I conclude that the best study of building is buildings themselves and that this is the surest basis for development. I suspect the overall creation of building programs based on theoretical concepts of building requirements to be crude (but full-size) models of reality, rather like the Frankenstein creation of man in a laboratory. I prefer the development of an existing type, the 'Best Buy' approach of DHSS perhaps.

Building is frozen data. Design is data-processing and calculation. Data is the raw material of market decisions, production, design and evaluation of performance. Its collection is undramatic, tiresome and expensive but it is vital. Models and simulations cannot be operated without reliable data.

Data acquisition is costly in relation to the construction of a model, and much less fun. It is important therefore, to avoid the expense of unnecessary accuracy for decision-making. A large sample is desirable, however. For example, it is not much use having 80 per cent of the possible information on 20 per cent of the available bricks: the reverse is to be desired. Similarly, a large sample of buildings is necessary for studies of user requirements. Effort has to be concentrated on hard (or conveniently hardened) information, and it is important that discretion is exercised initially in establishing the necessary units, bands of values and indicators. This is as true of buildings in use as it is for products.

It is desirable that the basis of data collection for control and evaluation is established at the inception of building programs. An example is the UNESCO Educational Code used in the IBRD Spanish project, which is capable of identifying spaces, functions and equipment and, by reference, performance, quantities and cost. Such methods are neutral to design and enable very different schemes to be compared. The development of data frameworks, such as the CIB Master List, is a necessary step for coordinating data.

Data banks for many purposes have been assembled by my firm. The techniques are well established and the results can be obtained on-line or manually (the latter has its own merits). Proprietary buildings were surveyed in 1966 and 1971 and a further revision is about to be carried out. Obviously, detailed results cannot be given in a paper of this kind but it is interesting to note that a claimed capacity of 10 million square metres in 1966 had fallen to 3 million in 1971, representing the kind of fluctuation the industry is prone to. Traditional building is economically very resilient and will survive on smaller returns than extensive prefabrication of low-cost elements.

To assess the degree of industrialisation, 49 elements were identified as being necessary for a complete building. No system offered all characteristics and the best score was 76 per cent. The most commonly occurring characteristic is the provision of structural elements followed by roof decks, suitability for single-storey construction and the provision of the vertical envelope. The only finish to be generally provided is the roof finish.

The percentages of products providing the following elements are:-

Element	1966 per cent	1971 per cent
Carcass		
Substructure	21	16
Structure	98	87
Roof: deck	91	81
finish	61	53
Cladding	85	75
Pre-glazed windows	25	24
Partition carcass	58	50
Pre-hung doors	15	14
Installations		
Heating	21	14
Water supply: cold	17	9
hot	16	8
Electrical	17	14
Gas	5	2
Sanitary	17	10
Rainwater disposal	51	41
Air treatment	8	7
Mechanical	1	1
Communications	2	1
Finishes		
Internal walls	12	12
Floor	5	6
Staircases	8	5
Ceilings	6	5
External frame	14	8
Wall	59	50
Windows	21	18
External doors	12	12
Infill panels	9	6
Fixtures and equipment		
Door fittings	45	42
Window fittings	53	50
Fitted furniture	10	12
Sanitary fittings	14	5
Kitchen fittings	15	12

The low percentages for installations, finishes and fixtures, and equipment are a fair measure of the, as yet, undeveloped nature of prefabrication in building. Most development work appears to have been devoted to the elements with the least effect on the user.

Conclusions

I conclude that the development of closed technical, material and economic solutions for building problems is inevitable and that the vernacular will reassert itself through industry and not through a necessarily independent design profession.

It is hoped that buildings will become entities again in a way not possible when the unit of repetition is too obviously the external wall components. The whole would then be less obviously the sum of the parts.

Evaluation is fundamental to prediction and selection and more effort should be devoted to collecting coherent data for this purpose.

Architects in particular must abandon an anomolous position in an industry which requires their talents but not their status.

Building users must make it their business to know their needs more thoroughly, specify them more precisely, select and encourage the best products available, and evaluate the results. Courage is then needed to present properly formulated requirements to industry and accept its proposals with an open mind.

□

Geometry and numbers in building systems

Paul Richens

Introduction

During the last two years my work has been largely on the implementation of a large computer-aided design project, called OXSYS, for the Oxford Method of construction. In the course of this work, I was much concerned to find a way of constructing a numerical model of building geometry, of sufficient power to support the wide range of applications that were to be built into OXSYS. Of especial concern was a particular function of OXSYS which is to act as a *detailing machine.* The idea is that an architect has a sketch design, which he describes to the computer, and gets back at the end a fully detailed set of working drawings, all thoroughly consistent with the rules of the method.

I suppose the *detailing* process can be subdivided into 3 parts with rather different characteristics. The first is a matter of communication between architect and machine, in order to describe the sketch design. This requires a language for interaction. The second stage consists of the internal detailing performed by the machine. This eventually· requires a model of building geometry, and the means to manipulate it. The third stage is the output of the resulting detailed building, most importantly by means of drawings.

I intend to concentrate in this talk on some features of the middle process, the manipulation of the model. However, some of the techniques are relevant to the production of drawings and, further, some of the properties of the geometrical model give important hints as to how the interactive language might communicate geometrical information.

Size, position and orientation of components

Oxford Method uses a tartan grid; its ground-rules permit components to have certain controlled relationships to the grid. This method of regulating a building system has an important result. Many components are rectangular boxes, and they are nearly always aligned parallel to the grid. Even components which are not strictly boxshaped are generally considered, at least for coordination purposes, to have a box-shaped envelope controlling their dispositions in the building.

The size of a rectangular box may be characterised in several ways *(Figure 1).* The most straightforward is simply to give its height, width and depth. This adequately describes the geometry of an isolated box. Once it is placed in a building, however, more information is required, to describe its position, and its orientation.

Position is easily defined by the 3-D coordinates of a corner; let us say the corner nearest the building origin, or one defined as the box origin (in this case identical).

Orientation of a box is more complicated. It may be rotated in three different planes (or about three different axes), as shown in *Figure 2.* When more than one rotation is involved, the situation becomes worse, as the order in which rotations are carried out becomes significant.

Rotations in plan

The effect of rotation on the coordinates of any point in the component may be obtained by pre-multiplying the component coordinates by a transform matrix, such as the one shown in *Figure 2* (for rotations in plan). Similar transforms exist for rotations about the other two axes.

Quite a lot can be done by describing geometry at this level, i.e. components as boxes defined by three dimensions, their positions as the coordinates of one corner, and their orientation by a 3 x 3 transformation matrix.

However, just as the use of a coordinating grid justifies the use of rectangular boxes for components, so it can largely justify the restriction of orientation to positions which line-up with the grid.

If we restrict rotations in plan to multiples of 90°, the transformation matrices become remarkably simple. You will notice that each row and each column contains only one non-zero digit, and that it is always plus or minus one. If you ignore the sign for a moment, what you have left is a *permutation matrix.* The result of multiplying a 3-element vector (such as the coordinates of a point) by a permutation matrix is another vector, whose elements consist of the same *values* but in a different *order.* The effect is to permute the order of the vector elements.

As permutation matrices are mostly zeroes, and therefore rather inefficient descriptions. of the transform, I have adopted an alternative representation (shown in the right-hand column of *Figure 3,* which I term a permutor.

The permutor corresponding to the identity transform (rotation through zero degrees) indicates that the first element of the result is equal to the first of the source, and similarly the second and third. The 90° permutor swaps the first and second coordinates, while the minus sign indicates that the first element of the result must be negated.

The geometrical interpretation of this operation for a 90° turn *(Figure 4)* shows that the a and b dimensions are exchanged, while the c dimension remains unchanged. Furthermore, the b dimension is running in the opposite direction to the original a, which is the significance of the minus sign.

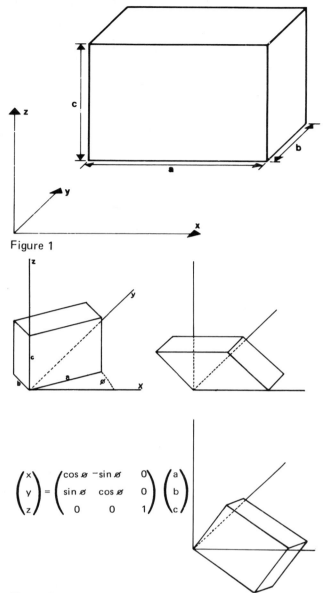

Figure 1

$$\begin{pmatrix} x \\ y \\ z \end{pmatrix} = \begin{pmatrix} \cos\varnothing & -\sin\varnothing & 0 \\ \sin\varnothing & \cos\varnothing & 0 \\ 0 & 0 & 1 \end{pmatrix} \begin{pmatrix} a \\ b \\ c \end{pmatrix}$$

Figure 2 Rotation of a Component About Principle Axes, with Transformation Matrix for Rotation in Plan

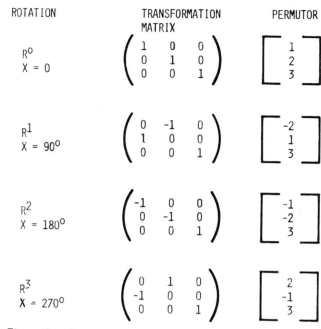

ROTATION	TRANSFORMATION MATRIX	PERMUTOR
R^0 $X = 0$	$\begin{pmatrix} 1 & 0 & 0 \\ 0 & 1 & 0 \\ 0 & 0 & 1 \end{pmatrix}$	$\begin{bmatrix} 1 \\ 2 \\ 3 \end{bmatrix}$
R^1 $X = 90^0$	$\begin{pmatrix} 0 & -1 & 0 \\ 1 & 0 & 0 \\ 0 & 0 & 1 \end{pmatrix}$	$\begin{bmatrix} -2 \\ 1 \\ 3 \end{bmatrix}$
R^2 $X = 180^0$	$\begin{pmatrix} -1 & 0 & 0 \\ 0 & -1 & 0 \\ 0 & 0 & 1 \end{pmatrix}$	$\begin{bmatrix} -1 \\ -2 \\ 3 \end{bmatrix}$
R^3 $X = 270^0$	$\begin{pmatrix} 0 & 1 & 0 \\ -1 & 0 & 0 \\ 0 & 0 & 1 \end{pmatrix}$	$\begin{bmatrix} 2 \\ -1 \\ 3 \end{bmatrix}$

Figure 3 Derivation of Permutors from the Transformation Matrices for Rotations in Plan

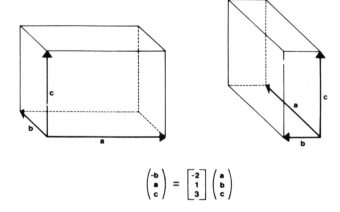

$$\begin{pmatrix} -b \\ a \\ c \end{pmatrix} = \begin{bmatrix} -2 \\ 1 \\ 3 \end{bmatrix} \begin{pmatrix} a \\ b \\ c \end{pmatrix}$$

Figure 4 Operation of Permutor for ¼-Turn in Plan on Order and Direction of Component Dimensions

We now move on to some properties of these permutors. The permutor for a 90° turn in plan I call the R or rotation permutor. As well as permuting coordinates, permutors may operate on each other. The table in *Figure 5* shows how the permutors may be combined to generate the permutors for 180°, 270° and finally 360° rotations. The end result, you will see, is the identity permutor as we have rotated the object back to its initial orientation.

Rotations about other axes

So far we have discussed plan rotations; however rotations about the other axes are equally amenable to representation by permutors. *Figure 6* shows the full set of basic permutors for 90° rotations about the 3 axes. The S permutor is a sideways rotation, the T a tilting forward through 90°.

We have achieved a numerical representation of the basic orientation operations that may be required on a component in our orthogonal world, and can proceed to investigate some general properties of our

model by algebraic means rather than geometrical.

We can now calculate a combination table for the basic permutors *(Figure 7)*. Here I show, in the columns, successive powers of the S and T operations, and in the rows the effect of pre-multiplying them by powers of R, or plan rotation.

The table has 28 entries, of which 4 are duplicates. So we have generated 24 different permutors. This is satisfactory as a box has 6 faces each with 4 sides, giving 24 possible orientations.

If you combine any two elements you will get another in the table, which again indicates its completeness. For the mathematician I would also point out that combination is associative; that there is an identity element I, and that every element has an inverse, for example R^3 is the inverse of R^1. The structure is, therefore, a non-commutative group.

The duplication which occurs is interesting. The root cause can be seen by the identity $R^2S^2 = T^2$. In fact any combination of 2 different squares gives the third. So $T^2S^2 = R^2$. In geometrical terms we are dealing here with 180° rotations.

The situation is shown in the 'triangular' diagram, *Figure 8*. Any apex can be reached by 1 half turn, or 2 half turns about the other two axes, in either order. This is an Abelian group, where the order of

combination of terms is immaterial. Further, each element is its own inverse. Two 180° turns bring you back to where you started.

The multiplication table has 24 terms, but the structure of the permutor indicates that 48 different cases could exist.

$$\left[R\right] = \begin{bmatrix} -2 \\ 1 \\ 3 \end{bmatrix}$$

$$\begin{bmatrix} -1 \\ -2 \\ 3 \end{bmatrix} = \begin{bmatrix} -2 \\ 1 \\ 3 \end{bmatrix} \quad \begin{bmatrix} -2 \\ 1 \\ 3 \end{bmatrix}$$

$$\left[R\right]^2 = \left[R\right] * \left[R\right]$$

$$\begin{bmatrix} 2 \\ -1 \\ 3 \end{bmatrix} = \begin{bmatrix} -2 \\ 1 \\ 3 \end{bmatrix} \quad \begin{bmatrix} -1 \\ -2 \\ 3 \end{bmatrix}$$

$$\left[R\right]^3 = \left[R\right] * \left[R\right]^2$$

$$\begin{bmatrix} 1 \\ 2 \\ 3 \end{bmatrix} = \begin{bmatrix} -2 \\ 1 \\ 3 \end{bmatrix} \quad \begin{bmatrix} 2 \\ -1 \\ 3 \end{bmatrix}$$

$$\left[R\right]^0 = \left[R\right]^4 \qquad \left[R\right] * \left[R\right]^3$$

Figure 5   Combination of Permutor for ¼-Turn in Plan

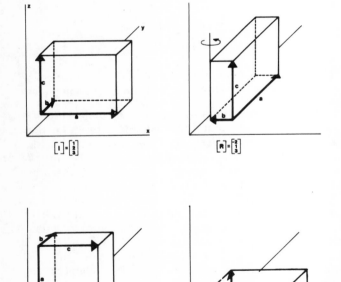

Figure 6   Standard Permutors for ¼-Turn Station About the Principle Axes

	$[I]$	$[S]^1$	$[S]^2$	$[S]^3$	$[T]^1$	$[T]^2$	$[T]^3$
$[R]^0$	$\begin{bmatrix}1\\2\\3\end{bmatrix}$	$\begin{bmatrix}3\\2\\-1\end{bmatrix}$	$\begin{bmatrix}-1\\2\\-3\end{bmatrix}$	$\begin{bmatrix}-3\\2\\1\end{bmatrix}$ $-[R]^2[T]^2$	$\begin{bmatrix}1\\-3\\2\end{bmatrix}$	$\begin{bmatrix}1\\-2\\-3\end{bmatrix}$	$\begin{bmatrix}1\\3\\-2\end{bmatrix}$ $-[R]^2[S]^2$
$[R]^1$	$\begin{bmatrix}-2\\1\\3\end{bmatrix}$	$\begin{bmatrix}-2\\3\\-1\end{bmatrix}$	$\begin{bmatrix}-2\\-1\\-3\end{bmatrix}$	$\begin{bmatrix}-2\\-3\\1\end{bmatrix}$ $-[R]^3[T]^2$	$\begin{bmatrix}3\\1\\2\end{bmatrix}$	$\begin{bmatrix}2\\1\\-3\end{bmatrix}$	$\begin{bmatrix}-3\\1\\-2\end{bmatrix}$ $-[R]^3[S]^2$
$[R]^2$	$\begin{bmatrix}-1\\-2\\3\end{bmatrix}$	$\begin{bmatrix}-3\\-2\\-1\end{bmatrix}$	$\begin{bmatrix}1\\-2\\-3\end{bmatrix}$	$\begin{bmatrix}3\\-2\\1\end{bmatrix}$ $-[T]^2$	$\begin{bmatrix}-1\\3\\2\end{bmatrix}$	$\begin{bmatrix}-1\\-2\\-3\end{bmatrix}$	$\begin{bmatrix}-1\\-3\\-2\end{bmatrix}$ $-[S]^2$
$[R]^3$	$\begin{bmatrix}2\\-1\\3\end{bmatrix}$	$\begin{bmatrix}2\\-3\\-1\end{bmatrix}$	$\begin{bmatrix}2\\1\\-3\end{bmatrix}$	$\begin{bmatrix}2\\3\\1\end{bmatrix}$ $-[R][T]^2$	$\begin{bmatrix}-3\\-1\\2\end{bmatrix}$	$\begin{bmatrix}-2\\-1\\-3\end{bmatrix}$	$\begin{bmatrix}3\\-1\\-2\end{bmatrix}$ $-[R][S]^2$

Figure 7   Combination Table for Standard Rotational Permutors

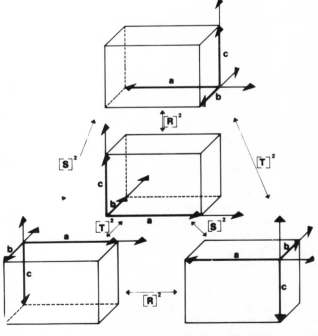

Figure 8   The Combination of Half-Turn Transforms

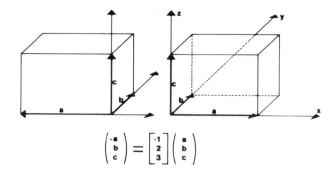

$$\begin{pmatrix} \text{-a} \\ \text{b} \\ \text{c} \end{pmatrix} = \begin{bmatrix} \text{-1} \\ \text{2} \\ \text{3} \end{bmatrix} \begin{pmatrix} \text{a} \\ \text{b} \\ \text{c} \end{pmatrix}$$

Figure 9   Permutor for Reflection in y-z Plane

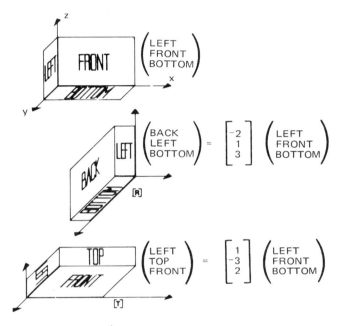

$$\begin{pmatrix} \text{BACK} \\ \text{LEFT} \\ \text{BOTTOM} \end{pmatrix} = \begin{bmatrix} -2 \\ 1 \\ 3 \end{bmatrix} \begin{pmatrix} \text{LEFT} \\ \text{FRONT} \\ \text{BOTTOM} \end{pmatrix}$$

$$\begin{pmatrix} \text{LEFT} \\ \text{TOP} \\ \text{FRONT} \end{pmatrix} = \begin{bmatrix} 1 \\ -3 \\ 2 \end{bmatrix} \begin{pmatrix} \text{LEFT} \\ \text{FRONT} \\ \text{BOTTOM} \end{pmatrix}$$

Figure 10

Take one which is not in the table; the identity permutor with the first term negated *(Figure 9).* If you draw the geometrical result of using it you find the result is a mirror-image, the box being reflected in the yz plane. In fact all the missing 24 cases turn out to be various orientations of the mirror image. From the modelling viewpoint, this is a bonus. Aiming for a simple way of describing orientation, we have achieved a means of describing handedness at the same time.

The model tells us so far what volume of space a component occupies in any orientation. Another question we would like to ask the model would be, "What is the disposition of the faces after rotation?" A box with labelled faces, unrotated, is shown in *Figure 10.* We can describe the faces as a vector, the elements being the faces facing to left, to the front, and to the bottom.

We then rotate this through 90° in plan, i.e. apply the R operation. If we permute the face vector by the same permutor as used for the dimensions we get the new disposition of faces. The minus sign is now interpreted as "take the opposite to," so *Front* becomes *Back.* This method works for all orientations, and incidentally for reflections as well.

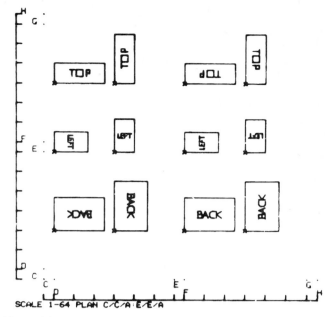

SCALE 1-64 PLAN C/C/A:E/E/A

Figure 11

Production of drawings

This system of making a numerical model of building geometry has been used very successfully in the OXSYS system. To demonstrate its use for drawing components I set up a demonstration component like this, with the faces labelled, and inserted it into a building in a variety of different attitudes. The result in plan *(Figure 11)* corresponds to part of the multiplication table. The top row shows rotations of the component the right way up, the second and third shows rotations applied after S, and after T.

The process of producing plans and sections in different views is very similar to that for locating individual components. Here we are in effect rotating the whole building with respect to the picture frame, not individual components with respect to the building. There are really 4 transforms to be applied to a coordinate point on the face of a component before it can be drawn. The first converts face coordinates to component coordinates, and depends on which face is visible, and the conventions used for describing face features. The next is the component transform, which converts the component coordinates to building coordinates. Then another converts the building coordinates to picture coordinates. Finally, coordinates are multiplied by a scalar factor to produce the desired scale of drawing *(Figure 12).*

$$\begin{pmatrix} x \\ y \\ z \end{pmatrix} = \text{SCALE} \begin{bmatrix} \text{PICTURE} \end{bmatrix} \begin{bmatrix} \text{COMPONENT} \end{bmatrix} \begin{bmatrix} \text{FACE} \end{bmatrix} \begin{pmatrix} a \\ b \\ c \end{pmatrix}$$

Figure 12   Transformation of Face Coordinates to Picture Coordinates

The transforms shown here are based on the permutors I have described, though there is also a translation component to account for the *position* of objects. This is simply related to the orientation permutor and the size of the object.

This concept of component geometry, consisting of

171

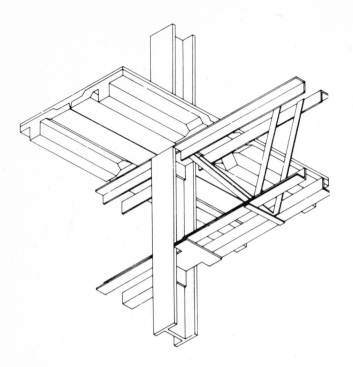

Figure 13

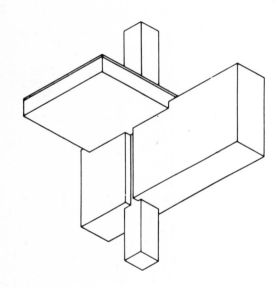

Figure 14

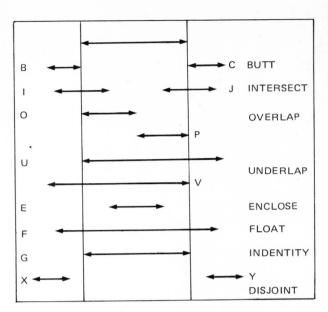

Figure 15   Adjacency Codes in One Dimension

rectangular boxes lined up on a grid, is happlily compatible with the Oxford Method. Many components really are box shaped (cladding panels, sink unit), others rather less so (WC, staircase), but they can still be conceived as occupying a box of space. Drawings are produced by OXSYS for graphical confirmation, and show components in isolation. The complete transformation system I have just described is used to produce plans and sections on a storage tube terminal during design.

Interrelationship of components

So far I have been talking of single components related to the spatial framework of the building. Now I would like to go on to show how we codify the relationships between one component and another.

We often have to deal with a jumble of components and a significant function of our geometrical model will be to avoid spatial clashes of this sort.

The isometric drawing *(Figure 13)* shows the intersection of beams, column and floor units. In terms of our model it reduces to a set of interpenetrating boxes *(Figure 14)*. The problem is now restated, omitting inessential detail, as a problem in the geometry of boxes. Their inter-relationships must now be reduced to a numerical form.

Figure 15 shows a 1 dimensional component (at the top), with all the different relationships that another could have to it. First we have butt joints, left and right-handed, where the components just touch. Then intersection, overlap and its inverse, which I have termed underlap. Then enclosure, its converse, and identity where the components exactly coincide. Finally they may be disjoint.

This system is easily extensible to more than one dimension. The tableau *(Figure 16)* shows a sample of the cases in 2 dimensions. In 3 dimensions there are too many cases to draw conveniently, but the same principles are applied. The method used to generate these is very simple. A matrix is formed *(Figure 17)* by calculating the end differences for the two components, once for each dimension. The actual values of the end difference are not significant for a qualitative description of the adjacency, and can be reduced to -1, 0 and $+1$.

I have shown *(Figure 18)* the end-difference matrices associated with each class of adjacency. These end matrices have some useful properties.

The product of elements e_{12} and e_{21} indicates the *degree* of the adjacency (disjoint, butt, penetrate). The sum $e_{11} + e_{22}$ indicates the *sidedness* (left, right or symmetrical). Finally penetrations can be further discriminated by $e_{11} - e_{22}$ which reveals whether it is a simple intersection, overlap or underlap *(Figure 19)*.

Application of modelling techniques

I have assigned various letters of the alphabet to the different classes of adjacency. So in 3-dimensions I can form a 3-character code completely defining the

172

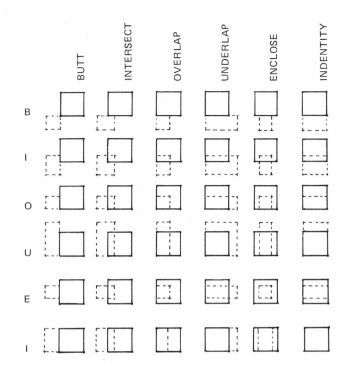

Figure 16   Tableau of 2D Adjacency Types

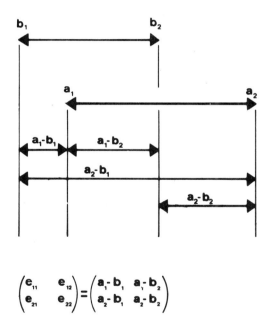

Figure 17

$$\begin{pmatrix} e_{11} & e_{12} \\ e_{21} & e_{22} \end{pmatrix} = \begin{pmatrix} a_1\text{-}b_1 & a_1\text{-}b_2 \\ a_2\text{-}b_1 & a_2\text{-}b_2 \end{pmatrix}$$

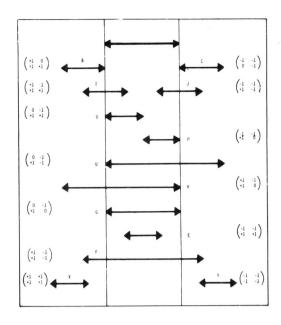

Figure 18   Relationship Between End-Difference Matrices
and Adjacency Codes

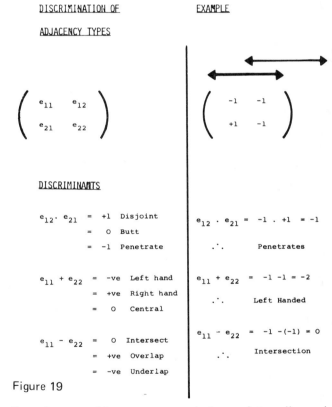

DISCRIMINATION OF ADJACENCY TYPES

EXAMPLE

$$\begin{pmatrix} e_{11} & e_{12} \\ e_{21} & e_{22} \end{pmatrix} \qquad \begin{pmatrix} -1 & -1 \\ +1 & -1 \end{pmatrix}$$

DISCRIMINANTS

$e_{12} \cdot e_{21}$ = +1   Disjoint

= O   Butt

= -1   Penetrate

$e_{11} + e_{22}$ = -ve   Left hand

= +ve   Right hand

= O   Central

$e_{11} - e_{22}$ = O   Intersect

= +ve   Overlap

= -ve   Underlap

$e_{12} \cdot e_{21}$ = -1 . +1 = -1

∴   Penetrates

$e_{11} + e_{22}$ = -1 -1 = -2

∴   Left Handed

$e_{11} - e_{22}$ = -1 -(-1) = 0

∴   Intersection

Figure 19

type of adjacency. A practical problem which makes use of these geometrical modelling techniques and is drawn from my experience with the OXSYS project will also indicate the kind of analysis and thinking required to solve computer-aided design problems of this sort, which are fundamentally geometrical.

The drawing on which the following examples are based, a plan grid in the form of a tartan, is a standard Oxford Method detail showing the disposition of steel required to support a rooflight. The main features are that tartans always contain steel, either beams or non load-bearing ties.

Several types of beams occur, main beams internally, perimeter beams at the edge of the roof, and expansion beams, which are split and very similar to a pair of perimeter beams, along an expansion joint. The rooflight frame is a rectangle of rolled-steel angle, and is supported, usually, on angle trimmers.

My technique, given a detail such as this, is to examine the geometrical implications concealed in it, and formulate a set of rules.

Rooflight rules

1.   Rooflights may not be located within 600mm of:

173

            perimeter
            expansion joint
            another rooflight
            the outside of a rooflight trimmer
            floor-roof junction
            floor-undercroft junction
2. Rooflights may not be located between an existing pair of trimmers unless of a size to be supported by them.
3. Rooflight frames may be supported by:
            rooflight trimmer
            main roof beam
            roof column tie
4. Rooflight frames may not be supported by:
            perimeter beams
            junction beams
            expansion beams
            beam ties
5. Rooflight trimmers must all span the same way in a bay.
6. Rooflight trimmers may be supported by:
            all types of roof beam.
7. Rooflight trimmers may not be supported by:
            ties
            other rooflight trimmers.

The writing of rules frequently provokes the architects involved in the building method into clarifying their details. I am particularly concerned to discover in what contexts the detail will work, and where it must be modified, or perhaps prohibited. For example the rooflight shown adjacent to a column in the detail is satisfactory on a flat roof, but would produce a clash if the column were extended because the diagonally opposite bay was a storey higher.

Now for the application of these rules to automatic design. I have chosen as an example a sketch design which calls for a rooflight in a certain position; the function of OXSYS is to check its legality, select the necessary components and locate them in the building. The position shown is in a bay already containing a rooflight, and bounded by an expansion beam, a perimeter beam, a column tie and a main beam.

The use of dummy components

The first problem is to select a direction of span, and test its legality. This is done by inventing a dummy component in the position shown, and testing its adjacencies. This dummy reaches up to the tartan edges in the direction of span, and is half a tartan wider than the rooflight opening in the other direction *(Figure 20)*.

Generating its adjacencies produces a number of highly significant results. The left end butts an expansion beam, so the trimmer would be supported. The bottom edge intersects a main beam, so a trimmer is not required, whereas the top edge has no adjacency and so will need a trimmer. These are all satisfactory results. However others are not. No adjacency is found for the right hand edge, as the column tie does not fill the tartan. No adequate support exists at that end. Worse still, the dummy is penetrated by an existing rooflight and its trimmers. The rooflight itself would be alright if it exactly fitted the dummy, as the two frames could then share trimmers. This is not the case. We have found an insuperable spatial clash

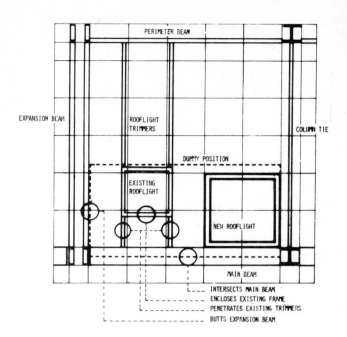

Figure 20   Adjacency Checks on Rooflight Dummy Component — Illegal Case

This position of the dummy is not usable. So OXSYS now tries the opposite rotation by generating a dummy spanning the other way *(Figure 21)*.

This has very satisfactory adjacencies; the ends of the span each butt suitable beams. One long edge has no adjacency, and so requires a trimmer. The other coincides with a column tie, which is an adequate substitute for the trimmer. There is now no clash with the existing light and its trimmer.

It is next necessary to do some checks on the rooflight frame itself. We have, as it were, obtained outline permission to place a light somewhere along the length of the dummy, we now need detailed clearance for the actual position. In this case we find it butts the main beam and the column tie both of which are permitted according to the rules. This would not have been the case if the light had been at the upper end of the bay, where it would have butted a perimeter beam, which is prohibited.

This process indicates the way in which standard details may be reduced to written rules, which in turn can be largely reduced to a list of permitted or prohibited adjacencies to components. Once this is achieved, the problems of computer-aided building assembly become tractable.

In this case we have now discovered all we need to know. Two directions of span have been examined, and one found suitable. We know we need one trimmer, on the left side, and we know which way it is to span. Our model of the building can therefore be enlarged by adding the new components to it.

Structural design and other applications

When the new components are added, all the individual adjacencies are determined *(Figure 22)*. These are stored in the computer as part of the building description. They will have wide application in subsequent processing of the model. For example, when we come to structural design, which involves

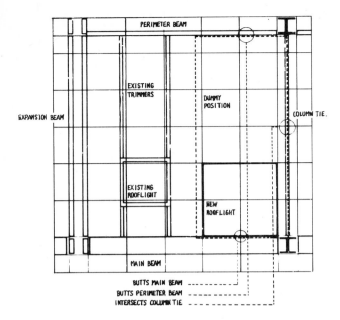

Figure 21   Adjacency Checks on Rooflight Dummy
Component — Legal Position

Conclusion

I hope this has given some idea of what can be achieved by the practical application of geometrical modelling in computer-aided building design. The success of the method depends entirely on the critical simplifications. We are fortunate to be dealing with a building method which is highly suitable for the 'box' approach. We have already developed systems for semi- or fully automatic input of beams and columns on similar lines. Here the type of component is often determined by its context. Floor slabs and cladding will be ready in the next few weeks. We have discovered that once you have achieved a modelling system such as I have described, it becomes a straightforward task to convert standard details to design algorithms.

Though more complicated geometrical descriptions could be employed you will find that the more complicated they are, the less usable. By discarding the fine detail of component structure we have achieved the ability to model, in more than adequate detail, the geometrical consequences of component relationships.   □

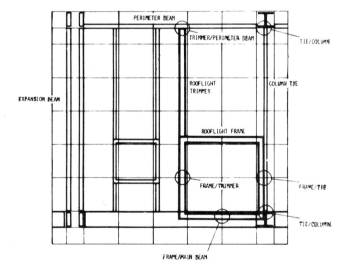

Figure 22   Significant Adjacencies Between Rooflight
Framing and Structural Steelwork

calculating the loads on the beams and columns in order to size them, we will find adjacencies between the beams and the trimmers. We will also find the adjacency between the trimmer and the rooflight it supports. This enables us to calculate the point loads generated by the rooflight. Similarly the columns are adjacent to the ties, which is adjacent to the frame. So we will get the direct load on the column.

Another case of the usefulness of these adjacencies would occur if the designer changed his mind and decided to delete the rooflight. Its adjacency to the trimmer would be found, so that would be deleted too, unless of course it was also adjacent to other rooflights (which must still be supported).

175

Cost/Performance: The key to a building systems approach

Ezra Ehrenkrantz

In the United States, to a great extent, our motivations are directly related to problems which come up within a relatively unconventional practice of architecture, where our basic concerns are building systems. The kinds of tools and methods that we develop are those that will help us do our job in a more effective way and, as a result of a number of years of work in the field, we have begun to develop a basic philosophy which, in effect, has evolved out of the 20:20 vision of hindsight. I will take advantage of that vision, so my comments result from actual problems that we have encountered in our projects.

Looking at any kind of a systems approach to design there is one thing that we have to recognise at the outset, and that is that what is one man's system is another man's component. As architects we may talk of a building as a building system, but to the superintendent of schools or to the chief surgeon at a hospital or an administrator, obviously the building is only a component. In the same way a mechanical engineer will talk about his air conditioning system, where we will say it is a sub-system or a component.

To be relevant within the society in which we operate we need to remind ourselves, when we talk of our system, that, to the person for whom we are designing, our system is just a component. We must get that sense across in the development of any kind of systems approach, recognising that *that* component of the user for whom we are doing the design work relates with *many other* components of his daily activities in order to provide a proper environment in which he may live and work and play, and so on. Within such a context our task is very much that of ordering the available resources to meet basic user requirements.

The user requirements we generally categorise as being a combination of needs and aspirations. If you design only for needs you may find, when your preliminary designs are presented, that the client will not accept them. If you design only for aspirations, you will go very quickly through the process but never visit after the building is completed.

On the other hand, the resources that you have to work with are essentially five in number for any type of construction: land, finance, management capability, technology and labour. I put land and finance first because no matter how good your management capabilities are, without those two you are not going to build. But assuming those resources are present, the most important single resource is the management capability by which the process is ordered. Then technology and labour are there in order, in fact, to do the job.

But you get some very interesting trade-offs in terms of, let us say, land densities which relate to technology. You may build higher, have greater cost per square foot, more fire protection and use a more expensive technology depending on the value of the land. Regarding another financial aspect, you may find that you can use a more expensive technology if you use phased construction to get the building up a year earlier. So again, obviously, one must consider all these factors, keeping in mind that the output of this process is measured in terms of *time, cost* and *performance.* We are looking at an ability to get a building constructed for the initial projected cost, to have it open at the planned time and to have it perform, in terms of characteristics of performance quality within the building, as predicted or projected initially in the programme brief.

If we can do that we are then able to control the building process and the credibility of the design professions will remain high. If the professions are not able to perform in terms of time, cost and quality, there will obviously be an ever-increasing dependence on other kinds of professional groupings to get the job done. This, unfortunately, is happening in great measure in the United States; I do not know what the case is here.

Looking at any particular project we might, however, find the need to control one or other of these three factors with greater certainty than the other two. If the prime criterion is *cost control* we find design/construct approaches have been developed, in which a design partner and a construction partner, in effect, give a price for doing the job. When that is done a client knows that a project will, in fact, be completed for that specific number of dollars. The obvious problem is that the designer is then working for the contractor to make sure that the building is completely detailed out within that price. If *time* is of the essence, we have phased construction techniques where we can break ground with a very limited amount of design information completed—perhaps only the schematic design plus working drawings on foundations—and work in a situation where we are providing the working drawings, or doing the working drawings, on the subsequent phases while the construction is going on. In this way we can reduce very considerably the time required to get a job done.

If we are trying to develop new powers within the industry to meet specific *user requirements* which are not easy to meet with available products, we may go out to bid on a basis of performance specifications.

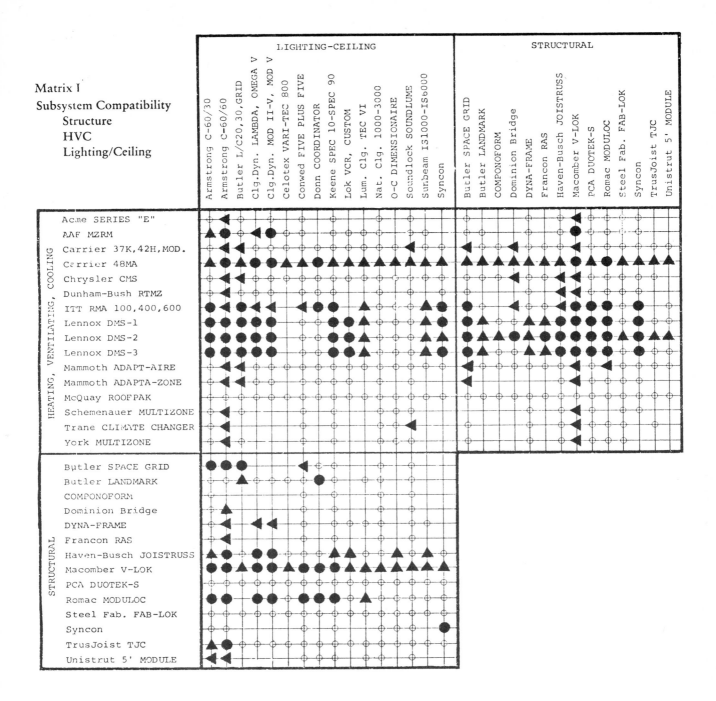

Matrix I
Subsystem Compatibility
   Structure
   HVC
   Lighting/Ceiling

Figure 1

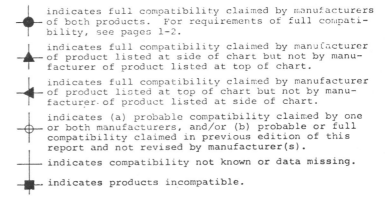

	indicates full compatibility claimed by manufacturers of both products. For requirements of full compatibility, see pages 1-2.
	indicates full compatibility claimed by manufacturer of product listed at side of chart but not by manufacturer of product listed at top of chart.
	indicates full compatibility claimed by manufacturer of product listed at top of chart but not by manufacturer of product listed at side of chart.
	indicates (a) probable compatibility claimed by one or both manufacturers, and/or (b) probable or full compatibility claimed in previous edition of this report and not revised by manufacturer(s).
	indicates compatibility not known or data missing.
	indicates products incompatible.

We have to recognise, however, that if we are going to expect people to do development work, we can't expect them to combine performance specifications and phased construction. There is no way to innovate quickly.

So you have a very wide range of strategies by which you can manage the building process. If one understands the way in which they work one can, in fact, develop a specific process for a specific project, and in doing this we must remember that unless the brief is properly related to the budget, there is no way that the job is going to work. A systematic approach does not provide a shoehorn to get a too-big brief into a restricted budget. All it does is to order the process so that you have an opportunity of seeing what options are available to you within the budget. I know that we in the United States are faced with the following kind of problem: we go in for an interview with, let us say, five other firms for a school commission and if the district arrangements are well organised we shall be given a brief and budget perhaps two weeks in advance. The first question the board will invariably ask is, "You have seen the brief; you know what the budget is; can you do the job?" You know that if you say you cannot do the job there are five other people being interviewed who will say that they can. So you obviously start off by saying,"Of course." Then if you are unlucky enough to get the job, you begin the time-honoured process of going into your schematic design in such a manner that you start talking about the multi use of space and which activities can be housed in the same space, and you go as far as you can to reduce the size of the brief. When the client really holds up his hand, you stop at that line. Then you submit for approval, and when the schematic design is approved you throw away the brief. Now you can begin the design development for the next series of compromises, and when that is approved you throw away the schematic design. Any architect worth his salt in the United States does a complete costing at the half-way stage in working drawings to get another cycle in this process of sub-optimisation. Then, if you have a recalcitrant client, the ultimate weapon available to you is the re-bid process when you go over the budget; at which point, if you have designed, for example, a deep plan school that requires air conditioning, you can take out the cooling component.

Examining this time-honoured process, we have to recognise that unless we develop tools for organising brief material at the outset of the job so that we can do cost/performance trade-offs, on every aspect of the brief, the profession will have very little relevance in the future. Thirty-five per cent of the components in Sweet's catalogue that we work with in the United States are new every five years. The old rules of thumb for both cost and product performance are things which we cannot rely upon any longer, and the traditional processes by which an architect worked to design a building are no longer relevant. Unless we have a good data base of information on both cost and performance and can take a look at the brief and cost that brief before we begin to design, we are in trouble, and that has become a major factor in any kind of systems approach to design.

We have to know how much it costs to provide different classes of lighting—let us say 50, 70, 100 ft. candles; how much it costs to provide air conditioning or different kinds of control of a thermal environment; whether all rooms facing a given orientation are on a single thermostat; whether all rooms in a given wing are on a single thermostat; or whether each room in the wing is on a separate thermostat. Unless we have that kind of data so that we can relate that to the brief, cost the brief and then go through a process of iteration before we begin design, we are going to be in great difficulty.

The problem is to balance resources and requirements before we begin the design, then a good designer will design a handsome building; a mediocre designer will do a mediocre building; but at least they will all be able to design buildings that function.

Adopting this kind of approach, we find that relatively complex buildings may require us to create certain kinds of new computer tools, and for this reason we have been developing some new tools for health facility planning which I will describe. Illustrations taken from a group of projects will help to explain different ways of organising the process.

A compatibility chart which has grown out of the SCSD process is shown in *Figure 1*. We consider lighting, ceiling, structure, and air conditioning components. The manufacturers who make those products and meet the performance specifications will attest to the fact that they have different levels of compatibility with the products of other manufacturers, but we are not involved in producing details of the components for which compatibility is assured. We had a job, about 3½ years ago, to do a student housing project for the University of Alaska, to be built in Fairbanks. We had four months to design and build 168 units of student housing. We succeeded in that case, and in the following year we had the task of managing the construction of nine projects on seven campuses. The period taken from the beginning of brief writing to occupancy was 20 months. Some of the buildings were of the order of $5 million to $5½ million. Bids were taken six weeks after we were hired, based on those compatibility charts. This gives a sense of the scale of the projects. It was obviously a phased construction approach based on previously developed and co-ordinated components.

The next project, that I will discuss very briefly, is one where we have designed a system for large academic buildings—science buildings. We spent a great deal of lead time on very careful user requirement studies. We have been on the project about five years, and have developed basic modules on an average of 10,000 sq.ft. of space. We have put these modules together to provide our building; our service elements are all on the perimeter, so we have full flexibility. Within that space the structure and the ducts are fixed. The adaptors from the ducts, the ceiling components, the partitions and case work are all completely flexible. There components go together with a walk-on ceiling that is really a catwalk approach but we also have ceiling access so that it is a relatively sophisticated kind of system. With it we have designed our first building, for which bids came in successfully. The job will be built in the Indianapolis campus of the Indiana University.

Figure 2 relates to when we were involved in the development of a technological system for housing, in Operation Breakthrough. This was the Fiber-shell

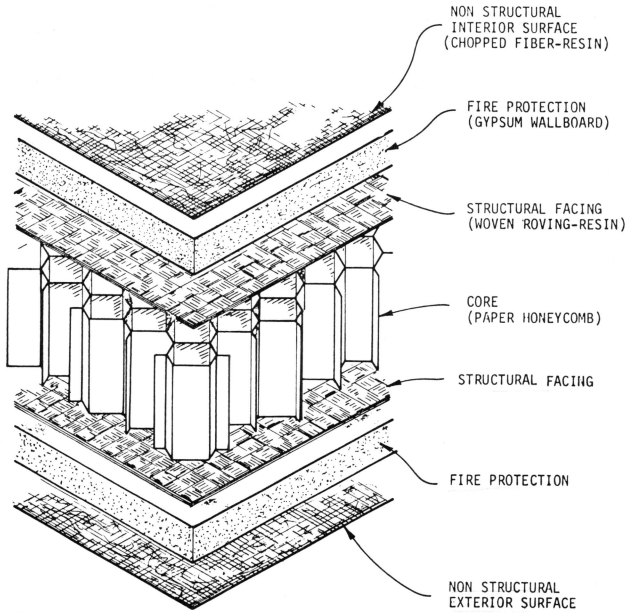

NON STRUCTURAL
INTERIOR SURFACE
(CHOPPED FIBER-RESIN)

FIRE PROTECTION
(GYPSUM WALLBOARD)

STRUCTURAL FACING
(WOVEN ROVING-RESIN)

CORE
(PAPER HONEYCOMB)

STRUCTURAL FACING

FIRE PROTECTION

NON STRUCTURAL
EXTERIOR SURFACE

Figure 2

system where we developed a process of making a sandwich, the centre being a honeycomb paper core. You can see beneath the corner of that honeycomb panel the fibreglass, which is a woven roving with a sprayed resin finish. The fibreglass is rolled on top of the honeycomb as well, and there is gypsum board outside the woven roving on both sides to provide fire protection for the fibreglass panels. These panels, made 21 ft. wide and any multiple of a 4 ft. module long, we assembled into boxes. When the boxes were put together to make town houses, all of the services were laid on the top of the lower box and we used a double wall approach for flexibility in getting our services through. Any interior partition was non load-bearing because we spanned between the outer walls.

This group of three projects shows, I think, that there are many different approaches that one can work with, whether it be a phased construction, as the first situation; trying to work to new performances, as in the second case; or doing what is primarily technological development.

I would now like to refer to the way in which we have developed a computerised briefing system program for hospital design. We ourselves are faced with problems which I am sure are widespread—rising costs, the time that it takes to construct the building and finding that it is obsolete by the time it is occupied, buildings which frequently do not meet some of the complex requirements, difficulties of financing projects, and many other problems. Our concern was to develop a communications system of the first order between the owner team, the community and the people who would get the building put up. In order to achieve this we needed a system which could provide for very quick cycling of information. Our concern was to go through the brief writing and design phases of the job with cost control, and with an ability to change various aspects of the design as more information came in. So we have developed an information base that contains 90 per cent of all the active medical facilities in the United States—some 7,000 health facilities are in our

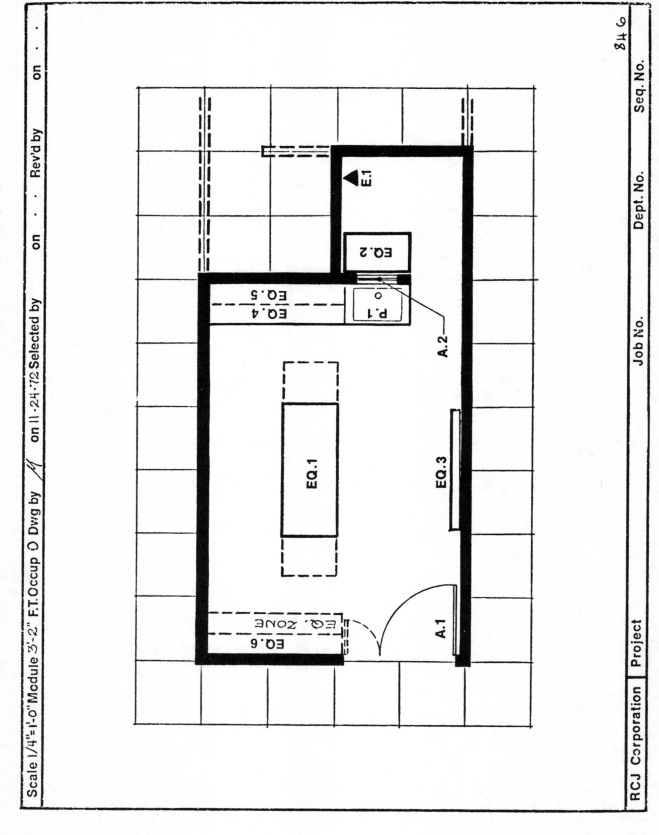

ROOM TYPE DRAWING

EXAM ROOM 280.A.1

Scale 1/4"=1-0" Module 3'-2" F.T.Occup O Dwg by ⟋⟍ on 11·24·72 Selected by on Rev'd by on

RCJ Corporation | Project | Job No. | Dept. No. | Seq. No.

Figure 3

180

program. From that we can take any type of job, and go back to its history and find out what would be relevant in a specific instance. We can develop this in many ways—such as by size, by location, or demographically. For instance, if we take a state to which old people are likely to retire, like Florida, we would have a brief which would relate to the medical problems of that population.

Our approach to design here is one that we have tended to call in the United States a Dick Tracy approach to programming, based on our comic book character whose police artist junior goes through exercises much like using an identikit when someone comes in and tries to describe a criminal. Working with an outline, the person will say that the face should be more sallow and the eyebrows more bushy, and little by little, proceed through a series of questions or steps until the 'client's brief', in effect, is total. For doing an average type hospital we have a programme of some 2,200 questions, but we can make our first cut with about six questions being answered. As more information comes in we can obviously keep revising the program.

Dealing essentially with medical facilities, we work at the functional level, whether it is a medical school, a teaching hospital or ambulatory care facility, or whatever. All the work is linked together. If, for example, one were going to put up a 300 bed hospital, and within the given catchment area there were extra requirements for radiology facilities, the program would automatically reduce the number of surgical beds because the demand for additional radiology effectively reduces the budget available for other departments.

So we can begin the brief initially on a functional grouping category. Radiology, for example, is part of diagnostic and therapeutic functions. With this we can begin to cut out a series of departmental requirements.

We can then take any single department, look at its history of use within the catchment area, and look also at other hospitals within that area to determine how they have grown and what the projections are for future growth. As a result we will plan facilities in quite a different way if we have an objective of 1980 rather than 1990. We will also try to join departments together so that as one department expands, given the kinds of growth characteristics that we look forward to in the future, others may be moved. The program develops a variety of scenarios for growth patterns within the basic space.

Also within the program is the capability of determining what already exists within a hospital or within a catchment area, what is needed and therefore what should be provided in new space and in altered space.

In our first job, in April 1973 when the program became operative, we had a series of medical requirements and general operating requirements for a hospital. We put these on the machine and came up with a $26 million cost to do the job. The hospital board immediately said that all they had available to them was $16 million, and within one day we were able to produce five other options. One of these was selected at $16 million, and the basic change in this case was in the operating characteristics of the

hospital where radiology, surgery and laboratory facilities would be used 54 hours a week, instead of 40 hours a week. So we can also program the operating characteristics and the finance characteristics of all the different departments on the computer, and 'play tunes' on the brief prior to beginning to design the building.

We had another case that we ran for John Hopkins, where they had done a nine month job of briefing for a radiology facility, costed out at some $10 million. We spent a day with them, put the program through the machine, and found that they had underestimated by 20 per cent; the cost should have been $12 million instead of $10 million. They had studied the brief. All we had done—by using the computer—was to pinpoint certain kinds of space of which they were in short supply. We said, "We do not know if we are right or wrong, but there are obviously some spaces that you should re-consider". Two weeks later we heard that we were right.

We have a basic cost pattern that is broken down by department, as well as by component area. With this, again, we can put in our first cost. It is tied in to national indices so we can cost in any part of the country. At later stages, when working with the construction manager or a general contractor, one can take any number out, modify it, and keep working. So our basic procedure is to start with rather gross factors and, little by little, to zero in on a particular job, trying to control the job within reasonable bounds from the outset.

We have 700 rooms detailed in our room type file. *Figure 3* shows just one of them. For each room we have an inventory of what is included in that room, so again, if one is looking at costs that are on the high side, one can go through this inventory and begin to economise in terms of finishes, furniture and a variety of other items.

This also provides a system for purchase orders, for inventory control and for running the total management system within the hospital, not only during construction but also when the facility is in use. Related to this we have a 300 page book that is really our critical path network, and a 28 ft. sheet of wallpaper on which it is all drawn up.

All of this gives us a software tool with which to work and programme hospitals. The briefing work goes right through the design stages, as you can see, from the room type files. We have developed the system to relate to a building method which our firm and Stone, Marraccini & Patterson of San Francisco developed for the Veterans Administration.

When working for the VA we had a series of requirements concerned with cost control, improving some of the operating performance within the hospital. A great deal of flexibility is required in the normal seven years that it took to get the hospital briefed, designed and built. The building was literally obsolete when first occupied. While concerned with flexibility, they also wanted a time reduction in the process, and wished to develop a method of building which could eventually be upgraded.

We went through the normal kinds of user study to determine what the dimensional criteria should be to meet a wide variety of different conditions. We took a look at the way the average hospital was built in the

THE PLANNING MODULES

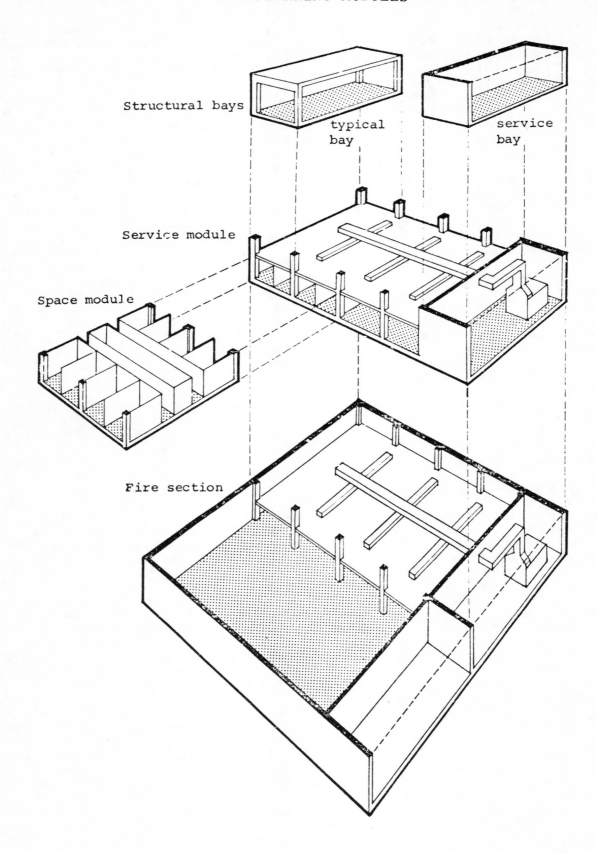

Structural bays

typical bay

service bay

Service module

Space module

Fire section

Figure 4

THE SERVICE MODULE AS A BUILDING BLOCK
FOR ALTERNATIVE BUILDING CONFIGURATIONS

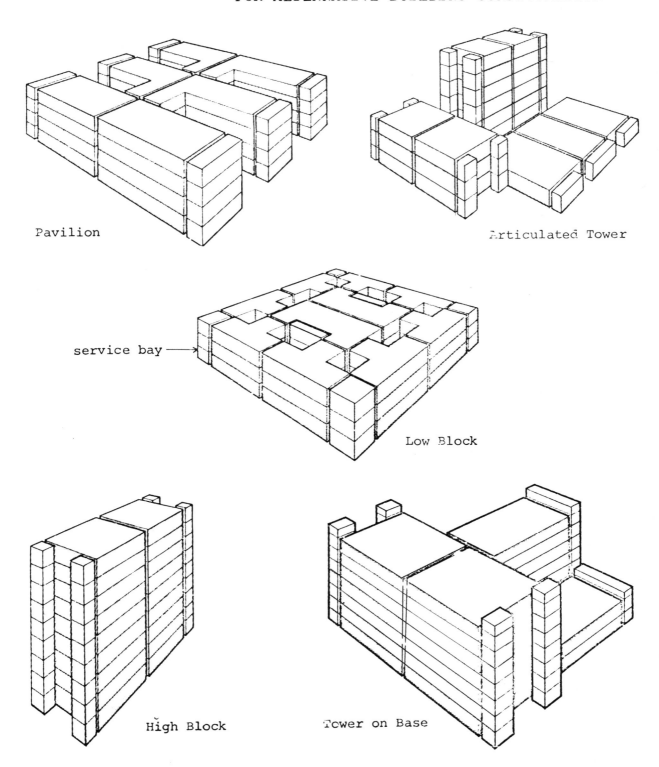

Pavilion

Articulated Tower

service bay →

Low Block

High Block

Tower on Base

Figure 5

United States, with partitions going from the floor to the underside of the structure; services were installed in such a way that each of the subtrades wanted to get there first and take the shortest run from wherever the service came into building to wherever it had to go, so that the next trade would have to fit services around or over those already in place (and if you could find any of the original valves you were lucky). So we began to look at planning in terms of a rather simple modular approach, with modules of the order of about 10,000 sq.ft. Basic structural bays were grouped together to make a space module. Space modules would then be grouped into a service module with a service bay for all vertical runs and an interstitial space for all horizontal runs. Code requirements necessitated fire walls at about 20,000 sq. ft. intervals.

The resultant basic service modules can be put together in a wide variety of ways. You have a basic structural shell, in which is hung a walk-on ceiling; the partitions, which come up to the ceiling, have all the services surface-mounted, to be covered by some type of cover plate or console. The services then fit through the horizontal and vertical spaces provided. We found we needed a range of 13 separate space modules in order to meet the user requirements—the different requirements for intensive care units as opposed to normal acute care requirements, different kinds of site conditions calling for different building forms, and so on. Seven separate structural components were required, with different load classes, for columns. These blocks can be put together as building blocks in a wide variety of different ways to build any shape or form of hospital.

So we have a very simple group of structural components; a hung ceiling; partitions which are demountable. We have, in our service area, the service systems organised so that no two services share the same space, with horizontal and vertical planning. This can be seen best, I think, in model form, where we have our air conditioning ducts in the centre, our plumbing on the left, and our electrical busbar ducts on the right, all coming out of the vertical service bay, and moving horizontally into the space above the modules. (The ducts are the same for each module, whenever it is used). There was concern as to whether we should still be able to scramble around in the space remaining, so we produced full size mockups of the most dense areas within the interstitial space, and proved that we could, in fact, get in to service the full facility.

The first building designed using this system is now under construction, and we are working on the first project for the Veterans Administration. Again Stone, Marraccini & Patterson and our firm are working in a joint venture, a 560 bed hospital which is a $43,000,000 project. The service towers are expressed on the perimeter of the hospital, which has a compact plan. Apart from the positioning of the service plant the building is fairly symmetrical. Because it is only a mile off the fault line for earthquakes in southern California, the design had to take this into account.

In this case we obviously have a system which was designed to innovate. We had to develop some new products, such as walk-on ceiling components. All the other products were quite readily available. So we were concerned here with developing a process by which we can proceed to do a job, to develop whatever kinds of tools are necessary, so that we can make decisions within an appropriate time span to get the job done.

Whether you are optimising on cost, performance or time, the key thing is that when you have accepted a brief you finally meet its requirements when the building is completed. It is only in this way that we have any chance of retaining the role that must be played by professionals in providing for the physical environment. □

Systems health building

A verbatim report of a talk by

Howard Goodman

In my capacity as both an architect and a civil servant I am going to try to explain the problems of introducing a systems approach into a Government Building Programme, and in particular into the National Health Service Building Programme. I shall try to explain why we decided to do this, what we thought were the advantages and what have been some of the pitfalls that we have come across. So to some extent it is going to be a series of random observations on the progress that we have made in the last few years.

The Hospital Building Programme

You must be familiar with the National Health Service in one form or another. Basically it is a centrally financed service, therefore its Building Programme receives its funds from central government. The money is allocated to fifteen different Regional Hospital Boards on an extended programme, and is allocated according to the service needs of each Region. By and large each Region determines its own priorities as regards building although The Department of Health and Social Security can and does comment on these priorities. The only mandatory constraint placed on the Boards is that the cost limits set by the DHSS are observed, in other words, that value for money be obtained; which is achieved to a greater or lesser extent. The obvious question to ask is why, with an efficient regional set up, there is need for central government's involvement in the Hospital Building Programme. The reason is really quite simple; the role of central government is a specialised one, being involved primarily in Research and Development. Although our programme is fairly large, say £150m a year, and each Region gets about £10m, the individual programmes are not big enough to carry their own Research and Development work. My role and that of the rest of my team, together with our engineering, surveying, medical and nursing colleagues, is to provide the R & D arm of the National Health Service Building Programme. We do this in a variety of ways, much is done directly within our Department within the various Building Divisions, and a lot is done by using outside bodies in both commercial and academic fields—you will have heard other speakers talking about work they have carried out which has been commissioned by the DHSS. Although some of the other papers may seem somewhat selective, they all are working within a broad master plan which comes together under the general heading of The Systems Health Building Programme.

The Reason for Systems

Another obvious question to be raised is, 'Why introduce systems into a Hospital Building Programme, as they are obviously not easy buildings to construct?' On the face of it, it would be easier to tackle schools or housing and yet this approach has not been introduced into either of these fields. There are in fact some very sound reasons. Firstly, because it is a National Building Programme consisting of large, vulnerable, complex buildings. The traditional progress of the schemes was slow and the clients themselves are complex groups and can be awkward to deal with, so to some extent we have a set-up ripe for revolution. Secondly, although hospitals on the face of it are frightening and complex organisations, rather like an ant's nest, with everyone appearing to rush about, nevertheless, just as in an ant's nest, there is considerably more order than there seems to be. If, in fact, we have a disciplined organisation which is susceptible to measurement then one can begin to see the reason for systemization.

The question of what to measure is the key to our current work on systems and standards. Like the ant's nest the hospital consists of people moving about, but this is only one aspect of the problem of communications because a hospital lives on movement, whether of people, goods, services, energy or information. What our studies have tried to do is to define, describe and measure all aspects of the movement in hospital and to extend these techniques into the field of other activities, bearing in mind that the same activity might occur many times over in different contexts in different parts of the hospital and yet basically require the same space, equipment, services and supplies. Here we can see the beginnings of simple statements about the measurement and the storage of activity data.

Development Work

Before we describe the picture today, perhaps I can go back a few years and try to show the logical progression from our earlier work into current activities. Apart from the overriding criterion of obtaining value for money, much of our work in studying the Hospital Building Programme has been concerned with problems of communication studies, briefing techniques, universal hospital structures, development of integrated building components and systematic techniques of handling data. We have always tried to practise what we preach, and an essential adjunct to our research work has been our development building projects, where we tried to show by demonstration some of our ideas. At Walton Hospital, Liverpool, we developed a universal structural envelope covering a wide range of hospital departments, hopefully very flexible in the long term, allowing a high level of service integration. Our project at Greenwich continued the early ideas from Walton although with greater emphasis on communication, measurement and movement and so on. To some extent Greenwich was a test bed rather than a prototype, and it has probably provided greater sources of knowledge on hospital planning than any other building in the world. We began to realise that the main problem was not one of buildings but of *programme* building, and that our studies should be extended into the implications of this on a national building programme. Whilst to some extent we could obtain the support of individuals in the DHSS for our specific projects, a great deal more support was needed in order to introduce a systems and standards programme applicable throughout the country.

Horizontal Communication Patterns

You will appreciate that in any bureaucratic organisation, be it government or commerce, 75% of the members have no positive views about anything. The technique is therefore to persuade the majority of the remainder that what one is doing is the right thing. In other words, if you can get 13% of the organisation on your side you win, and this is what we did. We identified those parts of the organisation which have a real role to play, put to them something that made sense from the economic, constructional, and political aspects and at the same time seemed to be realistic. The problem is to avoid developing too frantic a revolution, to avoid upsetting the various established Institutions, some of whom may see themselves threatened by this approach. One must persuade these people that there is something in it for them and the arguments we put forward go something like this: Hospitals should be efficient organisations and they should be susceptible to measurement. If we can measure them, then these measurements should indicate the sort of buildings we should be producing. Our early work leads us to think that the communication pattern is the key to the hospital and the item most readily measured. By and large this communication pattern tends to be horizontal, because people and supplies move economically and quickly horizontally. This type of development is flexible because hospital growth is usually by accretion and it is easier to obtain contiguous spaces in the horizontal plane. Virtually any type of 'pancake' development works fairly well as a hospital. Some years ago a warehouse was turned into a hospital at Boston and it worked extremely well because it consisted of large, flat, open spaces which were easily sub-divided. If one accepts horizontal hospitals with a pre-determined communication pattern then it is possible to indentify and generically type these communication patterns, and it was the identifying and typing of these patterns that led to the nickname Harness, the analogy being the electric harness pre-prepared for cars and aircraft. If in addition to identifying this communication pattern we can identify the essentials of the major hospital departments and dimensionally standardise these in some way then we have theoretical ability to clip these on to the Harness

in a fairly organised sort of way yet producing a very wide range of solutions.

Standardisation

This is the argument we put forward, which was accepted in principle and from which most of our current work stems. Our first attempts in this field were to say that each hospital consists of a number of standard departments and if we take these departments, identify them and join them together there is a hospital. In fact, we did design one or two standard departments and although they were quite good, when joined together they began to produce a random building with almost no discipline. The second stage was to refer back to earlier work at Walton and Greenwich in our search for a universal hospital structure, and hypothesise that it was possible to design this range of standard departments to fit within the same envelope. Once we satisfied ourselves, after a large number of exercises, that it was theoretically feasible then we had some geometric control of the building. If we can further extend this hypothesis into saying that we can stack unlike departments above each other then we have a far greater freedom in designing a hospital than in the traditional approaches. At this stage we still hadn't decided on the final dimensions and a very wide range of options was exhaustively examined. Sufficient to say that in the end we chose a dimension of 15 metres clear span because it seemed to be the most economic for most departments. We took a secondary dimension of 5 metres and this combination is the basic planning of the construction module, although in most instances we found we were using a 15 x 15 metres planning module.

Even at this embryonic stage there were also other constraints placed upon us. We are, after all, subject to the economic facts of life, and some highly desirable facilities could not be provided. For instance, all the evidence was that there was a steady progression towards totally air-conditioned hospitals, but this, it was felt, would place unacceptable increases in the field of both capital and revenue so that we had to find a development which would allow us to design hospitals which were predominantly naturally ventilated but could, on some subsequent occasion, be air-conditioned. We had to remember that whilst the life of the structure of a hospital may be 60 or 70 years the average life of the services within it is only twenty years. So our thoughts began to form along the lines of a medium density, low rise hospital with a very high level of servicing (resulting in the now familiar service space between floors) yet having courtyards every fifteen metres to give natural lighting and ventilation. We now had a geometry approaching that of a three dimensional chess board and all we had to do was to design the pieces in order that the game could commence. We developed a range of sizes for a department so that the hospital could be virtually tailor-made in terms of the medical need. This is where I quote a motto which we have had written on our walls for some time now, 'The criterion of any programme of standardisation is its ability to produce unique solutions'.

Data Bases

But the planning method is only part of our system. We were concerned with not only the reduction in the time that it takes to design a hospital but also a reduction in the time it takes to prepare the brief and the production material. The best average which was generally being achieved within the Service was $4\frac{1}{2}$ to 5 years between thinking about having a hospital and cutting the first sod on site. We wanted to offer a system which would reduce this time, bearing in mind that this was a very good selling point.

An overall approach to this system was to say that we would provide a series of data bases of information, running from very crude data which enables one to assemble a simple outline of a hospital to sophisticated data which allows one to produce the components needed to build it and join those components together. This information should be passed logically from one stage to another. Having developed the system in outline, we started work in a variety of different points in the system. As I said earlier, this is a progress report and parts of the system are still being developed, but in principle the major sub-systems consist of briefing, design, production material, construction, commissioning and evaluation.

Initially we concentrated on the Manufacturers Data Base (MDB) because it seemed obvious that development of a range of dimensionally related components with a sufficient variety to build a range of hospitals would need a long time to develop, and we extended work which had already been carried out on the Compendium of building components in the context of the Harness programme. At the same time we began to prepare standard draft operational policies for the hospital. In order that the potential customers could understand the way in which they were intended to operate we also had to get general clearance from the medical and nursing profession for these policies. The policies develop logically into descriptions of activity data, which in turn develop into activity spaces with all the required components and services.

Computer Applications

At this time it became obvious to the enthusiasts in the office that these techniques were highly susceptible to automatic data processing and it was then we started exploring ways in which we could automate the systems. It seemed that the highly disciplined geometry which we had developed mainly for constructional planning reasons was ideally suited for computer applications, and using the analogy of the three dimensional chess board it seemed fairly easy to use the computer as a spacial allocation tool by playing three dimensional chess. A lot of early work was done here at Cambridge by Applied Research of Cambridge (ARC) and the results came out fairly quickly. In a short time we began to get programs which would actually assemble hospitals and then by adding to these the other program which was already available, or by slight alteration to these programs, we could not only assemble them but we could measure them. We had then—and this is going back two years—crude working tools which have proved one of the biggest advantages of this pragmatic and fragmented approach in that we could take these tools out of the system and use them long before the system itself was complete. This crudeness of approach or, as we could say, the robustness in the

systems has meant that at a variety of stages, operational policies, activity data, user requirements, structural and constructural components, we were able to inject these into the Hospital Building Programme before the total system came into operation. Many of the processes had additional uses which were not envisaged when the work started. For instance the computer-aided assembly and evaluation programs are a useful tool for evaluating a site in comparative terms even when the hospital to be built on it ultimately is not a Harness hospital. It gives us a rapid way of applying norms to a situation where none was previously available.

Problem Areas

I am not attempting to describe the Harness method in any detail because you will have heard of this from other, more competent speakers but it will be obvious to you that a programme with such widespread implications must produce some problems. The first is the risk of political manipulation of this sort of system. One of the advantages of the present building programme is that the gestation period of any hospital is longer than the life of any Government and that successive Administrations continue the programmes of their predecessors. This means a fairly stable building programme. However, we are now in a position where, assuming maximum use was made of our systems, a building could be conceived and built within five years, and it isn't difficult to imagine situations where there is a rapid start of hospital buildings prior to an election, or schemes are accelerated in politically sensitive parts of the country. This worries me. Systems are splendid when they are being run by us, the professionals: they are not at all good when they are being run by politicians. The first point was perhaps only hypothetical, but the second, and from the architectural point of view perhaps the most dangerous, is the accusation that standardisation produces stereotype architecture. Last year perhaps my only real contribution to this system and standards programme was trying to produce a vocabulary of parts which enables a sensitive architect to produce a sensitive building and to write stages into the system where the man must intervene: where the machine has to stop. At the same time we try to offer the man as many options as possible. I think we are succeeding and hopefully some of the buildings we produce will be at least tolerable. (I am tempted to say that most of the hospitals being designed at the moment are so dismal architecturally that almost anything would be an improvement).

In the long run, perhaps the most serious problem is the danger of the system becoming fossilized, so that we continue into the '80's building hospitals which were good in the '70's. This is one of the risks we were aware of in the early stages and we have built into the system processes which enable us to update all relevant data whether it be on activities, components or production material.

There only remains the problem of bringing the professions and industry with us. So far we have had the general support of the building professionals. Indeed, in many cases, we have received a genuine welcome for these techniques which will improve the efficiency of the data provided to the building industry.

There are, of course, worries about the quality of the buildings and the environment we are producing, worries I think we can allay. I have far greater concern on whether the building industry will keep pace with us. It is, after all, still a cottage industry and its ways of handling data are crude in the extreme. In the early stages I think we will find enough forward looking sections of the industry which could handle our data fairly efficiently, but once it becomes generally used in the Hospital Building Programme I doubt the ability of the building industry to absorb the data in the form that we would prefer to put it. We must avoid a situation where data presented in a logically systematised, automated, coded way is translated back in traditional forms before it can be used by the industry.

Conclusion

This is, as I said, a progress report. As work progresses more and more data becomes available. Already prototype buildings using parts of the system are built and the first proper hospital using all the available parts of the system starts at Dudley next Spring. If this building lives up to expectations — and there is every sign that it will, then we shall be able to demonstrate how a modern hospital can be produced by these techniques and at the same time produce a work of architecture. □

Part 6

Review
of the conference

Open discussion

University of Strathclyde
SCHOOL OF ARCHITECTURE
INFORMATION ROOM

Chairman: Alex Gordon

I think it could be useful to take a look at the possible effects of the contents of this conference on education, research and practice. I thought we might have a discussion on these two groups of subjects among the panel first and then ask you to make your contributions—not just questions, but contributions.

Perhaps we ought to take a look first at where we have gone since the Architectural Association Computer Conference of about ten years ago, and where we are now, because I think that if we had been asked, in those heady days of ten years ago, to assess where we might be now, most of the people attending, that conference might have got the answer wrong. I think they might have anticipated that there would be much more general application of computers in the building world and in offices than there is now. Some of the enthusiasts in those days were even talking of design by computer, and although I believe that people soon saw the problems more clearly they were slower to accept that of the vast number of operations involved in bringing a building from conception to completion only a proportion lend themselves to computer aid. These had to be identified and clarified to discourage exaggerated, extravagant claims about a much wider coverage. I don't know what the figure is, but I feel that probably it is going to level off at five, ten, fifteen per cent, or something like that.

When a space capsule is going round, or landing on, the moon it is operating in a generally controlled environment. Everyone knows what should happen, and the computer plays a very large part in the operation. But one day the capsule comes back to earth, back into the earth's atmosphere. It comes down on three large parachutes (or maybe only one or two of them open) and dangles down into a choppy sea. Inside may be sick astronauts, with cameras falling on their heads as gravity once more asserts itself. It is a very complex situation where the computer plays no part at all. I feel that designing and building has more in common with the splash-down than it does with the capsule going round the moon in space. Even when programs with the potential to assess particular sections of the total design/build operation have become available, I think it must be said that the average architect, working on one-off jobs, has little or no incentive to stop the normal sequence of operations in order to provide the necessary input, and wait for the output to take advantage of computer aid. I welcome the fact that it seems to be accepted that only when freedom of design is channelled within limited bounds can data processing and analytical models of buildings be constructed simply enough to be attractive to the design team in comparison with their present working techniques.

The first thing on which we might find agreement is that for a good while we have got to look for development to the larger offices operating on a continuous programme of similar buildings, where, as Ed. Hoskins suggests, the design freedom is channelled within limited bounds. But, on the other hand, there should be an increase in 'fallout' from the work of the kind you have been talking about (hospitals, etc.) which may penetrate into the smaller offices working on one-off schemes. Is this something that should be just allowed to happen, or is it an area which encourages some activity to hasten it on? We have heard about the very real work which is taking place in the hospital field, but what of the other public offices and the local authorities? They are very interesting, because the old local authorities had the means and opportunities to do a lot of work, and one was aware of certain county opposition. What is the position now? So could we start with practice, and then to on to research and education. We can then see whether my colleagues accept Ed Hoskins' limitation regarding the kind of program and kind of office which is going to be involved, or believe that we should be thinking of the whole world, the multitudinous small jobs.

H. Goodman

I think it is really a question of getting this sort of work 'off the ground'. I am fairly committed to this systematic approach to building and the use of as many computer aids as we can handle. But I am also conscious of the fact that what we are producing in the early stages of this technology is rather simplistic huts. If we were not using this sort of technology, we would do far better by pragmatic means. But someone has to start, and this is why it is tending to depend on large organisations, such as the National Health Service, to make the first move. I don't think we are claiming that we are producing a better solution, it is just that unless someone starts, there can be no progress. I think it is inevitable that the start should be associated with programme building, because the one essential element is that of feedback. Learning from mistakes is important, and the mistakes in the early stages are enormous. Looking back over the four or five years since we have been seriously spending money on systems, I don't suppose ten per cent of it was worth spending. We wasted most of the money, but that was inevitable. We are now at the stage when three quarters of the money we spend actually produces something that is useful. This, in the Research and Development field, is extremely high compared with the speculation that a commercial firm in a totally different field may waste ninety per cent of their money every year. We have to use a programme with a hard, fast feedback, so it has to be a bureaucratic programme, not a democratic one, at this stage. Once the machine is rolling, then it can be used by other people whose use for it is only intermittent. If you take a private practice, one year it could have several jobs quite susceptible to these techniques, and the next year, none of the jobs would be. So the office has to make use of one of the programs that someone else has developed and I suspect this will be so for some time to come. It will be an opting in and an opting out for the private sector, with the main development being pushed along by the public sector. This is welcome because it will be these infusions from the private sector which will give it a little more impetus. There is this dreadful risk that we are going to produce rather a dreary machine and rather dreary buildings. On the other hand there is a stimulus from the "lunatic fringe" of private practice to do something a little different, and a balance has to be achieved between these two extremes.

A. Gordon

Can we simply accept what Howard Goodman has said, that the major initiative will be taken by the large organisations, particularly in the public sector, or should effort be directed towards encouraging the smaller offices to get moving?

E. Ehrenkrantz

Essentially, we are a smaller office and we have grown from six to fifteen people currently in the space of a year and a half. But we have a major investment in the development of the tools which I previously described. The reason for this is quite simple. If we did not develop that kind of tool we would not be able to compete with larger offices. I think this is something that is going to occur again and again as you deal with complex building types and complex situations, that in order to be able to participate effectively smaller offices are going to need to develop this kind of tool. The place where you are going to put your resources will be very heavily dependent on the needs of the market place in terms of that development, so that the value of the money invested should be rather high. In all areas we prepare material, cost, and performance data, etc., as though we had a computer to tie to. We only use the computer when we can no longer hand-manipulate the information that we have at our disposal, so it is a process reminiscent of a recommendation I made eight years ago after spending some time in India. I recommended that we export cardboard computers, so they should look real, so people thought that they were actually available and could begin to program information as for the machine. Once they did that, ninety per cent of the problems could be solved, and the other ten per cent couldn't afford to be solved. So I considered our relatively small office, which is undercapitalised, as an under-developed country. We began with the cardboard computers until we had enough data in an area to make it worth our while to put in a terminal. I think that both small offices and large offices are going to have to follow that approach.

A. Gordon

Are you aspiring, in the case of your hospitals, to handle the design and execution right through until you have a completed hospital, or are you giving a specialist service at a particular stage ?

E. Ehrenkrantz

Our concern is to do the whole job and our tools relate completely to that and we are now beginning to get commissions based on the fact that we have such tools.

W. Hillier

Can I extend the discussion on the diffusion of innovation, from the process to the product. It seems to me that new ideas can diffuse very quickly indeed in architecture. What is happening at present is that more and more buildings are coming into existence whose conceptual origins are at least partly in research. This is certainly happening in the environmental field, and many of these buildings, from the point of view of a whole architectural product, are very unsatisfactory, but the movement of ideas from research into built form is probably the most powerful diffusing agent that exists. It will not be, this time, just a diffusion of visual ideas, or technological ideas or general cultural ideas, but a transmission of concepts, ways of thinking about building. It will be much more of a theoretical viewpoint. This is one of the most important aspects of the diffusion problem.

A. Gordon

I always keep coming back to the thought, "What happens when I go back to my practice, to the variety of small jobs and the clients?" I work hard to see how one could adapt techniques like this to a practice of that type, and I find it extremely difficult.

W. Howell

I have a small practice and intend it to remain small, but like Howard Goodman I believe in systems, and I am, at the moment, designing a highly systematic bungalow for an Irish cliff top. This job must represent the most uneconomic enterprise we have ever been engaged upon, and I would guess that the actual development cost of this particular object must be nearly the same as the contract price. But, as for any product, the relationship between the thinking and development cost and the cost of the execution is something which must be a great concern to designers. One of the problems we have is that we are actually debarred from taking on all the work that we would love to do. We really love doing houses, for example, and it seems to me that one of the attractions in what we have been talking about is that in a way it will actually make possible the survival of the small, general practice. If one thinks of the field of conservation and doing the right thing to old buildings, this is going to become increasingly uneconomic from the design aspect. It seems to me that any aids we can produce to help people to do that and to survive will be welcome. I think, also, it will have a liberating effect on the big organisations. It was interesting to hear Howard Goodman talking about the way DHSS is involved in work with smaller outside groups, in a quite different way from what was the traditional way. I think the effect may be that the size of an organisation could become less important when there is the possibility of rapid intercommunication on a known basis with an organised and systematic arrangement of information. We may discover that very large programmes, based on continuity and on common development work, will actually be possible without their having to get quite as big as they did in the past.

L. March

Just a small point concerning practice. Quite a lot of the work which we have been engaged in over the last few years originated in a very small, private practice involved in a number of different kinds of problems. The design teams were very small, with not more than two or three people in each. Enquiring and questioning was assumed to be an essential part of the practice and I think this is true of the majority of offices. The difficulty seems to be that such questions have to be cut short because of the time horizon in the practice, and the problem is how some of those things can actually be transferred into a research environment where they can be thought about and nurtured in the way that we have found possible at the Centre.

D. Campion

I have been operating with one or two colleagues in private practice for many years and we have been trying to see how we can utilise the computer in the best way. Our practice numbers fifty, and it operates as a group of people, a small group of people on particular projects. As a larger than average practice we are able to afford certain amounts of overhead to develop our own programs, which a very small practice obviously cannot do. That is the first point. Going on to the education side, what has interested and worried me for years is the question of what happens in universities. There is the problem of taking something of the Harness scale into practices which are single disciplinary. The majority of the work that is done is where the engineer, the architect, the quantity surveyor are independent firms that get together for a project. Now, it would be a far more valid approach to be thinking of a common data base which they could all use. This introduces certain problems of fee scale, etc. It is a problem that has not been tackled in any way at a university research level, yet it is one of the biggest problems in practice. The costs to a practice of communicating with other people are surprisingly high. One can make considerable savings, even now, with computers through having a common data base for information. It is also possible to have general purpose programs that are not written for hospitals, or Harness, in particular. It is clear that techniques used in other fields can be applicable as they stand without the need to write special purpose programmes. Now it is possible to do a lot of work in practice with data base techniques and L* is an attempt to make some such techniques implementable and usable. We have written a data base language which we are using in practice, and it works very well, but the problems are computer problems of implementing it in an efficient way and no-one is tackling these problems. Most of the work in universities is done on small scale things and cannot be implemented in practice. I talked to Charles Eastman about his concept of linking a whole building of a million components, which might take six hours computing on the biggest computer available. That is a non-starter at the present time, so one has to think along other lines. Can I give you an example

which is brought out by Ezra Ehrenkrantz's views. Cost may not be so important here, but *time* is, and he has given a very dramatic example of costs. Thinking in terms of computers and time scales, if we can do a job quicker, it may cost a bit more by computer, but we are saving money by doing it quickly. We had a job abroad where someone was flying out to discuss with the clients the briefing information, and he wanted the data sheets giving the contents of each room. Five hundred sheets were printed within three hours. This is a remarkable saving of time, because conventional typing would have involved months of work. But what worries me is that although we now have programs available, no-one is using them. Why? People are coming out of universities and are going into practice and I thought that the practices would pick up these things. But they are not. Why? We are not getting through to practices an awareness of the benefits. I think time is the thing that is really going to sell this to practices.

W. Howell

Savings in time, if one is involved in a programme based on a series of one-off operations, isn't to me so interesting and dramatic as what actually happens if you are doing what Ezra Ehrenkrantz referred to as a phased operation. It has always been held up as an examplar of how one should behave in this country that in the U.S.A. you never start a project until you have got all the information, down to the colour of the lavatory ceiling. I never believed that that was the way practices operated, it was the way builders always told us they operated in America. I think it is very interesting to do the kind of operation where you move on to the site the day it is purchased and you start driving your piles, and, in fact, you base your planning application on a building which will fit that set of piles, and you go on from there. This has been the success of the whole Seifert operation. When it works, it works magnificently, and the client is very pleased, but it is entirely based on the availability of feedback and, obviously, on the speed. This is mainly to do with cost. At every stage, you must exercise your options, knowing precisely where you stand at that moment with regard to those options you have already closed up, from the point of view of cost expended. I think that is where both time and availability of accurate feedback really will help to produce a quite different mode of operation

A. Gordon

We have established the area of influence. We ought to move on to the future, graduates, etc. A reasonable proportion of the graduates in the future will find a ready home working on the programmed kind of buildings that Howard Goodman and larger local authorities and government departments are concerned with. I am a believer in changing the future through what graduates have got to offer and there have been encouraging signs of how the new graduates that are coming along, with a much better understanding of the building as a climate modifier and how to get the right kind of internal environments, are beginning to influence the offices which they are going into. So, this is the way ahead in the computer field as well.

The new E.E.C. commissioner, writing about how a commissioner going into Europe with bright ideas can or cannot influence change, drew another analogy from space which I think is very applicable to this situation. He said it is like the re-entry into space where you have got to get the angle absolutely right because, if you come in too steeply, you burn up, and if you come in too gently, you bounce off into space and are never seen again. I think this attitude is important as far as the graduates are concerned. If they come in with the right attitudes, have got their knowledge in perspective, know they are going to affect only a portion of the offices, and that their contribution is respected because of this awareness, they will have a much bigger influence than if they come in expecting everybody else to change.

W. Howell

I think students who don't immediately find that they walk straight from the level of activity at university into the same kind of operation in practice, perhaps can cheer themselves up with the feeling that they are going through a sort of 'voluntary service overseas' period. A lot of people involved in various disciplines are doing vast things at universities, and one of the interesting tasks that they have is to go to places where none of the hardware is available and perhaps there wouldn't be acceptance of the kind of thing they are trying to do. They have to find ways of bringing their mental disciplines to bear through an entirely different kind of technology, and that will have some very interesting effects in practice.

E. Ehrenkrantz

I think it is important to know where you want to go as you leave the university and enter an office. One of the problems we have is to take a look at what might be possible in terms of using the computer in ten or twenty five years' time, then look at the reality of how things are done today, and determine how to get from here to there. There will be a number of offices that will provide an environment in which that work will be done effectively and those offices will lead the way. One of the reasons why, in fact, we try to create that kind of atmosphere within our own office is that we think this is the way in which we can still be part of the profession and the industry ten or twenty five years from now, but one cannot expect that the people involved in the day to day activites are going to fully understand and appreciate what is possible. That bridge must be built.

H. Goodman

In principle, the raw material that I have to work with is the raw material that one finds in any traditional office. People came to the Department of Health for a variety of different reasons, and very few of them because of our technological reputation. I don't place quite as much faith as Mr Gordon does in the results of our educational system. If you look at the analogy of the medical profession, their education starts after they have left medical school. They do their stint at hospitals and then there is a series of supervised training education, all lasts quite a long time. They are becoming well aware of the need for continuing in-service education. As a profession, we are not. We assume that when someone comes out of university he is fit to take almost any role in architecture, and there is no real monitoring of what he actually does. There is no pressure or responsibility put on him to continue his education. So because of this incredibly inaccurate term "architect", the potential employer has no knowledge of the man presented to him. I would think, from the work we are doing now, and the sort of people that we are getting, that for the first year they are almost useless. This is a staggering thing to say when one is paying a lot of money to get apparently highly technically qualified people. I think the running-in period now due to this total lack of continuing education in the professions is a burden that we have to carry. The faster the rate of advance of the technology, I presume, the longer it will take to run people in, to retrain them and re-educate them. We run a very heavy educational programme because unless we do that, we cannot make the machines work. I said earlier that in the first year or two of our research commissions the money was wasted. It was not wasted in the sense that we educated a lot of firms into certain branches of technology, and they found the money very useful. But can practice afford this level of education? It is going to be quite high. If you look at the difference between what one needs to know now and what someone who graduated ten years ago was taught, the gap is very wide indeed. The cost is very high to bring that man up to date. Whilst within the large organisation one can afford to do it, I am not at all sure that others can. We have got to get right back to the root of the educational system. It has to be far more integrated with the practice of architecture. I regret the lack of a series of degrees in architecture, since I would rather, as in the medical profession, be able to see that the man has progressed, and has acquired further skills since he graduated. I know how this can be done in my own organisation, but not how it can be organised for the profession generally.

L. March

I was trying to make a case, earlier, for service education, showing that when you looked at the five points that Ezra Ehrenkrantz made there was a clear need for this continuing educational process in the design and architectural field. That throws back the question of what is the role of the university in the educational process, and I think essentially the role is to give a sound intellectual and theoretical base, as in medical science at the moment, for this developing of education throughout the career, in a more practical, practising situation. When Howard said, "Can the profession afford this kind of education?", surely the medical profession does not afford it, society affords it because we value our health. And earlier Mr. Ehrenkrantz pointed out to me that in the U.S.A. it is now clear, from certain economic studies, that the building industry is simply not valued highly enough by society. If that is the case, it follows that there is this lack of investment in education, and in particular in re-training and in-service education.

W. Hillier

I think the difficulty with architectural education is that there is no theory and no practice. Everything is in between these two. The movements towards better theory and application are really part and parcel of the same thing. It does raise a very fundamental question about what we mean by architectural education, and we should try to establish what we mean in detail about architecture because we have the question, is it just a vocation, is it just a practice, or is architecture a discipline? Which point of view we select is very important for how we see education and the future of architecture. For me, speaking from outside architecture, it seems obvious that the fundamental intellectual weakness of architecture is the source of its political weakness. This is the obvious lesson to be learnt from looking at how engineers look after themselves, and how various other disciplines manage to organise a body of knowledge which has both its theoretical development and its application. It seems to me that the fundamental intellectual aspect which is now the source of political weakness *could* be its greatest source of political *strength*. We have to be clear about this. Are we going to teach architecture as a vocational thing, in which case these questions arise of linking up the need to practise immediately with the need for education (and perhaps advanced practice with advanced education in certain instances). Or are we going to go for a much more fundamental development of architecture as a discipline in its own right. Speaking as a non architect, I am totally persuaded not only that architecture is a discipline in its own right, but also that it is one of the most fertile and rich that you can wish to have and will be increasingly at the centre of things in universities as compared with the current social sciences. The ideas of Herbert Simon, for example the idea of sciences of the artificial (having sciences to study the artificial things that we make), are going to be a big perspective-maker in universities in time to come, and architecture can be part of this.

E. Ehrenkrantz

I think the points I was making earlier relate first to the entire industry with which we are dealing, and then to architecture and aspects of it. This correlates with some work of a communist named Balmaal, who has done studies of productivity in industries and in social service areas. He has found that the cost of social services goes up as the productivity in industry increases. The reason for this is quite simple: if car manufacture has improved fifteen times since the end of world war two, the workers have got their share of the increase in pay for working on the assembly lines. A teacher, however, in 1890 may have had thirty students in a class and today also has thirty students in a class. Some methods may have changed, the quality of performance may have gone up somewhat, but the actual efficiency in the performance of the social services has not changed very much. However, as the car salaries go up, whether in Birmingham, Detroit, etc., since the teacher has the option of working on the assembly line as well, teachers salaries go up somewhat, but nevertheless as they go up so the actual cost of education goes up relative to the productivity. And society, unfortunately, does not expect to pay for this because the explanation of the way that service costs go up in direct relationship to industrial productivity is not made. The problem is compounded in the construction industry where we have a field that is expected to behave as an industrial concern, but whose productivity rate follows the curve of social service. As a result of this we have come, at least in the States, under increasing pressure. People are unwilling to pass bond issues for hospital, or education facility construction and we are, in fact, lagging behind very seriously. So we have a two fold problem, firstly, of trying to understand the way in which the building industry works and increasing its level of productivity (because if we do not do this we are going to find more and more industrialised activities providing shelter, and this is obviously beginning to take place in terms of motor homes of various sorts in the States). Secondly, we have to recognise that it is necessary to educate the public to realise that the total cost of providing social services, does, in fact, go up whenever we improve in terms of national productivity.

F. Battisti

I quite agree with the conception of architecture as a discipline; it is a study and a discipline, and there is a connection between architecture and the social services. For instance, we had in this conference several examples of hospital building and there have been studies of daily routines in hospitals. What all the studies show is that most attention has been paid to what the staff was doing, and most of the design and research related to the needs of the staff. If anyone has read the book "Asylums", which deals with psychological reactions in total institutions, he will understand that in a hospital there is not only a social network constituted by the staff, but there is also a social network constituted by the patients. In the design and in the research of hospital planning, it seems that we are repeating the same errors with computers as were made in simple manual projects, i.e., a study has been made of the staff activities, but no study has been made of the patients themselves, their social activities, interaction with other patients and with the staff.

J. Meunier

The title of this conference is Models and Systems in Architecture and Building and I came along as an outsider. It seems to me that what we have heard has been intellectually stimulating and I received some ideas that I will build on in the future. But what I have not heard is anything that calms some of the deeply felt worries that I have and, I think, a lot of other people have who are not completely commited to this area. These worries, whether you are talking about architectural education or architecture itself, focus on the price that you pay as a result of concerning yourself with new models and new systems. The price seems to be one of oversimplification. I am a little worried when someone like Bill Hillier, who is responsible for some of the more interesting ideas, talks about architecture as a discipline. Some aspects of architecture could be described as disciplines, but I have found it impossible to conceive of *architecture* as a discipline, with a set of rules that one understands and a set of connections that are tightly bound up. It is much too rich and diverse a subject for that, and I think the same is true of architectural education as well. The big fear that I have, and I am sure none of you is free of this either, is that in order to make architectural education and architecture respectable disciplines we will cut off absolutely vital limbs of both branches of work. I think the last point was made by Mr. Battisti. We have heard from people talking about the application of these systems to hospital design, that one of the reasons hospital desing has been the recipient of this attention is because there is so much factual data and measurement available from hospital design, and he has put his finger on the one vitally important part of hospital design, the welfare of the patient, his social welfare, and his morale, about which there is very little factual data, and therefore it does not get studied, it does not get involved. I would like to make it quite clear that I do not want to stop the work that is going on here. We are vitally interested in it, we feel that it holds tremendous promise for the future, but we would like to reinforce the slight worries that many of you have expressed that there is a great price being paid in the pursuit of these areas of work.

W. Hillier

There is no rule to say that discipline has to be tidy. Actually, I should have said set of disciplines. I do think because it is rich and untidy and is based on life blood relationships which exist in the real world it is a university subject of the future, capable of generating out of itself all kinds of vigorous, historical, mathematical and scientific areas of study, but out of *itself* rather than out of the contributions of particular disciplines from outside.

J. Chalmers

I was a bit taken back when the chairman suggested talking about education, since I was hoping to talk about practice, but perhaps we can come back to that. One thing that did strike me about the summing up of the conference was the suggestion for an overall scheme for education, which should include some sort of education on techniques, analysis, methods of analysis, and then some movement towards practice, or a situation similar to practice, afterwards. It interested me that some years ago when I was an undergraduate, it was the very thing they suggested and to some extent tried to carry out. Clearly, there are problems in implementing this sort of education at the moment, as there are whole sets of disciplines, both inside and outside architecture, which can be taught here, but they are by no means complete, they do not map out the whole picture. You have gaps, and the problem is what to do about those gaps. The other problem is to avoid the sort of educational difficulties that, say, engineers have, where the techniques they have been taught occupy only a small part of the total time in a practice, so that it takes a long time for them to adapt to real conditions. What one hopes for from education is that somehow it will fit people to see the wider aspects of any problem they undertake and bring the problem into context. Speaking from some small teaching experience, I found that the people who came at the beginning of the year had a great deal of work to do to reach the point where they could begin operating in the area and understanding the techniques involved. People get so involved in the techniques that they "disappear" and never see the surrounding world again. Most of the people I taught went into the kind of practice afterwards which bore no relationship to the things I taught them. One major requirement for getting people working on ideas is to give them the tools, the basic tools, of thinking in their early years of education.

A. Gordon

I would like to bring research into this, and how it can be integrated. I am not directly concerned whether education is vocational or not, I do not want to get involved in that argument, but I am concerned about the running-in period that has been mentioned, and I feel the running-in period need not be half as long as it is at the moment, if only the schools would do one thing. I am not concerned about the *skills* developed in the graduates, but the *attitudes* developed in the graduates. If one has to spend time redirecting people's attitudes in simple things, such as the importance of economic factors, or the role of the computer, etc., then I think this is a pity. I would think it reasonable that schools give the graduates the attitude of the moment. Then I believe that people will be accepted into offices with a very much shorter running-in period. Let us go on to this question of integration of practice, research and education.

L. March

There could be no academic discipline of architecture without the vocation of architecture and quite clearly vocation is what generates the rest. To that extent, it seems to me, vocation taken in its best sense is what will determine the shape of architectural education in the future. There is one other point. We are aware of the early work of the Bartlett School and it was the clearest statement of a plan for university education in architecture, made following the Oxford Conference. Clearly, Cambridge was also influenced very strongly by the Oxford Conference, but the tactics were different. No clear plan was laid out. No-one was so bold as to make a clear statement on how this architectural education would be structured. But one clear principle came through, and that was that whatever it was going to be, it would need a theoretical basis and research was going to provide that basis. It may have been that the early Bartlett experiment was a little premature. We could think of the areas, the cognitive areas, that architecture had and try to integrate these into the beginnings of the theoretical, intellectual base for architecture. I think you then get to the problem with engineering education that it tends to look like pure science, and not like the science of design, or design, as I would call it, without the science. I have tried to show that there is a clear distinction between mathematics and logic on the one hand, and science on the other, and design as another human activity requiring a different mode of thought, and so on. What we are looking for now, on the basis of some early work in theory, in theoretical approaches etc., is how we might be able to avoid the difficulties that engineering had a few years ago, when they were really just a natural science department, and become something that is really rather different. I share Bill Hillier's enthusiasm and I think we can now see that there is a new area opening up. Certainly it is going to be a very exciting area, rather like biology, perhaps. I think the design sciences, or design itself, will become quite central. Economists are finding that they cannot use just theoretical economics if they are going to plan. Engineers obviously cannot use just design sciences, if they are going to design. Lawyers, also, are in the same position, medical people too. That would give some general framework for discussion on practice, research and education. I have a fourth name to put in here, and I have tried to emphasise it in this conference. There is an absolutely critical role to be played by *development* and I must insist from my own experience, and what I have seen happening over the last few years, that development work must be isolated out and nurtured in its own right. We had expected far too much from research both in education and in practice. Research, which ever way round you go, has to be developed. If it is to go into education, there needs to be development work on it to turn it into educational material. It isn't educational material in its own right. To teach raw research to students, I think, is an appalling idea. It really does need to go through a whole process of thinking about the teaching process itself, how it will be received by the students, what it is doing in opening up their minds rather than merely the teaching of the latest idea. The same, of course, is true if you go the other direction, and we have heard a lot from, for instance, Applied Research of Cambridge of what happens in development work, and I am quite sure that we could have gone on making interesting, intellectual enquiries in our research, which took quite a lot of time to do. We showed that it was possible, however, to think a different way or to do something a different way, and to take that up really required a considerable amount of a different kind of expertise, a different kind of investment etc., and it really needed very strong contacts at that time with the potential users. We have been very fortunate, Applied Research particularly, in two major clients, the D.H.S.S. and the Oxford Regional Hospital Board.

W. Hillier

The situation that has developed in Cambridge is a very interesting one as regards development and theory. I would like to ask Mr. March one question, which I am sure he will answer in the affirmative, and that is, does he see Applied Research of Cambridge and Land Use and Built Form Studies as having feedback loops. I am sure he agrees that they do, and that the view of the Cambridge system from outside, is that you have a theory unit, an applied unit, and a school which are increasingly inter-related. I gather this is the intention now. This is exactly the kind of three way relationship that we should aim to develop, in and around schools of architecture and any school in ten years' time that has not got these three components in some degree of association with each other is likely to be behind the game. I would like to suggest a formula to him to try to reconcile our different views on what the relationship between the theory-based research and practice should be. I suggest the phrase 'autonomous contact'. I think the research worker must have contact, but it must be autonomous. It must be on his own terms. He must be generating the line of research. But, on the other hand, he must not be protected from feedback, from the effect of what he has done, because he himself can learn from it. I think we have got to regard this as a system necessarily having feedback between practice and education, a design cycle, if you like, of research and the educational process. It seems to me that the important thing is that as soon as you put a research unit in the middle of this it must become the most powerful force and should be the most powerful force if it is going to be any good.

L. March

Well, questions of power I would rather leave aside. There are four elements, obviously, we not only have the school but we have research, development and practice, and those four must work together. Do we have a feedback loop? I don't know. We do organise once or twice a year lunchtime discussion groups in which a person from Applied Research will present a paper and that is usually discussed quite seriously and puts people into contact who have not been in contact before. Obviously a commercial company like Applied Research has staff changes rather more than we do at the university, and new people certainly do not know various things until they come to one of those meetings. I will give an illustration of the diffusion from research that occurs, and then the feed-back. In response to the R.I.B.A., Philip Steadman and I wrote a book called *Geometry of the Environment,* which may well have surprised the Professional Literature Committee in the way that it turned out. They were very encouraging and were asking for something new, but some of the work that I did on *Geometry of the Environment* I thought was of purely theoretical interest. I was told by someone working in this field, that it was really a formalization that I developed that did not have anything much to do with anything else. Then I found that Paul Richens, of Applied Research, was, in fact, taking these ideas up directly in development with the Oxford Regional Hospital Board and we are now expecting to have the system operating next year. This is an incredibly quick time in which an idea diffused from something which was being toyed with purely intellectually, to something of practical use. On the other hand I have got the feedback from that because I have read papers from Paul Richens, and the most recent event is that an unpublished paper by me, which I gave them a copy of, contains ideas which are going into development work before the paper, in fact, is published. So there is some kind of connection, but it tends to be through papers, nothing formal.

W. Howell

I think it is also important to remember that the sort of development work that Applied Research of Cambridge have been doing is developing a part of the research work that has been done in the department. There is other work done at Land Use and Built Form Studies which has been developed in different ways. For instance, we have a technical research division whose main project has been an ecological one, doing the theoretical work in studying the possibility of the autonomous house. We have now got a grant to do the next stage of development work, actually to build such a house and live in it. But there is another aspect, too, of development work, and that is the sort of development work which is done by practitioners associated with a school, which will be greatly enriched if there is a very active 'bubbling up' of theoretical ideas taking place during, for example, mid-morning coffee breaks. The contact between those teaching, those involved in research, and those whose main activities are in practice is going to give rise to architectural work which will draw a lot of inspiration and material from the research work that is going on. I think that is something which certainly happened here arising out of work that Lionel March was involved in, some of which has resulted in things being built in a different way, with new ideas derived directly from the research. In that connection I would like to quote a slogan that John Meunier has coined, in which he said that he feels the motto for a practitioner involved in teaching should be, 'no bread and butter'. In other words, you do not take on something just to feed yourself, what you take on outside your teaching role is taken on because it makes a contribution towards the development of architectural ideas. This is very important, that the contribution you try and make in your practice, as somebody involved in teaching, should really be something that is a development of architectural theory demonstrated in practice.

A. Gordon

I ought to remind you, because the 1958 Oxford conference on education has been mentioned, that there was a Cambridge conference which didn't produce such clear-cut recommendations as the 1958 conference because times have changed, but its theme was just what we are talking about now and one hopes that it will begin to show effects in the next few years.

H. Goodman

I am getting rather worried that we are getting a long way from the real problems that I thought were going to be discussed at this conference. I think we ought to be looking at these in the context of the title of the conference. If you look at research, which we are talking about, and research specific to models and systems, then it is not necessarily the same sort of problem as research in a general way. The point made by most of the speakers is that we have reached a fairly high level of technology. In order to get a step further, we have got to put more money in. We get good value for our money now, but we do not push the frontiers of knowledge very far forward for the next hundred thousand pounds that we invest. This does tend to limit the sponsors of research in this particular field to very few bodies. The educational funds available are not enough to push things much farther forward so we have to rely on people like Government Departments, Regional Boards, etc. But when they do put money in, there are very strong strings attached and one of the things that I would like to have a few minutes on is whether those actually engaged in the field feel that the string is too strong. I know that when we put out research commissions we have very strong strings on them and I have seen no sign of resentment, but I pay the bills and this may be an element of significance. It would have been useful to have heard to what extent people doing this work feel that when they are working for a large bureaucratic organisation the strings are just too tight.

A. Gordon

Any views on this?

A. Beattie

I was also interested in meditating on the title of the conference, Models and Systems in Architecture and Building, in that I was trying to think of the missing element of this conference in terms of Bill Hiller's four functions model. I think several people have mentioned that the symbolic cultural function is missing. What exactly does that amount to anyway? Perhaps it is the same as the difference between architecture and building. A lot of people say that perhaps architecture is a term of approbation applied to buildings in retrospect. If you wait long enough, what would buildings be but architecture. On the other hand there is nothing in this conference about that aspect of what might be the uniquely architectural

contribution, if there is one. We have, essentially, building construction, environmental engineering and operations research. These are the three major areas, together with certain features of mathematics and computer science which enable us to cope with those things. The only suggestions we have had about the cultural symbolic have been historical, which is the traditional trap of the architectural profession, that it sees the light afterwards. Thinking about what things might be unique, I wondered whether I could pick up two things. Firstly, that the architect sees himself differently from engineers and other building scientists in that he feels free to question the brief, particularly at a social and cultural level. That is to say, given a brief for a hospital, he might decide that what you needed was a health centre, or what you needed was a health campaign. The second thing might be that of the impact of the buildings on the users, the aesthetic response, and I was wondering whether both these things are not things that we are still incredibly shy about. They are not in this conference, for instance, and is there any evidence that research in general and research on models and systems in particular is coming anywhere near these two things? Perhaps it is excluding them, and to take the case of the kind of research commissions that Howard is talking about, I certainly feel constrained by the terms of reference of the commission in precisely that first area. I don't feel at liberty to question the brief, because the constraints are so extremely tight. This is one of the more serious problems of models and systems, that it is hard to see any way in which you can manoeuvre to start reformulating the question, meaningfully, if you think that some of the assumptions are not quite correct.

J. P. Steadman

I would like to make a small point which perhaps does relate the question of education to the subject of the conference. It is something that we have seen as being a particular property of a models approach to architectural research, that this was an activity which brought people together, which provided both a central focus for education and a means by which students could be brought into a piece of work which was made clear by the model making process. A modelling approach lays information out with a clarity and openness to criticism and involves a whole diversity of people who can look at the model as one in terms of depicted knowledge.

D. Campion

Maybe this is stating the obvious, that models are a very integrating influence between research and practice and we are not making use of them. I was talking to Howard Goodman about the HAP model; a lot of work has been done producing models. I think his views were towards the theory of modelling without the use of computers, but it seems to me the models that are on a computer are very good teaching aids, not only at university level, but in practice. I remember having to calculate structures, and this seemed to be a very sterile operation. Nowadays one can put structures on the computer, simulating the bending from the loading on the beam and seeing the effect of it. You can do in a matter of hours what would otherwise take months. Why are we not having this sort of approach? The problem in practice is that one has to pay to play with models, but we have got enough hardware in universities to allow practitioners to come and play with these models and this is mid-career training, to play with environmental models and see what effect it has. This is the vital link between research and practice.

D. Hawkes

About two months ago, in Cambridge, we established a small committee of the faculty to look into this, to begin to make more generally available the types of modelling techniques being produced in the centre as teaching aids in the school.

C. Gray

I wonder if I could attempt to make a two point summary of Lionel March's summary which does address the research area. First, in order to know where research is going to go, we have to know where research is now. It is particularly appropriate here in the Charles Babbage Lecture Theatre to remember his remarks to John Herschel when they were working out some astronomical calculations, "I wish to God these calculations had been done by steam". We are now in the stage when these calculations *are* done by steam, at least *electronic* steam. In the calculations of stresses and the production of drawings, etc., there is probably now less research content and more development content. We know how things should be done, as opposed to actually getting down and doing the slog. If that is the current stage it is interesting to speculate about the future. I think that one thing has emerged, that a certain application of computers to the design process, as opposed to the production process, has run its course, and this is the original emphasis on the use of computers for optimisation. Initially, the idea was that Computer Aided Design would use computers to seek the best solution, and we hear papers by Tom Willoughby and others about programs that do this. I think that this branch of the application of computers may now be essentially over. There is a lot of momentum in this research and it will continue for some time but the next phase, and this is pure speculation, is that computers will be used to seek general robust solutions, not to seek optimum solutions to problems, but to help the designers to seek solutions which have a high degree of adaptability. I think the Harness type hospital is an example of this, and one can see other examples in a whole range of artifacts. People are demanding utility and adaptability in the environmental sense, in the genetic sense, of forms. So, instead of designing to the tightest possible constraint and achieving the optimum solution, one is indeed seeking the maximum usefulness of the solution. This will be a research line, it has hardly started, but it is just a feeling that I have, and I think conferences are the right vehicle for expressing one's intuitions about the future.

Dean Hawkes gave some idea that the models were hopefully going to be used in an educational situation. On the planning side we are going to run a whole week's workshop session, with planners, on using computer models and so on, and this is certainly educational. It is perhaps ironic that the Department of Architecture, that has nothing whatsoever to do with Planning (in the capital "P" sense) is actually running this particular course, but there seems to be a demand for it, we have developed quite a lot of the techniques for it, and I hope that this could be followed up with similar sorts of courses in architecture.

A. Gordon

I was reminded that I was charged with steering this session into looking at the effects that the whole conference might have on the outside world, and I don't think we ought to go away without trying to suggest simple, straightforward things that ought to be done.

H. Goodman

I think so. The real thing is to come and join us. A far harder commitment is needed on the part of people outside, because if you are going to improve the quality of architecture, which is what most architects are concerned with, then you must join or be left behind. But if you do join, then don't let us buy off your healthy scepticism.

W. Howell

One of the areas for useful debate on the subject would be more inter-connection between this centre and other similar centres. I know there are some people here who are involved in the communication of research, and I think that one of the things that would be useful as an activity in the future would be to have meetings with some of the other places with whom we have informal contacts. So far I do not think we have really tried to get together with them, and pool attitudes and present situations.

W. Hillier

Design needs models, but science is about testing models. If any generalisation could be made about this conference, I would say we have had rather more conjecture than refutation. We have not had much about refuting the basis of the models we are talking about, and what their relationship with real life is. And this is not just a matter of providing tools for the design, we have to separate that out. We have to watch for the Oedipean effect, that is, creating the world which you predicted, but through making the prediction. It is possible that by using models, we can actually make a simplified world in which they do operate, and are seen to operate. Now is the time to bring more refutations and more scientific testing into the foundations of our ideas about models.

L. March

Having been in research for six or seven years, and been involved in development, too, I realise that my own personal capacity is rather limited. I am determined to go into teaching and do my bit there. It is just impossible to do everything. I am also involved in editing a journal which has developed out of regional research, called *Environment and Planning*. This will be split into two series, A and B. Series B will be essentially involved with architectural research. I think Bill Howell's point about connections between research groups emphasises the fact that we have been badly served by high level journals in this field. Sponsors tend to say that research must address itself to practice. In actual fact, it is sometimes necessary to communicate in detail at a high research level, and that is where refutations will take place.

A. Gordon

To end, I would just say that we should avoid the danger of expecting more from the computer than it rightly can give and we should appreciate that it is still very difficult to quantify the intangible although some of the intangibles we have discussed here are very important.

Speakers

Delany, M. E.	Acoustics Section, National Physical Lab., Teddington, Middlesex.
Eastman, Charles,	Institute of Physical Planning, Carnegie-Mellon University, Schenley Park, Pittsburg, Pa. 15213 U.S.A.
Ehrenkrantz, Ezra D.	Ezra D. Ehrenkrantz Associates 232 Madison Avenue, New York N.Y. 10016, U.S.A.
Goodman, Howard,	Chief Architect, DHSS, Euston Tower, 286 Euston Road, London NW1
Gordon, Alex,	Alex Gordon and Partners, 6 Cathedral Road, Cardiff CF1 9XW
Gray, J. Crispin,	Applied Research of Cambridge Ltd. 5 Jesus Lane, Cambridge, CB5 8BA
Hawkes, Dr. Dean U.	Land Use and Built Form Studies, Department of Architecture, University of Cambridge, 1 Scroope Terrace, Cambridge.
Hayward, Dr. Peter,	Applied Research of Cambridge Ltd., 5 Jesus Lane, Cambridge, CB5 8BA
Hillier, Bill,	R.I.B.A., 66 Portland Place, London W1N 4AD
Hoskins, E. M.	Applied Research of Cambridge Ltd., 5 Jesus Lane, Cambridge, CB5 8BA
Howell, Professor William,	Department of Architecture, University of Cambridge, 1 Scroope, Terrace, Cambridge.
Hunt, Dr. Julian,	Department of Applied Mathematics and Theoretical Physics, Silver Street, Cambridge. CB3 9EW
Hutton, Geoffrey H.	Hutton and Rostron, 42 Claremont Road, Surbiton, Surrey.
Jacobsberg, Jennifer (Mrs.)	Applied Research of Cambridge Ltd., 5 Jesus Lane, Cambridge CB5 8BA
Leaman, Adrian,	R.I.B.A., 66 Portland Place, London W1N 4AD
March, Lionel J.	Land Use and Built Form Studies, Department of Architecture, University of Cambridge, 1 Scroope Terrace, Cambridge.
Milbank, Neil,	Building Research Establishment, Building Research Station, Garston, Watford, Herts.
Mitchell, Professor William J.	School of Architecture and Urban Planning, University of California, Los Angeles, Calif. 90024 U.S.A.
Ray, Keith,	31 Bateman Street, Cambridge, also Scicon, Sanderson House, 49 Berners Street, London W1
Richens, Paul,	Applied Research of Cambridge Ltd. 5 Jesus Lane, Cambridge CB5 8BA
Steadman, J. Philip,	Land Use and Built Form Studies, Department of Architecture, University of Cambridge, 1 Scroope Terrace, Cambridge.
Stibbs, Richard,	Computer Laboratory, University of Cambridge, Corn Exchange Street, Cambridge.
Tomlinson, Janet (Miss)	Computer Laboratory, University of Cambridge, Corn Exchange Street, Cambridge
Willoughby, Tom,	Meers and Wager, 49 Mount Street, London W1 5RE

U.K. Participants

University of Strathclyde
SCHOOL OF ARCHITECTURE
INFORMATION ROOM

Aldridge, R. J.	International Computers Limited, 17–27 John Dalton Street, Manchester 2
Anderson, G.	Scottish Development Dept., 83 Princes Street, Edinburgh EH2 2HH
Arschavir, A. L.	Oxford Regional Hospital Board, Old Road, Headington, Oxford OX3 7LF
Atfield, Mr.	Robert Matthew Johnson Marshall, Welwyn Garden City.
Baines George G., Professor,	Department of Architecture, University of Sheffield, Arts Tower, Sheffield S10 2TN
Barnard, David,	CAAD Studies, Department of Architecture, University of Edinburgh, 55 George Street, Edinburgh.
Beattie, Alan,	Polytechnic of North London, Holloway Road, London N7
Bowman, Dr. Neil,	School of Architecture, City of Leicester Polytechnic, Clapham Building, Oxford Street, Leicester.
Bright, Roy A.	Roy & Sheila Bright, 71 Carholme Road, Lincoln.
Burr, D. J.	Room F13, County Hall, Fishergate, Preston, Lancs.
Campion, David,	Cusdin, Burden and Howitt, 1–4 Yarmouth Place, Brick Street, Piccadilly, London W1Y 8JQ
Chalmers, J.	Room 1612, Lunar House, 40 Wellesley Road, Croydon CR9 2EI
Clements, Peter,	Huddersfield Polytechnic School of Architecture, Queensgate, Huddersfield.
Cradock, P. P.	c/o W. D. Dockeray, Associate Architect, John Laing Design Associates Limited, Pope Street, London NW7 2ER
Curtis, Robert,	Yorkshire and Humberside Regional Housing and Planning Office, City House, Leeds 1
Dalley, K. G.	Architects Co-Partnership Inc., Northaw House, Potters Bar, Herts.
D'Arcy, R. A.	Oxford Regional Hospital Board, Old Road, Headington, Oxford OX3 7LF
Davies, Olbris,	19 Charlotte Square, Rhinbina, Cardiff, Glamorgan CF4 6ND
Filmer, R. M. (Miss)	Building Research Establishment, Building Research Station, Garston, Watford WD2 7JR
Fisk, B. J.	Building Research Establishment, Garston, Watford.
Gaskell, B. J.	Department of the Environment, N.W.R.H. and P.O., Sunley Buildings, Piccadilly Plaza, Manchester M1 4BE
Gibbons, J. J.	Oxford Regional Hospital Board, Old Road, Headington, Oxford OX3 7LF
Gilleard, John D.	Department of Civil Engineering and Building, Lanchester Polytechnic, Coventry.
Grant, M.,	John Laing Design Associates Limited, Page Street, London NW7 2ER
Groak, Stephen,	Constrado, British Steel Corporation, 12 Addiscombe Road, Croydon CR9 3JH
Gusack, Philip M.	Environment Systems Consultants, 56 Doughty Street, London WC1N 2LS
Harrington-Lynn, John,	Building Research Establishment, Building Research Station, Garston, Watford WD2 7JR
Harrison, David J.	Brockhouse Steel Structures Limited, Birmingham Road, West Bromwich, Staffs.
Hawthorne, A. H.	Wessex Regional Hospital Board, Architects Department, "Highcroft", Romsey Road, Winchester, Hants.
Haywood, Michael E.	A.D.A.S. Lands Arm, Ministry of Agriculture, Fisheries and Food, Coley Park, Reading.
Hinton, Professor Denys.	Dept. of Architectural, Planning and Urban Studies, Handsworth Hall, 138 Friary Road, Handsworth, Birmingham B20 1NN
Holder, C.	Architects Co-Partnership Inc., Northaw House, Potters Bar, Herts.
Howard, Tony,	DHSS, Euston Tower, 286 Euston Road, London NW1
Howell, Peter,	Department of the Environment, Room G19, Five Ways House, Islington Row, Birmingham B15 1SN
Kernohan, D.	University of Strathclyde, Glasgow.
Leicester, Keith,	Greater London Council, Department of Architecture and Civic Design, Schools Division, Room N667, County Hall, London SE1
Maddison, John A. T.	Thames Polytechnic, Vercourt House, King Street, London W6.
Maguire, D. J.	Corporation of Dublin, Civic and Amenities Department, 6 Mountjoy Square, Dublin 1.

Mrowicki, A. D.	Gray and Walker, Chartered Architects, 227 High Street, Epping, Essex.
Murray, A. C.	Room 312, Postal Headquarters, St. Martins-le-Grand, London EC1A 1HQ
Mutter, J.	County Architect's Department, County Hall, Exeter, Devon.
Newman, Paul I.	92 Morningside Drive, Edinburgh EH10 5NT
Noble, Ann (Miss)	Vincent and Wynn, 45 Parliament Street, London SW1
Page, Peter Alan,	County Architects Department, County Council of Essex, County Hall, Chelmsford, Essex CM1 1LB
Portlock, Dr. Peter,	54 Merritt Road, Didcot, Berks.
Poodry, Deborah,	689A Finchley Road, London NW2
O'Connell, Dermot V.	School of Architecture, University College, Dublin 4.
Rabeneck, A.	Building Systems Development (UK) Limited, 38 Wigmore Street, London
Sears, Dan,	Joint Unit for Planning Research, 171 Tottenham Court Road, London WIP OBS
Shawcross, Graham,	Edinburgh CAAD Studies, University of Edinburgh, Department of Architecture, 55 George Street, Edinburgh.
Sheppard, D.	Building Systems Development (UK) Limited, 38 Wigmore Street, London.
Shoul, Michael,	School of Architecture, Kingston Polytechnic, Knights Park, Kingston-upon-Thames, Surrey.
Stone, D.	Scottish Development Department, 83 Princes Street, Edinburgh EH2 2HH
Thompson, B.	Department of the Environment, Room 1612, Lunar House, 40 Wellesley Road, Croydon CR9 2EI
Thurlow, David,	7 Essex House, Regent Street, Cambridge.
Town, P.	Building Systems Development Limited, 38 Wigmore Street, London.
Turner, John,	Department of the Environment, Room 251, Caxton House, Tothill Street, London SW1
Van Schaik, Paul,	Robert Matthew Johnson Marshall & Partners, Rosanne House, Bridge Road, Welwyn Garden City.
Vincent, Ronald,	Vincent & Wynn, 45 Parliament Street, London SW1
Wallace, Graham,	Department of Architecture and Building Science, University of Strathclyde, Glasgow.
Walters, Roger,	Department of Architecture and Building Science, University of Strathclyde, Glasgow.
Watts, John,	Haden Young Limited, Site B, Colindale Avenue, London NW9
Woodcock, Eric,	Robert Gordon's Institute of Technology, Garthdee, Aberdeen, AB9 2QB
Woodward, Brian,	Department of Architecture, Oxford Polytechnic, Gypsy Lane, Headington, Oxford.

University of Strathclyde
SCHOOL OF ARCHITECTURE
INFORMATION ROOM

Participants from abroad

Agger, Kristian,   School of Architecture in Aarhus, Norreport 20, 8000 Aarhus C, Denmark.
Aran, Kemel   Halici Sokak No. 2, Gaziosmanpasa, Ankara, Turkey.
Balint, Professor,   University of New South Wales, Sydney, Australia.
Battisti, Francesco,   Via dei 4 Venti 166, Roma, Italy.
Brown, F.   Technische Hochschule, Graz, Austria.
Chadirji, R.   Iraq Consult, PO Box 2291, Alivijah, Baghdad, Iraq.
D'Ambrosio, R.   Via Morgantini 3, Napoli, Italy.
Douqué, J. G. E. M.   Iber B. V. Delft, O.D. 180, Anthonie Van Dyck Straat 12, Amsterdam, Netherlands.
Fiorentino, Bruno,   Villa Lucia, Via Toma, Napoli, Italy.
Foti, Massimo,   Facolta di Architettura, Castello del Valentino, Torino, Italy.
Forte, Francesco,   Corso V. Emanuele 171, Napoli, Italy.
Hunt, Ian R.   Yuncken Freeman Architects Ptp. Limited, 27 Powell Street, South Yarra, Victoria 3141, Australia.
Piemontese, Antonietta Miss   Via Roma 256, Napoli, Italy.
Piemontese, Lugi,   Via Bonito 10A, Napoli, Italy.
P. L. de Matos, Julio Alexander,   Ecola Superior de Belas Artes do Porto, Rua Capitao Pombeiro 91, Porto, Portugal.
Portas, Nuno,   Laboratorio Nacional de Engenharia Civil, Av. do Brasil, Lisbon 5, Portugal.
Ramselaar, W. J.   Technische Hogeschool Eindhoven, Kol. Wilstraat 19, Ravenstein, Netherlands.
Reif, Benjamin,   Av. Andres Bello, Resid. Kennedy, Apt. 74, La Florida, Caracas, Venezuela.
Scarano, Rolando,   Via Roma 256, Napoli, Italy.
Spooner, T. W.   Department of Architecture, University of the Witwatersrand, Jan Smuts Avenue, Johannesburg, S. Africa.
Tagarro, Amaro,   Calle Balmes No. 84, at, 2a, Barcelona (8), Spain.
Yavus, Aysil T.   Middle East Technical University, Faculty of Architecture, Ankara, Turkey.
Zollo, Guiseppe,   Via Cupa Carbone 10, Napoli, Italy.

Discussants

Campion, David,   Cusdin, Burden and Howitt, 1–4 Yarmouth Place, Brick Street, Piccadilly, London W1Y 8JQ
Francesco, Battisti,   University of Naples, Italy. Postal Address: Via dei 4 venti 166 Roma, Italy.
Meunier, John,   Department of Architecture, University of Cambridge, 1 Scroope Terrace, Cambridge.
Chalmers, John,   Department of the Environment, Room 1612, Lunar House, 40 Wellesley Road, Croydon CR9 2EL
Beattie, Alan,   Polytechnic of North London, Holloway Road, London N7
Hawkes, Steadman, Gray   —already listed as speakers.

University of Strathclyde
SCHOOL OF ARCHITECTURE
INFORMATION ROOM